The novel is modernism's most vital and experimental genre. In this *Companion* leading critics explore the very significant pleasures of reading modernist novels, but also demonstrate how and why reading modernist fiction can be difficult. No one technique or style defines a novel as modernist, but these essays explain the formal innovations, stylistic preferences and thematic concerns which unite modernist diction. They also show how modernist novels relate to other forms of art, and to the social and cultural context from which they emerged. Alongside chapters on prominent novelists such as James Joyce and Virginia Woolf, as well as lesser-known authors such as Dorothy Richardson and Djuna Barnes, themes such as genre and geography, time and consciousness are discussed in detail. With a chronology and guide to further reading, this is the most accessible and informative overview of the genre available.

MORAG SHIACH is Vice-Principal (Teaching and Learning) and Professor of Cultural History in the School of English and Drama, Queen Mary, University of London. She is the author of *Modernism, Labour and Selfhood in British Literature and Culture, 1890–1930* (Cambridge University Press, 2004).

THE CAMBRIDGE
COMPANION TO
THE MODERNIST NOVEL

EDITED BY
MORAG SHIACH

CAMBRIDGE
UNIVERSITY PRESS

CAMBRIDGE UNIVERSITY PRESS
Cambridge, New York, Melbourne, Madrid, Cape Town, Singapore, São Paulo

Cambridge University Press
The Edinburgh Building, Cambridge CB2 8RU, UK

Published in the United States of America by Cambridge University Press, New York

www.cambridge.org
Information on this title: www.cambridge.org/9780521670746

First published 2007

Printed in the United Kingdom at the University Press, Cambridge

A catalogue record for this publication is available from the British Library

ISBN 978-0-521-85444-3 hardback
ISBN 978-0-521-67074-6 paperback

CONTENTS

NOTES ON CONTRIBUTORS

ANN BANFIELD teaches in the English department at the University of California, Berkeley. She is the author of *Unspeakable Sentences: Narration and Representation in the Language of Fiction* (1982) and *The Phantom Table: Woolf, Fry, Russell and the Epistemology of Modernism* (2000). She has published articles on Virginia Woolf and the problem of time in *Modernism/Modernity* (2000) and *Poetics Today* (2003).

REBECCA BEASLEY teaches in the School of English and Humanities, Birkbeck College, University of London. She is the author of *Ezra Pound and the Visual Culture of Modernism* and *T. S. Eliot, T. E. Hulme and Ezra Pound: Theorists of Modernist Poetics* (forthcoming).

PETER BROOKER is Professor of Literary and Cultural Studies at the University of Nottingham. He is the author most recently of *Modernity and Metropolis: Writing, Film and Urban Formations* (2002) and *Bohemia in London: The Social Scene of Early Modernism* (2004), and co-editor of *Geographies of Modernism* (2005). He is co-director of the AHRC-funded Modernist Magazines Project and co-editor of a forthcoming three-volume critical and cultural history of modernist magazines.

ANNE FERNIHOUGH is University Lecturer in the Faculty of English, University of Cambridge, and a fellow of Girton College. Her books include *D. H. Lawrence: Aesthetics and Ideology* (1993) and *The Cambridge Companion to D. H. Lawrence* (2001). She is currently writing a book on radicals and utopians in the Edwardian period.

HOWARD FINN teaches literature at Queen Mary, University of London. He has published widely on modernism, cinema and critical aesthetics, and is presently at work on a study of Dorothy Richardson.

JEREMY HAWTHORN is Professor of Modern British Literature at the Norwegian University of Science and Technology, Trondheim. He is the author of *Joseph Conrad: Narrative Technique and Ideological Commitment* (1990), and is editor of the new Oxford World's Classics editions of Joseph Conrad's *Under Western Eyes* and *The Shadow-Line* (both 2003).

MEG JENSEN is Field Leader of the Department of Creative Writing at Kingston University in London, where she also lectures in English and American Literature. She publishes both creative writing and literary criticism, and her recent work includes a study of Thomas Hardy, Katherine Mansfield and Virginia Woolf, among others, *The Open Book: Creative Misreading in the Works of Selected Modern Writers* (2002). She has recently completed her second novel.

CATHERINE GUNTHER KODAT, Associate Professor of English and American Studies, chairs the Department of English and directs the Program in American Studies at Hamilton College, Clinton, New York. She is finishing a book about the uses of culture during the Cold War.

LAURA MARCUS is Professor of English at the University of Sussex, where she teaches and researches in the fields of modern and contemporary literature, film and literary theory. Her most recent publication is *The Cambridge History of Twentieth-Century Literature* (2005), co-edited with Peter Nicholls, and she is currently completing *The Tenth Muse*, a study of film, literature and modernity.

KATHERINE MULLIN is Lecturer in Modern Literature at the University of Leeds and author of *James Joyce, Sexuality and Social Purity* (2003). She has also published articles on Joyce in *Modernism/Modernity* and *Textual Practice*.

LOIS OPPENHEIM is Distinguished Scholar, Professor of French, and Chair of the Department of Modern Languages and Literatures at Montclair State University. She is the author or editor of ten books, including *Directing Beckett* (1994), *The Painted Word: Samuel Beckett's Dialogue With Art* (2000) and *A Curious Intimacy: Art and Neuro-Psychoanalysis* (2005). She is a past president of the international Samuel Beckett Society and is a member of the advisory board of The Philoctetes Center for the Multidisciplinary Study of Imagination.

DEBORAH PARSONS is a senior lecturer in Nineteenth- and Twentieth-Century English Literature at the University of Birmingham and author of *Streetwalking the Metropolis* (2000), *Djuna Barnes* (2003) and *Three Critical Thinkers of the Modernist Novel: James Joyce, Virginia Woolf and Dorothy Richardson* (forthcoming).

ANNA SNAITH is a Lecturer in English at King's College, London. She is the author of *Virginia Woolf: Public and Private Negotiations* (2000), the editor of *Palgrave Advances in Woolf Studies* (forthcoming) and co-editor, with Michael Whitworth, of *Locating Woolf: The Politics of Space and Place* (also forthcoming). She is currently working on a monograph entitled 'Colonial Modernism: Women

Writing London 1900–1945' and editing *The Years* for the Cambridge Edition of Virginia Woolf.

HUGH STEVENS is Senior Lecturer in English at University College London. He is the author of *Henry James and Sexuality* (1998) and co-editor of *Modernist Sexualities* (2000). He is currently writing a monograph on D. H. Lawrence, nationalism and sexuality.

JEFF WALLACE, Professor of English at the University of Glamorgan, is the author of *D. H. Lawrence, Science and the Posthuman* (2005), and of the forthcoming *Beginning Modernism*. He is currently working on a study of the concept of abstraction in modern literature, criticism and the visual arts.

ACKNOWLEDGEMENTS

I would like to thank Dr Suzanne Hobson for her excellent work as editorial assistant on this volume. She created the Chronology and coordinated the Further Reading as well as dealing with the range of issues that arise when pulling together a volume of this sort. I am very grateful for her help in bringing this project to a conclusion.

It has been a pleasure to work with the contributors to this volume, who have approached the project with enthusiasm, have responded to requests for changes with alacrity and good humour, and have created a sense of shared intellectual engagement. I thank them for all their efforts.

I would like to acknowledge Queen Mary, University of London, which offered research funding that facilitated the final stages of work on this volume.

Thank you to Michael, James and John for not minding the many trips to the study at antisocial hours to work on this volume.

My thanks to Ray Ryan of Cambridge University Press who suggested that I might want to think about editing a *Companion to the Modernist Novel*. I am grateful to David Barnes for his assistance in creating the index. The editorial and production staff at Cambridge University Press have been helpful at all stages of this book's production and I would like to record my appreciation of their work.

CHRONOLOGY

SUZANNE HOBSON

1890   **James George Frazer,** *The Golden Bough* (1890–1915), suggests a historical progression from magic through mythology to science.
William James, *Principles of Psychology,* introduces 'mind-wandering', a precedent for 'stream of consciousness'.

1891   **Oscar Wilde,** *The Picture of Dorian Gray,* fictionalizes the pleasures and dangers of decadence.
Thomas Hardy, *Tess of the d'Urbervilles,* depicts a heroine destroyed by Victorian moralities.
George Gissing, *New Grub Street,* laments state of contemporary journalism.
Arthur Conan Doyle, Sherlock Holmes stories begin to appear in *Strand* magazine.

1893   **Sarah Grand,** *The Heavenly Twins,* and **George Egerton,** *Keynotes,* describe emergence of New Woman.

1894   Circulating libraries in Britain issue an ultimatum rendering three-volume novel obsolete. Between 1894 and 1897 the number published falls from 184 to 4.
Alfred Dreyfus, a Jewish officer on the French General Staff, is accused of treason. His case is taken up by Emile Zola and others and he is acquitted in 1906.

1895   Trial of **Oscar Wilde** in London puts issue of homosexuality on public stage.
Listing of 'best-sellers' begins in *The Bookman* magazine in the USA.
Lumière brothers' first projection of film to a paying audience in Paris.

| 1896 | Alfred, Lord Northcliffe founds *Daily Mail* in London. First modern Olympiad in Athens. |

1896   Alfred, Lord Northcliffe founds *Daily Mail* in London. First modern Olympiad in Athens.

1897   **Joseph Conrad**, *The Nigger of the 'Narcissus'*, published with an 'Author's Note' in which Conrad describes his impressionist aims.
Thomas Hardy, *The Well Beloved*, is his last and least realist novel.

1898   **H. G. Wells**, *War of the Worlds*, the most famous of his popular science fiction novels.
Isolation of radioactive element radium by Pierre and Marie Curie.

1899   Anglo-Boer War (1899–1902). Disastrous campaign throws ideals of British imperialism into doubt. Problems with recruitment lead to reports that British men have become physically degenerate.

1900   **Sigmund Freud**, *The Interpretation of Dreams*, demonstrates how to 'read' dreams.
Joseph Conrad, *Lord Jim*, concentrates on the 'invisible world' described in 'Note' to *Nigger of the 'Narcissus'*.
Theodore Dreiser, *Sister Carrie*, a naturalistic novel describing transformation of a working-class girl into an actress.
Max Planck elaborates quantum theory.

1901   **Rudyard Kipling**, *Kim*, his only well-known novel, describing adolescence of an Irish orphan in India.
B. Seebohm Rowntree, survey of poverty in York.
Death of Queen Victoria; Edward VII succeeds to the throne.

1902   **Joseph Conrad**, *Heart of Darkness*, portrays violence at heart of the colonial enterprise.
Frank Lloyd Wright's Willits House, one of his 'prairie houses', typifies geometric and organic emphases of his architectural style.

1903   **Samuel Butler**, *The Way of All Flesh*, attacks Victorian moral mores.
W. E. B. DuBois, *Souls of Black Folk*, describes 'double consciousness' of black Americans.
Henry James, *The Ambassadors*, anticipates point-of-view narration used by later modernist novelists.

Edward S. Porter, *The Great Train Robbery*, is first film to have a full-length narrative.

Foundation of Women's Social and Political Union by Emmeline Pankhurst and her daughters Christabel and Sylvia.

Wright brothers make first manned flight.

1904 Opening of Dublin's Abbey Theatre, a key moment in the Irish Literary Revival.

Outbreak of Russo-Japanese War (1904–5).

1905 **Albert Einstein** publishes 'On the Electrodynamics of Moving Bodies' introducing what will later be known as his special theory of relativity.

Fauvist exhibition in Paris includes works by Henri Matisse.

First movie-house opens in Philadelphia; 10,000 more open over next three years in the USA.

Russian Revolution forces Tsar to establish Duma.

1906 **John Galsworthy**, *The Man of Property*, is first novel of *Forsyte Saga* (1906–28) following in naturalistic tradition of Zola and Fyodor Dostoevsky.

Upton Sinclair, *The Jungle* is his first major novel, exposing conditions in the US meat-packing industry.

San Francisco earthquake.

1907 **Henri Bergson**, *Creative Evolution*, develops his theory of time as 'duration'.

Pablo Picasso, *Les Demoiselles d'Avignon*, marks beginning of Cubism.

Scout Movement founded in Britain.

1908 **Gertrude Stein** publishes her first novel, *Three Lives*.

Ford Madox Ford begins *The English Review* which publishes Henry James, Wells, E. M. Forster, Wyndham Lewis and others.

Arthur Schoenberg enters 'expressionist' or 'atonal' phase of his music.

National Association for the Advancement of Coloured People formed in America.

Aeroplane advertising used for first time to promote a Broadway play.

1909 **Sergei Pavlovich Diaghilev** begins Ballets Russes in France.

Henry Ford perfects assembly-line technique for Model-T Ford. By 1929 23 million cars are registered in the USA.

Lloyd George's 'People's Budget' rejected by House of Lords, leading to parliamentary reform.

1910 **E. M. Forster,** *Howards End.*
First Post-Impressionism exhibition in London.
Edward VII dies; George V succeeds to the throne.

1911 **Arnold Bennett,** *Hilda Lessways,* later provides Virginia Woolf with a key example of the 'Edwardian' novel.
Frederick W. Taylor, *The Principles of Scientific Management,* outlines theory of offering economic rewards to ensure greater productivity.
Complete English translation of **Friedrich Nietzsche** becomes available for first time.

1912 **Thomas Mann,** *Death in Venice,* a short novel tracing degeneration of an art lover.
1,500 die in sinking of *Titanic.*

1913 **D. H. Lawrence,** *Sons and Lovers* is his first popular success.
Marcel Proust, *Swann's Way,* first volume of *In Search of Lost Time* (1913–27).
Jacob Epstein, *Rock-Drill* sculpture portrays the 'Frankenstein's monster' that man has become.
Igor Stravinksy, *Le Sacre du Printemps* marks a controversial turning point in music, placing emphasis on rhythm rather than harmony.
Armory Show in New York shows Fauvists, Expressionists, Primitives and Cubists.

1914 *The New Freewoman* becomes *Egoist* (1914–18), which serializes James Joyce's *A Portrait of the Artist as a Young Man,* parts of *Ulysses* and Lewis's *Tarr.*
Outbreak of First World War.

1915 **Virginia Woolf,** *The Voyage Out,* her first novel.
D. H. Lawrence, *The Rainbow,* traces development of modern consciousness over three generations of a family.
Ford Madox Ford publishes his most celebrated novel, *The Good Soldier.*
Dorothy Richardson, *Pointed Roofs,* first of thirteen volumes of *Pilgrimage* (1915–67).
First transcontinental telephone call from New York to San Francisco.

1916   James Joyce, *A Portrait of the Artist as a Young Man*.
H. G. Wells, *Mr Brittling Sees It Through*, a patriotic war novel serialized in the *Nation*.
Georg Lukács, *The Theory of the Novel*, makes an influential diagnosis of the novel as a bourgeois form.
Easter Rising in Dublin.
Dada performances begin in Zurich.
Beginning of Great Migration in the USA in which 4.9 per cent of black population in the South move to the North.

1917   Leonard and Virginia Woolf found Hogarth Press as a diverting occupation which goes on to publish Freud, Eliot, Forster and Wells.
The USA enters the war on the Western Front.
Bolsheviks take power in Russia. Vision of popular revolution haunts literary imagination for some time to come.

1918   Willa Cather, *My Ántonia*, portrays pastoral life on prairies.
Wyndham Lewis, *Tarr*.
May Sinclair first applies the term 'stream of consciousness' to literature.
Marie Stopes, *Married Love*, introduces mechanics of sex to an ill-informed audience.
Armistice signed between Allies and Germany on 11 November.
Representation of the People Act in Britain extends vote to women over thirty.
Influenza pandemic in Britain (1918–19).

1919   May Sinclair, *Mary Olivier: A Life*, in which she follows Richardson in recreating the workings of the inner mind.
Virginia Woolf, 'Modern Novels', appears in *Times Literary Supplement*. Revised and retitled as 'Modern Fiction' in 1925.
William Somerset Maugham, *The Moon and Sixpence*, an 'outsider' novel following a painter's escape to South Seas.
Scofield Thayer and J. S. Watson purchase *The Dial*, which goes on to publish works by Lawrence, Eliot and Mansfield in the USA.

1920   D. H. Lawrence, *Women in Love*, a 'sequel' to *The Rainbow*.
Edith Wharton, *The Age of Innocence*, describes passing of an old generation in the USA.

Sigmund Freud, *Beyond the Pleasure Principle*, revises his model of the psyche to include the 'death drive' that he had identified in his study of war trauma.
Prohibition comes into effect in the USA.

1921 *The Little Review* prosecuted for obscenity over publication of *Ulysses*.
Shuffle Along using jazz music and dance is a huge Broadway hit.
Creation of Irish Free State.
Emergency Quota Act in the USA restricts immigration from Europe.

1922 **Virginia Woolf**, *Jacob's Room*, attempts to refashion *Bildungsroman*.
James Joyce, *Ulysses*, published in France in a luxury limited edition.
F. Scott Fitzgerald, *The Beautiful and Damned*, shows the corrupting influence of inherited wealth on the New York chic set of the 1920s.
T. S. Eliot, *The Waste Land*.
Report of War Office Committee of Enquiry into 'shell-shock' introduces the term to a wide audience in Britain.
Opening of Tutankhamen's tomb in Egypt.
Mussolini leads march on Rome and becomes Italian Prime Minister.

1923 **Jean Toomer**, *Cane*, a 'novel' comprised partly of poetry and drama, often described as literary high point of Harlem Renaissance.
Le Corbusier, *Towards a New Architecture*, describes buildings as 'machines for living'.

1924 **E. M. Forster**, *A Passage to India*.
Thomas Mann, *The Magic Mountain*, traces coming of age of hero alongside that of human race.
Virginia Woolf gives a talk to the Heretics in Cambridge, later published as 'Mr Bennett and Mrs Brown'.
First Labour government in Britain.
British Empire exhibition in London.

1925 **Virginia Woolf**, *Mrs Dalloway*.
Gertrude Stein, *The Making of Americans*, attempts to record every known human type.

F. Scott Fitzgerald, *The Great Gatsby*, shows dark side of 'American Dream'.

Franz Kafka, *The Trial*, published posthumously.

Exhibition of Arts Décoratifs in Paris.

Launch of first miniature camera, the Leica, at Leipzig fair.

1926   Ernest Hemingway, *The Sun Also Rises*, is his first success, describing life among expatriates in Paris.

André Gide, *The Counterfeiters*, reworks realist and naturalist traditions as represented by writers such as Dostoevsky and Honoré de Balzac.

BBC created by Royal Charter.

Imperial conference declares Australia, Canada, Irish Free State and South Africa 'autonomous communities' within Commonwealth.

General Strike raises 'spectre of communism' in Britain; *Daily Mail* describes it as a 'revolutionary movement'.

Chiang Kai-shek becomes President of China following revolution.

1927   E. M. Forster delivers Clarke lectures at University of Cambridge, published as *Aspects of the Novel*.

Hermann Hesse, *Der Steppenwolf*, a novel heavily influenced by psychoanalysis.

Wyndham Lewis, *Time and Western Man*, questions originality of modernist techniques.

Martin Heidegger, *Being and Time*, analyses mode of being-there in the world (*Dasein*).

Al Jolson stars in first successful 'talkie' film, *The Jazz Singer*.

German economy collapses.

1928   D. H. Lawrence, *Lady Chatterley's Lover*, published privately in Italy.

Djuna Barnes, *Ryder*, describing women's suffering under patriarchy, is a bestseller.

Claude McKay, *Home to Harlem*, becomes first bestseller by a black writer.

Kellogg-Briand pact between fifteen nations rejects war as a policy.

Alexander Fleming discovers penicillin.

1929   Ernest Hemingway, *A Farewell to Arms*, and Robert Graves, *Good-Bye to All That*, describe their wartime experiences.

William Faulkner, *Sartoris*, transforms his hometown, Oxford, Lafayette County, Mississippi, into Jefferson, Yoknapatawpha County.
Virginia Woolf, *A Room of One's Own*, is a key moment in feminist literary criticism.
Nella Larsen, *Passing*, describes black people who 'pass' for white in order to succeed in American society.
Edwin Powell Hubble demonstrates that the universe is expanding.
Wall Street Crash heralds Great Depression 1931–2. Average incomes in the USA decline by half.

1930   Evelyn Waugh, *Vile Bodies*, portrays postwar 'fast set' in 1930s London.
John Dos Passos, *U.S.A.* (trilogy 1930–6), provides a survey of American society 1900 to 1936.
Ford Madox Ford, *The English Novel*.
Private ownership of motor cars in UK passes a million, up from 200,000 in 1920.
Mahatma Ghandi begins campaign of civil disobedience against British rule in India.

1931   Virginia Woolf, *The Waves*, her most experimental novel.
Samuel Beckett, *Proust*.
Salvador Dali, *The Persistence of Memory*, in which his recurrent image of the clock makes its first appearance.
Oswald Moseley leaves Labour Party to found British Union of Fascists.

1932   Aldous Huxley, *Brave New World*, a dystopian novel.
Q. D. Leavis, *Fiction and the Reading Public*, criticizes effect of bestsellers on literary standards.
Atom split and neutron discovered at Cavendish Laboratory, Cambridge, England.

1933   Gertrude Stein, *The Autobiography of Alice B. Toklas*.
Claude McKay, *Banana Bottom*, his last novel, records conflict of local and European values in Jamaica.
Hitler becomes Reich Chancellor in Germany.

1934   Jean Rhys, *Voyage in the Dark*, mixes a woman's memories of childhood in Dominica with stark realties of her life as a chorus girl in London.

Mao Zedong leads Long March and becomes leader of Chinese Communist Party.

1935   **Patrick Hamilton,** *Twenty Thousand Streets Under the Sky: A London Trilogy,* records inner lives of three 'ordinary' visitors to a London pub.

Government of India Act grants responsibility in domestic affairs to provincial assemblies.

Nuremburg Laws enacted against Jews in Germany.

1936   **William Faulkner,** *Absalom! Absalom!,* described by readers as 'antinarrative'.

Djuna Barnes, *Nightwood,* edited and introduced by T. S. Eliot.

C. L. R. James, *Minty Alley,* his only novel.

John Maynard Keynes, *The General Theory of Employment, Interest and Money.*

International Surrealist Exhibition in London.

George V dies; Edward VII reigns briefly before abdication crisis brings George VI to the throne.

Spanish Civil War (1936–9) begins.

1937   **Zora Neale Hurston,** *Their Eyes were Watching God.*

Wyndham Lewis, *The Revenge for Love,* satirizes left-wing involvement in Spanish Civil War.

Mass Observation movement launched in Britain in which participants are encouraged to record their everyday lives.

Guernica destroyed in bombing in Spanish Civil War, immortalized in a painting by Picasso.

1938   **Samuel Beckett,** *Murphy,* capturing 'seedy' existence of its protagonist in London.

Elizabeth Bowen, *The Death of the Heart,* studies coldness and hypocrisy of middle-class life in London.

Graham Greene, *Brighton Rock.*

Orson Welles, radio broadcast of *War of the Worlds,* causes panic in America.

1939   **James Joyce,** *Finnegans Wake,* is his last and most experimental novel.

John Steinbeck, *The Grapes of Wrath,* described as a great 'proletarian' novel of the times.

Pan American Airlines begins commercial flights between the USA and Europe.
Second World War (1939–45) begins.

1940   **Charlie Chaplin,** *The Great Dictator*, his first 'talkie' film. Beginning of London Blitz.

1941   **Virginia Woolf,** *Between the Acts*, published three months after Woolf's suicide.
Japan bombs Pearl Harbor, leading to entry of the USA into the war.

1942   **Albert Camus,** *L'Etranger*, his most famous 'absurdist' novel. RAF begins bombing raids on German cities.

1944   **Saul Bellow,** *Dangling Man*, explores impact of society on the individual.

1945   **George Orwell,** *Animal Farm*.
Evelyn Waugh, *Brideshead Revisited*, shows decline of British upper classes.
Germany surrenders and Allies liberate Auschwitz. As many as six million Jews and other 'undesirables' have been exterminated.
America drops atomic bombs on Japanese cities Hiroshima and Nagasaki. Japan's surrender marks end of war.

MORAG SHIACH

Reading the modernist novel: an introduction

The aim of this *Cambridge Companion to the Modernist Novel* is to assist readers of modernist fiction, whether they are experienced or new readers of this challenging and stimulating body of literary work. The image of a 'companion' here suggests a kind of comradeship: a sharing of experiences as well as the illumination and pleasure gained through a conversation involving different viewpoints and diverse enthusiasms. This volume seeks, in that sense, to be a good companion to the reader. But it also aspires to be a challenging companion, offering new perspectives, teasing out difficult ideas, and drawing on the rich comparative and critical insights that can be gained through scholarship and research. Its contributors are experts in their field, and bring to their accounts of key ideas and key authors an extensive and deep knowledge of the period and the texts of modernism. The organization of this volume is intended to give the reader the greatest possible benefit from this expertise, and thus to help him or her to gain significant insight into whichever modernist novels they are reading.

The idea of 'modernism'

The focus of this *Companion* is the experience of reading English-language fictional narratives from the early years of the twentieth century. The second section of this volume is concerned explicitly with the challenges and the pleasures of reading the work of selected novelists who have been identified as key to modernist fiction. But in addition to such close readings of selected novels and novelists, some attention also needs to be given to the category that has shaped the analyses of these novels by the various contributors and also underpins the coherence of this volume: the category of 'modernism'. This category is the focus of the five chapters within the first section of the *Companion*. These chapters explore modernists' own understanding of the challenges of writing fiction in the modern world, discuss innovations in the representation of consciousness within the modernist novel, and analyse experiments with the representation of time in modernist fiction. They also map the beginnings of modernism and consider its legacy for later fiction writers. Because the idea of 'modernism' is now broadly familiar, being frequently and freely evoked in literary reviews and in academic curricula, this does not make its meaning or its significance in any sense obvious. What, the reader will want to know, makes these novels modernist? What kind of thing is 'modernism'? When did it begin, what is its scope, and why is it important for us to engage with?

Different contributors to this volume offer their own answers to some of these questions, but these are often tentative rather than definitive. As a response to a literary movement that is so fascinated by opacity and complexity, such critical scrupulousness or tentativeness is perhaps not inappropriate, but it leaves the task of satisfactory explication of 'modernism' for the aspirant reader of these novels a challenging one. Michael Levenson, who published a fascinating genealogy of 'modernism' that offers a map of some of its ancestry and its affiliations, writes of the tantalizing capacity of the idea of 'modernism' both to frustrate and to entice the critic and the reader. He writes of the term as 'at once vague and unavoidable. Anything more precise would exclude too much too soon; anything more general would be folly. As with any blunt instrument, the best that can be done is to use it for the rough tasks and to reserve the finer work for finer tools. As a rough way of locating our attention, "modernism" will do.'[1]

So in engaging with 'modernism' as a critical term, we are, according to Levenson, condemned to a certain roughness. This may indeed be a reassuring insight for the reader or the scholar who has searched in vain to pin down all modernism's defining characteristics once and for all. But we are also offered by Levenson a location for our attention, a way perhaps of bringing things together into comparative perspective, understanding a range of literary texts as having a more than accidental relationship to each other, and thinking about the literary culture of the years between the end of the nineteenth century and the end of the Second World War as having some sort of shape. In this sense the idea of 'modernism' forces us to ask questions about cultural forms as historical, and to think about the capacity of literary representation to express or to critique the period of its writing.

'Modernism' is not of course a term that would have been recognized and understood by the writers to whom we now apply it. There was certainly an intense consciousness among these writers of a need to be modern, in literary style as well as in life, and a developed perception that the modern world was, in important ways, unlike what had come before. In this sense the writers discussed in this *Companion* were, and knew themselves to be, modern. This much will be clear from the first chapter. But the idea of an abstract category of 'modernism' understood as a definable literary style, or as a grouping of texts that share central thematic and stylistic features, was essentially a critical creation of the second half of the twentieth century. There is no 'modernism' without institutionalized literary criticism and without a pedagogy of English that constitutes and disseminates its canon. In that sense the early twentieth-century writers discussed in this volume could not possibly have thought of themselves as modernists.

The retrospective quality of 'modernism' does not of course disqualify it as a critical term. Many connections, deep affiliations and historical trajectories can only be grasped at some distance from the urgency and messiness of their production. We may now indeed be able to see things about and in the early twentieth century that could be only fleetingly grasped then, and this may be what it is possible to invoke through the idea of 'modernism'. Certainly, we have the benefit as well as the handicap of knowing modernism's future, which means that we know both more and less about this period than those who lived through it. More in the sense that we can see where it led, but less in the sense that we cannot now recover the horizon of futurity within which that cultural moment was actually lived. The crucial differences between an early twentieth-century sense of the significant innovations of modern litera-ture and the later development of the more abstract idea of 'modernism' as a critical and to some extent a historical term, is very well captured in a study by Tim Armstrong: *Modernism: A Cultural History* (2005). Armstrong contrasts two distinct approaches to mapping the literature of the early twentieth century, one from the 1930s and one from the 1970s. The first approach he exemplifies through his discussion of a critical study of early twentieth-century literature published in 1935, with the title *The Georgian Literary Scene: A Panorama*. In this volume there is no sense of modern writing as a project, or of a coherent body of writing that can be understood as 'modernism'. Rather, a wide range of very diverse literary writing is evoked in terms of a literary panorama of what is new and striking in the period, which includes Ford Madox Ford, Katherine Mansfield, Virginia Woolf, Dorothy Richardson, Wyndham Lewis, and James Joyce (all of whom will be discussed within this *Companion*) but also H. G. Wells, Arnold Bennett, Somerset Maugham, Max Beerbohm and Compton MacKenzie, who would not now be thought of as standard 'modernist' fare. Armstrong argues that by the 1970s, on the other hand, in a text such as Hugh Kenner's *The Pound Era* (1971), there is a much more emphatic sense of a particular literary project of 'modernism'. For Kenner, this is revealed overwhelmingly in the work of Ezra Pound and in the stylistic innovations associated with writers such as T. S. Eliot, Lewis and Joyce.

Modernism has here become part of 'a heroic story in which Pound, armed with a philosophically and historically informed vision of the reform of language and technique ... creates the London Vortex from which flows the monumental works of "high modernism"'.[2] Kenner has thus given to 'modernism' a story, a cast of characters, and a definable project that will result in the production of significant cultural monuments.

A complementary critical history of the naming and mapping of 'modernism' as an abstract critical term and also as a literary movement is offered by Lawrence Rainey in his very interesting introduction to *Modernism: An Anthology*, which, like Armstrong's study, was published in 2005. Rainey produces a very persuasive narrative of the ways in which critical discussions of the idea of modernism have developed since the 1960s, and also indicates how this development itself intersects with broader cultural and social changes. Thus he shows how a critical identification in the 1960s of modernism with revolutions in literary technique and language and with the classicism and intensity associated with Imagism, gives way to a critical interest in modernism's creation of coherent and integral forms and its deployment of the legacy of European Symbolism. These critical approaches seem to look to modernism first as a point of resistance to the instrumentality and alienation of modern life and culture and then as a compensatory aesthetic, and even ethical, alternative to modernity's fragmentation and incoherence. They share a commitment to modernism as in some kind of oppositional relation to the dominant social and cultural forces within the modern world, but their emphases on the legacies of Imagism and of Symbolism lead them to foreground rather different texts and to theorize different forms of textual and artistic resistance.

Rainey goes on to discuss critical engagements with the idea of modernism which focus, for example, on the doctrines and philosophical systems that underpin this literary movement, best expressed in its polemical 'isms', including Vorticism, Surrealism, Imagism, Futurism, and Impressionism. In such critical approaches to modernism as an articulated and polemical project, there is a clear desire to connect the innovative energies and formal challenges of literary texts to broader cultural trends and aspects of modernization. More recent critical approaches to modernism also seek to reintegrate it within a historical narrative, either by stressing the ways in which modernist literature gives expression to historical changes or historical traumas (such as the First World War), or by looking at historical changes within the production and dissemination of culture itself, including the development of forms of literary mass production and distribution. This latter critical tendency leads to an investigation of the literary marketplace, and an analysis of the ways in which modernist literary fiction responds to the creation of new readerships through the expansion of education or the proliferation of affordable novels, journals and magazines.

Finally, Rainey shows how critical engagements with the literature of modernism are also in dialogue with the political concerns of the period from which they emerge. We might note, for example, the excellent historical and critical work on the idea of modernism that emerged from the context of feminism in the 1970s and 1980s. This led to the reinvigoration of critical discussions of relatively neglected writers such as Gertrude Stein or Richardson but also led to a fundamental challenge to the privileging of particular modes of experimental innovation within the canon of modernism. Following the publication of Bonnie Kime Scott's *The Gender of Modernism: A Critical Anthology* in 1990, indeed, a new consensus began to emerge that understood modernism less as the age of Pound, Eliot and Lewis and more as the age of Woolf, Richardson and Mansfield. This approach to modernism read literary texts not so much as heroic cultural project but rather as acute diagnostic of the faultlines of early twentieth-century culture. Such a transition, which seems to make the novelist particularly central to the drama of modernism, has its appeal for a volume such as this one that focuses particularly on the novel, and a number of the contributors to this volume write under the influence of this feminist reappraisal of the nature of modernism.

Every period, then, would appear to get the 'modernism' it deserves, or perhaps one might rather say the one it desires. This *Companion* is no exception to that and its mapping, too, is informed by a range of contemporary cultural, critical and political concerns, as will emerge in each of the chapters. Even so, across these various definitions, readings, and debates about modernism, which have unfolded since the 1960s, there are nonetheless some continuing themes, some consistent issues of style and form, and some texts that impose themselves as central to any attempt to map and to read modernism. In relation to modernist fiction, innovations in the representation of time; complex explorations of the nature of consciousness; formal experiments in narrative structure; and an intense use of the imaginative power of the image have always been understood as central. There are also few accounts that do not agree at least on the inclusion of Conrad, Joyce and Woolf. And across these many and various critical formulations of the name and nature of modernism there is also a continuing commitment to the importance of finding ways to read and to respond to these difficult, provoking and fascinating texts that offer an aesthetic experience in many ways quite unlike the experience offered by literature from other periods or in other styles.

How can we grasp the particularity of this aesthetic experience, or gauge its significance? To answer this we need to be able to discern the kind of changes that modernism brought to the writing and the reading of literary texts. Modernist texts demand a particular sort of reading that is intense and analytic, and often also informed by a wide knowledge of the history of European literature. Of the literary writer, understood overwhelmingly in this context as a significant and influential creative artist, modernism also made particular demands, charging him or her with the expectation of innovation and experiment, and weighting them with requirements of cultural renewal and a particular kind of psychological or historical insight. Malcolm Bradbury and James McFarlane argued in their very influential 1976 collection, *Modernism: A Guide to European Literature 1890–1930*, that European literary modernism had a cataclysmic effect on its writers and readers. They talk of 'those cataclysmic upheavals of culture, those fundamental convulsions of the creative human spirit that seem to topple even the most solid and substantial of our beliefs and assumptions, leave great areas of the past in ruins . . ., question an entire civilization or culture', and argue that this kind of convulsive, overwhelming change is part of the nature of modernism. They go on to say, 'that the twentieth century brought us a new art is undeniable . . . But we have also increasingly come to believe that this new art comes from, or is, an upheaval of the third and cataclysmic order.'[3]

More recent critics are wary of such claims of epochal transformations achieved through and in modernist literature. For example, Peter Nicholls's study, *Modernisms: A Literary Guide* (1995) stresses rather the multiplicity and the complexity of the various cultural innovations that come to be understood as different sorts of modernisms. He describes the beginnings of modernism in terms that seem very modest when compared to Bradbury and McFarlane's cataclysmic upheavals: 'The beginnings of modernism, like its endings, are largely indeterminate, a matter of traces rather than of clearly defined historical moments'.[4] These traces need to be deciphered and their connections mapped before a picture of the cultural impact of modernism can be discerned. On this model the impact of modernism was not one of epochal upheaval, but rather of gradually realized and complexly connected cultural transformations.

Nicholls suggests a historical moment at which these traces can first be glimpsed:

> in pursuit of those traces of modernism, then, we might return to Paris in the early 1840s, and specifically to a moment when visitors to the Champs-Elysées were entertained by the music of two young girls who begged their way between cafés, singing and playing the guitar. The striking beauty of one of them fascinated the writers and artists who frequented this part of the city. (1)

This trace of modernism is a momentary encounter between itinerant young women in the streets of Paris and the artistic sensibilities of writers and artists, including Charles Baudelaire. Baudelaire's aesthetic responses to the modern city, to the social figure of the outcast or derelict, and to the sensation of beauty and its momentary passing is here read as part of modernism's originary story. For Nicholls, however, although this story of origins begins with a social encounter in the streets of Paris, its meaning is crucially found within the development of a distinctive literary style. He writes of one of Baudelaire's poems that 'this early work already shows traces of what we might think of as a distinctively "modern" style. This is partly an effect of the glimpses the poem gives us of the new urban scene, and of the poet as one of its *déclassé* inhabitants; but mostly, I think, it has to do with a certain *tone*' (1).

There are a lot of issues in Nicholls's discussion here that resonate with our understanding of the nature of modernism: the urban setting, the emphasis on the power and the complexity of the momentary or evanescent experience, the invoking of different and disturbing social milieus and characters. But his emphasis is firmly on the question of poetic tone. For Nicholls, modernism begins when poetic writing develops a specific capacity for ironic distance, and it begins in nineteenth-century France. This is, of course, just one of many traces. Other stories could be told that begin with different encounters in different places. But what intrigues about Nicholls's account is the attempt to identify the moment when achieved aesthetic form has to give under the pressure of new social experience. The story Nichols tells here is of a cultural form that is driven by new forms of social experience, that responds to this through the creation of new kinds of poetic diction and idiom to produce a literary text that can be read as distinctively modern.

The beginnings of modernism are, unsurprisingly, the subject of extensive critical debate and many different stories have been told about when and why modernism began. Partly this is because the term embraces different forms of art: as well as the novel, 'modernism' is frequently attributed to music, architecture, painting, sculpture or poetry. 'Modernism' is also a critical term that refers to cultural works from a variety of different national traditions, each of which has its own requirements and constraints of periodization. The key moments will be understood differently within different national traditions, and translation is not always helpful here. Modernist architecture in Britain, for example, with its functional disdain of the decorative, has only selected points of contact with the colourful exuberance of the *modernisme* associated with an architect such as Gaudí, and the coincidence of names can at times be positively misleading.

The difficulty of establishing the moment when modernism began is not, however, just a matter of different national traditions but also one of the different disciplinary assumptions and approaches to periodization. For example, the beginnings of modernism in the visual arts, in architecture, or in music are thought of very differently, and consequently are generally located in different moments, though all are broadly understood as happening somewhere between the 1860s and the 1910s. Yet no sooner has one identified this modest degree of historical common ground than one can immediately think of an exception. In T. J. Clark's illuminating study of artistic modernism, *Farewell to an Idea: Episodes from a History of Modernism* (1999), modernism begins in 1793 with the exhibiting of Jacques-Louis David's painting *Death of Marat*. And this origin is crucial to the story Clark goes on to tell about the more familiar modernist landscape of Paul Cézanne and Pablo Picasso. But we must remember that Clark is making a quite particular argument here about the history of modernism and the history of socialism, which inflects the story he seeks to tell about the origins of modernism and generates an almost scandalous paradox of a modernism of the late eighteenth century.

Whatever story we are seeking to tell about modernism will, then, clearly inflect what we want to say about its beginnings. Nicholls looks to mid-nineteenth-century France as a point, or trace, of origin because he wants to tell a story that has at its centre the development of a particular modernist poetic sensibility and tone. T. J. Clark looks to 1793 as a point of origin because he wants to map the political and aesthetic energies associated with artistic modernism and to capture the faultlines between and within them. In this *Companion* the story of modernism is focused on the novel, and specifically the novel written in English in the early years of the twentieth century. It is a story about why and how particular innovations in narrative fiction were able to take place and also an assessment of what these novelistic innovations allow us particularly to know and to imagine. This approach leads to an 'origin' story beginning in the 1890s, and across the volume as a whole to a broader critical narrative that concentrates on the historical period between the 1890s and the 1940s (though the opening chapter on 'Modernists on the art of fiction' looks back to Henry James's 1884 essay on the art of fiction, while the closing chapter on Samuel Beckett looks at the development of his writing of and about narrative fiction from the 1930s to the 1960s). The claim implicit in this choice of period is partly a claim about an internal logic of literary history. Here the suggestion is that the development of the modernist novel is a response to difficulties or limitations within existing novelistic forms. For example, one might say that in the 1890s Thomas Hardy pushed novelistic realism as far as it could go, and in a novel such as *The Well-Beloved* (1897) was driven to such an excessive foregrounding of repetition and such a painful sense of an inescapable framework of causation that both theme and structure within a realist mode became impossible to countenance. Hardy's response to touching the limits of realism was, of course, to stop writing novels. But other novelists writing after him pursued the logic of density, repetition and excess and even made it the focus of their narrative fiction, which is perhaps one way of understanding the most disturbing aspects of a text such as Joseph Conrad's *Heart of Darkness* (1902). Conrad's allusiveness, his unease about narrative causation and his resistance to translatable symbolic or metaphorical figures all, as Jeremy Hawthorn notes in his discussion of Conrad in chapter ten, 'make of that story something quite on another plane than an anecdote of a man who went mad in the centre of Africa' (152).

On this model, the novelistic writings of Hardy, of James, or of Oscar Wilde in the 1890s are key to understanding the formal innovations of modernist fiction in subsequent decades, posing as they do particular questions about the limits of realism, while exploring the complexities of narrative voice and narrative point of view and raising questions about the relations between the metaphorical power of novelistic imagery and the analytic power of novelistic causality. Modernist fiction then becomes in some sense a complex and inventive series of responses to the formal questions raised by and in novels of the 1890s.

Yet the formal and stylistic challenges of novelistic writing in the 1890s are not just a matter of a literary style that had run its course. *Fin-de-siècle* novelists created their fictional texts at a moment when key social institutions were under particular pressure. They were writing at a moment of significant historical transition. Technological innovations, rapid urbanization, changing patterns of Empire, political realignments, and the destabilization of a range of social institutions all generated particular pressures on the literary imagination of the 1890s. The sense in reading novels of the 1890s of a literary form under pressure as it seeks both to register change and to capture the nature of a fluidity and an opacity that are experienced in new and pressing ways, makes this for me a persuasive historical moment from which to start mapping the origins of the modernist novel in English. For other writers, and for other historians, the key transition may come at a rather different moment; Woolf, as Jeff Wallace discusses in chapter one, argued for a slightly later date, insisting that it was 'in or about December, 1910, [that] human character changed' (20). Woolf's exemplification of this claim involves reference to significant modifications of class relations, to changes in the field of culture and also to transformations within the structure of the family. There is of course no absolutely identifiable beginning to such a complex set of changes, but there is nonetheless a broad recognition that the turn of the century saw transformations that generated a significantly, and often painfully, new social reality.

The choice of an ending for the story of modernism is also a matter of critical controversy, though the Second World War is commonly identified as the end of it as a coherent project. The deaths of both Joyce and Woolf during the war have been seen as bringing to an abrupt end the most distinctive phase of the modernist novel in English. But the choice of the Second World War as the possible end of modernism is more significant than this biographical coincidence suggests. Modernism is characterized both by a recognition of fragmentation and by a desire to resolve or overcome this through the integrity of aesthetic form. The urgency of achieving such integrity was apparently intensified by the traumas of the First World War, a fact Woolf registered so insistently in novels such as *Jacob's Room* (1922) or *Mrs Dalloway* (1925) and Lawrence figured rather differently in *Lady Chatterley's Lover* (1928). But the experience of the Second World War seems on the contrary to have been too great a challenge to the possibility of aesthetic wholeness and its promise, if not of redemption, then at least of a momentary insight and coherence. Something of the sense of an achievable project, of a shared aesthetic vision, was lost in those years of violent conflict and national and individual loss and dislocation. Thereafter, we are, if not exactly postmodern, at least in a period of late modernism whose dynamic remains to some extent still unresolved in the present. Modernism has not, as we shall see in Laura Marcus's chapter on its legacy, gone away, but it has certainly had to negotiate with new literary forms and to accept a more modest sense of its cultural possibilities. It is not, any more, our cultural dominant.

Making sense of the modernist novel

In creating this *Companion*, I have tried to concentrate on the issues and the texts that seem to me central to an understanding of the modernist novel in English, and also the most illuminating for the aspiring reader. The volume thus begins with a section that looks comparatively at a wide range of modernist writings and writers so that the relations between them can be better understood and the overall shape of the modernist project, or the modernist moment, can be more readily discerned.

In the first chapter Jeff Wallace discusses a range of modernist writers who reflected explicitly on the nature of narrative fiction and also sought to capture the distinctive qualities of modern prose. Wallace develops the idea discussed above of modernist innovation as facing in two directions: 'looking simultaneously inwards, towards form and language, and outwards, towards the changing material circumstances in which fiction was being produced and consumed' (15). He begins by discussing James's 1884 essay 'The Art of Fiction', in which James argues forcefully for the aesthetic seriousness of the novel as a form, and insists on its responsibility to capture the vastness and the variousness of the novelist's impression of 'life'. To do this, James argues, the novel must follow no received formula, but must rather capture the 'strange irregular rhythm of life' through a formal integrity that is both capacious and coherent (16). Wallace then turns to a discussion of Woolf's very influential reflections on the particular demands of and on modern fiction, which were developed in various essays written between 1919 and 1929. Woolf, like James, insists on the seriousness and the significance of the novel as a literary form. She challenges the aesthetic of literary naturalism associated with writers such as Bennett or John Galsworthy (who were highly successful in the period) and argues instead for a novelistic art that will capture the intangible, the transient and the allusive qualities and experiences that are for her the very stuff of being. Wallace's account of the developing aesthetic of novelistic modernism then turns to D. H. Lawrence's polemical identification of the novel as 'the highest complex of subtle inter-relatedness that man has discovered' (23) and to E. M Forster's very different sense that 'human beings have their great chance in the novel' (24). Woolf, Lawrence and Forster were all writing their most distinctive essays on the art of fiction at the same time, in the 1920s, and Wallace teases out both their shared assumptions and their very different aesthetic and social projects with great clarity. This chapter concludes with an analysis of two very challenging writers of and about modernist fiction: Samuel Beckett and Gertrude Stein. The key text here in relation to Beckett is his fascinating 1931 study of Marcel Proust, which is both a critical *tour de force* and something close to a personal manifesto, while the analysis of Stein focuses on her 'seemingly formless meditation', *How to Write*, published in that same year. Wallace keeps these diverse yet connected discussions of the art of modernist fiction in conversation with each other, and offers a persuasive overall argument, which might best be captured through Woolf's version of 'the modernist proposition, not only that the fiction will suffice, but that artistic autonomy is the very *guarantee* of its engagement with the real' (30).

Peter Brooker's discussion of 'early modernism' inevitably addresses the issues of periodization outlined above. Brooker identifies modernism explicitly as a literary movement characterized by a significant degree of formal experimentation, which can be understood, in however complexly mediated a fashion, as a response to the conditions of modernity. For Brooker, this definition assures that both Woolf and Joyce can be uncontroversially read as modernists. But the prehistory of modernism is a significantly more vexed issue. Brooker insists that 'the list of earlier novelists with some claim to be included under the heading of "modernism" is ... a long one' (32) and his candidates include Hardy, George Gissing, Wells, Forster and Ford Madox Ford. Brooker prefers the notion of 'early modernism' to any theory of a moment of origin for the complex modernist project, since 'it allows us to think of modernism as a process of change and development rather than an evolution "upwards" towards an achieved end' (32). Brooker notes how the aspiration to capture the complexity of social change drives Hardy towards new forms and new idioms, and argues that the 'awkwardness' this generates within Hardy's prose is in fact a mark of its modern qualities. He also explores the connections between literary experimentation, reflections on the nature of prose fiction, and networks of literary innovation in his reading of the influential role of Ford as an early modernist. Brooker notes Ford's friendships and alliances with a wide range of key modernist writers, his promotion of the seriousness of the art of fiction, and his support for the significant cultural mission of the novelist as modern artist. Ford's theorization of the techniques of literary impressionism, so important for Conrad, can be understood, Brooker suggests, as 'the hallmark of an emerging modernism in the English novel' (35). Finally, Brooker turns to May Sinclair and Mansfield, to assess the contribution they made to the development of modernist fiction, and in particular to their gendered constructions of the transitions and disruptions characteristic of the early modernist moment.

In the third chapter Ann Banfield analyses one of the most distinctive innovations characteristic of the modernist novel, experimentation with the representation of time. She focuses, in particular, on the development of a marked dualism in the experience and the representation of time, primarily manifested as a disjunction between public or objective and private or subjective time (48). She contrasts this dualism with the very influential philosophical current expressed in the work of Henri Bergson, for whom the only authentic human experience of time was one of 'duration', where time is lived as a series of flowing and interconnecting moments and memories. Banfield argues powerfully for the dynamic relation between these different conceptions of time, and shows their consequences for narrative structure and for narrative voice within a wide range of modernist novels, including those of Woolf, Proust, William Faulkner and Beckett. She also analyses the central role of the novel of a single day within modernist fiction, dwelling in particular on Joyce's *Ulysses* (1922), Woolf's *Mrs Dalloway* and Andrey Bely's *Petersburg* (1916) and develops an acute account of the complexity of grammatical tenses in the representation of novelistic time.

Innovations in the representations of time are, then, key to the development of modernist fiction. So, too, are the complex experiments with the representation of consciousness that are discussed in Anne Fernihough's chapter on 'consciousness as a stream'. Fernihough persuasively maps the relations between philosophical explorations of subjectivity, identity or the unconscious, and a range of formal and thematic developments within modernist fiction. For example, she discusses William James (brother of Henry) and his 1890 study, *Principles of Psychology*, and suggests that his concept of 'mind-wandering', understood as a psychological state in which the individual is open to the chaos and intensity of sense-impressions that bombard from minute to minute is a helpful one in reading both character and form in a range of novels. Thus, for example, we might understand the importance of physical and psychological 'wandering' in a novel such as *Ulysses* or *Jacob's Room*. Fernihough also explores the significance of the concept of 'stream of consciousness' often understood, and as often misunderstood, as a defining characteristic of modernist fiction. The phrase is probably borrowed directly from William James, but it is first applied in a literary context to the work of Richardson. Richardson had no fondness for the term, but its suggestion of fluidity, dynamism and complexity within human consciousness have made it a powerfully influential critical concept. Modernist fiction embraces such fluidity, and develops a series of narrative techniques to capture the pressure of impressions and memories as they are filtered through the consciousness of a character or of a creative artist. The modernist self is a complexly layered, conflicted and fluid subjectivity and the modernist novel has to develop new idioms and new forms to render this selfhood.

The first section of this *Companion* ends with Laura Marcus's mapping of the legacy of modernism and her exploration of the ways in which a range of writers responded to, argued with and rewrote key aspects of the modernist tradition. She ranges very widely across fictional writing from the 1950s to the present day and shows a continuing influence on narrative themes, or novelistic techniques, and on the understanding of the nature and the significance of the art of fiction. Novelists on whom she focuses particularly include B. S. Johnson, Paul Auster, Alan Hollinghurst, Doris Lessing, Saul Bellow, Ian McEwan, Salman Rushdie, Jeanette Winterson, Zadie Smith, Michael Cunningham, Colm Tóibín and David Lodge. The traces and tracks she follows are many and various, and the legacy that emerges is a complex one, but by the end of the chapter three novelists emerge with the strongest claim to have moulded, provoked and enabled their successors: Joyce, Woolf and Beckett.

The remaining chapters of this *Companion* offer the reader detailed critical accounts of the work of a range of modernist novelists. Each chapter offers local insights into the complexities of specific novelistic texts, but also situates the work of the authors they discuss in terms of larger arguments about the field of modernist literature. My choices for inclusion in this section may strike some readers as controversial. Detailed arguments for the significance of each of the writers discussed can, however, be found within the chapters that follow, as can careful and thoughtful analyses of their sometimes troubled relations to the critical understanding of 'modernism'. Thus, for example, Rebecca Beasley acknowledges that 'the inclusion of Wyndham Lewis in this *Companion* reflects a significant shift in our conception of the modernist novel over the past fifteen years' (126), while Hugh Stevens talks of Lawrence as modernist but also talks of Lawrence's 'unrestrained contempt for the modernist novel' (137). And Anna Snaith, in her discussion of the modernist fiction of the 'black Atlantic', talks of the global migrations and transatlantic crossings typical of the period and the contact between people of different races they generate, while insisting that 'attention to such contact puts pressure on many other frameworks within which modernism has been defined and debated' (207). The generation of such conceptual and critical pressure is, in the end, fundamental to the design of this *Companion*. Out of new juxtapositions and connections come new insights into this rich literary domain. Each novelist discussed in this volume in my view makes an important and distinctive contribution to modernist fiction. To understand the common ground and also the important differences between these writers is to have the tools for a complex but coherent mapping of the nature of modernist fiction in English.

Notes

1. Michael H. Levenson, *A Genealogy of Modernism: A Study of English Literary Doctrine 1908–1922* (Cambridge: Cambridge University Press, 1984), p. vii.
2. See Tim Armstrong, *Modernism: A Cultural History* (Cambridge: Polity Press, 2005), pp. 24–5.
3. Malcolm Bradbury and James McFarlane, 'The Name and Nature of Modernism', in Bradbury and McFarlane (eds.), *Modernism: A Guide to European Literature 1890–1930* (Harmondsworth: Penguin, 1976), pp. 19–55 (pp. 19–20).
4. Peter Nicholls, *Modernisms: A Literary Guide* (London: Palgrave Macmillan, 1995), p. 1. Further references cited parenthetically.

I

JEFF WALLACE

Modernists on the art of fiction

Between the 1880s and the 1930s, a new and fertile discourse on the art of fiction emerged alongside the extensive reshaping of fictional form itself. This interweaving of critical and creative activities typifies the self-consciousness we have come to find in modernism across all the arts. Manifestos, declarations, excurses and rationales are the inevitable accompaniments to modernist experimentation, just as reflexivity becomes lodged in the grain of the artwork: the Cézanne canvas cannot fail to be about the discourse of painting as much as it is about the pursuit of natural phenomena; the Imagist poem, stripping itself of the trappings of the 'poetical', succeeds in this very gesture in foregrounding the discourses of poetry. In the case of the art of fiction, the very use of the term 'art' is an emergent sign of this new self-consciousness.

It is important to recognize the influence of a particular historical context of aesthetic theory and practice, drawn mainly from France and Russia, in the development of Anglo-American modernist fiction, ranging from Gustave Flaubert's expressed desire to write a novel about nothing, to the coruscating naturalism of Emile Zola and the psychological intensities of Fyodor Dostoevsky. Through this context the idea of the modern novel comes to occupy a complex space bounded by the principles of abstraction on the one hand and realism on the other.

This essay presents a brief comparative survey of six representative writers and selected key texts on the art of modernist fiction. I want to suggest how far, through a cluster of recurrent concepts – art itself, but also life, experience, the human, realism, morality, freedom, democracy, readers – the discourse on modernist fiction is fundamentally Janus-faced, looking simultaneously inwards, towards form and language, and outwards, towards the changing material circumstances in which fiction was being produced and consumed.

Art and 'life': James and Woolf

Henry James settled in England in 1876, having gravitated from America to Europe a year earlier, and henceforth, in the words of Peter Keating, 'set about transforming the quality and status of modern fiction'.[1] In reviews, commentaries and prefaces to his own works of fiction, extending up to his death in 1916, James constructed a highly influential conceptual framework for the fictions of modernism. James's essay 'The Art of Fiction', published in *Longman's Magazine* in September 1884, echoes the title of a lecture delivered by the writer Walter Besant to the Royal Institution five months earlier. Besant was closely associated with the Society of Authors, founded in 1883 to maintain and defend the rights of authors in a rapidly expanding and diversifying literary marketplace, but also gained recognition for his own popular fictions of working-class East End London.

James's essay subtly inflects a sense of disparity between the cultured émigré and the stalwart champion of British literary craftsmanship. He begins by congratulating Besant on his contribution to the process of making the English novel more *discutable* and less *naïf*, 'if I may help myself out with another French word'.[2] The English novel was, in other words, aspiring to a theory of itself, not yet perhaps with the 'remarkable completeness' of the French, but at least with more sophistication than was contained in the warm and comfortably ascendant Anglo-Saxon feeling that a novel is a novel as 'a pudding is a pudding' (36, 24). The central insight of Besant's argument, for James, is that fiction is one of the *fine* arts. Arraigned against this view in late Victorian English culture are, James argues, two influential countertendencies, one residual, the other emergent: first, puritanical approaches to art in general as 'injurious' and the novel in particular as immoral; second, the omnivorous 'vulgarization of everything' in modern commodity culture.

Through the question of fictional art and its fineness, however, James carefully uncouples himself from Besant's position. Besant proposes that the 'laws' of fiction can be set out with precision: novelists must write from their own experience, and with a sense of moral purpose; characters should be 'real' and clearly outlined; story and style (or 'workmanship') should be of primary importance. James's gnomic response is that it is impossible unequivocally either to agree or to disagree with these aspirations. Instead, James maps out for modern fiction a highly influential, if somewhat more elusive, theory. The sole *raison d'être* of the novel, for which it should remain unapologetic, is to represent the novelist's direct impression of 'life'. An essential precondition is freedom, the absence of any limit on the novelist's technique or interest. A novel's 'air of reality' is a function of its ability to recognize that human life is immense and various, and to catch 'the very note and trick, the strange irregular rhythm of life' (38). 'Life' here bears, of course, enormous semantic weight, but in the context of the later nineteenth century it was at least partly a biological category. The novel for James must be 'a living thing, all one and continuous, like any other organism, and in proportion as it lives it will be found, I think, that in each of the parts there is something of each of the other parts' (34).

James's organicism places almost impossible strictures on analysis. Composition is not 'a series of blocks'; distinctions between aspects of description and narration in fiction are futile, those between different genres of fiction – for example, the novel and the romance – equally so. Good novels have life, bad novels do not; these, the only fictional classifications James claims to 'understand', are ultimately determined by the equally inscrutable quality of the author's intelligence: 'no good novel will ever proceed from a superficial mind' (44). The fineness of the fictional aesthetic, and whatever moral value fiction might possess, are both therefore determined by the untrammelled intelligence and sincerity of the individual novelist.

The powerful resonance of James's fictional aesthetic for the development of modernism might be located in its unresolved contradictions. In the conclusion to the essay, James places before the young novelist the alluring prospect of unlimited freedom and experimentation, in a form whose 'magnificence' makes other arts seem restricted by comparison. In one sense this is entirely consistent with the history of the novel which, since the eighteenth century, had been the preeminent art form of a secular modernity, bypassing the formal conventions of poetry and drama in order to open out aesthetic space for a post-Enlightenment age in which knowledge is no longer esoteric.[3] However, while the openness and flexibility of the Jamesian novel suggests an essentially *democratic* art, a challenge is posed to James's concept of fictional art by the actual extension of democracy in the late nineteenth century, through the widening of literacy and print culture as well as via the political modes of a widening franchise and the rise of the labour and suffrage movements. James's discourse on the novel coincides with a fragmentation or diversification of the literary marketplace. As popular fictions proliferate in the expansion of newspapers, magazines and periodicals, alternative initiatives seek to mark out a space for 'literary' art: specialist literary periodicals anticipate both the formation of the discipline of literary criticism and the construction of fiction as an object of study, in the early twentieth-century university.

James is therefore strictly ambivalent about the 'innumerable opportunities' open to the modern novelist, whose freedom is part of the trajectory of the novel as a democratic form, yet whose 'art' must be forged in contradistinction to a general 'vulgarization' which, in the realm of art itself, is signified by any resort to categorization, convention or cliché. The novelist must be liberated from Besant's 'laws', yet James fails to acknowledge the democratic possibility that laws, if transmissable as technique, might themselves liberate, creating the conditions for the proliferation of writing. His organicist aesthetic shrouds fictional value in the achievement of 'life' as a measure of the superior intelligence of the writer – a standard perhaps more intimidating and constricting in its inscrutability than any laws could be. There is then a disjunction between James's radical individualism and his insistence on absolute standards of taste and judgement. The same contradiction was to reemerge later in the ideological formation of F. R. Leavis's Cambridge school of criticism from the 1930s onwards.

Virginia Woolf qualifies as one of the 'young writers' to whom James's discourse on fiction was often addressed, and the influence of James on her earliest fictions has often been observed. Like James, Woolf was born into a family of some intellectual distinction, and created a corpus of work combining experimental fiction of profound importance with a prodigious output of criticism and theory. In two of her most famous and often anthologized essays, 'Modern Fiction' (1919) and 'Mr Bennett and Mrs Brown' (1924), Woolf seems to conduct a silent dialogue with the Jamesian aesthetic; more explicitly, the argumentative form of 'The Art of Fiction' is echoed, as is a discourse in which social class and the definition of art are subtly entwined. Woolf's targets are, however, more daunting. While James could take on Besant with a degree of confidence, even complacency, Woolf's critical subjects are Arnold Bennett, H. G. Wells and John Galsworthy, three of the most popular and bestselling male novelists of the Edwardian period. Along with a certain patrician Jamesian tone in Woolf's treatment of her subjects, then, there is also an element of courage, inseparable from the pursuit of a gender politics which decisively differentiates Woolf's discourse on fiction from that of her predecessor.

'Modern Fiction' includes a noticeably robust configuration of the 'art of fiction'. With gentle irony, the art is mythologized as a female goddess; should she appear among us, however, she would insist on being broken and bullied as well as honoured and loved. The unsettling image of female maltreatment is a mark of the uncompromising stand taken by Woolf, in this and in the later essay, on the need for rigorous and constantly renewed fictional realism. Wells, Bennett and Galsworthy are 'materialists', and this is the source of 'our' constant disappointment with them: they 'are concerned not with the spirit but with the body', and 'write of unimportant things', spending immense 'skill' and 'industry' on making the 'trivial' and 'transitory' appear 'true' and 'enduring'.[4] Echoing yet outdoing James on Besant, Woolf develops a clear distinction between the manual or industrial labour of the 'materialists' and the intellectual work of those dedicated to the true art of fiction. Woolf draws here perhaps from Arthur Symons's *The Symbolist Movement in Literature* (1899), in which Symons had consolidated the Flaubertian notion of the autonomous novel by accusing Zola and the naturalists of trying to 'build in brick and mortar inside the covers of a book'.[5] Woolf's Bennett is the best workman/craftsman of her three *bêtes noires*, building such substantial fictional edifices that there are no draughts from the windows or cracks in the floorboards. And yet – 'if life should refuse to live there'? ('Modern Fiction' 147). House property, Woolf wryly notes, 'was the common ground from which the Edwardians found it easy to proceed to intimacy'.[6]

'Life' is, however, an elusive proposition; tentatively, Woolf suggests that this 'essential thing' has indeed narrowly eluded the Edwardians, has 'moved off, or on'. What is clearer is that the established form of the novel is no longer appropriate to a modern epistemology in which the notion of objectivity has been problematized by relativity physics and the subjective sciences of psychology and psychoanalysis. What, Woolf asks, is life actually like? To examine 'an ordinary mind on an ordinary day' is to realize that experience is a bewildering bombardment of diverse stimuli. The notion of a fictional realism based on narrative omniscience or distance must be replaced by a more complex model, emphasizing the liminality of the boundaries between inner and outer:

> Life is not a series of gig lamps symmetrically arranged; life is a luminous halo, a semi-transparent envelope surrounding us from the beginning of consciousness to the end. Is it not the task of the novelist to convey this varying, this unknown and uncircumscribed spirit, whatever abberration or complexity it may display, with as little mixture of the alien and external as possible?
>
> ('Modern Fiction' 150)

Woolf constructs life as 'spirit' here through a delicate counterbalancing of the mystical and the naturalistic, 'luminous halo' seeming to belong simultaneously to religious imagery and the science of optics, 'semi-transparent envelope' to biology and spiritualism.

Woolf thus updates James's impressionistic insistence on 'catching . . . the strange irregular rhythm of life', correspondingly toughening up the task of the novelist in the final call to arms, where the proposal is clearly not simply for modernist fiction to repudiate realism, but to achieve a more authentic engagement with the real than *realism*, so called, could possibly attain. The preconditions for this task remain resolutely Jamesian: if the novelist is to be able to realize the 'infinite possibilities of the art', she must be freed from the 'powerful and unscrupulous' tyranny of realist fictional convention and its 'embalming' air of probability. Thus liberated, the only things forbidden to the novelist are falsity and pretence. The ethical drive is further reinforced by Woolf's bold use of the spiritual, confirming a sense that, for both her and James, consecration was a large part of advocacy. James had witheringly described Anthony Trollope's tendency to confide in the reader as the 'betrayal of a sacred office' (26).

Yet in Woolf's case this strategic attack on 'materialism' is at the same time misleading. Two distinctly materialist emphases lie at the centre of Woolf's foundational contribution to modern feminist criticism, *A Room of One's Own* (1929). Woolf argues in this essay that to be able to write, a woman must have material support, time and space, a room; and she must inherit a set of 'tools'. Looking back across the history of modern prose, however, the woman writer finds at her disposal only *masculine* tools of grammar, syntax, vocabulary, sentence structure, even when these were deployed by her female predecessors.

Woolf's attack on the realist novel in the name of the 'spirit' of life is thus an encoded reflection on the thoroughly *ideological* nature of the realist tradition. Fittingly, the substance of the essay 'Mr Bennett and Mrs Brown' is crystallized in a single challenge: how does the novelist depict, or express the life of, the small anonymous woman sitting opposite in the railway carriage? Framing the enquiry is Woolf's revision, along the lines of a new relativity, of the old cliché that all novels deal essentially with character. Not only might character mean one thing to you, another to me, but, as Woolf claims in one of her most notorious and enigmatic assertions, 'in or about December, 1910, human character changed' ('Mr Bennett' 113). Beneath the gender-neutral terms in which this debate is conducted, however, we know that it is a woman who is being looked at, and that the material history of the realist gaze might also be that of a male gaze. '"Stop! Stop!"' exclaims Woolf, interrupting her imagined Edwardian materialist's attempt to describe Mrs Brown in terms of her father's shop in Harrogate and the wages of shop assistants in 1878. If Mrs Brown is the archetypal 'spirit we live by, life itself' (128), the ability to render her might require something more than the placing of new fictional tools at the disposal of Arnold Bennett – something, for example, like women writing with modernist tools of their own invention.

Lawrence and Forster: modernism as antimodernism

Woolf intriguingly assessed the effect, on 'young Georgians' such as D. H. Lawrence and E. M. Forster, of their inheritance of Edwardian fictional tools. Their early work, she claims, was spoilt by the attempt to effect a compromise between social or materialist realism and the need to break out into radical, modernist experimentation ('Mr Bennett' 125). It may, however, have been an easier proposition for both James and Woolf to carve out a theoretical space for modernist fiction as a fine and sacred art. In the work of

Lawrence and Forster, the problematic position of the aesthetic in a class-based society looms larger, producing complex fusions of identification and distance. Neither writer, it seems, could shake off either the allure of the aesthetic as a mode of emancipation in its own right, or the responsibility to use art as a mode of social investigation and critique. The result is that both remain ambivalent figures *vis à vis* the kind of 'official', high modernist fictional aesthetic of James and Woolf. In their own discourses on fiction, the novel attains a life and agency of its own, as if to anticipate a later 'death of the author' syndrome – or as if to attest to a lack of that ownership which in James and Woolf is constantly affirmed by an emphasis on the agency of the writer.

A sense of the novel's independent power as a form is glimpsed in Lawrence's early, and extraordinary, excursus, the *Study of Thomas Hardy*, which he began to write in 1915 'out of sheer rage' at the onset of war.[7] Hardy's novels figure relatively lightly, and appear to be a mere pretext for the first extended outline of a Lawrentian metaphysic of modernity as a long historical process of psychic and bodily repression. In contemporary terms, for Lawrence, this was exemplified by the 'self-preservation' ethic of capitalist economics and political democracy. In the longer view, it had been encapsulated in the rise of Christianity and the steady triumph of the ethic of Love over the old Mosaic Law of the Father. Boldly theoretical in his grasp of Hardy's fictional oeuvre, Lawrence asserts that all Hardy's heroes and heroines figure this pattern in the struggle, against the limits of social convention, to burst into 'flower' or being, while their subsequent failure, and banishment to the wilderness, constitute the tragedy of the novels. Enclosing this tragedy, however, and revealing its modern 'weakness', is the greater elemental context of nature, within which the human and social dramas are played out. Lawrence's Hardy is thus divided against himself. The explicit prevalence of the social system as the source of morality and retribution is 'almost silly' as a metaphysic, and makes some aspects of Hardy's writing 'sheer rubbish'.[8] But the novels expose what Hardy is powerless to conceal: that he has a deeper, instinctive and sensuous understanding of nature or the Law, an 'unconscious adherence to the flesh', which is somehow always overridden by his sense of social tragedy (94).

Several aspects of this reading of Hardy demonstrate a theory of fictional autonomy and impersonality which is nevertheless quite distinct from the modernist aesthetic of James and Woolf. There is initially a surprisingly collective treatment of the novels, almost cursorily listed and summarized, as if their individual characteristics were of far less importance than the shared pattern they reveal; and there is the sense that the novel possesses an unconscious dimension which might be antithetical to its author's motives. Hardy, the individual, is almost bracketed out of the account, as if merely the cipher through which the art of fiction comes into being. This impersonality, then, constitutes a different kind of artistic truth-telling from the cool detachment of the author in pursuit of the minute data of experience; rather, it is a revelation of broader human and cultural truths, in patterns possibly unavailable to the individual consciousness.

This thinking about the art of fiction reaches its fullest expression in *Studies in Classic American Literature* (1923), where Lawrence famously announces:

> Art-speech is the only truth ... The artist usually sets out – or used to – to point a moral and adorn a tale. The tale, however, points the other way, as a rule. Two blankly opposing morals, the artist's and the tale's. Never trust the artist. Trust the tale. The proper function of a critic is to save the tale from the artist who created it.[9]

This view of art as antithetical to its own morality confers upon the critic the hermeneutic task of uncovering the 'symbolic meaning' of the work. In the case of American literature, this meant revealing the extent to which writers were enslaved to the ideal of democratic equality, whether in terms of race, class or gender. In James Fenimore Cooper's 'white' novels, for example, all the characters are, Lawrence claims, fixed by the 'pin' of a social contract, 'never real human beings'; in the Leatherstocking novels, however, 'dreaming' close bondings between white and native Indian men, an unconscious belief in a natural inequality or *dis*quality reasserts itself (49, 58). Repeatedly, Lawrence subsumes the question of individual artistic genius beneath a model of the novel as a cultural document of profound revelation. Edgar Allan Poe is 'doomed' to register a process of 'white' psychic disintegration, and then to be reviled for performing this 'necessary' task by moralists; Herman Melville is similarly bound, in his loathing of the human and helpless fascination with the impersonal movements of matter, to produce in *Moby-Dick* (1851) an epic of 'esoteric symbolism of profound significance, and of considerable tiresomeness' (66, 146).

A series of essays written in the mid-1920s crystallize the peculiar amalgam of modernist and antimodernist thinking in Lawrence's discourse on the art of fiction.[10] The strains of the modern, democratic and emancipatory are familiar: the novel is 'the one bright book of life' (195). As in Woolf, 'life' is a condition of complete aesthetic freedom to convey the relativity of all things and the uniqueness and unpredictability of individual character. As we have seen, however, the novelist for Lawrence is no freer, as he put it, than a rooted tree is free; he or she is grounded in culture and history, and obliged by the novel itself to express situated truths which lie beyond individual consciousness. The novel may then remain, in an age of rapidly developing technologies of communication and representation, 'the highest complex of subtle inter-relatedness that man has discovered' (172), but to maintain this condition the novelist's own relatedness must be insouciant, for as soon as the relationship becomes *willed*, the novelist trying to 'fix' or 'nail' the novel by organizing character into 'pattern', the novel either falls dead, or walks off with the nail.

Here, however, in what constitutes an extraordinary reversal of James's and Woolf's readings, Lawrence proposes that it is precisely in the most acclaimed of contemporary modernist fiction that the novel's demise along these lines is threatened. In an unforgettable satire, Lawrence characterizes the concerns of every character in Joyce, Dorothy Richardson and Marcel Proust: "'Did I feel a twinge in my little toe, or didn't I?'…'Is the odour of my perspiration a blend of frankincense and orange pekoe and boot-blacking, or is it myrrh and bacon-fat and Shetland tweed?'" (151). The novel's intense self-consciousness, he asserts, is an expression of childish egotism and a death blow to the possibility of an open and flexible approach to human identity seen as a whole. Once the novelist-surgeon has reduced the self to thousands of pieces, it cannot be reassembled; analysis arrests the organism in stasis, no longer to be seen as a living process or 'man alive'. This of course is a different stasis from the kind that Lawrence detected and condemned, in scrupulously modernist fashion, in the moral systems of nineteenth-century realism; both are, however, *immoral*, according to Lawrence's own Nietzschean inversion or transvaluation of values, because both upset the 'trembling balance' of interrelatedness between humans and the universe which was, for him, the very definition of the moral purpose of art. A bomb, he concluded, was the only solution, followed by modern fiction renewing itself through an alliance with philosophy, developing the courage once again to 'tackle new propositions without using abstractions' (155).

Forster's scepticism about modern fiction carried more of diffidence than of Lawrence's revolutionary zeal. Flattered to be invited to give the annual Clark lectures at Trinity College, Cambridge, in 1927, following T. S. Eliot in 1926, Forster nevertheless realized that the generous remuneration would require him not only to undertake a heavy course of reading, but to speak from within the developing profession or institution of literary criticism whose validity he had often questioned and whose inferiority to the creative process he had often upheld. However, once he had committed to the lectures, Forster's reflections fell obediently into the accessible headings of the student textbook: 'the story', 'people', 'the plot', 'pattern and rhythm'. *Aspects of the Novel* (1927) quickly became, and remained, a staple item on undergraduate reading lists, and deposited a homely and now deeply familiar vocabulary for fictional analysis: 'flat' and 'round' characters; 'bouncing' the reader between narrative perspectives; and '"Yes – oh dear yes – the novel tells a story."'[11]

It is thus, initially, difficult to read *Aspects* as the work of a modernist, until we remember that the combination of friendly and accessible, prosaic, common-sense liberal humanism, and the wry, ironic sense of the potential fragility of this whole humanist project, is precisely what might be identified as modernist in Forster's fiction. Ostensibly, *Aspects* charts a middle way between the respective virtues of popular and experimental fiction. The factor of mediation, connecting with Woolf's pursuit of Mrs Brown and Lawrence's search for 'relatedness', is the sovereign condition of the 'human'. Like his peers, Forster saw the novel's lack of formal constraint, its openness and flexibility, as the ideal mode for recording the rich incalculability of human life. 'Human beings have their great chance in the novel', and they prevail at the *expense* of form; the novel's artistic development is hindered, in comparison with the drama, by 'its humanity or the grossness of its material': the novel is 'sogged by humanity' (149, 145, 39). Accordingly, Forster borrows some of this soggy humanity to help distance himself from the kind of critical and scholarly method that might be expected of him: he will 'attack' the novel with no system or apparatus, but with 'the human heart', because the final test of a novel always consists in our 'affection' for it.

It would be unsurprising if Forster's 'soggy' novel called to mind James's oblique association of the English novel with a pudding. In *Aspects* a critique of James's fiction is the means by which Forster distances himself from the Jamesian aesthetic. Forster is content to follow the orthodox line that novels essentially deal with character, even to the extent of signalling as the central idea of his lectures that there are only two 'forces' in fiction, 'human beings and a bundle of various things not human beings' (101). James is initially identified as an 'extreme case' of the inverse tendency to put those various things before the human, and the advantage of this aesthetic is found in the hourglass-shaped beauty of James's novel *The Ambassadors* (1903). However, Forster then invokes the extended public debate between James and Wells, in which the claims of 'art' and 'life' in fiction had become polarized, in order to align himself unequivocally with the latter. The beauty of the aesthetic pattern in James's fiction requires enormous, and literally human, sacrifices; 'most of human life has to disappear before he can do us a novel', the 'we' in this case representing Forster's implicit alliance with readers who cannot get interested in James's 'gutted' and 'castrated' characters, the 'common stuff' that fills other books (143). In James a 'heavy price' is paid for the aesthetic; it is a narrow path that leads, ultimately – the modern novel having struggled to shake off the straitjackets of formula – to the return of 'tyranny' in a new guise.

It is part of Forster's forging of a common cause with an expanding mass readership of fiction that he should call into question the boundary line between Jamesian art and writing of greater popularity. 'Has not a passage like this', he writes, as part of an analysis of Max Beerbohm's *Zuleika Dobson* (1911), 'a beauty unattainable by serious literature?' (111). However, the quarrel with James was not a quarrel with modernism as such, but a reconfiguration of modernism in which it is extricated, *à la* Lawrence, from the preciousness of Jamesian 'art'. Despite his humanistic protests against 'pseudo-scholarship' and analysis – protests which, of course, ironically align him with James – the project of *Aspects* itself compels Forster into a distanced assessment of technique, sometimes bringing distinct and surprising glimpses of a modernistic impersonality. Characters, the beating human heart of the Forsterian anti-aesthetic, are for example intriguingly seen as the author's 'word-masses', ripe for manipulation and modification. The universal aspects of human experience with which fiction deals are also open for defamiliarization – food, for example, and the curious 'stoking-up process' by which the individual 'goes on day after day putting an assortment of objects into a hole in his face without becoming surprised or bored' (58). These emphases might be mistaken, without too much difficulty, for something distinctly Beckettian.

Finally, then, Forster makes a cautious embrace of experimentalism, for example in the work of Gertrude Stein. Stein's fictive attempt to abolish narrative time fails, he argues, but the failure is both instructive and admirable; the impulse to 'emancipate fiction from the tyranny of time' is far more important than trying to rewrite the Waverley novels, for example. When the attempt involves the most fundamental disruption of language and form, the abolition of sequence in sentences, in syntax, and even in letters and sounds in words, then she is, however, 'over the precipice' (53). Forster himself declined to go over this precipice, but how might the art of fiction appear to those who did?

Beckett and Stein: theory as practice

'The Proustian equation is never simple'. From the opening challenge of Samuel Beckett's long essay on Proust (1931), we are conscious of a discourse in which creative intellectual work on the nature of fiction is striving to overcome the distinction between criticism and fiction, theory and practice.[12] Proust's multivolume work, *In Search of Lost Time* (1913–27), itself calls such a distinction into question, the narrative enfolding itself into the narrator's aspiration to write. It is indeed common to find extracts from Proust's novel anthologized alongside reflections on the theory of fiction.

The value of Proust, for Beckett, lay in the reconfiguration of two central preoccupations in modern discourse on fiction, character and realism, through the concept of time. Much of Beckett's essay is a meditation on the significance in Proust of the famous, epiphanic moments of involuntary memory: the taste of the madeleine cake steeped in tea, for example, or the hearing of a phrase of Vinteuil's music. For Lawrence, such moments may have epitomized the excesses of a maudlin, analytic self-consciousness. For Beckett, they herald the deconstruction of the concept of the self, under the pressure of Bergsonian theories of time and memory, Freudian psycho-analysis and relativity physics.

Time, Beckett explains, is the means by which the Proustian equation does not add up. Proust's characters are, in a conventional sense, 'victims and prisoners' of time, as bodies determined within a particular lifespan. But time is also inhabited in a different way from that suggested by the chronological measure of days and years, a way which allows us to occupy a 'much greater place' than that allotted by space (12–13). This distinctively modernist *spatialization* of time is confirmed by Proust's illustrations of involuntary memory, in which the slightest sensual stimulus triggers a memory so vivid that the individual might be said to inhabit, simultaneously, both the present moment and the recollected scene. In *Matter and Memory* (1911) the philo-sopher Henri Bergson had begun to question the concept of recollection itself, tied as it was to a model of memory as a set of images in the brain, selected for projection in the private cinema of consciousness. Rather, Bergson theorized, memory was an *actualization* of the past in the body, a complex physical event or evocation through which the individual does not 'have' memory but 'is' memory. Thus, for example, the opening pages of Woolf's *Mrs Dalloway* (1925), with their subtle manipulation of tense and careful ambiguity surrounding the question of 'now', vividly suggest a sense in which Clarissa Dalloway is simultaneously a menopausal and a teenage woman.

Beckett's endorsement, then, of the Proustian epiphany, and of the infer-iority of voluntary memory as 'of no value as an instrument of evocation' (14), closely resembles the theory of art as 'defamiliarization' in Russian Formalist criticism. Habit, 'the ballast that chains the dog to his vomit', is temporarily suspended by involuntary memory, and we see things afresh; we feel the true 'suffering of being', which is equivalent to 'the free play of every faculty' (20). Beckett is unafraid to designate this as contact with the 'real', that which 'the mock reality of experience' cannot reveal. Habit and voluntary memory thus enable the strictly retrospective, and false, construction of the self as stable, unitary and continuous. According to the Bergsonian conception of *durée*, what this idea of the self necessarily obstructs is the *experience* of being, as a continuous process of strictly unforseeable becoming. If, therefore, we are prisoners of time, this is also, curiously, because we are condemned to be 'other, no longer what we were before the calamity of yesterday' (13). The human subject dies and is reborn anew every moment, whereas the seeming historical inevitability of the 'personality' or 'old ego' (terms similarly used by Lawrence to designate a false idea of the self) can only ever be constructed once these changes have occurred. Like Proust's Albertine, we are beings 'scattered in space and time', multiple not only in our capacity for simultaneity, but in the constant, creative unfolding of new selves; in a formulation that resonates through Beckett's own oeuvre and on into deconstructive philosophy, it is indeed common to be present at our own absence.

Needless to say, the established art of realist fiction, for Beckett-Proust, is inadequate to account for these conceptions of time and selfhood. Here Beckett rejoins for a moment the sceptical debate around realism which had animated the discourse on fiction since Flaubert and James. To an extent, he asserts, Proust follows a kind of impressionist realism, recording phenomena 'in the order and exactitude of their perception'; but Proust's contempt for the 'grotesque fallacy' of realism lies in the refusal to fit such recordings into the retrospective patterns of cause and effect (86, 76). This undoubtedly constitutes a strain of romanticism in Proust, a preference for intuitive over intellectualistic perception, though only insofar as 'intellectual' signals the tendency to make sense of things which are of necessity out of date. At the same time, however, Proust is thereby distanced from the abstraction of Charles Baudelaire and the Symbolists, his singular and lonely pursuit of a tenacious new contract between the imagination and reality figured in an enigmatic formula: 'real without being merely actual, ideal without being merely abstract' (64, 75).

The writing of Walter Benjamin, whose work on and around Proust forms a close parallel with that of Beckett, might helpfully, if indirectly, summarize in two main ways the extent to which Beckett's discourse on Proust, despite its instinctive avoidance of heroic or pious polemic, remains a discourse about emancipation. First, Benjamin maintains that the Proustian emphasis on involuntary memory counteracts the tendency of modern imaging technologies, such as the camera and cinema (which themselves infiltrate the forms of modern fictional realism), to 'reduce the scope for the play of imagination' and to degrade the role of *practice*. Second, in this manner the Proustian novel restores the value and communicability of *experience*, steadily devalued by the modern triumph of information over narrative, and embodied in the rise of the novel itself.[13]

Beckett's exacting study of Proust implies that the modernist novel might become progressively unrecognizable in its pursuit of Bergsonian insights.

Stein was also familiar with the work of Bergson, and strove to embody this in the creation of a fictional 'continuous present'. The character of Melanctha Herbert in Stein's much-admired early work *Three Lives* (1909) is renewed in every pulse of her reiterative sentences, as if nothing of Melanctha can ever be taken for granted as established. Stein, however, did not stop at jumping off the precipice with fiction: she took the discourse on the art of fiction with her. *How to Write* (1931) is a long, seemingly formless meditation in eight chapters whose headings, with their allusions to sentences and paragraphs, grammar, narrative and vocabulary, attest to Stein's longstanding preoccupation with the nature and philosophy of language and its relation to the idea of representation.[14] Critics have regarded *How to Write* as one of the most hermetic texts of a writer always working at the farthest verge of avant-garde modernism, and have tended to conclude, from its ironic subversion of the idea of an instructional and inclusive manual, that it was never intended for a wide readership.

The difficulty for any critical account of *How to Write* is that of avoiding a kind of bad faith implicit either in paraphrase or in extrapolation. Both of these strategies have of course been deployed, and might be defended as standard methods of 'making sense' of an otherwise recalcitrant text. Stein's 'discovery' that a paragraph is emotional but a sentence is not is often cited as the key insight of *How to Write*, while '[i]t is natural to suppose that a rose is a rose is a rose', can be extracted as a familiar Steinian reflection on the redundancy of descriptive or referential writing. *How to Write* requests of its reader, however, a way of reading quite peculiar to itself, and a mode of intellectual engagement which, as in Bergson's critique of the logic of cause and effect, refuses the retrospective imposition of a structure of meaning, as if to translate the text as it is into an explicatory metalanguage. In *practice*, as it were, what might this look like?

> Grammar is undated because furlows and furrows are avaricious with hunting hares in partial referring to enable utter with renown come distaste unable.
> How can beginning and end beginning with white in iron end whom with lent.
> A grammar colors reddened. (79)

> Well well is he. Explain my doubts, well well is he explain my doubts.
> Could he get used to a city.
> Explain my doubts.
> Well well is he explain my doubts. Well well is he explain my doubts. (217)

Let us assume that the reader is learning not to identify and retain points of central significance in *How to Write*, but instead to become immersed in Stein's playful linguistic flow. The flow is aided by the almost complete exclusion of any punctuation other than the full stop. This exclusion also has the effect of focusing the mind on decisions of meaning that are usually made for us; the utterances seem protean, not simply unrelated fragments, but units of sense that shift through the action of hingeing words which can perform more than one grammatical function. Is 'colors' a verb or a noun? Can 'in partial referring' be allowed to continue the sentence or is it the source of a new, fugitive unit of sense? The middle section of the first example, 'How can . . .', might be recomposed, with judicious punctuation, into a meditation on the strange disjunction between beginnings and endings of utterances, and more generally seems to reflect Stein's fascination with the way grammatically correct utterances might be nonreferential, and with the lapsing of language in and out of sense (she reflects elsewhere on the interesting impossibility of *not* making sense in language for any length of time). With the alliteration of 'furlows and furrows' and 'hunting hares', poetic affect also unsettles grammatical sense. 'Explain my doubts' in the second example is a surreal intrusion into its sentence, like the murmuring of a subconscious. In the general context of punctuation, the rare comma only intensifies a questioning of the relationship between text and subtext, just as repetition intensifies the autonomy of the phrases.

The longer the reader is able to sustain this attention, the more we realize that the text is working according to a logic of the glimpse or of peripheral vision, as of something held just out of reach; what we glimpse, perhaps, are the underlying rules that make and constrain sense. This of course is precisely how *not* to write in an orthodox way, but another sense of the proposition 'how to write' is released, in which writing is a transitive act – literally, an act of contiguity, of placing one letter after another and one word after another. In 'Proust' Beckett observes that the 'enchantment' of reality can only be apprehended when objects can be seen in their singularity, 'independent of any general notion and detached from the sanity of a cause' ('Proust' 22–3). In *How to Write* Stein performs a similar service for words. In direct contrast to Lawrence's aesthetic, nothing is more inappropriate to Stein's text than the hermeneutic gesture: as attention is diverted from conventional sense and reference, it is focused with a peculiar tenacity, perhaps enchantment, on the texture of words and their effects, or on what Stein called 'wordness'.

It would be tempting to read in Stein's astonishing text a certain logical extension of James's call for an autonomous art of modernist fiction.[15] Autonomy in this sense has often proved capable of acquiring a bad name; James can be seen to demonstrate, 'in the saddest possible way, that the modernist novel was ruthlessly determined to be about nothing but itself', and satirized for giving up on the reader only when 'he was finally persuaded that he had almost no readers to address'.[16] At its most extreme, this critical approach produces the misunderstanding of modernism apparent in George Orwell's 'Inside the Whale' (1943). At a time of unprecedented turmoil in world history, Orwell complains, the modernists can only look elsewhere, and primarily into their own art. This critique is founded, however, on a false dichotomy. In Benjamin's theory of artistic 'correspondence', contemporaneity has nothing to do with content, or with the recording of reality in literary form; it consists, rather, in the direct correspondence of the *form* of art with its context, such that what is discovered could not have taken any other form. 'In order to complete them', Woolf mused, on the sense of incompleteness left by the novels of the Edwardian materialists, 'it seems necessary to do something – to join a society, or, more desperately, to write a cheque' ('Mr Bennett' 119). Woolf here voices for her peers the modernist proposition, not only that the fiction will suffice, but that artistic autonomy is the very *guarantee* of its engagement with the real. The fact that an extensive discourse on fiction seemed increasingly necessary to sustain this autonomy becomes less paradoxical in the light of what we might see in modernism as a will-to-literature or 'one of the fiercest campaigns ever mounted in favour of literature'.[17] The campaign is nevertheless shadowed by a fear that the future of the novel will depend upon the existence of a world not yet 'grown alien to it'.[18]

Notes

1. Peter Keating, *The Haunted Study: A Social History of the English Novel 1875–1914* (London: Fontana, 1991), p. 13.
2. Henry James, 'The Art of Fiction', in Leon Edel (ed.), *The House of Fiction: Essays on the Novel by Henry James* (London: Hart-Davis, 1957), pp. 23–45 (p. 23). Further references cited parenthetically.
3. See, for example, Ian Watt, *The Rise of the Novel: Studies in Defoe, Richardson and Fielding* (London: Chatto and Windus, 1957).
4. Virginia Woolf, 'Modern Fiction', in Woolf, *The Common Reader: First Series*, ed. Andrew McNeillie (London: Hogarth Press, 1984), pp. 146–53 (pp. 147–8). Further references cited parenthetically.
5. Arthur Symons, *The Symbolist Movement in Literature* (New York: Haskell House, 1971), p. 5.
6. Virginia Woolf, 'Mr Bennett and Mrs Brown', in Peter Faulkner (ed.), *A Modernist Reader: Modernism in England 1910–1930* (London: Batsford, 1986), pp. 112–28 (p. 123). Further references cited parenthetically.
7. D. H. Lawrence, letter to J. B. Pinker, 5 September 1914, in *The Letters of D. H. Lawrence*, 8 vols., *Volume II: 1913–1916*, ed. George Y. Zytaruk and James T. Boulton (Cambridge: Cambridge University Press, 1981), p. 212.
8. D. H. Lawrence, *Study of Thomas Hardy and Other Essays*, ed. Bruce Steele (Cambridge: Cambridge University Press, 1985), p. 93. Further references cited parenthetically.

9. D. H. Lawrence, *Studies in Classic American Literature*, ed. Ezra Greenspan, Lindeth Vasey and John Worthen (Cambridge: Cambridge University Press, 2003), p. 14.

10. See 'The Future of the Novel', 'Morality and the Novel' and 'Why the Novel Matters' in Lawrence, *Study of Thomas Hardy*, pp. 149–55, 169–76, 191–8.

11. E. M. Forster, *Aspects of the Novel* (Harmondsworth: Penguin, 1982), p. 40. Further references cited parenthetically.

12. Samuel Beckett, 'Proust', in Beckett and Georges Duthuit, *Proust and Three Dialogues* (London: John Calder, 1965), pp. 7–93. Further references cited parenthetically.

13. See 'On Some Motifs in Baudelaire' and 'The Storyteller', in Walter Benjamin, *Illuminations*, ed. Hannah Arendt, trans. Harry Zohn (London: Fontana/Collins, 1982), pp. 157–202, 83–109.

14. Gertrude Stein, *How to Write* (New York: Dover, 1975). Further references cited parenthetically.

15. See Ira B. Nadel, 'Gertrude Stein and Henry James', in Shirley Neuman and Ira B. Nadel (eds.), *Gertrude Stein and the Making of Literature* (Basingstoke: Macmillan, 1988), pp. 81–97.

16. Keating, *Haunted Study*, pp. 358, 397.

17. David Trotter, 'The Modernist Novel', in Michael Levenson (ed.), *The Cambridge Companion to Modernism* (Cambridge: Cambridge University Press, 1999), pp. 70–99 (p. 74).

18. Milan Kundera, 'The Depreciated Legacy of Cervantes', in Kundera, *The Art of the Novel*, trans. Linda Asher (New York: Harper and Row, 1988), p. 16.

2

PETER BROOKER

Early modernism

To talk of 'early' modernism immediately raises questions of definition and periodization. Such questions have indeed been key to the long 'postmodernist' period of retrospective construction and reconstruction of 'modernism' itself. The recent tendency has been to stretch the term to neglected figures and literatures. 'It should surely be clear by now', Andrzej Gasiorek contends, 'that modernism is a portmanteau concept, which comprises a variety of often mutually incompatible trajectories.'[1] Accordingly, the periodizing dates of modernism have shifted this way and that; from, for example, the years 1890–1930 adopted by Malcolm Bradbury and James McFarlane in 1976 to Jane Goldman's 1910–45 in 2004.[2] Critics have of course selected specific years and episodes within these bookends, but at its widest, the period of modernism could on this reckoning evidently run for fifty-odd years, from the 1890s to 1945.

The list of novelists with some claim to be included under the heading 'early modernism' is therefore a long one. Did Thomas Hardy in some ways anticipate modernism? Does the 'naturalism' of George Gissing belong to the modernist project? Were H. G. Wells or E. M. Forster modern or modernist? What is our estimate now of the undoubted newness of D. H. Lawrence's fiction? Was this primarily a matter of new social content rather than artistic form? And what of contemporary examples of gothic fiction, or the advent of science fiction or the detective novel? Do we think of these as generic 'popular fiction' and are they opposed from the outset to modernism? Bradbury and MacFarlane's volume indexes all the named writers here (which is not to say they are regarded as modernist). Goldman numbers only Lawrence in a list of nearly forty of 'the most important writers (in English)' of her period, topped by ten 'giants'; Wells she references simply as one of the Edwardians dismissed by Virginia Woolf.[3] Neither volume mentions *The Strange Case of Dr Jekyll and Mr Hyde* (1886), *Dracula* (1897) or Sir Arthur Conan Doyle's fictional Sherlock Holmes, who made his first appearance in 1887.

One further guiding consideration in this debate about the
modernism is modernism's relation to varieties of realism. I want
this issue below and also to invite some general reflection on
should look not for a 'before' or even 'after' modernism but rath
ments *within* modernism. My starting point is the conventional one: the
belief that 'modernism' best refers to works exhibiting a high degree of
conspicuous formal experiment where this can be understood as a response,
one way or the other, to the conditions of modernity. The most honoured
examples of this experimental modernism in English fiction, namely James
Joyce and Woolf, remain immensely interesting. We should, however, resist
the automatic valorization of this particular mode and associated moment of
writing, since, while other fiction may seem to anticipate this type, it may
also vary and counter it in ways which extend our understanding of modernism's rationale and rewards.

Even within a limiting period definition, we are likely to conclude with
Goldman that modernism was 'transitional'. The designation 'early modernism' we can then see as having a distinct advantage over its apparent syno-
nym 'premodernism', since it allows us to think of modernism as a process of
change and development rather than an evolution 'upwards' towards an
achieved end from which there is then a falling away. We need this understanding if we are genuinely to see modernism as a dynamic 'movement' and
appreciate the simple fact that individual writers (Joyce and Woolf among
them) became 'more modernist', along with the more complex fact that a
'more modernist' text, by Henry James or Joseph Conrad, for example,
might have appeared before the early 'less modernist' Joyce or Woolf.

We might think that 'realism' belongs to this transitional period and that
it, too, passed through various modes, early and late. Some of the figures
named above (Hardy, Gissing, Forster, Lawrence) then come back into view.
The common judgement is that modernism, understood as a self-referential
mode, alert to its own formal composition and the constructedness of the
'real', defined itself against realism's assumption of a pregiven external
reality. Hardy's late fiction – to go no further – might make us question
this distinction. Both *Tess of the d' Urbervilles* (1891) and *Jude the Obscure*
(1895) deal with transitional figures and experiences and it is Tess who, in a
much-quoted phrase, feels 'the ache of modernism'.[4] If we cannot think
comfortably of Hardy and the Joyce of *Ulysses* (1922) in the same breath,
we might remember that Hardy was a significant influence upon Lawrence
and detect a different modernist lineage here.[5] Above all, however, we are
likely, in reading Hardy, to think of character and theme: tradition and
mobility, poverty and frustrated ambition, and the difficult encounter with
newer sexual and social attitudes, especially in the new towns. These things

make Hardy 'modern', but they are not simply thematic. For the struggle to depict a contemporary changing reality pushes a conventional realism into a new form and idiom. The result is an often remarked upon 'awkwardness' in Hardy's prose style which is itself a sign of the 'modern' or 'new' and anticipates the more deliberate formal experiment of later writers. We appreciate, that is to say, that realism and modernism can coexist in the same text or author and need to be weighed in the balance if we are to appraise changes of degree and kind.

An individual who encapsulates much of the transitional character of this period, and some of the mutations in fiction, is Ford Madox Ford: for Max Saunders 'a central transforming force of early English modernism'.[6] Ford was born Joseph Leopold Ford Hermann Hueffer and changed his surname from Hueffer to Ford in 1919. This set of names is in itself a compound sign of a changing personal and literary identity in a changing period. Behind it lies the rich literary and artistic history associated with Ford's grandfather, the Pre-Raphaelite painter, Ford Madox Brown, and his uncle William Michael Rossetti. There followed Ford's acquaintance with James, Stephen Crane and Conrad, as well as with Wells, John Galsworthy and Arnold Bennett; his friendships and liaisons with contemporary writers and artists, among them May Sinclair, Rebecca West, Violet Hunt, Stella Bowen and Jean Rhys, and his role as patron to '*les jeunes*', including Ezra Pound and the Imagists, Lawrence and Wyndham Lewis. Over his whole career, Ford published more than eighty volumes (thirty-six between 1900 and 1914) comprising novels, poetry, memoirs and social and critical commentary, and was editor of the *English Review* between 1908 and 1910. Here he published Hardy, James and Conrad, as well as younger, though very few women, authors, making the *Review* itself a compendium and symptom of a shifting agenda from one generation to the next.

Ford anticipated the 'new' and actively encouraged '*les jeunes*' while simultaneously promoting the conscious artistry of European prose fiction and denigrating the arid didacticism, as he saw it, of the English novel. George Eliot, for example, he judged as sententious and 'unreadable': she was as 'a moral force practically extinct' and 'has as an artist no existence whatever'.[7] Ford's alternative, poised against both the moralizing Victorian and the present-day commercial author, was the writer who 'engrosses himself strictly in his art and thinks of nothing else' (97). An emphasis such as this opened the way for the kind of internationalist purview and commitment to formal innovation and artistic autonomy which appealed to younger writers such as Pound. Also, although Pound's association with Ford has become part of the history of modernist *poetry*, the latter's arrival on the London scene arguably consolidated the earlier achievements in prose fiction. Thus Pound consistently deferred to Ford's criterion that 'poetry should be written at least as well as prose'.[8] And for both men there lay behind this precept the examples of James and Conrad, and in a further widening of the modernist tradition, Gustave Flaubert, Guy de Maupassant and Ivan Turgenev.

What Ford himself admired in these authors developed into his account of the techniques of impressionism, for many commentators the hallmark of an emerging modernism in the English novel.[9] Impressionism, Ford repeated, rendered the world dispassionately as it appeared to the perceiving mind of the individual artist.[10] The writer should accordingly eschew the overtly moralizing role of the Victorian novelist in the interests of an accurate and succinct portrayal of incident and character. Narrative, following what Ford termed the 'time-shift', should observe the aberrant movement of events and the eccentric timekeeping of storytelling itself. Language should be direct and economical and dialogue necessarily selective (a narrator could not plausibly remember all that had been said) and follow the distractions and interruptions of real-life conversation. The experience of the reader was a prime consideration and Ford suggested that the reader should be kept 'interested', through style, cadence and the accelerating momentum that Ford termed *'progression d'effet'*.[11]

Above all, the rationale for these techniques was to present a faithful and unbroken illusion of reality. The ambiguity of this is plain. On the one hand, Ford appeared to be calling for an unmediated depiction of the world; on the other he advocated an 'accuracy as to impressions'.[12] The 'objective' purpose, admired by Pound, was, as Michael Levenson points out, coupled to a subjectivist, indeed idealist, epistemology and aesthetic. The two could be reconciled, after a fashion, only by Ford's view of the modern world as being like this. The modern period, he argued, had done with the 'Great Figures' and the degraded moral certainties of the past. Self and society were therefore disunited – there was no viable political consensus and no stable basis of knowledge, only an awareness of 'how little of all that there is, is the much that we know' (*Critical Attitude* 178). The 'real world' was conceived not as an external foundation, therefore, verified by consensus or factual evidence – 'I have for facts a most profound contempt', Ford said (*Ancient Lights*, xviii) – but as given by the impressions upon an individual and rendered, in turn, in a compelling way in the novel.

In a further ambiguity, while impressionism and the emphasis on artistic autonomy appeared to owe something to the 'art for art's sake' movement of the 1890s, Ford's disdain for the moralizing author did not mean that for him literature should not engage with issues of moral concern. The impressionist novel would therefore show the world as it was – meaning as it was perceived – and, while abstaining from didacticism, would offer its readers the means for determining their own moral attitudes. We might think the result was an undeveloped hybrid which was 'not yet modernism'. I suggest rather that we view impressionism as a mode within modernism's wide orbit, one which in its own right cultivated conscious craft and encouraged an active exploration of inward psychology while retaining realism's grasp upon pertinent contemporary social themes. Impressionism emerges, therefore, as not simply a transitional artistic mode on its way to something else but as an examination of the instabilities of this very experience of transition at this particular cultural moment. As such it was 'already a modernism' – a doubly symptomatic and analytic mode whose particularly striking feature was a fascination with the unknown: 'the opacity and unknowability of other people' conjoined with 'the subjective and often unreliable nature of our cognitions' ('Ford's Modernism' 13–14).

Ford found prose fiction he admired preeminently in the work of Flaubert, James and Conrad. Conrad shared his views to the extent of collaborating on at least two novels and, if Ford is to be believed, seeking the latter's assistance throughout his writing career (a claim strongly denied by Conrad's wife).[13] In his memoir of Conrad, Ford talks of their common pursuit of *le mot juste* and the need to suppress the author so as to present an unmediated world; a project which, in Conrad, led to the innovation of the intermediary narrator and storyteller, Marlow, in three novellas and the novel *Lord Jim* (1900).[14]

We might thus deem Conrad too an impressionist, as Ford did (*Critical Attitude* 90). But it was a description Conrad avoided, and there were, in truth, firm differences between the two writers. In particular, Conrad viewed the vocation of writing with a high seriousness and strenuous devotion to art which could make Ford seem like a casual entertainer. While Ford wanted above all to retain the reader's interest, Conrad wished to reveal the underlying fundamental truths ('before all, to make you *see*!') which would unite readers in humanitarian fellowship.[15] But perhaps this is to reveal Conrad as more a Victorian and less a modern author; a late aspirant to the role of sage and critic of society which Ford felt the modern author must discard. The notorious result in Conrad's prose can be an air, or 'impression', of profundity, the accumulation of mystery below which there lies some great redemptive truth. There is much of this in *Heart of Darkness* (1902), often recognized as a 'classic of modernism'.[16] Conrad has Marlow brood on 'the stillness of an implacable force brooding over an inscrutable intention . . . a vast grave full of unspeakable secrets . . . the unseen presence of victorious corruption, the darkness of an impenetrable night'.[17] For Allon White, Conrad's obscurity comprises a sententious and mystificatory patina of sound whose significance lies less in any underlying truths than in the air of wisdom it confers upon the novel and novelist. It serves nevertheless as a modernist device, for the texture of Conrad's prose serves to confer a seriousness and worth upon its demonstrable 'art'.

Ford's analysis of literary trends in this period draws a clear division between those few novelists (James, Conrad and George Moore) united by 'an extreme literary conscientiousness' working in 'the great mainstream of European International Literature' and 'the more insular and amateur' writers (Rudyard Kipling, Wells, Bennett, Galsworthy) who make a 'sociological contribution' (*Critical Attitude* 107, 89, 99). Similarly, Woolf's essays 'Modern Fiction' (1919) and 'Mr Bennett and Mrs Brown' (1924), where she distances herself from the external 'materialist' treatment of character in the 'Edwardians' Bennett, Wells and Galsworthy, are taken as a virtual manifesto of modernist fiction. The names of the 'moderns' have changed, but the pros and cons of the argument are much as they are drawn up in Ford's analysis of 1911. 'Look within', Woolf famously urges in 'Modern Fiction': 'The mind receives a myriad impressions ... Life is not a series of gig lamps symmetrically arranged; life is a luminous halo, a semi-transparent envelope surrounding us from the beginning of consciousness to the end.'[18] This, too, is reminiscent, surely, of James's 'Experience is ... a kind of huge spider web of the finest silken threads suspended in the chamber of consciousness.'[19]

The modernizing Woolf was not, after all, immediately a modernist, and did not altogether abandon the 'impressionist' view of the world when she rejected 'materialism'. What in fact distinguished writers across these generations, I suggest, was not so much whether they were or were not 'impressionists', but what kind of 'realists' they were. For if we associate James with an 'aestheticist modernism', it is difficult all the same to see the characteristic themes of his fiction – the American in Europe, the mores of upper-class society, the role of money and property, or the position of women – as belonging to anything other than a tradition of social realism. The same goes for Conrad's concern with power, innocence and corruption in the era of colonialism. These themes relate less to 'modernism', as we know it, than to the 'modern' world in transition. Like Ford, Conrad responded, too, to the new character of urban life and mass society. In *The Secret Agent* (1907) the small world of would-be anarchists is defined physically and politically by the larger urban nexus of the modern press, police and governments. Even Conrad's 'modernist' obscurity has an everyday contemporary reference in the fog and darkness of the city's byways. White finds a 'symbolist *brume*' in Conrad.[20] Elsewhere, too, across a long period – from J. A. M. Whistler's canvasses to Alvin Langdon Coburn's photographs, from Arthur Symons and W. J. Henley's poetry and Conan Doyle's stories to T. S. Eliot's verse – fog, haze, and mist function not only as a textual effect but as a psychological and social referent in the contemporary metropolis. Linked to this is the recognition, indicated above, of the force of chance and contingency, of alterity and the unknown, 'the opacity and unknowability' of both the self and the other. Charles Baudelaire had associated one half of modernity with 'the ephemeral, the fugitive, the contingent'.[21] And it was just this foggy unknowability, drifting in and out of focus in the modern real, which impressionism grasped and which could not be grasped but in this way.

It is in the nature of 'movements' – such as impressionism and modernism – that, on inspection, they comprise different strands and even contrary emphases. We might view what Fredric Jameson terms impressionism's 'de-realizing' aestheticization of the real as a prelude to modernist internalization and abstraction, or simply conclude that impressionism did not come up to the new (really new) modernist requirements.[22] On the other hand, we might view impressionism as a distinctive 'realist-modernism' which did not simply prefigure modernism, nor 'transform' reality into impressions, nor suppress history in favour of abstraction,[23] but record an impressionistic modern reality as perceived history. Certainly this was these writers' paramount aim: 'Fiction is history, human history or nothing', insisted Conrad. The artist, said Ford, is 'the only unbiased voluminous and truthful historian of our day'.[24] And both praised James as simultaneously the artist of consciousness and 'historian of fine consciences'.[25] Thus art, consciousness, morality and history are joined in an impressionist strategy to create, in James's phrase, an 'air of reality'.

A novel which puts this doctrine to the test is Ford's *The Good Soldier* (1915). From the beginning, Ford's novel has kept very good modernist company. The opening chapter, then titled 'The Saddest Story', was included in the first issue of Wyndham Lewis's magazine *Blast* in 1914 and subsequently read at a house party along with episodes of James Joyce's *A Portrait of the Artist as a Young Man* (1916).[26] Since then its canonical status has been confirmed by a number of critics.[27] Ford said that he put '*all* that I knew about writing' into the novel.[28] Its narrative is told as if in a room 'in a country cottage with a silent listener' (119–20) by a storyteller, John Dowell, who is also its principal subject. Dowell's narrative mimes the movement back and forth of his memory across a story of intrigue and adultery among his associates, including his wife and best friend, and of his progress towards a degree of self-awareness. The novel's author is duly suppressed, the illusion of reality is uninterrupted, the narrative moves through 'time shifts' in a '*progression d'effet*' which maintains the reader's attention. It conforms, therefore, to impressionist dicta and if it is at the same time regarded as a 'quintessentially modernist' text, this only confirms how these modes are implicated together.[29]

The story presents some well-rehearsed difficulties, however, principally having to do with the figure of Dowell who *as a character* is too inept to double as conscious artist in his role *as narrator*. Praise for Ford's artistry, that is to say, will not transfer to his storytelling character, who remains a passionless actor in what is subtitled 'A Tale of Passion', and strikes most readers as implausibly obtuse. Above all, among other failures of insight, Dowell astonishingly does not know or suspect that his wife, Florence, has been committing adultery for several years with 'the good soldier', Dowell's best friend, Ashburnam. As Ashburnam's wife knows, this has been only one of his affairs. Dowell tells us all we know while he repeatedly admits that events and 'the oddities of the human psychology' are beyond him (125). 'It is all a darkness', he confesses (109).

The various explanations of this – that Dowell has colluded with Ashburnam, that he is asexual or unwittingly homosocial, or a symptom of wider cultural enervation[30] – seek to reconcile us to Ford's deeply unreliable narrator, who must presumably know 'his' own story but appears to know and feel nothing but his own bewilderment. This problem is aggravated if we consider the 'realist' side of the story and its analysis of 'the English "gentleman"' and 'the "black and merciless things" which lie behind that façade', in Graham Greene's words.[31] In this respect the novel might be said to show the cruel and distorted sexual emotions which break though a world of suffocating social forms embodied in a residual system of feudal patronage and hierarchy embodied in Ashburnam. It is difficult, however, to attribute such insights to Dowell, an American outsider and shallow observer, seduced by Ashburnam's example. Even at the end, he flatters himself that he is a faint version of the model of Englishness that Ashburnam represents (151, 161) when it is he, Dowell, we are led to believe, who has seen the destructive pretence and ugliness behind it all.

We find, I suggest, a more productive way of reading Ford's character and novel if we regard Dowell's naivety and obtuseness as belonging to the 'modern' theme of the instability and uncertainty of knowledge and selfhood. A range of writings, including Conrad's tales, the reportage of the 'social explorers', and the new form of detective fiction, staged the encounter with the psychological, social and racialized unknown in a symbolic conjunction of submerged regions of the capital city and the colonial hinterland.[32] Dowell's striking naivety, in Ford's novel, finds a similarly broader context. Thus Levenson points to Dowell's 'childlike credulity, asexuality and trust' and links this with Ford's own 'I never seemed to have grown up' and the conception of the child in the period; on the one hand (in the Boy Scout Movement) promoting an idea of the male child as a young, efficient, upstanding adult and on the other (as in J. M. Barrie's *Peter Pan*) encouraging an idea of the epicene, fantasizing child who never grew up.[33] In their antagonism these ideas of the child express a divided attitude towards the family, the moralizing Victorian parent, national identity and imperial purpose. We can therefore read Dowell's failings as a protest against his Victorian forebears and contemporary associates who were more sexually and socially knowing than himself.

Examples of sexual, social and cultural innocence or 'unknowingness' occur frequently in other contemporary 'transitional' fiction, associated in James, as in *The Good Soldier*, with Americans abroad, or otherwise with those marked by their youth, gender or foreignness as outsiders and prone to, or accused of, error, immorality or crime. We think of John Kemp in Ford's and Conrad's *Romance* (1903), of Flora in Conrad's *Chance* (1913), of Maisie in James's *What Maisie Knew* (1897), of Miles and Flora in his 'The Turn of the Screw' (1898) and of Oscar Wilde's Dorian Gray, who in the eponymous novel (1891) remains youthful looking while his crimes are transferred to his portrait. At the same time, these characters are motivated by romantic daring, vanity and a quest for freedom from the suffocations of childhood, the constraints of time and ageing, and the stubborn, filigreed conventions of Victorian society. The angelic, haunted Miles, expelled from school for some unnamed, unnameable misdemeanour, yearns 'to see more life ... to get away' and for his governess 'to let me alone'.[34] Lord Jim, who can stand for much of this sentiment, once free from the authority of his father who 'possessed such certain knowledge of the unknowable', day-dreams from his station aloft in the foretop upon a life of derring-do just 'as a hero in a book'.[35] In their nonconformity, in other words, these characters risk being modern, youthful and new. In so doing, although their stories are 'moral' through and through, and although they prove fallible or even in some way corrupt, they challenge the moralizing literary and social conventions of an earlier generation.

In 'The Art of Fiction' (1884) James takes issue with Walter Besant's proposition that a novelist must write from experience. 'Experience is an immense sensibility ... the very atmosphere of the mind', says James, and an imaginative mind, especially that of 'a man of genius' will convert its 'faintest hints' into 'revelations' (*Selected Literary Criticism*, 85–6). Interestingly, James follows this comment with the example not of a man but of 'a woman of genius', identified as the English novelist Anne Thackeray Ritchie.[36] In one fictional text Ritchie develops a portrait of French Protestant youth derived, James reports, from a glimpse merely of young Protestants at a table as she passed an open door. She had her 'direct personal impression' (James's broad definition of the novel), which, aided by her general knowledge and 'power to guess the unseen from the seen', she converted 'into a concrete image and produced a reality'.[37] In James's own fiction, women and, in examples such as *What Maisie Knew* (1897) and *The Awkward Age* (1899), the figure of the young girl or young lady, herself at a point of transition, serves to 'experience' that society's changing mores and morality. The 'young lady', Jesse Matz argues, becomes James's 'exemplary aesthetic imagination'.[38] The consequences are ambiguous. Thus James presents Maisie, her perceptions 'almost infinitely quickened', as the '"ironic centre"' of his tale. But while delegated to 'register ... the whole complexity' of the story's action, Maisie can do so only through her 'child's confused and obscure notation of it'.[39] James seeks to create an advantage out of what remains a disadvantage. For while a limited experience enables a girl or woman of genius to imagine 'more', the accumulated insight is linked, indeed dependent upon, an 'infant mind', restricted by its 'great gaps and voids' which can only guess (wisely or unwisely) at 'the implication of things'.[40]

This gendered construction, fundamentally of the transitional relations of art and life, is an important preoccupation of women writers themselves in this period. In a conspicuous example, May Sinclair's novel *The Creators* (1910) is directly concerned with the impediments to artistic creativity of a woman's conventional 'experience' of the domestic life of marriage and children. Five authors in this novel – three women and two men – share the doctrine that the commitments of a married life and any sign of popular fame will degrade the consuming force of their 'genius'. All but one of the creators (a male poet) become successful and all are drawn into romantic attachments and marriage. The novel follows their struggle, and in particular that of the woman novelist, Jane Holland. Her married life and children compromise her art but the nature of genius is ambiguously gendered – defined by the male novelist Tanqueray as 'feminine ... humble and passive in its attitude to life', but by the author Nina as 'another sex inside you and a stronger one' which makes you fight for what you want 'as a man fights'.[41] Also, although these creators agree that '*The* unpardonable sin is separating literature from life' (8–9), when Mary embarks on a new novel she realizes that 'the world of vivid and tangible things' including her house, husband and child could not compete with 'the ungovernable resurgence of her vision' (249). To be a woman of genius, therefore, a woman must annul her identity as a sexualized woman in the world. 'If a woman is to do anything stupendous', declares Nina, 'it means virginity' (75).

Sinclair returned to this theme in other work, including her study of the Brontës (1914), the book *Feminism* (1912), and the later semi-autobiographical novel *Mary Olivier: A Life* (1919) whose story ends in 1910. Here she explores the frustrations of a life regulated by the conventional standards of the mother and a possible alternative world of ideas, creativity and romance.

Her solution to this tension draws on Sigmund Freud's concept of sublimation and on contemporary mysticism. Thus, having sublimated her sexual energies into poetry and the world of ideas, Mary finally achieves a state of beatific happiness divorced from people and things: a 'flash point of freedom', knowing reality and her inner self in a 'consciousness of God'.[42]

These preoccupations and Sinclair's own strenuous intellectual life made her a modern author. Indeed, in her reflections on celibacy and an independent, creative life for women she helped to author the themes of this period. As a novelist she learnt the virtues of a clear, direct prose from the Imagists whom she openly supported, but otherwise, with the exception of *Mary Olivier*, she retained the forms of a conventional realism. Here she was to attempt the method she had named in a review in 1918 of Dorothy Richardson as the 'stream of consciousness'. This method has of course been associated with James Joyce and with Woolf, who was to find in Richardson's prose a model of 'the psychological sentence of the feminine gender'.[43] Sinclair, described by her most recent biographer as 'A Modern Victorian', therefore embodied the transitions out of which one of the established features of literary modernism emerged.[44]

One writer, at least, with her own credentials to be considered an early modernist was ambivalent about this device. In her reviews of Richardson, Sinclair's *Mary Olivier* and Woolf's *Night and Day* (1919), Katherine Mansfield objects that this 'novel of the future', as it seems to be, is superficial and in fact out of date. Mansfield tends to view the 'stream of consciousness' as an intensification of subjective impressionism and critiques it as such. In Richardson everything is 'of equal importance' and so 'of equal unimportance'.[45] Richardson and Sinclair alike isolate but do not discriminate or explore the endless stream – 'the vast barn of impressions' (312). Sinclair's novel is 'too late in the day' (312) while Woolf's *Night and Day* appears like an updated Jane Austen novel in a world where 'we had never thought to look on its like again!' (314).

Hermione Lee shows how important Mansfield was to the 'debate about modernism' Woolf was at this time having with herself and with the texts of Eliot, Joyce and Richardson, along with Sinclair's 1918 review, discussed above.[46] Famously, Woolf viewed Mansfield's work as 'the only writing I have ever been jealous of'.[47] Mansfield kept her distance from the example of Joyce and the other male modernists, whom she found by turns 'loathsome' and 'unspeakable'.[48] Her own modernism developed through an exploration, over three main collections, of the form of the short story, itself an answer, we might think, to the long novel or novel series, practised by Richardson and admired by Sinclair, in which 'Nothing happens. It is just life going on and on.'[49]

Mansfield's first short story collection, *In a German Pension*, appeared in 1911. In these stories there was a different relation between art and modern experience than in James or Sinclair: neither the glimpse of a limited consciousness, nor the transcendence of worldly demands, but rather the full glare of the real and its oblique, submerged rather than expanded, imaginative rendering. Mansfield later dismissed these earlier stories as inadequate juvenilia and contemporary readers have found them venomous and unbalanced, but they present an instructive comparison with Mansfield's later work and with contemporary fiction.[50]

Sydney Janet Kaplan notes Mansfield's 'powerful impressionism' and 'cinematic' imagination and finds in a description of an unemployed crowd in London '"hundreds of them – monotonously, insistently – like a grey procession of dead hours"' an anticipation of Eliot.[51] *In a German Pension* sets the young woman narrator in a company which reveres family life ('Germany', booms one guest, 'is the home of the Family'), childbearing (a woman with nine children cannot compare with her friend who had four at the same time) and fawns upon the outward signs of rank and status.[52] The stories are reminiscent of, though more genial than, George Grosz's satirical cartoons of the German bourgeoisie. In addition to the portraits of bourgeois greed, complacency and snobbery, the stories critique male violence, in and outside marriage, and pretension and vanity in both men and women. In this respect two stories especially, 'The Modern Soul' and 'The Advanced Lady', reflect on the question of being the 'self' who is a modern woman in the face of male brutality and the dogmas of the pension matriarchs. The actress who embodies the 'modern soul' (who is 'curiously sapphic' and cursed by her 'genius' which 'cannot hope to mate' 719, 720) faints at the narrator's 'helpful' suggestion that her widowed mother should marry the modern soul's present admirer. To 'the Advanced Lady' who is a novelist writing on 'the Modern Woman' – described as 'the incarnation of comprehending love' (758, 759) – the narrator replies 'very sweetly' that her own book would be on '"caring for daughters ... and keeping them out of kitchens!"' (759); and more pointedly, since '"Ignorance must not go uncontradicted!"', that her advanced theory '"about women and LOVE – it's as old as the hills – oh, older!"' (762). The narrator in all this is the very modern, independent, ironically deferential, and sweetly acerbic young woman whose tone and personality is markedly different from the unguardedly passionate Mansfield we find in her early earlier letters.

Mansfield later came to think of herself as leading a 'double life' as a writer and in her lived experience.[53] A number of other women artists and writers express a similar sense of self-alienation or adopt a performative sense of self in the period, including Sinclair and Woolf.[54] Mansfield, however, did not appear to anguish over this condition, nor to separate her life from her writing, as Sinclair was led to do. She speaks rather of the estranging experience of being in a hotel room and *simultaneously* in a story, 'in the villa of fiction', as Bennett puts it (1). Once more, however, if this is a late realization on the theme of the self, it is prefigured in the early stories where an unexpected reversal, contrary undertow or other world frequently comes to the narrative surface. The themes, moods and movement of these stories are startling. They draw on melodrama and the crime story – without the latter's usual consolations – and estrange the cultural forms and attitudes of an English or European realism. One can find an emergent technical 'modernism' here in the depiction of Rosabel's inner fantasies ('Of course they rode in the park next morning, the engagement had been announced in the *Court Circular*, all the world knew, all the world was shaking hands with her' (*Stories* 518), but we remember Mansfield's reservations about the use of 'stream of consciousness' and the boredom and flatness of 'nothing happening' which others admired. Mansfield in fact wanted something like James's 'revelation', the significant, telling detail (as did Woolf), but this comes in her writing with a jolt. Thus the story 'A Birthday', which tells of a husband's fretting while his wife suffers the difficult birth of their third child, ends, without comment, when he knows she has survived to produce a boy: '"Well, by God!' he says, 'nobody can accuse *me* of not knowing what suffering is"' (*Stories* 743).

'[R]eality', said James, 'has a myriad forms' (*Selected Literary Criticism* 85). There were, and still are, accordingly, different ways of being modern, and different ways and times of being modernist. I have emphasized the transitional nature of this period and drawn attention to a double-sided version of modernism in impressionist-realism. Like other modernisms, this version emerged through an active response to new metropolitan social forms and modern philosophies and their impact upon conceptions of identity, newly perceived by age and generation, class and occupation, gender, sexuality and nation. Hence the concern with consciousness, invariably ambivalent and divided, especially in those youthful men and women who experienced change most keenly, and hence the indeterminacies of this fictional mode.

The newness of this subject matter and theme made these writers modern but did not consistently accompany the newness of form and structure we associate with Joyce and Woolf in the 1920s. Sometimes an adherence to narrative conventions and pressing contemporary themes, including the anguished reflections on creativity, can seem modern only in a narrowly historical sense. We should be wary, therefore, as we review the period, of reinforcing an evolutionary history and modernist orthodoxy which rides roughshod over this uneven development. What makes this fiction modernist, across a wide range, is its self-consciousness, in the different senses of these writers' deliberation on art and the artist, the attempted narrative registration of consciousness, and an awareness of the instabilities shaping and enabling contemporary identities. In this respect some of those discussed provide an instructive comparison with more developed kinds of 'internalized' experimental modernism. Some, too, we might find, speak not only to their own period but to a readership well after what we take to be the modernist moment of the early twentieth century.

Notes

1. Andrzej Gasiorek, 'Ford Madox Ford's Modernism and the Question of Tradition', *English Literature in Transition, 1880–1920* 44:1 (2001), p. 3. Subsequent quotations cited parenthetically.
2. Malcolm Bradbury and James McFarlane, *Modernism: A Guide to European Literature 1890–1930* (Harmondsworth: Penguin, 1976), and Jane Goldman, *Modernism, 1910–1945: Image to Apocalypse* (London: Palgrave Macmillan, 2004).
3. Goldman, *Modernism, 1910–1945*, pp. xiv, 66, 156.
4. Thomas Hardy, *Tess of the d'Urbervilles* (London: Dent, 1993), pp. 114–15.
5. See D. H. Lawrence, *Study of Thomas Hardy and Other Essays*, ed. Bruce Steele (Cambridge: Cambridge University Press, 1985), and Rosemary Sumner, *A Route to Modernism: Hardy, Lawrence, Woolf* (Basingstoke: Macmillan. 2000).
6. Max Saunders, *Ford Madox Ford: A Dual Life*, 2 vols., *Volume I: The World Before The War* (Oxford: Oxford University Press, 1996), p. vi.
7. Ford Madox Ford, *The Critical Attitude* (London: Duckworth, 1911), pp. 55, 57. Further quotations cited parenthetically.
8. Ezra Pound, *Literary Essays of Ezra Pound* (London: Faber, 1960), p. 373.
9. H. Peter Stowell, *Literary Impressionism, James and Chekhov* (Athens: University of Georgia Press, 1980); Michael H. Levenson, *A Genealogy of Modernism: A Study of English Literary Doctrine, 1908–1922* (Cambridge: Cambridge University Press, 1984), p. 48; and Gasiorek, 'Ford Madox Ford's Modernism', p. 22.
10. Ford Madox Ford, 'On Impressionism' (1914), in Ford, *The Good Soldier*, ed. Martin Stannard (New York and London: Norton, 1995), pp. 257–74. Further quotations cited parenthetically.
11. Ford Madox Ford, *Joseph Conrad: A Personal Remembrance* (1924), excerpted in Ford, *The Good Soldier*, pp. 281–5.
12. Ford Madox Ford, *Ancient Lights and Certain New Reflections: Being the Memories of a Young Man* (London: Chapman and Hall, 1911), p. xviii. Further quotations cited parenthetically.
13. Ford Madox Ford, *Ford Madox Ford*, 5 vols., *Volume I: The Good Soldier, Selected Memories, Poems* (London: Bodley Head, 1962), pp. 291–5, and Frank MacShane (ed.), *Ford Madox Ford: The Critical Heritage* (London: Routledge, 1972), pp. 131–2. Further quotations cited parenthetically.

14. Sondra J. Stang (ed.), *The Ford Madox Ford Reader* (Manchester: Carcarnet, 1986), pp. 211–12, 220, 229–30, and Ford, *The Good Soldier*, p. 297.

15. Joseph Conrad, *The Nigger of the 'Narcissus'/Typhoon and Other Stories* (London: Penguin, 1968), p. 13.

16. Andrew Michael Roberts (ed.), *Joseph Conrad* (London: Addison Wesley Longman, 1998), p. 110.

17. Joseph Conrad, *Heart of Darkness*, (London: Penguin, 1978), pp. 48, 89.

18. Virginia Woolf, 'Modern Fiction', in Woolf, *The Common Reader: First Series*, ed. Andrew McNeillie (London: Hogarth Press, 1984), p. 150.

19. Henry James, *Selected Literary Criticism*, ed. Marcus Shapira (London: Penguin, 1968), p. 85. Further quotations cited parenthetically.

20. Allon White, *The Uses of Obscurity: The Fiction of Early Modernism* (London: Routledge, 1981), p. 115.

21. Charles Baudelaire, *The Painter of Modern Life and Other Essays*, ed. and trans. Jonathan Mayne (London: Phaidon Press, 1964), p. 13.

22. Fredric Jameson, *The Political Unconscious* (London: Routledge, 1989), p. 214.

23. *Ibid.*, p. 210, and Marianne DeKoven, *Rich and Strange: Gender, History, Modernism* (Princeton: Princeton University Press, 1991), p. 13.

24. Joseph Conrad, *Notes on Life and Letters* (London: Dent, 1970), p. 17, and Ford Madox Ford, *Henry James* (London: Martin Secker, 1913), p. 66.

25. Conrad, *Life and Letters*, p. 17.

26. Ford Madox Ford, *Return To Yesterday* (New York: Liveright, 1932), pp. 416–17.

27. Gasiorek, 'Ford Madox Ford's Modernism', pp. 19–20, and Robert Hampson and Max Saunders (eds.), *Ford Madox Ford's Modernity* (Amsterdam: Rodopi, 2003), pp. 1, 71–158.

28. Ford, *The Good Soldier*, p. 3.

29. David Trotter, 'The Modernist Novel', in Michael Levenson (ed.), *The Cambridge Companion to Modernism* (Cambridge: Cambridge University Press, 1999), p. 70.

30. Gasiorek, 'Ford Madox Ford's Modernism', 19, and Peter Nicholls, *Modernisms: A Literary Guide* (London: Palgrave Macmillan, 1995), pp. 185–6.

31. Graham Greene, 'Introduction', in Ford Madox Ford, *The Good Soldier* (London: Heinemann Educational Books, 1970), p. 10.

32. Peter Keating (ed.), *Into Unknown England, 1866–1913: Selections from the Social Explorers* (London: Fontana, 1976).

33. Levenson, *Genealogy of Modernism*, pp. 57–8.

34. Henry James, *The Turn of the Screw*, ed. Peter G. Beidler (New York: Bedford/ St Martin's Press, 1995), pp. 82, 90, 91.

35. Joseph Conrad, *Lord Jim: A Tale*, ed. Cedric Watts and Robert Hampson (London: Penguin, 1986), pp. 46, 47.

36. Jesse Matz, *Literary Impressionism and Modernist Aesthetics* (Cambridge: Cambridge University Press, 2001), p. 94.

37. *Ibid.*, p. 86.

38. *Ibid.*, p. 95.

39. Henry James, 'Preface', in *What Maise Knew* (London: Penguin, 1966), pp. 8, 11, 9.

40. *Ibid.*, p. 9, and James, *Selected Literary Criticism*, p. 86.

41. May Sinclair, *The Creators*, ed. Lyn Pykett (Birmingham: University of Birmingham Press, 2004), pp. 12, 74. Further references cited parenthetically.
42. May Sinclair, *Mary Olivier: A Life* (London: Virago, 1980), p. 377.
43. Virginia Woolf, *A Woman's Essays*, ed. Rachel Bowlby (London: Penguin, 1992), p. 51.
44. Suzanne Raitt, *May Sinclair: A Modern Victorian* (Oxford: Oxford University Press, 2000).
45. Katherine Mansfield, 'Review of Richardson's Interim', in Scott (ed.), *Gender of Modernism*, p. 310. Further references cited parenthetically.
46. Hermione Lee, *Virginia Woolf* (London: Vintage, 1997), pp. 390–1.
47. Virginia Woolf, *The Diary of Virginia Woolf*, ed. Anne Olivier Bell, 5 vols. (London: Harvest, 1980), vol. II, p. 227.
48. Katherine Mansfield, *The Collected Letters of Katherine Mansfield*, 4 vols. *Volume II: 1918–1919*, ed. Vincent O'Sullivan and Margaret Scott (Oxford: Oxford University Press, 1987), p. 343.
49. These are May Sinclair's words. Mansfield commented that 'things just "happen" one after another' (Scott (ed.), *Gender of Modernism*, pp. 444, 309).
50. Andrew Bennett, *Katherine Mansfield* (Tavistock: Northcote House, 2004), pp. 2, 72. Further references cited parenthetically.
51. Sydney Janet Kaplan, *Katherine Mansfield and the Origins of Modernist Fiction* (Ithaca: Cornell University Press, 1991), pp. 208–9.
52. Katherine Mansfield, *The Collected Stories* (London: Penguin, 2001), p. 685. Further references cited parenthetically.
53. Katherine Mansfield, *The Letters of Katherine Mansfield*, 2 vols., ed. John Middleton Murry (London: Constable, 1928), vol. II, p. 218.
54. Peter Brooker, *Bohemia in London. The Social Scene of Early Modernism* (London: Palgrave Macmillan, 2004), pp. 102–12.

3

ANN BANFIELD

Remembrance and tense past

This chapter will explore the link between time, modernism and the novel. In literary modernism it is the novel, almost alone among genres, which is typically linked to time and to innovations in the representation of temporality. Despite T. S. Eliot's *Four Quartets* (1944) being about time, time is not a structural concept for poetry (excluding narrative poetry). This chapter will not discuss innovations in temporality as a response to aspects of modernity external to the novel itself, whether developments in the other arts, in philosophy, in scientific theory, in technology (including train travel, the synchronization of clocks, the telegraph, photography and the cinema)[1] or in the organization of the work day under capitalism. Our specific concern is rather what in the formal properties and history of the novel makes it the one among literary genres in which the modernist preoccupation with time is worked out. The answers to this question will necessarily select among the various external theories of modernism and time those that best explain the novel's internal development. For time is not simply a subject of the modernist novel; it governs its formal experiments. Just as, according to Michel Foucault, 'philology was to untie the relations that the grammarian had established between language and external history in order to define an internal history', a history internal to the novel can be isolated, alongside the novel's role *in* history.[2]

Dualism of history and private life

Modernist time-thinking manifested an increasingly marked dualism: a disjunction between public/objective and private/subjective time. Henri Bergson criticized this dualism, asserting that time was really experienced 'duration', that is, a flow of interpenetrating moments, by contrast with scientific or physical 'spatialized' time, the 'time' measured by clocks, in which the units are discrete. Bergson held that only duration constitutes real time, which is not divisible into discrete moments. Most modernists have been called Bergsonian at one time. William Faulkner stated his agreement 'with Bergson's theory of the fluidity of time'.[3] Virginia Woolf's conception of time is frequently called 'Bergsonian', though she claimed to 'have never read Bergson'.[4] Marcel Proust certainly knew Bergson's work, but none-theless discounts his influence. The real questions, however, are whether time as it operates in the modernist novel is dualist, and also whether it is conceptualized as duration or as a series of discrete moments.

The dualism between a mind or interiority and the external world is already built into the novel's structure, with a dualist temporality the result. The nineteenth-century novel saw this dichotomy as the confrontation between private and public history: history disrupted private life, invading the novel's traditional domestic sphere. History in nineteenth-century novels is revolutionary history, proceeding by ruptures in the timeline, when, as Georg Lukács says, 'everything changes in a flash'.[5] Lukács saw the cause in the French Revolution and revolutionary war, 'which for the first time made history a *mass experience*'.[6] In revolutionary periods the most private, most quietist, of individuals is swept into history.

A key text here is Sir Walter Scott's *Old Mortality* (1816); the key moment the forcible entrance of the king's light guardsmen into a Scottish manor house in the 1680s, projecting its proprietor, the young Morton, someone with no inclination to join the anti-English forces, into the Covenanters' ranks. 'His character was for the moment as effectively changed as the appearance of a villa, which, from being the abode of domestic quiet and happiness is, by the sudden intrusion of an armed force, converted into a formidable post of defence.'[7] The event Scott takes from late seventeenth-century history was emblematic of the period just before the novel's 1816 publication. The poet Goethe's house had been similarly invaded by Napoleon's army after the Battle of Jena.[8] This metaphor for history's invasion of private life leaves its trace in Woolf's *Jacob's Room* (1922) and *Mrs Dalloway* (1925), where aproned old women, 'figure[s] of the mother whose sons have been killed in the battles of the world', stand at their door, scanning the horizon for war ships, defending the threshold between history and domesticity'.[9]

But Lukács found the twentieth-century novel's preoccupation with time divorced from history: 'Subjective Idealism had already separated time, abstractly conceived, from historical change ... Bergson widened it further. Experienced time, subjective time, now became identical with real time; the rift between this time and that of the objective world was complete.'[10] Time's dualism in modernist experiments indeed presents abstract versions of domesticity and history. Privacy is conceived as interiority rather than domestic life; history is reduced to time's irreversibility. When history in the modern novel bursts into private life, it increasingly breaks into a character's train of thought, disturbs an abstracted, distracted state, because history itself has receded to such an incomprehensible distance, become an impersonal force.

The modernist novel does not omit history; it shows its new face. History's ruptures, however distanced in time and space, continue to have their repercussions. In Faulkner's *Absalom, Absalom!* (1936), where subjective time might seem the only reality, a date (1865, the end of slavery, the defeat of the southern secession) establishes a division in the novel's history, private and public, just as Miss Dunne's 'click[ing] on the keyboard' anchors private events to '16 June 1904' in James Joyce's *Ulysses* (1922).[11] And the question of Scott's survival is even put at the centre of Woolf's *To the Lighthouse* (1927). Mr Ramsay and William Bankes worry that the young do not read him. In the novel's middle section, the experimental 'Time Passes', an old woman with a Scottish name 'fetched up from oblivion all the Waverley novels'.[12] It is 'Time Passes' that marks the break in time, the division of this novel and of its characters' lives into a before and after.

In Woolf's *Mrs Dalloway* 'an indescribable pause; a suspense ... before Big Ben strikes' (4–5) makes the boom of the hour sudden, unexpected, suggesting 'something tremendous [is] about to happen' (104). Here time is *experienced* as freedom. By contrast, public time sounds the fateful hour. The hour strikes '[f]irst a warning', 'then the hour, irrevocable' (5). Leo Tolstoy wrote that 'Every man ... us[es] his freedom to attain his personal aims, and feels with his whole being that he can at any moment perform or not perform this or that action; but, so soon as he has done it, that action accomplished at a certain moment in time becomes irrevocable and belongs to history'.[13] Perhaps because the promise of freedom renewed from 1789 to 1917 in fact returned continually new prison-states worse than any *ancien régime*, modernism saw the dualism as the single life confronting the past's finality.

A single experience does not suffice to locate one in history. Modernism increasingly confronted histories so large in scale, so distant or hidden, that the understanding of them escaped individual experience. Even if the details of these histories passed some individuals by, it might, however, still be the case that for them 'all [had] changed, changed, utterly'.[14]

Dualism of time and tense

The dualism of history and the private world is embedded in the novel's very language. There is the purely narrative sentence. This typically contains no terms such as *now*, *today* and *yesterday*, which locate time with respect to the speaking subject and speech act, but only objective temporal markers such as dates, for example, 16 June 1904, which denotes the same day, regardless of when it is uttered. The narrative sentence recounts events independent of a subject. In contrast, there is the sentence of free indirect style or represented thought, representing third person subjectivity.[15] An example is the following sentence from *Mrs Dalloway*: 'No, the words meant absolutely nothing to her now' (51). Note the exclamation 'No', representing Clarissa Dalloway's point of view. Crucial is the cotemporality of temporal deictics like *now*, denoting a private time, with the past tense ('meant ... now'), a combination not possible in the spoken language. Subjectivity is thus here represented as a now-in-the-past.

This dualism is also one of verbal tense. Tense is generally considered to pattern with words like *now* and *yesterday*. However, the so-called 'historical past' (aorist or preterit) demonstrably does not: for example, the French *passé simple* does not cooccur with *hier* 'yesterday', but with temporals like *on the previous day*. Hence there are two tense systems, one centred in the now = present of a subject in time and the second independent of a subject, yielding a sequence like the integers.[16]

The relation between tense and the novel is significant enough to have merited various well-known treatments.[17] The same is not true of 'tense and the lyric' or 'tense and the drama'. For once the novel distances itself from the structure of spoken communication, as lyric and drama do not – essentially when it abandons the formal framework of letter and journal – it develops its own repertoire of tenses.

Time will tell: the past recounted

Defining a story as 'a narrative of events arranged in time sequence', E. M. Forster sees it as eliciting the question 'And then? ... And then?'.[18] This is pure narration, giving the 'objective' passage of time. Its basic unit is the sentence in the historical past, what *Ulysses*'s 'Ithaca' episode calls an 'aorist preterite proposition' (734). Its unwritten, censored example ('parsed as masculine subject, monosyllabic onomatopœic transitive verb with direct feminine object') is *Ulysses*'s ur-event: he (Blazes Boylan) fucked her (Molly Bloom). Usually in the novel, sentences in the historical past alternate with sentences of represented thought representing experienced time. But sequences of sentences all in the historical past tense can also occur. Such pure diegesis, the narratologist Genette says, is 'what English-language critics call *summary*', 'that is, the narration in a few paragraphs or a few pages of several days, months, or years of existence, without details of action or speech'.[19]

But summary can equally well recount events not widely separated in time, as in *Jacob's Room*:

> A window tinged yellow about two feet across alone combated the white fields and the black trees ... At six o'clock a man's figure carrying a lantern crossed the field ... A load of snow slipped and fell from a fir branch ... Later there was a mournful cry ... A motor car came along the road shoving the dark before it ... The dark shut down behind it.[20]

It is the isolated, random, contingent nature of events and the objective nature of their recounting that these sequences convey. Time passes without regard for the subject. Narrative is emptied of 'story', its reassuring subjectivity. While nothing historically momentous occurs in the last example, it certainly does in the novel itself, albeit tragically offstage: Jacob dies in the First World War – as contingent as any event in the series. These sequences potentially flatten time's passage, making no distinction between world-historical and private events. Each event is discrete, so between any two a rupture from some point of view is possible. But if, as Woolf says, 'the moment of importance came not here but there', it is only because a subject at some point confronts time's inexorability.[21]

Forster asserts of Scott that 'to make one thing happen after another is his only serious aim' (37). Such is not the motor driving the modernist narrative forward, but this is not to say that it disappears, as *Ulysses* attests. Woolf's pronouncement that 'this appalling narrative business of the realist: getting on from lunch to dinner' is 'merely conventional' only means to dispense with the characters' full set of movements.[22] Instead, a few events suffice to convey time's passing. Woolf punctuates the middle section of *To the Lighthouse*, 'Time Passes', with a sequence of sentences in brackets starkly recounting events of these passing years in the historic past tense, alternating with sentences in the *now*-in-the-past of represented subjectivity – in this case empty viewpoints on an empty house and landscape. Arguably the only 'aorist preterite propositions' in *To the Lighthouse*, their scarcity endows them with a skeletal abstractness. Modernist experimentation strips away everything superfluous to the measuring of time's passing.

The bracketed sentences in 'Time Passes' recount Mrs Ramsay's, Prue's and Andrew Ramsay's deaths and the war itself, but flattened alongside trivial, albeit symbolic events, such as the snuffing of a candle. 'The epic past is called the "absolute past" for good reason', Mikhail Bakhtin observes. 'It is walled off absolutely from all subsequent times.'[23] The significant events of the night of 'Time Passes' (seven years) – three deaths, the war – take place while the characters are asleep and thus unaware of them. Yet, Woolf suggests, the unavailability of historical change to immediate perception in no way minimizes the reality of its consequence for those who sleep through the night of time: they awake to reality.

The city as the multiplicity of experiences synchronized

Lukács charged that modernism had substituted an abstract, subjective *time* for *history*'s concreteness and objectivity. The critic Roland Barthes's answer to this charge is that the historical past tense in the novel functions 'to reduce reality to a point in time, and to abstract from the depth of a multiplicity of experiences, a pure verbal act, freed from the existential roots of knowledge'.[24] Barthes sees this tense as in complementary distribution with represented thought, or what he calls the 'third person of the novel'. Represented thought, exploited by novelists such as Jane Austen from at least the early nineteenth century, was increasingly used by the modernists, sometimes giving the passage of time almost exclusively, but never entirely, as private time – as in parts one and three of *To the Lighthouse* and throughout *Mrs Dalloway*. *Ulysses* alternates statements of both types, along with interior monologue. Proust's narrative, as Genette observes, is frequently in the habitual aspect, recounting a plurality of events – 'We used always to return from our walks in good time to pay aunt Léonie a visit'[25] – but these appear alongside the recounting of singular events or sentences in a now-in-the-past.

Barthes's formulation maps historical narration on to two possibilities of represented thought that the modernists exploited: frequent shifts in point of view and the arresting of the moment. The former is illustrated in the following jump from Lily Briscoe's consciousness to Augustus Carmichael's in *To the Lighthouse*: 'Gently the waves would break (Lily heard them in her sleep); tenderly the light fell (it seemed to come through her eyelids). And it all looked, Mr. Carmichael thought, shutting his book, falling asleep, much as it used to look' (214). Unless direct speech is used, as in *The Waves* (1931), such shifts are possible only with the suppression of the first person. In represented thought in the first person, as in Proust's first person narration, each *now*-in-the-past represents a shift from one moment to another and hence to a different version of the narrator's past self.

It is not surprising that the novelists who pushed the possibilities of this style to their limits should find analogies for the novel's disintegration into a collection of points of view in private space-time in modern physics, modern transportation (the train, the motor car), in the linkage of two different points in space-time by the telegraph and the telephone, but above all, in the organization of the city. The great modernist novels of multiple viewpoints and moments set them ticking in the geography of the modern city: *Ulysses* and *Mrs Dalloway*, as well as *The Years* (1937) and parts of *Jacob's*

Room and *The Waves*. The crowded urban spaces become the obvious correlative of the multiplication of points of space-time in constant motion; the slowness of time Proust claims that the novel speeds up is there accelerated and made visible.

A single day, reduced to a waking day, i.e. the conscious part of the day, in a single city, offered a device to gather the proliferation of moments. *Ulysses* provided the model; Woolf in *Mrs Dalloway* and Mulk Raj Anand in *Untouchable* (1935) followed it. *Untouchable*, significantly, begins with the protagonist Bakha's awakening – his is, furthermore, a working day. (*Finnegans Wake*, 1939, and *To the Lighthouse*'s 'Time Passes' fill in the missing night.) Modernism's unity of time is far from the classical drama's twenty-four hours, which, Ian Watt maintains, denied 'the temporal dimension in human life', asserting that reality's timelessness meant that the truth of existence is as fully revealed in a day as in a lifetime.[26] Still, the modernist day is datable – like *Ulysses*'s 16 June 1904, *Mrs Dalloway* is set on a particular day in mid-June in the postwar period. It is thus one of a series, something that *To the Lighthouse*'s tripartite structure underscores. Clocks further divide it into smaller units and connect it to public time.

This is strikingly apparent in the similarities between *Ulysses* and *Mrs Dalloway*, on the one hand, and Andrey Bely's *Petersburg* (1916) on the other, though neither Joyce nor Woolf knew *Petersburg*. These can be explained by responses to the same scientific and technological discoveries, but even more so to the novel's internal development. Instead of traditional chapter divisions, all three novels' highly fragmented subparts are motivated by their adoption of multiple points of view, set in motion in the city streets. Bely uses captions to title his brief sections much as Joyce in *Ulysses*'s 'Aeolus' episode. In *Petersburg* the jumps between sections indicate Apollon Apollonovich's movements in time and space. The little breaks in the text of *Mrs Dalloway* indicate shifts from one subjectivity to another, but also from one point in space-time to another: when Mrs Ramsay leaves the dining room and enters another present moment, the effect is cinematic, as if characters pass from frame to frame. The representation of time's passing is hardly Bergson's interpenetrating duration.

Such discrete events must be ordered with respect to one another in terms of before and after and typically correlated with public time via clocks, to establish an objective timeline. Besides 'the wall cuckoo clock' in *Petersburg*,[27] there is the 'clock mechanism' attached to a bomb (163); in *Ulysses* the 'Heighho! Heighho!' of the 'bells of George's church' marks 'Quarter to' (70) and 'The Right Honourable William Humble, earl of Dudley, G. C. V. O., passed Mickey Anderson's all times ticking watches' (253) – 'Five to three' (219); in *Mrs Dalloway* the striking of two clocks, Big

Ben and St Margaret's, 'shredding and slicing', 'dividing and subdividing', along with the clocks of Harley Street, 'nibbled at the June day' (154). There is also the liturgical division of the day in *Ulysses*, beginning with Buck Mulligan's mocking introit and moving to the 'little hours' of Father Conmee's breviary (242). There are 'tides in the body' (*Mrs Dalloway* 171): breakfast, lunch and dinner. For the body is a clock. The timeline is even projected into the future: 'Ten years, he [Buck Mulligan] said, chewing and laughing. He [Stephen] is going to write something in ten years' (*Ulysses* 249).

In the streets the private worlds are in motion relative to one another. It is a postrelativity world: each has its own clock, keeping its own time – 'separate and immanent dynamisms related by no system of synchronisation', Samuel Beckett comments in speaking of Proust's characters' mutual relations.[28] The public clocks in the cityscape of *Ulysses*, *Mrs Dalloway* and *Petersburg* confirm the importance of public clocks in cities such as Bern, where Albert Einstein in May 1905, a year before *Ulysses* is set, began to define simultaneity by the electrocoordination of clocks, for 'there were but real times given by clocks'.[29] The striking of clocks catch characters at different points on the map consulting the time and connect the private moments. All of *Ulysses*, Vladimir Nabokov observed, patterns the 'synchronization of trivial events'.[30] The 'Cuckoo/Cuckoo/Cuckoo' of '[t]he clock on the mantelpiece in the priest's house' is also heard by Gerty MacDowell (*Ulysses* 382). 'On Newcomen bridge' father John Conmee S. J. 'stepped on to an outward bound train' as '[o]ff an inward bound tram stepped the reverend Nicholas Dudly C. C. ... on to Newcomen bridge' (221–2). In Woolf's *The Years* '[t]ravellers watched the hands of the round yellow clocks as they followed porters, wheeling portmanteaus, with dogs on leashes'.[31] The choreography of movement in space-time maps out abstractly the traditional novel's chance or missed encounters. Samuel Beckett, reader of Joyce and Proust, would himself schematize this as the brief meeting of the 'two wayfaring strangers' A and C in the opening of *Molloy* (1951).[32]

A momentary group of sensations in the perpetual flux[33]

The novel as a genre also increasingly exploited represented thought to slow down experienced time by magnifying its smallest units: the day, the moment. 'Newton and Locke presented a new analysis of the temporal process; it became a slower and more mechanical sense of duration which was minutely enough discriminated to measure the falling of objects or the succession of thoughts in the mind', Ian Watt comments (24). The moment opens to reveal myriad microscopic, random, trivial events. Woolf's writer of 'modern fiction' is enjoined to record them 'as they fall, ... shape themselves into the life of Monday or Tuesday' or, in the words Woolf uses of Dorothy Richardson's multivolume novel *Pilgrimage* (1915–67), 'to register one after another, and one on top of another, words, cries, shouts, notes of a violin, fragments of lectures, to follow these impressions as they flicker through Miriam's mind'.[34]

The impressions meant 'the immediate sensations of the moment'.[35] Woolf would write in *To the Lighthouse* of 'any turn in the wheel of sensation' having 'the power to crystallize and transfix the moment upon which its gloom or radiance rests' (9). In a novel whose plot rests on the instability of Scottish weather – 'if it's fine tomorrow' the excursion to the Lighthouse will take place – the line invokes those momentary meteorological changes of light and season that Impressionism aimed to capture.

Early accounts of represented thought understood it in the light of recent innovations in painting as a literary impressionism. Charles Bally, who coined the term 'free indirect style' in 1912, related impressionism and time: impressionism 'seized a fugitive moment and fixed it' ('d'en saisir un moment fugitif et de le *fixer*'), stopping time's movement to isolate one unit.[36] Bally concludes that impressionism is 'static', giving 'substantive form to processes' and so 'crystallizing them'.[37] His language is strikingly reminiscent of Woolf's. Similarly, in *Absalom, Absalom!*, Faulkner spoke of a 'forever crystallized instant'.[38] Bergson had invoked crystallization for what was not duration, so the image suggests the modernists' non-Bergsonian conception of time, even at the level of experience.[39] Lukács had objected that 'separating time from the outer world of objective reality' transforms 'the inner world of the subject' into an 'inexplicable flux' which 'acquires, paradoxically ... a static character', finding modernism thereby both Bergsonian and anti-Bergsonian.[40]

These arrested moments punctuate the novels of the city. Traffic may flow continuously, 'motor cars, tinkling, darting', 'overwhelmed by the traffic and the sound of all the clocks striking', crowds rush by, '[m]urmuring London flowed up to her' (*Mrs Dalloway* 245, 72, 169). 'In the swing, tramp, and trudge; in the bellow and the uproar; the carriages, motor cars, omnibuses, vans', the characters pause, 'even in the midst of the traffic' (*Mrs Dalloway* 4), 'the random uproar of traffic', little islands of arrested time (*Petersburg* 5, 4, 79). 'By lorries along Sir John Rogerson's quay, Mr Bloom walked soberly' (*Ulysses* 71). Within the moment, all becomes still, like W. B. Yeats's stone in the midst of the living stream in his poem 'Easter 1916'.

If subjective, sense impressions are at the interface between inner and outer reality, experience enters interiority as present impressions. Arresting time allows otherwise 'evanescent' impressions to be 'engraved with the sharpness of steel', as Woolf says in 'Modern Fiction' (150), extracted from experience to become history by the process Barthes describes – 'something happened so violently that I have remembered it all my life', Woolf records of her past.[41]

But, in the midst of traffic, the mind may also be simultaneously elsewhere, elsewhen. Father Conmee reads Nones out of sequence with the time (*Ulysses* 224). So, as '[t]he sun was nearing the steeple of George's church' in the western world, Bloom's mind is '[s]omewhere in the east: early morning: set off at dawn, travel round in front of the sun, steal a day's march on him. Keep it up for ever never grow a day older technically. Walk along a strand, strange land ... Wander through awned streets. Turbaned faces go by' (57). The emancipation from present surroundings transforms Peter Walsh into the solitary traveller, occupying a time and place independent of Mrs Dalloway's sequence of hours, nowhere in the interstices of two wakeful moments, presided over by a knitting nurse.

Time's arrow passes through still moments

Nonetheless, the moment's stillness does not escape time: modernist time passes through arrested moments. For there to be time, more than one now is required; there must be a sequence of moments. If Impressionism, painting the effects of light, painted only one moment, it captured change by painting series such as Claude Monet's of the façade of Rouen cathedral or of haystacks. So Woolf, in the interludes of *The Waves*, gives sequential descriptions of appearances through changes of light throughout a day, which also becomes a season.

This can be conveyed by jumping from *now* to *now* in subjective time, i.e. by shifting point of view, either to another character's simultaneous or subsequent point of view or from one now to another, as in Katherine Mansfield's 'At the Bay' (1922): 'Now a stone on the bottom moved, rocked, and there was a glimpse of a black feeler; now a thread-like creature wavered by and was lost ... And now there sounded the faintest "plop".'[42] With their 'nows-in-the-past', these examples of represented thought reduce to represented sensations. This formalization of temporal change, broken down into a sequence of 'frames' or discrete moments – Bergson's example is a cinematograph – is not Bergson's *durée*, but it corresponds with novelistic practice, which modernism seized in its abstract form. As Franco Moretti comments of William James's notion of a 'stream of consciousness', James's own language, where 'a succession of states, or waves, or fields' is in apposition with 'stream', is at odds with the stream metaphor. So, Moretti concludes, Bloom's experience in *Ulysses* consists of 'discrete, and almost absolute, moments'.[43] The moment, the hours, night and day, the years, the waves – the titles of Woolf's novels record this conception of time as discrete units in sequence.

Linguistically, the multiple points of view in different *nows* are reduced to past-tense statements in chronological sequence. This is possible because each *now* can be correlated with a date and the series of *nows* has the same order as a series of dates. Even the mind's escape from time occurs only against the background of time's passage: when absence of mind ends, often interrupted by a striking clock, the revenants discover, like Lily Briscoe waking at the end of 'Time Passes', that time has not waited for them. Swann at the end of Proust's *Swann in Love* (1913), waking from a dream, realizes he has wasted years of his life for a woman not his type. The mind's temporary freedom from time only returns it to time's reality.

The space of a forgetting

From the mid-nineteenth century to the period of modernism, the novelist typically writes from the vantage point of midlife. Midlife is identifiable not as a quantity of time but as a crisis, a perceivable break. Modernism incorporates this break *within* the novel as a lapse of time or memory. The blank in memory marks the break from which suddenly the life which was being lived is seen from a distance. Perhaps this is why Jean-Paul Sartre claims that 'for Faulkner, as for Proust, time is, above all, *that which separates*'.[44]

'Time Passes' in *To the Lighthouse* emphatically divides the text. As the characters sleep, time passes in leaps and bounds. What separates past from present, then, is the space of a forgetting, the unconsciousness of the characters. It is followed by a sudden awakening to the fact that time *has* passed unbeknownst to the subjects. Suddenly, at the distance of 'middle age', looking back across the divide, Lily Briscoe discovers that something is over: what she awakes to is the postwar world. 'Time', Lukács says in his *The Theory of the Novel* (1920), 'can become constitutive only when the bond with the transcendental home has been severed.'[45] Home is thus always located in the past, and the existential nostalgia or homesickness that Lukács sees as distinguishing novel from epic longs to recover a past: 'Man is conscious of his fate, and calls this consciousness "guilt".' 'Through guilt a man says "Yes" to everything that has happened to him; by feeling it to be his own action and his own guilt, he conquers it and forms his life.'[46] Guilt is the persistence of a forgotten or repressed memory that must be recovered.

Identity and memory

To reconnect present with past, two differently tensed propositions must be reconnected. The connection between such past moments and the present remembering self holds the key, Proust thought, to the problem of personal identity: 'Locke had defined personal identity as identity of consciousness through duration in time; the individual was in touch with his own continuing identity through memory of his past thoughts and actions.'[47] But not all is remembered, nor remembered reliably. Waking to himself, Proust's narrator 'could not be sure who I was' until memory drew him 'up out of the abyss of non-being'.[48]

In *The Waves* the characters begin as undifferentiated, blank slates; they become distinguished one from the other by the accumulated events that happen to them. The question of whether their distinctiveness is a result of their different experiences or whether each has its own innate way of registering experience is raised by the novel. If subjects caught in the present receive impressions from without, thoughts and images spontaneously arise in the mind. Among the latter, besides Leopold Bloom's imaginary wanderings 'through awned streets', are memories of past moments: his of Molly, Clarissa Dalloway's of Bourton, Mrs Ramsay's of 'the Mannings' drawing-room at Marlow twenty years ago' (*To the Lighthouse* 140). The moment is endowed with a historical depth; on 'the moment of this June morning ... was the pressure of all other mornings' (*Mrs Dalloway* 54). Woolf's *Jacob's Room* had limited the characters' represented subjectivity to their present sensations and thoughts. In *Mrs Dalloway* and *To the Lighthouse*, the characters' represented thoughts include memories. Woolf uses her 'tunnelling process' to give 'the past by instalments', making *Mrs Dalloway* a kind of *Time Regained-In Search of Lost Time* compressed in one volume. (Proust's last volume interestingly also ends in a last soirée reassembling the major characters, showing their final metamorphoses in time.) Woolf's method is to 'dig out beautiful caves behind my characters'. The idea was 'that the caves shall connect, & each comes to daylight at the present moment'.[49] In the represented thoughts of one character are contained references to times and places in other characters' thoughts, which take on an independent existence. With Peter Walsh and Sally Seton, Clarissa 'shared her past; the garden; the trees; old Joseph Breitkopf singing Brahms without any voice; the drawing-room wallpaper; the smell of the mats. A part of this Sally must always be; Peter must always be' (*Mrs Dalloway* 277). 'Odd affinities she had with people she had never spoken to' (231). The connections are not necessarily conscious, though Clarissa has such intimations. It is largely the novel's style that establishes these affinities. The style's ability to shift point of view and follow the mind's wanderings establishes relations between points of view and builds up a common impersonal past independent of the individual mind and even beyond human memory – it is this that the chiming of the hours in public time signals. It is in such terms that Woolf imagines modern technologies of communication: 'the streets of any large town', Woolf writes,

[are] cut up into boxes, each of which is inhabited by a different human being who has put locks on his doors and bolts on his windows to ensure some privacy, yet is linked to his fellows by wires which pass overhead, by waves of sound which pour through the roof and speak aloud to him of battles and murders and strikes and revolutions all over the world.[50]

What is most important is not the moments of communication between two subjectivities but the establishment of real correlations between experiences and events.

The historical past remembered

In the nineteenth-century historical novel, the stretch of time that counts as history is a past within living memory, the author's own remembered past or that handed down from the previous generation, parents or grandparents. Again, Scott's *Old Mortality* sets it out emblematically at the start. The series of frames that begin it and give it its title connect the novel, preeminently written genre, to oral tradition. Oral storytelling, Benjamin says, is 'experience that goes from mouth to mouth'.[51] Old Mortality, the itinerant raconteur, is the living link between the novel's late seventeenth-century past, and the contemporary frame. 'He considered himself as ... renewing to the eyes of posterity the decaying emblems of the zeal and sufferings of their forefathers' (64):

> He was profuse in the communication of all the minute information which he had collected concerning them, their wars and their wanderings. One would almost have supposed he must have been their contemporary, and have actually beheld the passages which he related, so much had he identified his feelings and opinions with theirs, and so much had his narratives the circumstantiality of an eye-witness. (66)

Not accidentally, the historical novel, a written form, appears at the moment when a European oral culture is rapidly disappearing. The bard who sings in *Waverley* (1814) belongs to Highland culture and not the lowland world of the future. The process mirrors the transformation of memory into history, that other nineteenth-century written genre.

The frame bridging orality and the writing of the novel that introduces the story of *Old Mortality* disappears from nineteenth-century historical novels, even if it remains part of the circumstances of their composition. But it reappears as a structuring principle in Faulkner, as also in Conrad. Modernist experiments with time, like Faulkner's in *Absalom, Absalom!*, the novel in which Thomas Sutpen's black stallion is 'named out of Scott' (63), locate in Scott's chain of living memory an epistemological missing link. The recovery of the past Faulkner undertakes so as to discover 'the incontrovertible fact which embattled' (269) the brothers Charles Bon and Henry Sutpen – not the Northern and Southern brothers that orthodox history sees pitted against one another in civil war but two Southern brothers divided by race (91) – requires moving through layers of subjective experience, generations of narrators, chronology, genealogy – even the latter has to be determined. Who is father to whom? Faulkner's chain of memory's multiple links – 'Sutpen *may* have told your grandfather ... your grandfather *might* have told me and I *might* have told you' (8), Quentin's father Mr Compson recalling what 'Father' said, including what Thomas Sutpen told him – forges a chain of suppositions acknowledging the uncertainty of the past: 'That's what Miss Rosa heard. Nobody knows what she thought' (62). 'She *must* have told Mr Coldfield that there was nothing wrong and evidently she believed that herself' (63). '"*Maybe* I can read it here all right," Quentin said. "*Perhaps* you are right," Mr Compson said' (71) (my italics).

In taking over Old Mortality's anecdotes, 'far from adopting either his style, his opinions, or even his facts, so far as they appear to have been distorted by party prejudice', Scott has no compunction in 'correct[ing] or verify[ing] them from the most authentic sources of tradition, afforded by the representatives of either party' (68). For Scott, not only is the truth now known, it is separable from opinion and acknowledged without controversy. Faulkner's past is, as Sartre remarked, 'full of gaps'. Faulkner pieces together oral histories in which a repressed past is allowed to speak through each narrator. From these testimonials it is surmised that Thomas Sutpen uncovered miscegenation. The multiplication of viewpoints serves less to shut out the external world of history as to underscore the difficulty of arriving at a single incontrovertible account of it. But it would be a mistake to conclude that Faulkner thinks the truth will not out, any more than W. G. Sebald, returning in *Austerlitz* (2001) to a chain of narrators, could be accused of entertaining negationism as a valid hypothesis. Indeed, Sebald's return to modernist experimentation is compatible with his allusions to Stendhal, i.e. to the historical novel.

For the modernist novel's reduction of the confrontation between history and private life to that between the tragic irreversibility of time and the brief instant of individual freedom (call it 'youth') was not a simple retreat to quietism. It sought to discover, through an analysis of the past, the exact moment when the course of history could have been otherwise. The brief moment of freedom is seized as it is already congealing into a past. Could we not hypothesize that the trace of this fact can be discovered in the peculiar *now*-in-the-past of represented thought's retrospective language?

It was necessary now to carry everything a step further. With her foot on the threshold she waited a moment longer in a scene which was vanishing even as she looked, and then, as she moved and took Minta's arm and left the room, it changed, it shaped itself differently; it had become, she knew, giving one last look at it over her shoulder, already the past.   (*To the Lighthouse*, 167–8)

'Was it goodbye? No. She had to go but they would meet again, there, and she would dream of that till then, tomorrow, of her dream of yestereve' (*Ulysses*, 367).

Notes

1. See Stephen Kern, *The Culture of Time and Space: 1880–1918*, (Cambridge, MA: Harvard University Press, 1983), p. 12, and Peter Galison, *Einstein's Clocks, Poincaré's Maps* (New York: Norton, 2003).
2. Michel Foucault, *The Order of Things: An Archaeology of the Human Sciences* (London: Tavistock, 1970), p. 294.
3. James B. Meriwether and Michael Millgate (eds.), *Lion in the Garden: Interviews with William Faulkner, 1926–1962* (New York: Random House, 1968), pp. 70, 255.
4. Virginia Woolf, *The Letters of Virginia Woolf*, 6 vols., *Volume V: 1932–1935*, ed. Nigel Nicolson and Joanne Trautmann (New York: Harcourt Brace Jovanovich, 1979), p. 91.
5. Georg Lukács, *Soul and Form* (Cambridge, MA: MIT Press, 1974), p. 159.
6. Georg Lukács, *The Historical Novel* (London: Merlin Press, 1965), p. 20.
7. Walter Scott, *Old Mortality* (Harmondsworth: Penguin Books, 1975), p. 192. Further references cited parenthetically.
8. R. J. Hollingdale, 'Introduction', Johann Wolfgang von Goethe, *Elective Affinities*, trans. R. J. Hollingdale (Harmondsworth: Penguin, 1971), p. 7.
9. Virginia Woolf, *Mrs Dalloway* (New York: Harcourt Brace Jovanovich, 1985), p. 87. Further references cited parenthetically.
10. Georg Lukács, 'The Ideology of Modernism', in Lukács, *Realism in Our Time: Literature and the Class Struggle*, trans. John and Necke Mander (New York: Harper and Row, 1964), p. 35.
11. James Joyce, *Ulysses* (New York: Vintage, 1990), p. 229. Further references cited parenthetically.
12. Virginia Woolf, *To the Lighthouse* (New York: Harcourt Brace Jovanovich, 1927), p. 209. Further references cited parenthetically.
13. Leo Tolstoy, *War and Peace*, trans. Rosemary Edmonds (Harmondsworth: Penguin, 1978), p. 717.
14. W. B. Yeats, 'Easter 1916', in Yeats, *Poems*, ed. Daniel Albright (London: J. M. Dent, 1994), p. 228.
15. In Charles Bally's 1912 term '*style indirect libre*', '*libre*' means 'independent', as in 'independent clause'. I prefer 'represented thought', alongside Otto Jespersen's 'represented speech'. See Ann Banfield, *Unspeakable Sentences* (London: Routledge and Kegan Paul, 1982).

16. See Emile Benveniste, *Problems of General Linguistics*, trans. Mary Elizabeth Meek (Coral Gables: University of Miami Press, 1971), pp. 205–15.

17. See W. J. M. Bronzwaer, *Tense in the Novel* (Groningen: Wolters Noordhoff, 1970), and Roland Barthes, *Writing Degree Zero*, trans. A. Lavers and C. Smith (New York: Hill and Wang, 1967).

18. E. M. Forster, *Aspects of the Novel* (New York: Harcourt Brace, 1927), pp. 30, 37. Further references cited parenthetically.

19. Gérard Genette, *Narrative Discourse: An Essay in Method*, trans. Jane E. Lewin (Ithaca: Cornell University Press, 1980), pp. 94–6.

20. Virginia Woolf, *Jacob's Room* (New York: Harcourt Brace Jovanovich, 1950), pp. 98–9.

21. Virginia Woolf, 'Modern Fiction', in Woolf, *Collected Essays*, 4 vols. (London: Hogarth Press, 1966), vol. II, p. 106.

22. Virginia Woolf, *The Diary of Virginia Woolf*, ed. Anne Olivier Bell, 5 vols. (Harmondsworth: Penguin, 1982), vol. III, p. 209.

23. M. M. Bakhtin, *The Dialogic Imagination: Four Essays* (Austin: University of Texas Press, 1981), p. 15.

24. Barthes, *Writing Degree Zero*, p. 30.

25. Genette, *Narrative Discourse*, p. 136.

26. Ian Watt, *The Rise of the Novel* (Berkeley: University of California Press, 1965), p. 23. Further references cited parenthetically.

27. Andrey Bely, *Petersburg*, trans. Robert A. Maguire and John E. Malmstad (Bloomington: Indiana University Press, 1978), p. 5. Further references cited parenthetically.

28. Samuel Beckett, *Proust* (London: Chatto and Windus, 1931), p. 7.

29. Galison, *Einstein's Clocks*, p. 47.

30. Vladimir Nabokov, *Lectures on Literature*, ed. Fredson Bowers (London: Weidenfeld and Nicholson, 1980), p. 289.

31. Virginia Woolf, *The Years* (New York: Harcourt Brace Jovanovich, 1937), p. 193.

32. Samuel Beckett, *Molloy*, in Beckett, *Three Novels* (New York: Grove Press, 1955), pp. 8–11.

33. The phrase is used by Roger Fry in 'The Philosophy of Impressionism', in Christopher Read (ed.), *A Roger Fry Reader* (Chicago: University of Chicago Press, 1996), p. 16.

34. Woolf, 'Modern Fiction', p. 106, and 'Dorothy Richardson', in Woolf, *Virginia Woolf: On Women and Writing*, ed. Michèle Barrett (London, Women's Press, 1979), p. 189.

35. Fry, 'Philosophy of Impressionism', p. 18.

36. Charles Bally, *Linguistique générale et linguistique française* (1932; rev. edn Berne: Francke, 1944), p. 362.

37. 'L'impressionisme est d'une essence *statique*, et ce n'est pas un hasard s'il donne la forme *substantive* aux procès et aux qualités; c'est une manière de les cristal-liser.' *Ibid.*, p. 362.

38. William Faulkner, *Absalom, Absalom!* (New York: Vintage, 1990), p. 127. Further references cited parenthetically.

39. See Henri Bergson, *Time and Free Will: An Essay on the Immediate Data of Consciousness* (New York: Harper and Row, 1960), p. 237.

40. Georg Lukács, 'The Ideology of Modernism', in Lukács, *The Meaning of Contemporary Realism* (London: Merlin Press, 1963), p. 39.
41. Virginia Woolf, *Moments of Being*, ed. Jeanne Schulkind (San Diego: Harcourt Brace Jovanovich, 1985), p. 71.
42. Katherine Mansfield, *Stories*, ed. Elizabeth Bowen (New York: Random House, 1956), p. 115.
43. Franco Moretti, *Modern Epic: The World-System from Goethe to García Márquez*, trans. Quintin Hoare (London: Verso, 1996), p. 136.
44. Jean-Paul Sartre, 'On *The Sound and the Fury*: Time in the Work of Faulkner', in Sartre, *Literary and Philosophical Essays*, trans. Annette Michelson (New York: Criterion Books, 1955), pp. 84–93 (p. 89).
45. Lukács, *Theory of the Novel*, p. 122.
46. Lukács, *Soul and Form*, p. 165.
47. Watt, *The Rise of the Novel*, p. 21. See also John Locke, *An Essay Concerning Human Understanding*, Book II, ch. 27, sections ix, x.
48. Marcel Proust, *Swann's Way*, trans. C. K Scott Moncrieff (New York: Penguin, 1998), pp. 3–4.
49. Virginia Woolf, *The Diary of Virginia Woolf*, 5 vols., ed. Anne Olivier Bell (Harmondsworth: Penguin, 1981), vol. II, p. 263.
50. Virginia Woolf, 'The Narrow Bridge of Art', in Woolf, *Collected Essays*, vol. II, p. 222.
51. Walter Benjamin, 'The Storyteller', in Benjamin, *Illuminations*, ed. Hannah Arendt, trans. Harry Zohn (New York: Schocken Books, 1969), p. 84.

4

ANNE FERNIHOUGH

Consciousness as a stream

In 1911 the French philosopher Henri Bergson wrote an impassioned preface to a new edition of William James's *Pragmatism* (1907). James, the distinguished American psychologist, had recently died, and Bergson paid homage, in his preface, to the mind with which he had felt such a strong affinity.[1] He stressed the centrality of *redundancy* and *superabundancy* to James's vision of reality: 'While our motto is *Exactly what is necessary*, nature's motto is *More than is necessary* – too much of this, too much of that, too much of everything ... Reality, as James sees it, is redundant and superabundant' (267).

Bergson then went on to draw an essentially literary analogy between traditional (pre-Jamesian) philosophy and the artifice of the stage play:

> Between this reality and the one constructed by the philosophers, I believe he would have established the same relation as between the life we live every day and the life which actors portray in the evening on the stage. On the stage, each actor says and does only what has to be said and done; the scenes are clear-cut; the play has a beginning, a middle and an end; and everything is worked out as economically as possible with a view to an ending which will be happy or tragic. But in life, a multitude of useless things are said, many superfluous gestures made, there are no sharply-drawn situations (268).

A chaotic superabundancy *versus* a literary economy and contrivance: the terms are strikingly suggestive of the famous passage in Virginia Woolf's essay 'Modern Fiction' (1919), in which Woolf defends her own evolving 'stream-of-consciousness' technique:

> The mind receives a myriad impressions – trivial, fantastic, evanescent, or engraved with the sharpness of steel. From all sides they come, an incessant shower of innumerable atoms; and ... if [the writer] could base his work upon his own feeling and not upon convention, there would be no plot, no comedy, no tragedy, no love interest or catastrophe in the accepted style.[2]

Three years later, in *Jacob's Room* (1922), Woolf would attempt to capture in novelistic form this 'mind receiv[ing] a myriad impressions', as in this description of a London dawn, where the 'trivial' and 'evanescent' (a blade of grass, a discarded coffee cup) compete for attention with the historic and magisterial landmarks of the capital:

> But colour returns; runs up the stalks of the grass; blows out into tulips and crocuses; solidly stripes the tree trunks; and fills the gauze of the air and the grasses and pools.
>
> The Bank of England emerges; and the Monument with its bristling head of golden hair; the dray horses crossing London Bridge show grey and strawberry and iron-coloured. There is a whir of wings as the suburban trains rush into the terminus. And the light mounts over the faces of all the tall blind houses, slides through a chink and paints the lustrous bellying crimson curtains; the green wine-glasses; the coffee-cups; and the chairs standing askew.[3]

In his *Principles of Psychology* (1890), James had coined the phrase 'mind-wandering' to describe a mental state in which we open ourselves up to the swarm of sense data bombarding consciousness at any given moment.[4] 'Mind-wandering' indeed seems an apt description for Woolf's technique in this passage. It brings to mind that quintessentially modernist literary persona, the *flâneur* ('stroller' or 'wanderer'), who idly roams the streets of the city, surrendering to its aesthetic fascinations and delights.[5] In *Principles* James distinguished between this errant mental state and what he called 'selective attention', a more discriminating faculty of mind which made practical, everyday life possible by singling out the particular things which might be useful to us and suppressing or editing out the rest.[6]

Published in the same year as *Jacob's Room*, James Joyce's *Ulysses* also placed 'superabundancy' and 'mind-wandering' at the heart of its agenda. In chapter six, for example, Leopold Bloom, attending Paddy Dignam's funeral, finds his mind wandering back in time to the conception of his son, Rudy, who died in infancy. The tragedy of his son's death and thoughts of how Rudy might have turned out had he lived ('Walking beside Molly in an Eton suit. My son ... I could have helped him on in life') mingle with tiny details from the scene of the conception, such as the rip in Molly's cream gown which she had never got round to stitching, or the sight through the window of a pair of dogs mating. These memories compete with half-formed observations in the present moment about the other funeral guests and half-digested fragments of the funeral service, all coexisting in higgledy-piggledy fashion.[7] Joyce's technique in this particular passage is more naturalistic than Woolf's, in that it attempts to render as closely as possible the *chaos* of the inner life, and the raw, unfinished quality of our thoughts and impressions, as well as the sheer speed with which they meld into one another. The technique is taken yet further in Molly Bloom's soliloquy in the final chapter of the novel, where there is a complete absence of punctuation and an almost complete lack of paragraphing. The unbroken flow of words on the page embodies an undiscriminating and unstoppable consciousness in which there is no editing out and no hierarchy of thought:

> first I want to do the place up someway the dust grows in it I think while Im asleep then we can have music and cigarettes I can accompany him first I must clean the keys of the piano with milk whatll I wear shall I wear a white rose or those fairy cakes in Liptons I love the smell of a rich big shop at 7½d a lb or the other ones with the cherries in them and the pinky sugar 11d a couple of pounds of those a nice plant for the middle of the table ... (642)

Thoughts and impressions are connected more by free association than logic, and there is no privileging of the portentous (Molly's thoughts of infidelity) over the trivial (her penchant for the fairy cakes at Lipton's shop).

James was no advocate of 'mind-wandering', in life or in art: we could not thrive, or even survive, he argued, if we gave in to this 'promiscuous' faculty of mind; we would find ourselves 'lost in the midst of the world' (444). In Woolf's *Mrs Dalloway* (1925) it is the mentally ill, shell-shocked soldier, Septimus Smith, who is most vulnerable to it, and least able to cope with life (he eventually jumps to his death from a window). His shell shock has opened him up to a richly synaesthetic, yet also bewildering, experience of the world around him; he is alert to sounds, patterns and sensations to which others are oblivious:

> he would not go mad. He would shut his eyes; he would see no more.
> But they beckoned; leaves were alive; trees were alive. And the leaves being connected by millions of fibres with his own body, there on the seat, fanned it up and down; when the branch stretched he, too, made that statement. The sparrows fluttering, rising, and falling in jagged fountains were part of the pattern; the white and blue, barred with black branches. Sounds made harmonies with premeditation; the spaces between them were as significant as the sounds.[8]

There is common ground between this so-called 'madness' and the experience of the very young child who has not yet learnt to conceptualize and categorize in conventional and practical ways. Woolf recognized this in the early sections of *The Waves* (1931), where she uses interior monologue to convey the small child's extraordinary capacity for synaesthesia: '"Now the cock crows like a spurt of hard, red water in the white tide," said Bernard.'[9] In May Sinclair's novel *Mary Olivier* (1919), we meet the same sensory keenness and receptivity when Mary, as a tiny girl, experiences snow for the first time: 'White patterns on the window, sharp spikes, feathers, sprigs with furled edges, stuck flat on to the glass; white webs, crinkled like the skin of boiled milk, stretched across the corner of the pane; crisp, sticky stuff that bit your fingers.'[10]

Sinclair was in fact the writer who first used the phrase 'stream of consciousness' in a literary critical context, in a review of Dorothy Richardson's work which was published in 1918.[11] She is generally thought to have taken the phrase from James, who had used it in his *Principles*, but Suzanne Raitt has argued persuasively that the actual phrase 'stream of consciousness' might have come from a whole range of texts, psychological and biological, that Sinclair had read, and not necessarily from James.[12] Whether or not Sinclair was referring directly here to James, Woolf's 'Modern Fiction' certainly does resonate with echoes of James, particularly in her assertion that 'life is a luminous halo, a semi-transparent envelope surrounding us from the beginning of consciousness to the end' (160). James, when writing of consciousness as a stream, had used this same term, 'halo'. He emphasized that consciousness was not divisible into clear-cut sections, or, as he phrased it, into 'pailsful, spoonsful, quartpotsful, barrelsful, and other moulded forms of water'. He went on:

> Even were the pails and the pots all actually standing in the stream, still between them the free water would continue to flow. It is just this free water of consciousness that psychologists resolutely overlook. Every definite image in the mind is steeped and dyed in the free water that flows round it ... The significance, the value, of the image is all in this halo or penumbra that surrounds and escorts it. (255)

Woolf's use of the term 'halo', then, seems to suggest a knowledge of James. There is also reason to believe that Woolf would have known of Bergson's work, on which her sister-in-law, Karin Stephen, had published a monograph.[13] Bergson's notion of *dureé* ('duration') was a major influence on the cultural climate from which the stream-of-consciousness novel emerged.

Richardson, whose work Sinclair was reviewing when she used the phrase 'stream of consciousness', actually took umbrage at what she called this 'death-dealing metaphor'.[14] Throughout her life she railed against it, seeing it as inappropriate for what she was trying to do. Perhaps she disliked it because it failed to capture the way in which consciousness *accumulates* rather than merely flows in her writing. *Pointed Roofs*, the first volume of her epic thirteen-volume, semi-autobiographical novel *Pilgrimage* (1915–67) was drafted in 1913, and the philosopher whose work was being most widely canvassed in Richardson's circles at this time was Bergson. Bergson had used the image of a snowball, rather than a stream, to evoke his 'time-philosophy': 'My mental state, as it advances on the road of time, is continually swelling with the duration which it accumulates: it goes on increasing – rolling upon itself, as a snowball on the snow.'[15] For Bergson, memory was all-important as the condition of our free will: it is through memory, he argued, that our actions transcend predictable mechanical responses to the extent that we bring our accumulated experiences to bear on a given situation. Consciousness or 'duration', in which the present is swollen with the past, is the essential feature of our humanity.

Bergson's analogy between consciousness and an unbroken sentence, 'this single sentence that was begun at the first awakening of consciousness, a sentence strewn with commas but in no place cut by a period', seemed to be a clarion call to writers in this period.[16] Richardson later acknowledged Bergson as someone who 'was putting into words something then dawning within the human consciousness'.[17] In an article written in 1918, she wrote of the relationship between past and present in distinctly Bergsonian terms: 'It is a characteristic vice of the intellect to see the past as a straight line stretching out behind humanity like a sort of indefinite tail. In actual experience it is more like an agglomeration, a vital process of crystallization grouped in and about the human consciousness, confirming and enriching individual experience.'[18]

A snowball; an unbroken sentence: Bergson's metaphors for human consciousness suggest an 'agglomeration' that is not implicit in the idea of a stream. When Sinclair writes, of *Pilgrimage*, 'It is just life going on and on. It is Miriam Henderson's stream of consciousness going on and on', she fails to convey any sense of meaningful accumulation.[19] Both the snowball and the unbroken sentence are more appropriate for the idea of the self as a developing entity that is so central to the work of both Richardson in *Pilgrimage* and Sinclair herself in *Mary Olivier*. Both novels are semi-autobiographical in nature, charting the consciousnesses of their female protagonists from youth (or babyhood, in Mary Olivier's case) into maturity.

It was the self-obsessed, self-analytical nature of stream-of-consciousness writing that D. H. Lawrence pounced on in his essay on the modern novel: 'Through thousands and thousands of pages', he grumbled, 'Mr Joyce and Miss Richardson tear themselves to pieces, strip their smallest emotions to the finest threads.'[20] Yet Lawrence was just as capable as these writers of excessive and finely nuanced psychological analysis, and for Lawrence, as for Bergson (whom he had read), consciousness *is* the individual; it is what makes each of us unique and free, redeeming us from purely deterministic or materialist explanations of human identity. As Bergson writes in *Creative Evolution* (1907):

each of [our acts of attention] is borne by the fluid mass of our whole psychical existence. Each is only the best illuminated point of a moving zone which comprises all that we feel or think or will – *all, in short, that we are at any given moment*. It is this entire zone which in reality makes up our state. Now, states thus defined cannot be regarded as distinct elements. They continue each other in an endless flow (my italics).[21]

The lynchpin of Bergson's philosophy, then, was his belief that each individual consciousness has its own uniqueness and its own *durée*. It was his conviction that philosophy, and culture as a whole, had refused to recognize this by confusing time with space. Our understanding of time as a sequence of hours and minutes, of interchangeable, measurable units, was, he argued, really a spatial notion. It artificially broke up time, severing the continuity of *durée* and effacing its uniqueness. This was all part of our mistaken tendency to approach psychic experience, consciousness, in terms borrowed from the perception of physical objects. The faculty responsible for this deleterious confusion, according to Bergson, was the intellect, which could deal with the mind only in terms of physical, measurable entities. In 1907 he wrote to James in a spirit of mutual congratulation. Their philosophical projects were, he believed, 'destined to take the place of intellectualism', and he was, of course, using the term 'intellectualism' in a specific, and pejorative, sense.[22]

Woolf, in a number of novels, exploits what is essentially Bergson's distinction between *durée* and a (merely) spatial time. She does it most obviously in *Mrs Dalloway*, a novel which, like Joyce's *Ulysses*, takes place within the confines of a single day, but which, in terms of 'real time' as opposed to spatial time, is 'swollen' with memory, and ranges freely over experiences widely separated in time. When Big Ben strikes the half-hour 'as if a young man, strong, indifferent, inconsiderate, were swinging dumb-bells this way and that' (41), the word 'indifferent' seems to carry Bergsonian overtones, suggesting the identical, undifferentiated, *indifferent* units of clock time. The same tolling of Big Ben is heard by the various characters (Clarissa, Septimus, Peter Walsh), but serves only to accentuate the way in which their individual consciousnesses diverge from the commonality imposed by clock time.

In *To the Lighthouse* (1927), time as a linear sequence of days and months and years is similarly subordinated to the tissue of individual consciousnesses. In the middle section, 'Time Passes', we are told of a number of deaths, all in parenthetical asides. They are related with what appears to be brutal nonchalance on the part of the narrator: '[Mr. Ramsay stumbling along a passage stretched his arms out one dark morning, but, Mrs. Ramsay having died rather suddenly the night before, he stretched his arms out. They remained empty.]'[23] Mrs Ramsay's death would traditionally have been made into a climactic point in the novel. Instead it is downplayed as a random and unexpected occurrence which must, like other random occurrences, be absorbed into the fabric of consciousness. That consciousness, for the survivors, is ongoing; death does not halt it any more than trivial occurrences do. This is not to say that Woolf is belittling death: the memory of Mrs Ramsay reverberates throughout the remainder of the novel. But even in bereavement, there will always be the ongoing, multifarious tissue of consciousness, subject to the pressures of everyday, trivial concerns.

Bergson, then, is an unspoken presence in these novels by Woolf, just as he is in some of her best-known critical writing, including the essay 'Character in Fiction', also published in pamphlet form as 'Mr Bennett and Mrs Brown' (1924). Here as elsewhere, Woolf defines herself against a trio of older contemporaries, Arnold Bennett, H. G. Wells and John Galsworthy. Of these it is Bennett, author of *The Old Wives' Tale* (1908) and the *Clayhanger* novels (1910–18), who is her chief bugbear. Ironically enough, Bennett had published in 1908 a self-help book entitled *How to Live on 24 Hours a Day*, which reads like an unintentional parody of Bergson's concept of spatial time. Addressed to the typical, newspaper-reading suburbanite who has to travel to the office by train and tube, it teaches him how to 'balance a budget of the hours', and to squeeze the most out of every spare five minutes.[24] Bennett treats time as a sequence of physical, measurable entities. He also, according to Woolf, mistakes solid objects for the human subject, which is why she dubs him a 'materialist': 'He [Bennett] is trying to hypnotise us', she says, 'into the belief that, because he has made a house, there must be a person living there.'[25] To support her case against Bennett, Woolf cites a passage from his 1911 novel, *Hilda Lessways*, in which he describes the eponymous heroine's home:

> It was one of the two middle houses of a detached terrace of four houses built by her grandfather Lessways, the teapot manufacturer; it was the chief of the four, obviously the habitation of the proprietor of the terrace. One of the corner houses comprised a grocer's shop, and this house had been robbed of its just proportion of garden so that the seigneurial garden-plot might be triflingly larger than the other. The terrace was not a terrace of cottages, but of houses rated at from twenty-six to thirty-six pounds a year; beyond the means of artisans and petty insurance agents and rent-collectors. (430)

Woolf resolves to take a different approach to the 'Mrs Brown' of her essay title. She will rid her novelistic space of the physical and material clutter that the Edwardians have bequeathed to her, and unlike them, she will find a way of capturing Mrs Brown without needing to know 'whether her villa was called Albert or Balmoral' or 'what she paid for her gloves' (433).

We have already seen, however, that there is a sense in which the stream-of-consciousness writer transmutes *physical* into *psychological* clutter, into a superabundancy of impressions and memories. Unredeemed, apparently 'objective' descriptions of the material world, such as Bennett's in the passage above, are replaced by accounts of the material as filtered through consciousness, and permeated with memory. The opening of James Joyce's *A Portrait of the Artist as a Young Man* (1916), for example, is written from a baby's perspective ('his father looked at him through a glass: he had a hairy face'); in the infant Stephen Dedalus's consciousness, certain material objects, trivial in themselves, loom large, such as the velvet-backed brushes belonging to 'Dante' – his childish rendition of 'Auntie'. While away at boarding school, the young Stephen involuntarily recalls the brushes when he sees their colours echoed in a friend's painting: 'he had coloured the earth green and the clouds maroon. That was like the two brushes in Dante's press.' Almost unconsciously, for Stephen the brushes signify a lost, childish sense of security. The thought of them in turn triggers a memory of a family quarrel in which Dante ripped the velvet off the green-backed brush, saying that Parnell was 'a bad man'. With Stephen's growing awareness, the brushes have become the repository of painful memories involving family tensions and a dimly understood, foreboding sense of Ireland's troubled politics.[26]

The opening of Sinclair's *Mary Olivier* is strongly reminiscent of the opening of Joyce's *Portrait* in its recreation of a baby's physical and psychological perspective. It opens with the big bed that Mary's parents sleep in, seen from Mary's vantage point in the adjacent cot: 'The curtain of the big bed hung down beside the cot. When old Jenny shook it the wooden rings rattled on the pole and grey men with pointed heads and squat, bulging bodies came out of the folds on to the flat green ground. If you looked at them they turned into squab faces smeared with green' (3). The 'polished yellow furniture: the bed, the great high wardrobe' (13) of her parents' room serves throughout the novel as one of the markers of Mary's psychological and emotional growth. Initially offering Mary sanctuary and a comforting sense of symbiosis with her mother, it soon starts to resonate with a sense of loss and disillusionment. Before long, it is wielding the same emotional tyranny over Mary that her mother wields over her, however unconsciously, and that Mary simultaneously resents and succumbs to: '"There's a part of me that doesn't care and there's a part that cares frightfully." The part that cared was not free. Not free. Prisoned in her mother's bedroom with the yellow furniture that remembered. Her mother's face remembered. Always the same vexed, disapproving, remembering face' (170). The bed, then, evolves with Mary and even remembers with her: 'the yellow furniture that remembered'.

On the face of it, those philosophies and artforms that place the delicate vagaries of the individual consciousness at their centre might seem to be progressive in a loosely left-wing sense, a celebration of the uniqueness and the unlimited potential of every human being. In certain contexts they undoubtedly do take on this political colouring: Bergson was used, for example, by the Marxist critic Georg Lukács to criticize the dehumanizing conditions of factory labour.[27] Bergson's philosophy was, however, double-edged, and those writers and cultural theorists who took up his work with enthusiasm often drew a very fine and dangerously permeable line between criticizing a culture based on quantifiable things, and deploying a rhetoric whereby 'the masses' *could* be dehumanized and presented as, precisely, quantifiable things. The individual, in other words, could be opposed to the masses, and indeed the very concept of the masses, with its suggestion of bulk, of quantity rather than quality, could be seen as a logical outcome of Bergson's philosophy. This helps us to understand, I believe, why stream-of-consciousness fiction often risks the charge of elitism, as I hope to show below.

In the late nineteenth and early twentieth centuries, when stream-of-consciousness writing and philosophy were emerging, the physical and cultural textures of life were changing at a bewildering rate, through major advances in technology, for example, and the rapid growth of suburbia. Increasing mechanization, organization and centralization at every level of society were contributing to a paranoid sense on the part of some intellectuals that private space was being surrendered to the public space of the masses. Stream-of-consciousness writing was just one facet of the complex cultural response to this sense of invasion and contamination, as were movements and trends centring on food reform and on the 'simple life'. Such movements were driven by notions of purity and vigour, and by anxieties about the unwholesomeness of mass, urban living. In magazines like the *New Age* and the *Egoist*, in which so much early modernist writing first appeared, advertisements for 'nonflesh' restaurants and nature cures appeared alongside pieces on philosophers such as Bergson and Friedrich Nietzsche, and articles on aesthetics.

In such a cultural environment, it was easy to harness Bergson's philosophy to attacks on democracy. It was easy to do so because of the reductive way in which democracy was being understood and presented by its opponents at this time. They argued that democracy was premised on a false assumption of a quantifiable sameness, a lack of differentiation, between individuals, just as Bergson's intellect reduced the world to a quantifiable sameness. Dora Marsden, for example, the pugnacious editor of the *Freewoman* (which became the *Egoist* in 1914) used Bergson's distinction between a real time and an unreal space to denounce the suffragettes (even though she was a former suffragette herself). Suffrage, she argued, 'seeks to establish in space – in the static – that which has an existence only in time'. The vote may, she went on, be fit for what she termed 'bondwomen', those women who were content to remain hidebound by social and political convention, but for the 'freewoman' the vote was an irrelevance, a chimera. 'Bondwomen are distinguished from Freewomen by a spiritual distinction,' Marsden explains. 'Bondwomen are the women who are not separate spiritual entities – who are not individuals. They are complements, merely.'[28] Bergson is not the only philosopher she draws on here: she also produces a feminized version of Nietzsche's distinction between the superman and the common herd. Casting aside the false securities of the democratic state, Marsden's freewoman will 'push open the door of the super-world'.[29] Bondwomen, it seems, will by contrast be left behind in the ordinary world, the world of suburbia perhaps, that world of the identical, interchangeable, Edwardian villas that were sprawling out from the big cities during this period.

Marsden, then, throws Nietzsche as well as Bergson into the antidemocratic pot. In fact, her favourite concoction is a heady mixture of Bergson, Nietzsche and a third philosopher, Max Stirner. Stirner's treatise *Das Eigen und Sein Eigentüm* (1844), translated into English in 1907 as *The Ego and His Own*, was an anarchistic attack on all governments and institutions on the grounds that the only reality was the self, the ego. Stirner argued that abstractions such as 'equality', 'humanity' and 'law' were unrealities, mere phantoms leading to the 'sacrifice of real individuals to the non-existent and impossible Perfect Man'.[30] Following Stirner, Marsden argues that a democracy based on the concepts of equality and fraternity is not real freedom; it is merely an intellectual construct preventing the 'freewoman' from realizing herself.

Through a potent fusion of Bergson, Nietzsche and Stirner, then, writers such as Marsden blamed the intellect for a whole range of obsolete and oppressive social and political movements and institutions, including marriage, the family unit and conventional schools which, unlike the new breed of progressive school, did not allow 'proper scope for the play of instincts and impulses'.[31] Freewomen and supermen were not to be straitjacketed by marriage, and it is worth noting here that a significant number of stream-of-consciousness heroines, including Miriam Henderson, Mary Olivier, Woolf's Lily Briscoe and Lawrence's Ursula Brangwen in *The Rainbow* (1915), all resist the constraints of marriage, either refusing to marry at all or choosing partners who will not compromise their personal freedom. Towards the end of *Mary Olivier*, Sinclair's heroine abruptly and seemingly brutally terminates her love affair with Richard Nicholson in favour of her 'real', authentic self. Reflecting on her decision, Mary has no regrets: 'If I had to choose now – knowing what reality is – between losing Richard in the way I have lost him and losing reality, absolutely and for ever, my real self, knowing that I'd lost it? . . . Knowing reality is knowing that you can't lose it. That or nothing' (379). Throughout her life Mary has battled to protect what she calls her 'sacred, inviolable self', a self constantly besieged by 'inscrutable hostility, hindering, thwarting, crushing you down' (290). At times in agonizing doubt as to whether such an inviolable self really does exist independently of the 'net' of heredity, she decides by the end that she is prepared to take the risk that it does, and that the risk is what makes it worth while (312, 379).

Mary Olivier ends with an epiphany, as Mary comes to a mystical awareness that her 'real self' is there and worth living by. The ending of the novel bears comparison to that of *To the Lighthouse*, where the artist Lily Briscoe turns towards the canvas that she has been working on through the course of the novel, her portrait of Mrs Ramsay, and has 'her vision':

> She turned to her canvas. There it was – her picture. Yes, with all its greens and blues, its lines running up and across, its attempt at something. It would be hung in the attic, she thought; it would be destroyed . . . With a sudden intensity, as if she saw it clear for a second, she drew a line there, in the centre. It was done; it was finished. Yes, she thought, laying down her brush in extreme fatigue, I have had my vision. (225–6)

The pronoun is telling: '*my* vision'. It is Lily's solitary, private moment. No matter that the picture may be hung in an attic where no one can see it, or simply destroyed. Like Sinclair's Mary, Lily could be accused of drifting into solipsism. But it is Richardson's Miriam in *Pilgrimage* who most clearly embodies a particular kind of egoism to be found in stream-of-consciousness writing, one that stems from the potent combination of Bergson, Nietzsche and Stirner described above. Richardson's narrative is spun entirely from Miriam's consciousness, and in its adherence to the precise contours of that consciousness, and its refusal to engage directly with any consciousness other than Miriam's, it silently delineates a rejection of democracy and a horror of the masses. The lofty Miriam is all too convincing as a literary version of Dora Marsden's 'freewoman', despising the 'bondwomen' around her with their compliant, feminine smiles: 'They would smile those hateful women's smiles – smirks – self-satisfied smiles as if everybody were agreed about everything. She loathed women. They always smiled.'[32] When not being assaulted by women's smiles, Miriam is the target of predatory, invasive eyes, eyes that threaten to violate the integrity of her own hypersensitive ego. Eyes seem to crop up once every few pages throughout *Pointed Roofs*, 'dreadful eyes – eyes like the eyes of hostesses', 'expressionless' eyes, 'evil' eyes, eyes that trigger nausea or even murderous feelings in Miriam. 'Is there anywhere where there are no people?', she asks herself in desperation. (21, 89, 171).

Joyce's *Portrait*, which was first serialized in the pages of Marsden's *Egoist* from 1914, also seems in some ways to follow this trajectory towards the unfettered ego. Stephen's right to individuality becomes ever more important to him as he matures, to the extent that, as a fledgling young writer, he starts to foster Nietzschean fantasies of 'forging anew in his workshop out of the sluggish matter of the earth a new soaring impalpable imperishable being' (183). Lawrence's *The Rainbow*, too, written between 1912 and 1915, projects a sense of selves restlessly striving to reach their full potential, particularly through the figure of Ursula, who rejects both marriage and suffragist campaigning in favour of a more mystical notion of 'woman becoming individual'.[33] All the female friends that Ursula makes during the course of the novel are involved in suffragism: we are told of Maggie Schofield, for example, that she is 'a great suffragette, trusting in the vote'.[34] One by one, Ursula turns her back on them, suggesting, again, Marsden's freewoman who refuses to be constrained by the carapace of an ideology: 'Ursula broke from that form of life wherein Maggie must remain enclosed' (382).

Lawrence's version of stream-of-consciousness writing is more *bodily* than that of his contemporaries. His distinctive version of free indirect discourse is shown in the following passage from *The Rainbow*, where Ursula, ill with fever, has decided to break off her engagement to Anton Skrebensky:

> And again, to her feverish brain, came the vivid reality of acorns in February lying on the floor of a wood with their shells burst forth and discarded and the kernel issued naked, to put itself forth. She was the naked, clear kernel thrusting forth the clear, powerful shoot, and the world was a bygone winter, discarded, her mother and father and Anton, and college and all her friends, all cast off like a year that has gone by, whilst the kernel was free and naked and striving to take new root, to create a new knowledge of Eternity in the flux of Time. And the kernel was the only reality: the rest was cast off into oblivion. (456)

The repetition with variation, centring on the image of the kernel, conveys a circling and an overlapping rather than a neat sequence of thoughts; but it also creates a pulsing, incantatory rhythm suggestive of the breathing and the heartbeat of the human body. The argument implicit in *The Rainbow* is a vitalist one about the need to assert 'life' and to be able to separate what is real from the inauthenticity of conventional social structures. In *Women in Love*, completed in 1916, the case is made in more overtly elitist terms. Birkin in that novel remarks that some people are individuals, while others are just part of 'the common ruck', and he goes on to make the by now familiar distinction between the 'real' individual and the unreal masses: 'Not many people are anything at all … Essentially they don't exist, they aren't there.'[35]

In spite of this disturbing sentiment, Lawrence's novels, like Woolf's and unlike Richardson's, consist of multiple streams of consciousness rather than a single one, thereby forcing the reader to identify with several points of view. The presence of more than one consciousness means that any given character cannot simply absorb others into himself or herself, as Richardson's Miriam appears to do; instead they are absorbed in turn by others, giving us a multifaceted perspective. In this respect Joyce's *Ulysses* is a very different species of novel from his earlier *Portrait* which, like Richardson's *Pilgrimage*, had been confined to a single consciousness. *Ulysses* seems indeed to offer a rare example of a democratically motivated stream-of-consciousness novel. As Declan Kiberd has argued, much of it is set in the streets and the public spaces that the poorest Irish people could claim as their own even if they could claim nothing else; it celebrates the civic and the collective.[36] The novel gives us access to those parts of Dublin frequented by ordinary people, and to the consciousnesses of those same people.

Woolf's stream-of-consciousness writing, like *Ulysses*, is dispersed among a range of consciousnesses, though her claims to being democratic are more open to question. Of the writers discussed in this chapter, she is the one who flits most readily and rapidly from one mind to another, often traversing three or four consciousnesses within the confines of a single page. Her characters and narrators, like their creator, often express a reluctance to summarize other people on the grounds that their consciousnesses will always remain closed to us. Twice we are told of Clarissa Dalloway that she 'would not say of any one in the world now that they were this or were that' (8, 9), and twice in *Jacob's Room* we are cautioned, 'It is no use trying to sum people up. One must follow hints' (24, 135). Yet in spite of this, it is possible to see in Woolf's novels residues of the distinction between the fully realized 'freewoman' and the less complex 'bondwoman'. In *Mrs Dalloway* the suffragette Miss Kilman is rendered with less complexity than Clarissa, Septimus or Peter Walsh. Clarissa sees Miss Kilman as the stereotypical embittered spinster (indeed the parodic name, Miss Kilman, invites such a response), and there is little evidence to suggest that the narrator sees her otherwise. When we are first introduced to Miss Kilman, her mind is closed off from us; instead, we are given Clarissa's response to her:

> Miss Kilman would do anything for the Russians, starved herself for the Austrians, but in private inflicted positive torture, so insensitive was she, dressed in a green mackintosh coat. Year in year out she wore that coat; she perspired; she was never in the room five minutes without making you feel her superiority, your inferiority; how poor she was; how rich you were; how she lived in a slum without a cushion or a bed or a rug or whatever it might be ... poor embittered unfortunate creature! (12)

In many ways this reads as if an Edwardian character has been dropped into Woolf's modernist novel, complete with the necessary material and economic details (the green mackintosh, the slum with no cushions). Of course, Clarissa's snobbery is being mocked here, yet even when we do have direct access to Miss Kilman's psyche, it is presented in rather reductive terms, as limited and thwarted by socioeconomic concerns (135). Like the psychiatrist Bradshaw or the upper-class busybody Lady Bruton, Miss Kilman remains in the mind as a 'type' rather than a fully individuated consciousness.

Stream-of-consciousness writing, then, is *in itself* neither politically neutral nor politically stable. Its fluidity led right-wing intellectuals such as T. E. Hulme, Ezra Pound and Wyndham Lewis to spurn it, rather lazily, as the undifferentiated slime of democracy.[37] They confused a fluid literary form with a social fluidity and mobility. Perhaps in a novel such as *Ulysses* there is a felicitous coincidence of formal with social fluidity, as it were, with a free 'circulation of social energies' in Declan Kiberd's phrase.[38] But some of the best-known practitioners of the form set themselves *against* a democracy they saw not as fluid, but as quite the reverse, as the embodiment of reified abstraction.

The issue of gender highlights similar complexities and contradictions. Richardson's *Pilgrimage* is scathing about 'women' in the collective, yet paradoxically opposes them to the 'authentic' individuality embodied by Miriam, herself a woman. Both Miriam and Richardson herself argue on numerous occasions that true individuality is the prerogative of women. In *Deadlock*, for instance, Miriam complains that 'men invent systems of ethics, but they cannot weigh personality; they have no individuality, only conformity or nonconformity to abstract systems' (III, 37). Like Woolf's writing, Richardson's is peppered with wry observations on the limitations of the male psyche. For both writers, the vitalist distinction between realities and rational systems is gendered in favour of women, and both writers see the elastic, minimally punctuated sentence often used in stream-of-consciousness writing as 'the psychological sentence of the feminine gender'.[39]

Ever since its inception, then, there has been this tendency to gender stream-of-consciousness writing 'feminine', and this has been the case even when the author has been male. The French feminist writer Hélène Cixous, famous for her formulation of an *écriture féminine* that would subvert the dictates of a 'masculine' logic, wrote her doctoral thesis on Joyce, and was at pains to stress that the practice of a 'feminine' writing was not tied to biological sex. In the same spirit of freedom, Roland Barthes, writing in the 1970s, drew an influential distinction between the 'readerly' (*lisible*) and the 'writerly' (*scriptible*) text.[40] The 'readerly' text, associated with nineteenth-century realism, was, he argued, a conservative literary form: it passively reproduced a bourgeois reality that could be effortlessly consumed by the reader. The 'writerly' text, by contrast, was liberating and progressive, freeing the reader from the endless repetition of the received or conventional view of the world. According to Barthes, realism dealt in a perpetual recycling of the same, and his critique of realism was in this respect not unlike Bergson's critique of the intellect.[41]

Barthes's notion of the 'writerly' text seems particularly appropriate for understanding parts of Joyce's *Ulysses* and especially for *Finnegans Wake* (1939), which is first and foremost a piece of linguistic fabric. We should, however, beware of homogenizing stream-of-consciousness writing, and of dehistoricizing it. In its earlier manifestations stream-of-consciousness 'form' was the sign of the real (Bergson's *durée*); more specifically, it was the sign of the individual's reality, understood to be incommensurable with anyone else's. The literary historian who looks back at it has to come to terms with the way in which Bergson's distinction between a (real) time and an (unreal) space too easily elided into a distinction between superior and inferior beings, between the individual and the mass. At the same time, paradoxically, stream-of-consciousness writing brought to literature, via Bergson, James and others, a psychological subtlety and complexity that it had never known before, at its best forcing us to acknowledge, with Woolf, 'It is no use trying to sum people up.' Its legacy is double-edged, and in this sense no different from the legacy bequeathed to us by modernism as a whole.

Notes

1. Henri Bergson, 'On the Pragmatism of William James: Truth and Reality', in Bergson, *Henri Bergson: Key Writings*, ed. Keith Ansell Pearson and John Mullarkey (New York: Continuum, 2002), pp. 267–73. Further references cited parenthetically.
2. Virginia Woolf, 'Modern Fiction', in Woolf, *The Essays of Virginia Woolf*, 4 vols., ed. Andrew McNeillie (London: Hogarth Press, 1988), vol. IV, pp. 157–65 (p. 160). Further references cited parenthetically.
3. Virginia Woolf, *Jacob's Room*, ed. Sue Roe (London: Penguin, 1992), p. 143.
4. William James, *Principles of Psychology*, 2 vols. (New York: Dover Publications, 1950), vol. I, pp. 417, 447. Further references cited parenthetically.
5. See Walter Benjamin, 'The Flâneur', in *Charles Baudelaire: A Lyric Poet in the Era of High Capitalism*, trans. Harry Zohn (London and New York: Verso, 1997), pp. 35–66.
6. James, *Principles of Psychology*, vol. I, pp. 284–9.
7. James Joyce, *Ulysses*, ed. Hans Walter Gabler (London: Bodley Head, 1986), pp. 73–4. Further references cited parenthetically.
8. Virginia Woolf, *Mrs Dalloway*, ed. Stella McNicholl (London: Penguin, 1992), p. 24. Further references cited parenthetically.
9. Virginia Woolf, *The Waves*, ed. Kate Flint (London: Penguin, 1992), p. 6.

10. May Sinclair, *Mary Olivier: A Life* (London: Virago, 1980), pp. 8–9. Further references cited parenthetically.

11. May Sinclair, 'The Novels of Dorothy Richardson', *Egoist* 5 (April 1918), pp. 57–9, and *Little Review* 4 (April 1918), pp. 3–11; reprinted in Bonnie Kime Scott (ed.), *The Gender of Modernism: A Critical Anthology* (Bloomington and Indianapolis: Indiana University Press, 1990), pp. 442–8.

12. Suzanne Raitt, *May Sinclair: A Modern Victorian* (Oxford: Clarendon Press, 2000), pp. 218–20.

13. See Karin Stephen, *The Misuse of Mind: A Study of Bergson's Attack on Intellectualism, with a prefatory letter by Henri Bergson* (London: Routledge, 1922).

14. Dorothy Richardson, Letter to Bryher, 1 January 1949, in Gloria Fromm (ed.), *Windows on Modernism: Selected Letters of Dorothy Richardson* (Athens: University of Georgia Press, 1995), p. 597.

15. Henri Bergson, 'The Endurance of Life', in *Key Writings*, pp. 171–86 (p. 171).

16. Bergson, quoted in *Egoist*, 1 January 1914, p. 7.

17. Dorothy Richardson, Letter to Shiv K. Kumar, 10 August 1952, quoted in Shiv K. Kumar, *Bergson and the Stream of Consciousness Novel* (London and Glasgow: Blackie, 1962), p. 37.

18. Dorothy Richardson, 'Comments by a Layman', *The Dental Record*, 38: 8, 1 August 1918, pp. 350–2.

19. Sinclair, 'Novels of Dorothy Richardson', p. 444.

20. D. H. Lawrence, 'The Future of the Novel', in *Study of Thomas Hardy and Other Essays*, ed. Bruce Steele (Cambridge: Cambridge University Press, 1985), pp. 149–55 (p. 152).

21. Bergson, 'Endurance of Life', p. 172.

22. Bergson, Letter to James, 27 June 1907, in *Key Writings*, p. 361.

23. Virginia Woolf, *To the Lighthouse*, ed. Stella McNichol (London: Penguin, 1992), p. 140.

24. Arnold Bennett, *How to Live on 24 Hours a Day* (London: Hodder and Stoughton, 1908), p. 133.

25. Virginia Woolf, 'Character in Fiction' (often referred to as 'Mr Bennett and Mrs Brown', the shorter piece from which it evolved), in Woolf, *Essays*, vol. III, pp. 420–38 (p. 430).

26. James Joyce, *A Portrait of the Artist as a Young Man*, ed. Seamus Deane (London: Penguin, 1992), pp. 3, 3–4, 12, 13. Further references cited parenthetically.

27. See, for example, Georg Lukács, *History and Class Consciousness: Studies in Marxist Dialectics*, trans. Rodney Livingstone (London: Merlin Press, 1971), p. 90.

28. Dora Marsden, *Freewoman*, 23 November 1911, p. 3.

29. Dora Marsden, quoted by Francis Grierson in the *New Freewoman*, 15 June 1913, p. 11.

30. This is a paraphrase of Stirner's argument, taken from a review of *The Ego and His Own* in the *New Age*, 15 August 1907, p. 251. It is quite probable that Marsden had read the *New Age* review as there are striking parallels between the *New Age* and the *Freewoman*.

31. *New Age*, 4 November 1909, p. 21.

32. Dorothy Richardson, *Pointed Roofs*, in *Pilgrimage*, 4 vols. (London: Virago, 1979), vol. I, p. 21. Further references cited parenthetically.

33. D. H. Lawrence, Letter to Edward Garnett, 22 April 1914, in *The Letters of D. H. Lawrence*, 8 vols., ed. George J. Zytaruk and James T. Boulton (Cambridge: Cambridge University Press, 1981), vol. II, p. 165.

34. D. H. Lawrence, *The Rainbow*, ed. Mark Kinkead-Weekes (London: Penguin, 1995), p. 377. Further references cited parenthetically.

35. D. H. Lawrence, *Women in Love*, ed. David Farmer, Lindeth Vasey and John Worthen (London: Penguin, 1995), pp. 25, 20.

36. Declan Kiberd, 'The Circulation of Social Energies in James Joyce's *Ulysses*', paper delivered at a colloquium on 'Energie, intensité, régime', Sorbonne Nouvelle, Paris, 23–4 September 2005.

37. See, for example, Wyndham Lewis, *Time and Western Man* (New York: Harcourt, Brace, 1928), p. 214. I discuss this issue in '"Go in Fear of Abstractions": Modernism and the Spectre of Democracy', *Textual Practice* 14 (2000), pp. 1–19.

38. See endnote 36.

39. Virginia Woolf, 'Romance and the Heart', in *Essays*, vol. III, pp. 365–8 (p. 367).

40. Roland Barthes, *S/Z*, trans. Richard Miller (Oxford: Blackwell, 1990), p. 4.

41. *Ibid.*, p. 20.

5

LAURA MARCUS

The legacies of modernism

'The fact is that every writer *creates* his own precursors. His work modifies
our conception of the past, as it will modify the future.'
Jorge Luis Borges[1]

The question of the legacies of modernist fiction for the generations of
writers that followed could lead us in a number of different directions. As
perspectives on the literary and cultural history of the past century shift and
alter, maps will be differently drawn. In particular, the literary-historical
narrative in which 'high modernism' gave way (after the extreme experiment
of James Joyce's *Finnegans Wake* (1939) and with the coming of the Second
World War) to postwar realism, and cosmopolitanism to parochialism,
requires, and is receiving, substantial revision. The 'realisms' of many mid-
twentieth-century writers and beyond are beginning to look not only more
interesting and more complex, but closer to the 'modernisms' that they are
conventionally held to have displaced. There is much new work to be undertaken on this and related questions. The focus of this chapter is a little
different, in that it explores the legacies of modernism as a question of direct,
rather than diffuse, influences. It discusses writers of the mid-twentieth
century (including B. S. Johnson, Saul Bellow and Doris Lessing) and their
relationship to their modernist predecessors, but its primary focus is on the
ways in which recent and contemporary novelists (including Paul Auster,
Alan Hollinghurst, Don DeLillo, Ian McEwan, Salman Rushdie, Jeanette
Winterson, Zadie Smith, Michael Cunningham and Colm Tóibín) are engaging with modernist fiction and its creators.

The British writer B. S. Johnson, whose fiction was published in the 1960s
and early 1970s, wrote that literature is 'a relay race, the baton of innovation
passing from one generation to another'. The problem, as he saw it, was that
'the vast majority of British novelists had dropped the baton, stood still,
turned back, or not even realized that there is a race'.[2] The image of the 'relay
race' is a curious one, contrasting clearly with Ezra Pound's warcry, now so
associated with modernist culture in general, 'Make it new'. For Johnson,
'innovation' was a quality that could be transmitted as the legacy of one

generation of writers to another. Does the baton of literary innovation change its form, however, in the race through time and space?

For Johnson, as for many of the novelists and critics discussed in this chapter, Joyce was the most significant shaper of the forms and possibilities of twentieth-century fiction. He was, Johnson asserted, 'the Einstein of the novel':

> His subject-matter in *Ulysses* was available to anyone, the events of one day in one place; but by means of form, style and technique in language he made it into something very much more, a novel, not a story about anything. What happens is nothing like as important as how it is written, as the medium of the words and form through which it is made to happen to the reader. And for style alone *Ulysses* would have been a revolution. . . .
>
> But how many have seen it, have followed him? Very few. It is not a question of influence, of writing like Joyce. It is a matter of realizing that the novel is an evolving form, not a static one, of accepting that for practical purposes where Joyce left off should ever since have been regarded as the starting point. (152)

We might suggest, following Johnson, that the proliferation of styles in *Ulysses* (1922) opened up the possibility of an inexhaustible number of languages for the novel. Christine Brooke-Rose, for example, has explored the styles or languages of science, computing and simultaneous translation; Ali Smith's *The Accidental* (2005), has made highly inventive use of the new language of 'texting' and of the format of question-and-answer in which there are echoes of the 'Ithaca' section of *Ulysses*.

Joyce's most immediate and significant legatee, Johnson argued, was Samuel Beckett. Johnson's novel *Alberto Angelo* (1964) opens with an epigraph from Beckett's *The Unnamable* (1958), in which the narrator seeks continuously to distance himself from his invented characters and to confront the reader with the unadorned self, even though a self of 'my own skin and bones' produces no self-certainty. For Johnson, 'the only thing the novelist can exclusively call his own is the inside of his own skull: and that is what he should be exploring' (152). He thus uses Beckett's image of entrapment and ceaseless repetition – 'the inside of my distant skull where once I wandered, now am fixed, lost for tininess, or straining against the walls'[3] – to articulate a belief in the possibility of the novel's authenticity, predicated on the abandonment of 'stories' and made-up characters: 'Fuck all this lying.'[4]

'I can't go on. I'll go on' are the final words of *The Unnamable*. Writers from the generation following Johnson's have met these lines as a challenge, asserting both the impossibility and the necessity of literature. Beckett may be seen as Joyce's closest affiliate, but the work of the two writers has also been radically opposed, with Joyce placed at the pole of abundance and accumulation and Beckett at that of entropy and exhaustion. Beckett's 'reduction' of personhood, in the *Trilogy* (1959) and in his late plays in particular, to a disembodied voice, condemned to ceaseless articulation, has served later writers as a profound image for the solitariness of writing and for the transmutation of 'autobiography' into 'autography', a self-writing or self-inscription without 'a life' to come between the self and the page.

The American writer Paul Auster has also paid homage to Beckett throughout his writing career, echoing his words in order to interrogate, while ultimately confirming, the role of the author. In an essay on Knut Hamsun's novel *Hunger* (1890), Auster writes, 'Hamsun's character systematically unburdens himself of every belief in every system, and in the end, by means of the hunger he has inflicted upon himself, he arrives at nothing. There is nothing to keep him going – and yet he keeps on going. He walks straight into the twentieth century.'[5] Auster's phrasing echoes the last lines of *The Unnamable*: 'where I am, I don't know, in the silence you don't know, you must go on, I can't go on, I'll go on'. Before Beckett, though, there was the modernist Franz Kafka, another maker of the 'hunger artist' and the elaborator of 'the aesthetics of hunger'. In Kafka's short story 'A Hunger Artist' (1924), the eponymous protagonist 'goes too far', starving himself to death in a 'performance' in which, as Kafka writes, he was 'bound to be the sole completely satisfied spectator of his own fast'.[6] 'But that', Auster writes, 'is the risk, the danger in any act of art: you must be willing to give your life ... I do not believe that we have come any farther than this' (324).

Explicit references to the legacies of modernism can also be found in the work of Alan Hollinghurst. The youthful hero of Hollinghurst's novel *The Line of Beauty* (2004), Nick Guest, is writing a PhD on 'style at the turn of the century – Conrad, and Meredith, and Henry James, of course ... style that hides things and reveals things at the same time'. Nick amuses a group of friends by recounting the details of a gay sexual encounter in the language of late James. Hollinghurst deploys a Jamesian style to describe feelings, sensations and desires that James's text itself could never have articulated:

> It was all new to Nick, this being with another man, carried along on the smooth swelling current of mutual feeling – with its eddies sometimes into shop door-ways or under the awnings of the bric-à-brac stalls. There was no more talk of lunch, which was a good sign. In fact they didn't say anything much, but now and then they shared glances which flowered into wonderful smirks. Lust prickled Nick's thighs and squeezed his stomach and throat, and made him almost groan between his smiles, as if it just wasn't fair to be promised so much.[7]

At this point the question of the literary 'legacy' and its relationship to 'parody' and 'pastiche' becomes a pressing one.[8] To what extent is Hollinghurst exploring, or exposing, style as repression, with the defining obliquity of James's prose represented as a veiling of homosexual desire? British writing has seen new relationships developing between the contemporary novelist and his or her modernist predecessors, which raise complex issues of rein- . scription and of ways of negotiating literary legacies. The sense of a radical break between the modernist novel and the fiction of later decades has weakened. Nonetheless, novels such as *The Line of Beauty* are as concerned with dramatizing their distance from their modernist precursors as with their proximity.

The legacy of the one-day novel

One particular and powerful modernist way of structuring the fictional work – the use of the single day – can serve as a route into an exploration of the continuities and differences between the modernist text and the fiction that followed it. The one-day novel, as exemplified by Joyce's *Ulysses* and Virginia Woolf's *Mrs Dalloway* (1925), was central to modernist fiction, serving, as Steven Connor has noted, as both 'less and more at once: less than the world in its concentration and condensation . . . and yet containing more than the world in its accumulation of allusion and interconnection'.[9] 'Examine for a moment an ordinary mind on an ordinary day', Woolf wrote in her essay 'Modern Fiction' (1919), defining the reception by the mind of 'a myriad impressions – trivial, fantastic, evanescent, or engraved with the sharpness of steel' as both the substance of 'life' and as the materials of the modern novel.[10]

The structure of the day has subsequently been deployed in a range of texts across the century, including Mulk Raj Anand's *Untouchable* (1935), Saul Bellow's *Seize the Day* (1956) and Christopher Isherwood's *A Single Man* (1964). Isherwood's novel owes a clear debt to *Mrs Dalloway*, but here the single day in the life of its protagonist – a middle-aged, gay university teacher living in California – is also his last. The novel opens with the protagonist wakening: 'Waking up begins with saying *am* and *now*. That which has awoken then lies for a while staring up at the ceiling and down into itself until it has recognized *I*, and there-from deduced *I am, I am now*'. It concludes at the end of this same day with the loss of that '*I*' in the 'instant, annihilating shock' of a heart attack.[11]

Doris Lessing's *The Golden Notebook* (1962) also incorporates an experiment in recording the events of a single day. Anna, one of the two women with whom the novel opens, records in a notebook that 'I shall write down, as truthfully as I can, every stage of a day. Tomorrow. When tomorrow ends I shall sit down and write.' The next entry begins, 'I could not write last night because I was too unhappy. And now, of course, I am wondering if the fact that I chose to be very conscious of everything that happened yesterday changed the shape of the day.'[12]

The day Anna records is both an ordinary and an extraordinary day, like that of Mrs Dalloway in Woolf's novel. In *The Golden Notebook* Anna's day includes not only the care of her child and her work routines, but her decision finally to leave the Communist party and her recognition that her love affair is at an end. Anna's account of her day is also shaped by the fact that her menstrual period begins in the morning:

> And so I begin to doubt the value of a day's recording before I've started to record it. I am thinking, I realize, about a major problem of literary style, of tact. For instance, when James Joyce described his man in the act of defeca-ting, it was a shock, shocking … I realise it's not basically a literary problem at all. For instance, when Molly said to me, with her loud jolly laugh: I've got the curse; I have instantly to suppress distaste, even though we are both women. (291)

Lessing's novel could be seen as a 'writing back' to Joyce, both in her simulta-neous construction and erasure of the account of a single day and in her suggestion of its inadequacy to record Anna's own, highly gendered, experi-ences. *The Golden Notebook* is fragmented at the level of structure (the four different notebooks) rather than, as in *Ulysses*, style and language. In Lessing's novel the imbrications of dailiness, bodily processes and writing entail, for Anna, a tortuous process of articulation and analysis, in which she veers between physical, emotional and cerebral states. At the close of the record of her day, there is no affirmation of her experiences. Instead we read: 'The whole of the above was scored through – cancelled out and scribbled underneath: No it didn't come off. A failure as usual.' Underneath the long entry is written a terse alternative account: 'A normal day' (314).

In Bellow's *Seize the Day* (1956), Tommy Wilhelm confronts, or fails to confront, the failure which is his life during the course of one day. He is estranged from his wife and children, jobless and living in a New York residence hotel also occupied by his elderly, emotionally distant father. Bellow structures the first half of this short novel around Tommy's purchase of a newspaper, the collection of mail and the eating of breakfast. The components match, one for one, those that animate the physical and mental life of Leopold Bloom in the early sections of *Ulysses*, but in Tommy's world the potential – imaginative, bodily, sensory – of each event is severely curtailed, subordinated to his anxieties over the commodities market and the money he has been persuaded to invest 'in lard' by the charismatic, untrustworthy Dr Tamkin.

The injunction to 'seize the day', the novel's title, is placed in the mouth of Dr Tamkin: 'The spiritual compensation is what I look for. Bringing people into the here-and-now. The real universe. That's the present moment. The past is no good to us. The future is full of anxiety. Only the present is real – the here-and-now. Seize the day.'[13] The multiple ironies at work here include Tamkin's induction of the hapless Tommy into the world of commodity 'futures'. Such a relationship between time and money is taken to its limit in Don DeLillo's *Cosmopolis* (2003), in which, as one character states, time has become a 'corporate asset. It belongs to the free market system. The present is harder to find. It is being sucked out of the world to make way for the future of uncontrolled markets and huge investment potential. The future becomes insistent.'[14]

In DeLillo's one-day fiction the only flow in the city is the circulation of capital; for much of the novel, Eric, the central protagonist, is stalled in his stretch-limousine as the traffic sits at a standstill. We could trace such images of 'paralysis' back to Joyce and his *Dubliners* (1914) and to the moments in *Mrs Dalloway* in which the 'prime-minister's car' halts the circulation of the modernist city. The hollowed-out moments or intervals of the modernist novel, however, in which subjectivity, desire and memory are allowed space and time to burgeon, are almost entirely lacking in DeLillo's text, which represents a world in which time has become split into smaller and smaller units – 'Yoctoseconds. One septillionth of a second' (79).

Ian McEwan's one-day novel *Saturday* (2005) is prefaced by an excursus on 'what it means to be a man', where McEwan cites a passage from Bellow's novel *Herzog* (1964): 'In a city. In a century. In transition. In a mass. Transformed by science. Under organized power. Subject to tremendous controls. In a condition caused by mechanization. After the late failure of radical hopes. In a society that was no community and devalued the person. Owing to the multiplied power of numbers which made the self neglible.' The epigraph has, presumably, been chosen in part because Bellow's words seem to apply so directly to the context in which McEwan is writing, half a century later. Beyond this, however, McEwan is also acknowledging a debt. As he wrote on the occasion of Bellow's death in 2005:

> He set himself, and succeeding generations, free of the formal trappings of modernism, which by the mid-20th century had begun to seem a heavy constraint. He had no time for Virginia Woolf's assertion that in the modern novel character is dead. Bellow's world is as densely occupied as Dickens', but its citizens are neither caricatures nor grotesques ... Bellow's city, of course, was Chicago, as vital to him, and as beautifully, teemingly evoked as Joyce's Dublin; the novels are not simply set in the 20th century, they are about that century.[15]

The trajectory traced by McEwan moves from Dickens through Joyce to Bellow. Joyce is thus split off from a 'modernism' identified with Woolf and characterized only by its formal properties and its alleged rejection of 'character' in the novel.

In *Saturday* McEwan opens the day in the life of his hero before daybreak: 'Some hours before dawn Henry Perowne, a neurosurgeon, wakes to find himself already in motion, pushing back the covers from a sitting position, and then rising to his feet. It's not clear to him when exactly he became conscious, nor does it seem relevant.' Opening his bedroom shutters, he looks out at the London landscape, recalling the events of the preceding day, until he sees 'something amazing'. Henry finally understands that he is looking at a burning aeroplane: 'the spectacle has the familiarity of a recurrent dream'.[16] Going downstairs, and watching the television news with his son, he discovers that what he had seen was not part of a terrorist attack but rather 'a simple accident in the making. Not an attack on our whole way of life then.' Both father and son go up to their bedrooms. Henry and his wife make love: 'And so his night ends, and this is where he begins his day, at 6.a.m' (50). Henry falls asleep and wakes again to begin his Saturday, and the novel continues with the events of this new day.

There are echoes in this opening of the 'Ithaca' section of *Ulysses*: father and (surrogate) son conversing in the kitchen; the human encounter overlaying a universe governed by scientific and natural laws; the return to the bedroom, where Henry Perrowne's sexual desire for his wife will be satisfied, though Leopold Bloom's was not. Woolf's 'day in the life of London' novel, *Mrs Dalloway*, also reverberates throughout *Saturday*, whose elements include the watching of the spectacle in the sky; the preparations for an evening party; blockades in the city, on the day of the antiwar protest; the embedding of memories which back the present with the past; the world seen by the sane and the insane, side by side.

McEwan's 'one-day novel', like *Ulysses* or Woolf's *To the Lighthouse* (1927), poses the question of the length of a day, and of whether nighttime is the close of one day or the beginning of the next. For a number of modernist writers, the permeable boundaries between day and night were mapped on to the transitional states between sleeping and waking, in which subjectivity is dispersed and the self has to be remade, every day. *To the Lighthouse* is bound up with the representation of reduced attentiveness and lowered wakefulness and the central section of the novel, 'Time Passes', begins and ends with the processes of going to sleep and awakening – the last word of the section being 'Awake'. In McEwan's writing we find a continuation of this preoccupation with the relationship between narrative and mental processes.

James Joyce and the postcolonial novel

McEwan's suggestion that Bellow enhanced Joyce's legacy while avoiding a restrictive modernism suggests one way in which Joyce has been claimed as a 'postmodernist' writer who transcended the formal limitations of the modernist text. Joyce himself called his movement through different styles in *Ulysses* a 'scorching' method: 'each successive episode, dealing with some province of artistic culture (rhetoric or music or dialectic) leaves behind it a burnt-up field'.[17] The 'scorching' suggests destruction rather than inclusion, though something in the image remains of Stephen Dedalus's 'forging' himself in the white heat of artistic creation. For later twentieth-century writers, Joyce comes to stand for the energies – linguistic, vernacular, metropolitan, sexual – that apparently both literary formalism and the cultural project of Bloomsbury had suppressed or denied. Angela Carter celebrated the legacies of Joyce in her *Expletives Deleted* (1993), writing that *Ulysses*, whose 'magisterial project: that of buggering the English language, the ultimate revenge of the colonialized', had set Carter herself free to 'treat the Word not as if it were holy but in the knowledge that it is always profane'.[18] The coexistence of a multiplicity of styles and languages in Joyce's fiction has also been engaged, in diverse and complex ways, by postcolonial writing up to the present.

The writing of Salman Rushdie is exemplary here. *The Satanic Verses* (1988) engages in a dialogue with *Ulysses* and, in its dreamscape, with *Finnegans Wake*. In the 'aesthetic of the dream', Joyce is recorded as saying, 'the forms prolong themselves and multiply themselves, where the visions pass from the trivial to the apocalyptic, where the brain uses the roots of vocables to make others from them which will be capable of naming its phantasms, its allegories, its allusions'.[19] In *The Satanic Verses* dream visions unfold one upon another, while the 'vocables' of Rushdie's text are, like those of Joyce's writing, exuberant plays with onomotopoeia, portmanteau words and the sounding of language. 'Ellowen Deeowen' represents, for Rushdie's Saladin Chamcha, 'the six letters of his dream-city', 'Proper London itself, Bigben Nelsonscolumn Lordstavern Bloodytower Queen'.[20]

Many of the fantastical elements of Rushdie's novel contain very direct echoes of *Ulysses*, in particular its 'Nighttown' episode. Rushdie's unhappy hero Saladin Chamcha grows 'cuckold's horns', which also represent the 'goatishness' into which he mutates, in the image of the racist's nightmare projections. Like Leopold Bloom, Saladin occupies the world of advertising jingles. Rushdie plays with the way in which, as in Joyce's text, everything has a voice, while at the same time suggesting that Saladin's talent for mimicry – 'He made carpets speak in warehouse advertisements, he did celebrity impersonations, baked beans, frozen peas' – has made him into a colonial 'mimic man' (60). *Ulysses* and *The Satanic Verses* have also opened up, at different ends of the century, the cultural meanings of 'obscenity' and 'blasphemy' respectively. For Homi Bhabha, 'Blasphemy goes beyond the severance of tradition and replaces its claim to a purity of origins with a poetics of relocation and reinscription.'[21] In an interview, 'Bonfire of the Certainties' (broadcast 14 February 1989, the day on which the fatwa against Rushdie was declared by the Iranian religious leader Ayatollah Khomeini), Rushdie spoke of his fascination with the conflict between 'the sacred text and the profane text, between revealed literature and imagined literature'. He also explored the significance of the notion of 'doubt' as a defining aspect of cultural modernism:

> Doubt, it seems to me, is the central condition of a human being in the twentieth century. One of the things that has happened to us in the twentieth century as a human race is to learn how certainty crumbles in your hand. We cannot any longer have a fixed certain view of anything ... Everything we know is pervaded by doubt and not by certainty. And that is the basis of the great artistic movement known as Modernism.[22]

At the opening of part four of *The Satanic Verses*, 'Ayesha', Rushdie writes of his character Gibreel Farishta's 'serial visions' and of the ways in which he has been tranformed by them. 'Who is he? An exile. Which must not be confused with, allowed to run into, all the other words that people throw around: émigré, expatriate, refugee, immigrant, silence, cunning' (205). The terms 'silence', 'cunning' and 'exile', and those 'hollow, booming words, *land, belonging, home*' (4) which reverberate emptily as the plane in which Saladin and Gibreel are travelling splits into two at the novel's opening, create a direct link to Joyce's *A Portrait of the Artist as a Young Man* (1916), and to the imbrications of language, nation and colonial relations in Joyce's work.

In *Portrait* Stephen famously compares his speech to that of the English dean of studies: 'The language in which we are speaking is his before it is mine. How different are the words *home*, *Christ*, *ale*, *master*, on his lips and on mine! I cannot speak or write these words without unrest of spirit. His language, so familiar and so foreign, will always be for me an acquired speech.'[23] Rushdie, writing of the central importance of the English language for the British Indian writer, argues that 'it needs remaking for our own purposes'. There is, however, no possibility of rejecting it: 'we are translated men'.[24]

Relationships between metropolis and colony lie at the heart of much modernist literature and culture. Joseph Conrad's *Heart of Darkness*

(1902) was described by the critic Edward Said as 'a kind of relentlessly open-ended, aggressively critical inquiry into the mechanisms and presuppositions and situatedness and abuses of imperialism', and as a work that 'has obviously compelled many, many other writers to write in its wake'.[25] *Heart of Darkness* revolves around ambiguity, ambivalence and the unsayable. This has been one of the most significant conditions for its various rewritings, and for the fact that it has created a literary and cultural legacy both complex and unresolved.

Said noted that the African novelist Chinua Achebe has been both a severe critic of Conrad's 'racism', and yet profoundly influenced by his novella: 'he can't stop talking about it, and he can't stop writing about it. Some of his early work, like *Things Fall Apart*, is unintelligible without *Heart of Darkness*.' Said points out that Graham Greene's *The Heart of the Matter* (1948), Alejo Carpentier's *The Lost Steps* (1953), Ngugi wa Thiong'o's *A Grain of Wheat* (1967), Tayeb Salih's *Season of Migration to the North* (1970) and V. S. Naipaul's *A Bend in the River* (1979) are 'all rewritings of *Heart of Darkness*, in one way or another' (228, 303). Similarly, as the critic John Marx argues, the Guyanese novelist Wilson Harris, writing of the legacy of *Heart of Darkness*, 'uncovers affiliations between figures as far-flung as the Nigerian Wole Soyinka and the American Jean Toomer ... collating the various versions of this fiction is, in fact, an act tantamount to cataloguing and arranging the field of postcolonial prose as a whole'.[26]

Virginia Woolf's influence on women's writing

Much modernist writing represented a disturbance of fixed sexual identities, as in the Tiresias figure at the heart of T. S. Eliot's *The Waste Land* (1922) and the surreal sexualities represented in *Ulysses* or in Djuna Barnes's *Nightwood* (1936). These texts, and, perhaps most significantly, Woolf's *Orlando* (1928), underlay some of the most interesting feminist writing of the final decades of the twentieth century. While *Orlando*, in its own time, was a popular success, it did not receive the same amount of serious critical attention as many of Woolf's other novels, and it could be argued that it truly found its audience only in this later period. Androgynous sexualities, cross-dressing and transsexualism are strikingly central themes in the work of women writers of the 1980s and 1990s. The twists and turns of gender and other identities in the work of Angela Carter, Patricia Duncker, Jackie Kay and Rose Tremain arose from a context in which the self-evidence of 'speaking as a woman' was no longer a given.

Jeanette Winterson has written at length about Woolf's work, and about the significance of the modernist legacy more broadly. Her *Art Objects*

(1996) is both a manifesto and a sternly pedagogic reader's guide to modernist writing: 'The Waves is not Blackpool beach. There is no use in diving in here and splashing out there'. It is also a defence of 'Art' and of modernist 'difficulty'. Winterson writes:

> [Joyce] is difficult. Woolf is difficult. Eliot is difficult. A poet's method, because it works towards exactness, is exacting on the reader. The nineteenth-century novel, and I include in there 95 per cent of English novels written now, in the late twentieth century, is a loose overflowing slack-sided bag ... To assume that Modernism has no real relevance to the way that we need to be developing fiction now, is to condemn writers and readers to a dingy Victorian twilight. To say that the experimental novel is dead is to say that literature is dead.[27]

Woolf's *Orlando* and Gertrude Stein's *The Autobiography of Alice B. Toklas* (1933) are central for Winterson's discussion in that they are, in her terms, fiction masquerading as memoir, the category in which Winterson would place her own first novel, *Oranges Are Not The Only Fruit* (1985), which was, for the most part, received as relatively unmediated autobiography. 'Like Stein,' Winterson writes, 'I prefer myself as a character in my own fiction, and like Stein and Woolf, what concerns me is language'. Autobiography becomes a matter of 'performance' or 'masquerade': 'It may be that to understand ourselves as fictions, is to understand ourselves as fully as we can' (53, 60).

Angela Carter, unlike Winterson, was ambivalent towards Woolf and her legacy. Hermione Lee, a biographer of Woolf, notes that Carter 'appeared on a Channel Four *J'accuse* programme attacking Virginia Woolf, and made a memorably satirical remark about *Orlando*'s "brown-nosing" of the aristocracy'. Yet Carter's unfinished work included a draft libretto for an opera based on *Orlando*, in which 'Carter leaps at all the possibilities the novel offers of pageantry and farce'.[28]

Reinscribing the modernist novel

Such ambivalence towards the Woolfian text is also to be found, though in a very different fictional context, in Ian McEwan's *Atonement*. Woolf is directly named twice in this novel. Bryony, the novel's central protagonist, and, it transpires, its 'author', writes a novella in a style based on tenets that strongly echo those of Woolf.

> [Bryony] no longer really believed in characters. They were quaint devices that belonged to the nineteenth century. The very concept of character was founded on errors that modern psychology had exposed. Plots too were like rusted machinery whose wheels would no longer turn ... It was thought, perceptions,

sensations that interested her ... If only she could reproduce the clear light of a summer's morning, the sensations of a child standing at a window, the curve and dip of a swallow's flight over a pool of water. The novel of the future would be unlike anything in the past. She had read Virginia Woolf's *The Waves* three times and thought that a great transformation was being worked in human nature itself, and that only fiction, a new kind of fiction, could capture the essence of the change.[29]

Bryony receives a letter from *Horizon* magazine rejecting the novella, entitled 'Two Figures by a Fountain': 'Something unique and unexplained is caught. However, we wondered whether it owed a little too much to the techniques of Mrs Woolf' (296).

In reviews of *Atonement* John Updike wrote that 'a Virginia Woolfian shimmer overlays [its] Austenish plot', while Michiko Kakutani described the language of the novel's first section as 'lambent Woolfian prose'.[30] Barbara Apstein argued that Woolf's influence on McEwan's novel 'extends beyond the shimmer and lambency of poetic descriptions', and found strong echoes of *Mrs Dalloway*. She suggested that the fountain scene in the novel's first section 'alludes to a similar, emotionally charged encounter in *Mrs Dalloway*': 'The heat of the day, the country estate, the flowers, the opening of French windows, all echo the details of Bourton which flood Clarissa Dalloway's memory as she steps out into the London sunshine on a June morning.'[31]

But *Atonement*'s most powerful modernist echo is in fact *To the Lighthouse*. *Atonement* deploys a version of its tripartite structure: a single day in the world of the house in the country, the middle section – time passes and the war – and, finally, the return to the house, when everything that happens is an attempt to complete what was left unfinished. In its central section *Atonement* gives us the experience of war. It transmutes the empty house and the passage of time in *To the Lighthouse* into a profoundly realized and experienced representation of war and its impact upon bodies. One might be tempted to say that this is the male novelist, supplementing, filling in, or giving flesh – albeit of a torn and wounded kind – to the sort of events and experiences at which Woolf would not look directly, in her refusal to make heroes of the protagonists in a war to which she was profoundly opposed.

In *Atonement* McEwan turns back to Woolf, and, in particular, to the ways in which she continued to play out the dissolution and the recreation of character in the novel. McEwan suggests that the creation of narratives adequate to the complexity of human consciousness and subjectivity emerges from a refusal to leap to moral judgement: 'She could write the scene three times over, from three points of view ... She need not judge. There did not have to be a moral' (40). Bryony's 'atonement' for her childhood 'crime' – the false identification of her sister's lover as a rapist – takes the form of her writing her novel over and over again. The final version of the novel takes 'a stand against oblivion and despair':

> All the preceding drafts were pitiless. But now I can no longer think what purpose would be served if, say, I tried to persuade my readers, by direct or indirect means, that Robbie Turner died of septicaemia at Bray Dunes on 1 June 1940, or that Cecilia was killed in September of the same year by the bomb that destroyed Balham Underground station . . . The problem these fifty-nine years has been this: how can a novelist achieve atonement when, with her absolute power of deciding outcomes, she is also God (370–1).

A number of critics and writers have argued that we are seeing the emergence of an 'ethical turn' in contemporary literature, and there have been some very interesting turns by contemporary novelists to modernist texts – in particular those of James, Forster, Lawrence and Woolf – as spaces in and through which questions of art, life and value can be reposed and reconfigured. Zadie Smith prepared the way for her novel *On Beauty* (2005), which is deeply interwoven with Forster's *Howards End* (1910), with literary essays in which she explored the significance of Forster for her own writing and for an understanding of ethics and the novel more broadly: 'It is Forster who shows us how hard it is to will oneself into a meaningful relationship with the world; it is Forster who lends his empathy to those who fail to do.' The question of 'character', at the heart of Forster's own literary manifesto *Aspects of the Novel* (1927), is central here. 'It seems', Smith concludes, 'that if you put people on paper and move them through time, you cannot help but talk about ethics.'[32]

Smith's *On Beauty* pays not just 'a debt' to Forster but also, in her words, '*hommage*'. This term encompasses Smith's close reworkings of the structure and plot elements of *Howards End*. The first line of *On Beauty* – 'One may as well begin with Jerome's e-mails to his father' – echoes that of Forster's novel: 'One may as well begin with Helen's letters to her sister.'[33] One question opened up here is whether the emphasis is to be placed on the repetition or the difference. Smith does not appear, for example, to be 'rewriting' Forster. Nonetheless – and the touch is a light one – Smith does endow her version of Forster's Leonard Bast with a culture which *is* a culture and not merely composed of what Frank Kermode has called 'pathetic aspirations'.

For Kermode, the resemblance between *Howards End* and *On Beauty* 'goes beyond the plot allusions everyone talks about. What lies behind both is an idea of the novel as what Lawrence called the one bright book of life – a source of truth and otherworldiness and prophecy.'[34] Yet the 'plot allusions' are not merely an obvious surface concealing the profounder elements of something like a moral influence: they raise central but complex issues of reinscription and of the ways in which contemporary fiction is negotiating literary legacies. The relationship is neither that of 'parody' nor that of 'pastiche', but one in which the author sets up a dialogue with a literary predecessor, and in so doing explores questions of proximity and distance, as matters of style, voice, history, authorship and biographical identity.

Fictionalizing the modernist author

Michael Cunningham's *The Hours* (2002) is both a rewriting of Woolf's *Mrs Dalloway* and an incorporation of 'biography' into the genre of the novel. There is a strong affinity between *The Hours* and many other texts in which authors stage encounters between historical and fictional characters. Yet the structure of Cunningham's novel, with its interwoven but separate stories, does not require him to place his historical characters in the same frame as his fictional ones. His 'Virginia Woolf' may indeed be as much of a construction as his Clarissa Vaughan or his Laura Brown. As Tory Young notes, the opening of *The Hours* is 'an amalgamation of poetic license and documentary evidence', and even this category of 'evidence' raises within the novel the issue of citation as a fictionalizing reinscription.[35]

Colm Tóibín's *The Master* (2004) explores four years in James's life, between 1895 and 1899. The novel, which appears to aspire to inhabit James's consciousness, collapses the distance between narrator and subject and then recreates or reinstates distancing through the representations of perspective, watching and witnessing, from threshold and liminal spaces, from doorways and windows. The troping and tropism of 'the window' is a turn that animates *The Master* (playing on James's assertion that 'the house of fiction has many windows'), and is linked to the image of the witness as the watcher at the window, to be found in other contemporary novels, including *Atonement*, *Saturday* and Kazuo Ishiguro's *The Remains of the Day* (1989) and *Never Let Me Go* (1995). As in Woolf's fiction, and in particular *Mrs Dalloway* and *To the Lighthouse*, the window, or the windowpane, also suggests transparency and opacity, connection and separation, clarity and distortion, and the relationship between past or present, or the ways in which the present becomes the past.

Tóibín goes beyond any of James's biographers in his representations of James's homosexual desire, and it is here that the image of looking up at, and down from, windows and of being watched from windows is at its most concentrated. 'He realized now', Tóibín writes of his 'Henry', 'that this was something he had described in his books over and over, figures seen from a window or a doorway, a small gesture standing for a much larger relationship, something hidden suddenly revealed.'[36] We find here, and throughout the novel as a whole, a repetition of some of the central tenets of the modernist 'new biography' of the early twentieth century: the gesture that stands in for the whole, the concept of a key to the self, the notion of human life as made up of motifs, as in Tóibín's representations of the women who ask James for comfort and from whom he turns away to his writing. In *The Master*, however, these are given a new self-consciousness, as things that the subject knows about himself. As in *The Hours*, and indeed *Atonement*, we have to ask who is writing whom, and who is living out whose story.

David Lodge's novel about James, *Author, Author*, appeared in 2004, shortly after the publication of *The Master*, and James is also a central figure in Michael Wood's collection of critical essays *Literature and the Taste of Knowledge* (2005), in which Wood explores what it might mean to pose the question: 'What does this work of literature know?'[37] Following Wood, we could reframe the issue of literary legacy as one of literature's knowledge, and ask to what ends such knowledge is transmitted from one text to another and across the decades. Contemporary fiction's return to modernist novels, whether through reinscription, or the fictional-biographical depictions of their authors, suggests that the interplay of modernist knowledge and obliquity continues to play a powerful role in shaping the fiction of the present.

Notes

1. Jorge Luis Borges, *Labyrinths: Selected Stories and Other Writings* (Harmondsworth: Penguin, 2000), p. 236.
2. B. S. Johnson, 'Introduction', in Johnson, *Aren't You Rather Young to be Writing Your Memoirs?* (London: Hutchinson, 1973), p. 30. Reprinted in Malcolm Bradbury (ed.), *The Novel Today: Contemporary Writers on Modern Fiction* (Manchester: Manchester University Press, 1977), pp. 151–68 (p. 167). Further references cited parenthetically.
3. Samuel Beckett, *The Unnamable*, in *The Beckett Trilogy* (London: Picador, 1976), p. 277.
4. B. S. Johnson, *Albert Angelo*, in *B. S. Johnson Omnibus* (London: Picador, 2004), p. 167.
5. Paul Auster, *The Art of Hunger* (London: Faber and Faber, 1983), p. 324. Further references cited parenthetically.
6. Franz Kafka, *Complete Short Stories of Franz Kafka*, ed. Nahum N. Glatzer (London: Allen Lane, 1983), p. 270.
7. Alan Hollinghurst, *The Line of Beauty* (London: Picador, 2004), p. 111.
8. See Fredric Jameson for parody and pastiche in relation to modernist and postmodernist cultures. Jameson, *Postmodernism, or, the Cultural Logic of Late Capitalism* (London: Verso, 1991), p. 17.

96

LAURA MARCUS

something he had described in his books over and over, figures seen from a window or a doorway, a small gesture standing for a much larger relationship, something hidden suddenly revealed.'[36] We find here, and throughout the novel as a whole, a repetition of some of the central tenets of the modernist 'new biography' of the early twentieth century: the gesture that stands in for the whole, the concept of a key to the self, the notion of human life as made up of motifs, as in Tóibín's representations of the women who ask James for comfort and from whom he turns away to his writing. In *The Master*, however, these are given a new self-consciousness, as things that the subject knows about himself. As in *The Hours*, and indeed *Atonement*, we have to ask who is writing whom, and who is living out whose story.

David Lodge's novel about James, *Author, Author*, appeared in 2004, shortly after the publication of *The Master*, and James is also a central figure in Michael Wood's collection of critical essays *Literature and the Taste of Knowledge* (2005), in which Wood explores what it might mean to pose the question: 'What does this work of literature know?'[37] Following Wood, we could reframe the issue of literary legacy as one of literature's knowledge, and ask to what ends such knowledge is transmitted from one text to another and across the decades. Contemporary fiction's return to modernist novels, whether through reinscription, or the fictional-biographical depictions of their authors, suggests that the interplay of modernist knowledge and obliquity continues to play a powerful role in shaping the fiction of the present.

Notes

9. Steven Connor, 'Postmodernism and Literature', in Connor (ed.), *The Cambridge Companion to Postmodernism* (Cambridge: Cambridge University Press, 2004), p. 68.
10. Virginia Woolf, 'Modern Fiction', in Woolf, *The Crowded Dance of Modern Life*, ed. Rachel Bowlby (Harmondsworth: Penguin, 1993), pp. 5–12 (p. 8).
11. Christopher Isherwood, *A Single Man* (London: Methuen, 1964), pp. 7, 157.
12. Doris Lessing, *The Golden Notebook* (London: Michael Joseph, 1962), p. 283. Further references cited parenthetically.
13. Saul Bellow, *Seize the Day* (Harmondsworth: Penguin, 1996), p. 66.
14. Don DeLillo, *Cosmopolis* (London: Picador, 2003), p. 79. Further references cited parenthetically.
15. Ian McEwan, *Guardian*, 7 November 2005, G2, p. 2.
16. Ian McEwan, *Saturday* (London: Jonathan Cape, 2005), p. 15. Further references cited parenthetically.
17. James Joyce, *Letters of James Joyce*, 3 vols., ed. Stuart Gilbert and Richard Ellmann (New York: Viking, 1957–66), vol. I, p. 129.
18. Angela Carter, *Expletives Deleted: Selected Writings* (London: Vintage, 1993) pp. 208, 210.
19. Joyce to Edmond Jaloux, quoted in Richard Ellmann, *James Joyce* (Oxford: Oxford University Press, 1959), p. 559.
20. Salman Rushdie, *The Satanic Verses* (Harmondsworth: Penguin, 1988), pp. 37–8. Further references cited parenthetically.
21. Homi K. Bhabha, *The Location of Culture* (London: Routledge, 1994), p. 225.
22. Cited in David Smale (ed.), *Salman Rushdie* (Basingstoke: Palgrave Macmillan, 2001), p. 31.
23. James Joyce, *A Portrait of an Artist as a Young Man* (Harmondsworth: Penguin, 1960), p. 189.
24. Salman Rushdie, *Imaginary Homelands* (London: Granta, 1992), p. 17.
25. 'An Interview with Edward W. Said', in Carola M. Kaplan *et al.* (eds.), *Conrad in the Twenty-First Century: Contemporary Approaches and Perspectives* (New York: Routledge, 2005), pp. 288–9. Further references cited parenthetically.
26. John Marx, 'Postcolonial Literature and the Western Canon', in Neil Lazarus (ed.), *The Cambridge Companion to Postcolonial Literary Studies* (Cambridge: Cambridge University Press, 2004), p. 90.
27. Jeanette Winterson, *Art Objects: Essays on Ecstasy and Effrontery* (London: Vintage, 1996), pp. 82, 176.
28. Hermione Lee, ' "A Room of One's Own, or a Bloody Chamber?": Angela Carter and Political Correctness', in Lorna Sage (ed.), *Flesh and the Mirror: Essays on the Art of Angela Carter* (London: Virago, 1994), pp. 308–20 (pp. 317–18).
29. Ian McEwan, *Atonement* (London: Jonathan Cape, 2001), p. 282. Further references cited parenthetically.
30. John Updike, 'Books: Flesh on Flesh', *New Yorker*, 4 March 2002, pp. 80–2, and Michiko Kakutani, 'Books of the Times: And When She Was Bad She Was . . .', *New York Times*, 7 March 2002.
31. Barbara Apstein, 'Ian McEwan's *Atonement* and "The Techniques of Mrs. Woolf" ', *Virginia Woolf Miscellany* 64 (Fall–Winter 2003), pp. 11–12.

32. Zadie Smith, 'Love, Actually', *Guardian Review*, 1 November 2003, http://
books.guardian.co.uk/print/0,3858,4786273-110738,00.html.
33. Zadie Smith, *On Beauty: A Novel* (London: Hamish Hamilton, 2005), p. 3.
34. Frank Kermode, 'Here She Is', *London Review of Books* 27:19, 6 October 2005,
p. 13.
35. Tory Young, *Michael Cunningham's 'The Hours': A Reader's Guide* (London:
Continuum, 2003), p. 50.
36. Colm Tóibín, *The Master* (London: Picador, 2004), p. 34.
37. Michael Wood, *Literature and the Taste of Knowledge* (Cambridge: Cambridge
University Press, 2005).

6

KATHERINE MULLIN

James Joyce and the languages of modernism

James Joyce's (1882–1941) reputation can be daunting for the first-time reader. The term 'Joycean' is readily adopted to suggest impenetrability, bewildering experimentalism, obscurity and inaccessibility. Although *Ulysses* (1922) regularly makes it into the top four of '100 Books of the Century' polls, it is famously a book more talked about than read. Its predecessor, *A Portrait of the Artist as a Young Man* (1916), is often seen to offer a route into *Ulysses*'s formal experimentations. But *Finnegans Wake* (1939), with its lack of a discernible plot and its invented language saturated with multilingual puns, far exceeds *Ulysses*'s resistance to navigation. Any baffled reader who turns to literary criticism for help might well be further disconcerted. Joyce once boasted, 'I've put in so many enigmas and puzzles that it will keep the professors busy for centuries arguing over what I meant, and that's the only way of insuring one's immortality.'[1] His prophecy has come true in the ever increasing critical studies of Joyce which crowd library shelves, offering fresh perspectives on a writer discussed almost as frequently as Shakespeare. Yet Joyce's perceived difficulty, and the range of analyses responding to that difficulty, need not be so daunting. For 'difficulty' is a product of the richness of his fictions, a richness of form, of content, of wit and of pleasure which makes Joyce and the 'Joycean' command such influence over both his contemporaries and the many writers in his wake.

Joyce is commonly perceived to stand at the centre of his aesthetic moment, the 'father of high modernism', the protégé, friend and inspirer of T. S. Eliot, Ezra Pound and other modernists, whose long shadow hangs over later writers.[2] However, Joyce's centrality should not distract us from the many ways in which he spoke from the periphery of the literary culture he would come to dominate. Born in Dublin in 1882, the eldest child in a rapidly increasing and increasingly impoverished Catholic family, the young Joyce self-consciously wrestled with questions of poverty, class, faith and nation. In the opening episode of *Ulysses*, Stephen Dedalus tells the English cultural tourist Haines 'I am a servant of two masters', going on to identify these as '[t]he imperial British state ... and the holy Roman catholic and apostolic church'.[3] Dublin, the predominantly Catholic second city of the British Empire, was, to Joyce, 'the centre of paralysis', largely populated by the 'gratefully oppressed' who too often demonstrated their servility to London or to Rome.[4] His collection of short stories, *Dubliners* (1914), offered 'a chapter in the moral history of my country', for, as Joyce protested, 'It is not my fault that the odour of ashpits and old weeds and offal hangs round my stories.'[5] These are stories of frustrations great and small, of illusions lost, of deep loneliness, of fractured marriages, of lives of 'commonplace sacrifices closing in final craziness'. They are peopled with a cast of destitute conmen, failed artists, timid spinsters, bullied shopgirls, misanthropic celibates and belligerent, lonely drunks. These are stories of desperate lives lived on the margins; the lives Joyce knew.

Joyce's position as a writer from the margins was confirmed when, in 1904, he left Dublin for Europe, eloping with Nora Barnacle, a Galway chambermaid. He and Nora would spend the rest of their lives on the continent, living in Pola, Trieste, Zurich and Paris, often moving house within those cities several times a year. Yet while Joyce had self-consciously chosen this nomadic exile from his homeland, his imaginative exile would never be accomplished. Letters home to family and friends requested local newspapers and gossip; Ireland's fraught literary and political heritages became the subject of Joyce's lectures in Trieste; most importantly, the Dublin of his youth became the unvarying location of his fiction. In *Portrait* Stephen Dedalus's artistic sensibilities are so indelibly mapped on to the landscape of his city 'that as he passed the sloblands of Fairview he would think of the cloistral silver-veined prose of Newman'.[6] *Ulysses* is set on one day, 16 June 1904, in commemoration of Joyce's first date with Nora, and the cityscape of that year is so accurately inscribed within that novel that Joyce later boasted that the city, were it ever demolished, might be reconstructed from his account. *Finnegans Wake* turns the Dublin landscape itself into characters; the novel's central protagonist, Humphrey Chimpden Earwicker, is allegorically connected to Dublin and its surroundings, 'Howth Castle and Environs', while his wife, Anna Livia Plurabelle, is on one level a personification of the River Liffey flowing through the city. Throughout his fictions Joyce was a writer simultaneously in exile and at home. When, in later life, Joyce was asked if he would ever return to Ireland, he replied, 'Have I ever left?'[7]

Joyce's sense of his own marginality was further compounded by the difficulties of circulating his work. He struggled to publish both *Dubliners* and *Portrait*, since publishers and printers were wary of passages of sexual explicitness, fearing prosecution. *Ulysses* was embroiled in a famous obscenity trial, and banned in 1921 in the USA and the United Kingdom. Doubly notorious for its obscurity and its obscenity, the novel was eventually rescued by the Parisian modernist publishing house Shakespeare and Company, and only furtively distributed in the USA and elsewhere as pirated pornography. Yet, perversely, these experiences of exile and dispossession fuelled Joyce's creativity. His peripheral position arguably creates the richness of his stylistic experimentations. In an oft-cited passage from *Portrait*, Stephen Dedalus, who is a college student at Dublin's recently established Catholic university, disputes the meaning of an unfamiliar word with his Dean of Studies, an English-born 'countryman of Ben Jonson':

> The language in which we are speaking is his before it is mine. How different are the words *home*, *Christ*, *ale*, *master*, on his lips and on mine! I cannot speak or write these words without unrest of spirit. His language, so familiar and so foreign, will always be for me an acquired speech. I have not made or accepted its words. My voice holds them at bay. My soul frets in the shadow of his language. (189)

Stephen's linguistic unease was shared by his creator. Unable and unwilling to write in Irish, a language systematically eroded a generation earlier, Joyce rose to the challenge of expressing himself in a 'borrowed' tongue. His allusive, experimental prose responds by refashioning English into a form transcending the boundaries of national identity. As if in revenge, Joyce created a hybrid language of his own at once 'so familiar and so foreign'. This was a project he was to extend into the curious Esperanto of *Finnegans Wake*, composed from silted layers of puns in sixty-three different tongues. Not only is this novel's language barely recognizable as English, its obscurity might be read as an ironic retaliation to censorship.

If we turn to the opening passage of Joyce's first novel, we can clearly see how these themes of national and cultural marginality conspire to create a radically new 'portrait of the artist'. It begins: 'Once upon a time and a very good time it was there was a moocow coming down along the road and this moocow that was coming down along the road met a nicens little boy named baby tuckoo' (1). Immediately, Joyce locates his novel somewhere between the familiar and the strange. 'Once upon a time' is the standard beginning of folk stories, yet this is no fairy tale. Instead we occupy the consciousness of a very young child – the artist of the title – who longs to insert himself into the narrative his father tells:

> He was baby tuckoo. The moocow came down the road where
> Betty Byrne lived: she sold lemon platt.
> *O, the wild rose blossoms*
> *On the little green place.*

He sang that song. That was his song.
O, the green wothe botheth. (1)

'Baby tuckoo' is Stephen Dedalus, and even in infancy his imagination is engaged in the artistic processes of narrative transformation. The 'wild rose' from the popular song 'Lilly Dale' is refashioned through Stephen's lisping into a 'green wothe'; a simple mistake, perhaps, but a mistake brimming with ideological undercurrents. Green is Ireland's national colour. Can we read into Stephen's error a hint of his later determination to transform an English into an Irish rose and thereby 'forge in the smithy of my soul the uncreated conscience of my race' (253)? A green rose also suggests the green carnations worn by Irish dramatist Oscar Wilde as emblems of artificiality, and thereby associated with Wilde's criminalized homosexuality. Is Joyce covertly reminding us of another Irish artist whose meteoric career ended in censorship and disgrace? A further hint that censorship and artistic practice might be inevitably entangled is implicit in the corrupt version of the song Stephen knows. The lines from 'Lilly Dale' should read 'O, the wild rose blossoms / O'er the little green grave'; the substitution of 'place' for 'grave' bleaches the grief out from the song, bowdlerizing an elegy into a nursery rhyme. These buried meanings offer just one example of the political dynamism of Joyce's art. This passage implicitly rejects the apolitical aestheticism of Wilde and his fellow *fin-de-siècle* writers, who insisted on 'art for art's sake'. Instead here and elsewhere, Joyce's aesthetic is also ideologically laden, as his art acknowledges its roots in historical and political realities.

This opening passage of *Portrait* does more, however, than simply offer an instance of the multilayered, ideologically resonant nature of Joyce's writing style. It also exemplifies one of Joyce's most significant formal innovations. For *Portrait* announces from its first page Joyce's radical break with the conventions of the nineteenth-century realist novel. There is no omniscient narrator here, who directs the reader's response. Instead the narrative focuses on a particular consciousness, and is articulated through the kind of language that such a consciousness would use. If we compare the passage with the opening lines of Charles Dickens's *Great Expectations* (1861), another novel concerning a young man's coming of age, the difference is striking. *Great Expectations* begins: 'My father's family name being Pirrip, and my Christian name Philip, my infant tongue could make of both names nothing longer or more explicit than Pip.'[8] The sentence immediately announces that this is not the voice of a child; the grammatical complexity of the opening clause, the use of the distinctively adult words 'infant tongue' and 'explicit', tell us that this narrator is an older man looking back at his childhood, not a child telling his own story. In contrast, Joyce's use of simple words, baby-talk and childish diction erases this overseeing, distancing narrative presence from the text, leaving us in intimate relation to Stephen's consciousness alone.

Joyce was not the first writer to move from omniscient narration to a narrative style shaped by the interior life of his character. Novelists as diverse as Henry James, George Meredith, Joseph Conrad and Marcel Proust had already experimented with free indirect discourse and interior monologue to express the psychologically complex inner lives of their narrators. Yet Joyce pushed these experiments further in order to create a pointed separation between author and text, in an attempt to emancipate his fiction from an overbearing and inauthentic authorial presence. Later in *Portrait*, the young Stephen hypothesizes that 'the artist, like the God of creation, remains within or behind or beyond or above his handiwork, invisible, refined out of existence, indifferent, paring his fingernails' (215). This Joycean technique of secession from the text is often described as 'stream-of-consciousness' writing, yet it is more accurately labelled 'coloured narrative' – narrative infected by the idiom of the character and thereby achieving a curious independence from its author. Hugh Kenner has named this feature of Joyce's prose 'The Uncle Charles principle'[9] after Stephen's elderly uncle, encountered at the start of chapter two of *Portrait*:

> Uncle Charles smoked such black twist that at last his nephew suggested to him to enjoy his morning smoke in a little outhouse at the end of the garden.
> – Very good, Simon. All serene, Simon, said the old man tranquilly. Anywhere you like. The outhouse will do me nicely: it will be more salubrious.
> – Damn me, said Mr Dedalus frankly, if I know how you can smoke such villainous awful tobacco. It's like gunpowder, by God.
> – It's very nice, Simon, replied the old man. Very cool and mollifying.
> Every morning, therefore, Uncle Charles repaired to his outhouse but not before he had creased and brushed scrupulously his back hair and brushed and put on his tall hat. (60)

What is at stake here is Joyce's curious use of the word 'repaired'. The rather affected term provoked Wyndham Lewis to criticize Joyce's slipshod style. Yet, on closer inspection, the word is no slip; its faux gentility is closely akin to Uncle Charles's reported use of the words 'salubrious' and 'mollifying'. It is surrounded by invisible quotation marks, since it is the kind of word Uncle Charles himself might choose.

Joyce's extension of the established modernist literary technique of free indirect discourse is crucial to *Portrait*'s ironic mode. While Joyce avoids the explicit narrative commentary associated with classic realist fiction, the quasi-autobiographical nature of his novel invites us to puzzle over the nature of the author's relationship to his creation. At one level, Stephen is a portrait of Joyce as a young man; any glance at a biography of Joyce's early years will show how closely the two share their family background, education and youthful religious, political and sexual experiences. Yet Joyce's authorial retreat from the text destabilizes any reading of the novel as straight autobiography, since Joyce is scrupulous in allowing ironic distance to problematize his depiction of Stephen. The novel's episodic rhythms underscore this irony. Divided into five chapters, each episode apparently ends with an epiphany – a moment of sexual, religious or artistic revelation which could be seen to deepen and enrich Stephen's character. Yet each concluding epiphany is abruptly followed by a moment of bathos: Stephen's confrontation with the rector at Clongowes at the close of Part One leads on to the foul smell of Uncle Charles's tobacco at the start of chapter two; sexual bliss in a prostitute's arms gives way to pedestrian dreams of stew for dinner; his epiphanic vision of the bird-girl bathing at the end of chapter four is undercut by the breakfast squalor of 'watery tea' and rifled pawn tickets at the beginning of the final chapter. The absence of explicit authorial commentary leaves these juxtapositions open to dispute, but they arguably unsettle Stephen's artistic aspirations. Even the diary structure of the novel's close queries Stephen's ambitions to leave Dublin to 'forge in the smithy of my soul the uncreated conscience of my race', since a diary is a necessarily inconclusive literary form, always awaiting the next day's entry (253). *Portrait* is thus a radically unstable text, since Joyce deliberately avoids giving his readers an unequivocal picture of his chief protagonist.

If in *Portrait* Joyce insisted upon his own authorial absence from the text, and flirted with the ambiguities thereby released, *Ulysses* evades fixed meanings with far greater emphasis. To work out what *Ulysses* 'means' is, Joyce took care to ensure, an impossible and, more importantly, an irrelevant task. For resistance to a finite reading is one of the novel's many points, a point its author wilfully made by encoding within the text minor puzzles which can never be resolved. (Who is the stranger in the mackintosh at Paddy Dignam's funeral? What does U.P. on the anonymous postcard maliciously sent to Denis Breen mean?) Early readers of Joyce strove to master the novel by tracing the parallels between *Ulysses* and Homer's *Odyssey*. Bloom, like Odysseus a father bereft of a son, seeks his Telemachus in Stephen, a son without a satisfactory father; meanwhile, at home Bloom's wife Molly, like Penelope, is besieged by suitors while awaiting her husband's return. Indeed, Joyce invited such parallels by informally naming his chapters, or episodes, after Homer's, so that it is now an established convention to label the first chapter 'Telemachus' and so on, through to the final chapter, 'Penelope', yet he also insisted on the unreliability of this crutch by deliberately erasing these Homeric chapter titles from the final draft. If all this is confusing, then first-time readers may be consoled by the thought that it is confusing by design. Joyce challenges our ability to make sense of his novel by putting in place one frame of meaning – the Homeric parallels – and then inviting us to query why this form of knowledge should necessarily be privileged over any other. For, as a glance at Dan Gifford's compendious *Ulysses Annotated* (1988) quickly reveals, knowledge of Homer is as about as useful as knowledge of Irish history, of popular fiction, of the detailed geography of 1904 Dublin, of rebel ballads and music hall songs, of contemporary social crusades and theological wranglings, of Dublin brothel etiquette, of early Edwardian fashions, of early cinema, of popular theatre, of Dublin slang.[10] The point is that one might attempt to read *Ulysses* armed with these knowledges, most plausibly in the shape of a good annotated edition or a reliable guide; one can also read *Ulysses* straight through, relishing its rich pleasures while acknowledging that it is impossible to catch every nuance.

What, then, is *Ulysses* about? In the simplest of terms, its plot traces one day – 16 June 1904 – in the lives of two men, the penniless, frustrated artist Stephen Dedalus, still in Dublin despite his earlier aspirations to leave for the continent, and the middle-aged Jewish advertising canvasser, Leopold Bloom. Both awake at around eight in the morning, Stephen in a Martello Tower rented by his friend Buck Mulligan on Dublin's south coast, Bloom in his matrimonial home at 7 Eccles Street in north Dublin. Both, once breakfasted, leave home to travel around Dublin, at business and at leisure. Stephen's morning is spent teaching; Bloom's attending the funeral of his friend Paddy Dignam, then arranging for the placing of a newspaper advertisement on behalf of a client, Alexander Keyes. Their paths cross in the newspaper offices of *The Freeman's Journal*, in the National Library, and in the Rotunda Maternity Hospital, but they finally meet in the small hours of the next day while drinking in the parlour of Bella Cohen's brothel in Dublin's 'Monto' red-light area. Bloom rescues Stephen from the attentions of the police and takes him home to Eccles Street for the night, attempting to sober him up with hot drinks and discussions of religion, social problems, politics and art. As the two finally drift off to sleep, the final chapter of *Ulysses* inhabits the mind of Bloom's wife Molly, who, woken by the late arrival of her husband, drowsily reminisces about the affair with Blazes Boylan she had begun that afternoon, about her youth in Gilbraltar, and about her marriage to Bloom, among other things. This briefest sketch of *Ulysses*'s plot is, of course, an extreme over-simplification, since Joyce's novel far exceeds the conventions of formal plot structure. The first three chapters, for example, trace Stephen's day from eight until noon, while the fourth chapter, 'Calypso', abruptly leaps back four hours to begin the day of the novel's other central protagonist with the strikingly unheralded observation that 'Mr Leopold Bloom ate with relish the inner organs of beasts and fowls' (4: 1–2). *Ulysses* thus starts afresh, with a new character and a new consciousness; readers might as plausibly begin the novel at 'Calypso' as at its beginning.

Despite this volatility, however, character and consciousness offer as good a path into *Ulysses* as any, particularly since one of the most immediate and obvious pleasures that *Ulysses* has to offer is uniquely generous access to its central protagonists. Joyce, notoriously, allows his readers to glimpse aspects of his characters' lives that previous novelists would have flinched from documenting, and one of the novel's most infamous scenes occurs at the close of 'Calypso'. Bloom, feeling 'a gentle loosening of his bowels', visits the outside toilet, silently accompanied by the narrator: 'Quietly he read, restraining himself, the first column and, yielding but resisting, began the second. Midway, his last resistance yielding, he allowed his bowels to ease themselves quietly as he read, reading still patiently that slight constipation of yesterday quite gone. Hope it's not too big bring on piles again. No, just right' (4: 506–10).

For the first time in the history of fiction, we are invited to witness our hero 'at stool' (4: 465), as we will later join him in the bath, or observe his wife Molly seated astride her chamber pot, vexed at the unexpected onset of menstruation. Joyce's meticulous surveillance of these bodily functions still has the power to disconcert, yet this frankness is only one instance of the many ways in which Joyce makes it possible to know Leopold Bloom better than any previous character in fiction. Such intimacies are balanced in a narrative style which moves fluidly between the more conventional omniscient third-person narration, and Bloom's unmistakable interior monologue. Here, we see Bloom attending to the needs of his cat:

> – Mrkrgnao! the cat said loudly.
>
> She blinked up out of her avid shameclosing eyes, mewing plaintively and long, showing him her milkwhite teeth. He watched the dark eyeslits narrowing with greed till her eyes were green stones. Then he went to the dresser, took the jug Hanlon's milkman had just filled for him, poured warmbubbled milk on a saucer and set it slowly on the floor.
>
> – Gurrhr! she cried, running to lap.
>
> He watched the bristles shining wirily in the weak light as she tipped three times and licked lightly. Wonder is it true if you clip them they can't mouse after. Why? They shine in the dark, perhaps, the tips. Or kind of feelers in the dark, perhaps. (4: 32–42)

Aspects of this passage are clearly written in the third person: the metaphoric richness of the second paragraph, animated by the resonant phrases 'avid shameclosing eyes', 'her eyes were green stones', 'warmbubbled milk'; the careful observation 'she tipped three times and licked lightly'. Indeed, Joyce's descriptive virtuosity is most clearly evident in his meticulous transposition of the cat's cries, in contrast to Bloom's more conventional interpretation:

> The cat mewed to him.
> – Miaow! he said in answer. (4: 461–2)

Yet, as Bloom's 'Miaow' implies, these almost self-consciously poetic elements of 'Calypso's' narrative are interrupted by Bloom's own idiom. As Joyce moves beyond 'Miaow' to something more accurate in describing a cat's voice, so, too, he strives for greater accuracy in depicting his central protagonist by capturing the tone of Bloom's inner thoughts. With 'Wonder is it true if you clip them they can't mouse after', Joyce takes us inside Bloom's mind, as the narrative becomes coloured by the telegraphic texture of Bloom's idiosyncratic thoughts.

Character, then, is one very compelling way of orientating ourselves within *Ulysses*, since the novel creates a peculiarly intense bond between those who read and those who inhabit its pages. Yet the attractions of character are nonetheless gradually diffused. The first six chapters of the novel can, more or less, be understood as, firstly, the thoughts inside Stephen's mind, and, from 'Calypso' onwards, the thoughts inside Bloom's. But with the seventh, 'Aeolus', the reader who has grown familiar with, even fond of Stephen and Bloom, is abruptly knocked off course. Set inside the newspaper offices of *The Freeman's Journal*, 'Aeolus' introduces not only a host of new characters – the editor Myles Crawford and his contributors – but also a radically new style, a parody of contemporary journalese, punctuated with stark headlines summarizing the action: 'IN THE HEART OF THE HIBERNIAN METROPOLIS' (7: 1), 'WE SEE THE CANVASSER AT WORK' (7: 120), 'LIFE ON THE RAW' (7: 938), 'INTERVIEW WITH THE EDITOR' (7: 970). 'Aeolus' sets the tone for later chapters, in which Joyce moves beyond the aspiration voiced by Stephen in *Portrait* that 'the artist, like the God of creation, remains within or behind or beyond or above his handiwork, invisible, refined out of existence, indifferent, paring his fingernails'. Whereas until this point Joyce's abstraction from his creations chiefly takes the form of experimentation with interior monologue and coloured narrative, from 'Aeolus' and beyond, any consistency of style – even a style which 'belongs' far more to Stephen or Bloom than it does to Joyce – is entirely renounced. Instead of sustaining the kind of stable narrative voice we can glimpse surrounding Bloom's thoughts in 'Calypso', Joyce borrows from the styles of others to weave a complex, allusive fabric from pastiche.

Borrowed styles supply both the delights and the difficulties of much of the rest of *Ulysses*. Among the more accessible are the chapters devoted to women; the 'lovely seaside girl' Gerty MacDowell in the thirteenth 'Nausicaa' episode, with whom Bloom enjoys an attenuated, voyeuristic sexual adventure, and Molly Bloom in 'Penelope'. Molly's interior monologue is, perhaps, closest in style to the first six chapters, since it offers unmediated access to her inner thoughts through a continuous stream of unpunctuated reminiscences: 'not that I care two straws now who he does it with or knew before that way though Id like to find out so long as I dont have the two of them under my nose all the time like that slut that Mary we had in Ontario terrace padding out her false bottom to excite him' (18: 53–6). 'Nausicaa' elaborates on the Uncle Charles principle by narrating Gerty in the language she would herself deploy, a language derived from the romantic fiction, advertising discourse and women's magazines she voraciously consumes:

> Her figure was slight and graceful, inclining even to fragility but those iron jelloids she had been taking of late had done her a world of good much better than the Widow Welch's female pills and she was much better of those discharges she used to get and that tired feeling. The waxen pallor of her face was almost spiritual in its ivorylike purity though her rosebud mouth was a genuine Cupid's bow, Greekly perfect. (13: 83–9)

Other chapters, however, offer still more challenging experiments with the relationship between form and content. The eleventh, 'Sirens', set in the bar of the Ormond Street hotel where Bloom dines as Simon Dedalus and friends sing popular airs, follows the intricate musical patterns of a fugue; it begins with an initially baffling 'overture' section of key words and phrases ('Bronze by gold heard the hoofirons, steelyringing Imperthnthn thnthnthn' – 11: 1), later explicated through musical techniques of recapitulation and variation. Chapter fourteen, 'Oxen of the Sun', narrates a meeting between Bloom and Stephen at the Rotunda maternity hospital, where the elder man has come to enquire after Mina Purefoy, a friend suffering a long and perilous labour, and the younger to drink with medical student friends in an anteroom. There, characters boozily discuss the ethics of contraception, pregnancy and abortion while the themes of the chapter are echoed in its protean form. For the chapter can be loosely divided into nine sections (in allusion to the nine months of pregnancy), tracing the gestation of the English literary canon through pastiches of major literary styles, so that Bloom is variously named as 'Some man that wayfaring was ... Of Israel's folk' (14: 71–2), 'the traveller Leopold' (14: 126), 'childe Leopold' (14: 160) and 'Sir Leopold' (14: 169–70). 'Circe', the fifteenth chapter, set in Dublin's red-light district or 'Nighttown', expresses Bloom's subliminal fears, or fantasies, of exposure through its form, since it is presented as a drama or, more plausibly, a film script,[11] while 'Eumaeus', the sixteenth, takes the Uncle Charles principle to its logical extreme by adopting the kind of style that Bloom himself might use, were he to fulfil his dreams of authorship.

Ulysses's mercurial shifts in literary styles, particularly in its second half, push the novel form to new extremes. Indeed, the book challenges attempts to define it as fiction at all. Not only might some chapters – 'Circe' in particular – more plausibly be categorized within other genres, but chapters might well also be read discretely, relatively independent of the larger text in which they stand. As *Dubliners* is a collection of short stories tending towards a novel in its structure and unity of theme, so, with curious symmetry, *Ulysses* invites deconstruction into its constitutive chapters. In *Finnegans Wake*, Joyce's final project, the limits of the novel form are pushed further still, but we cannot say we are not warned. '[L]ook at this prepronominal *funferal*, engraved and retouched and edgewiped and puddenpadded, very like a whale's egg farced with pemmican, as were it sentenced to be nuzzled over a full trillion times for ever and a night till his noddle sink or swim by that ideal reader suffering from an ideal insomnia', the novel admonishes, though whether the admonition is directed towards reader or creator is tricky to discern.[12] This tangled fragment of a sentence gives some flavour of the *Wake*'s ceaselessly inventive, amusing and infuriating style, which delights in polyglottal punning and portmanteau words, thereby transforming language from a mode of communication into an arena of endless play. It is also, in fact, one of the easier sentences to interpret. 'Prepronominal' flirts with 'preposterous' before moving on to '*funferal*', a term simultaneously recalling the funeral wake suggested in the title and suggesting a festival of celebration. This promise of fun for all might seem far-fetched, but Joyce, in acknowledging the difficulty by imagining an 'ideal reader' suffering from an 'ideal insomnia', invites us to take the book less seriously. Joyce's definition of his 'ideal reader' might be playfully ambitious, yet playful ambition more obviously applies to *Finnegans Wake* as a whole. Explaining the novel to a friend, he wrote, 'One great part of every human existence is passed in a state which cannot be rendered sensible by the use of wideawake language, cutanddry grammar and goahead plot', and, as Colin MacCabe observes, 'Joyce attempted to write a book which took all history and knowledge for its form, and all workings of the dreaming mind for its subject.'[13] The novel's resistance to conventional reading practices is one response to the impossibility of its subject.

It is, then, useless to ask what *Finnegans Wake* is about. 'His writing is not *about* something; *it is that something itself*' insisted Joyce's disciple Samuel

Beckett, and its subject is inseparable from its style, for its style is its subject.[14] As Margot Norris notes, '*Finnegans Wake* might be said to be "about" not being certain what it is about; its subject is the nature of indeterminacy itself.'[15] Indeed, the novel abounds with self-reflexive observations on its jumbled, borrowed, multiply allusive, radically interderminate form: for instance, fascinated with narrative as a process of borrowing, recycling and even plagiarism, *Finnegans Wake* proclaims itself to be '[t]he last word in stolentelling!' (424, line 35). Nonetheless, traces of character and even plot can be discerned under the novel's 'middenheap' of extravagant linguistic play. The novel is often interpreted as a dream, perhaps taking place in the unconscious mind of a dreamer, named through the initials HCE, which variously stand for Humphrey Chimpden Earwicker, Howth Castle and Environs, Haveth Childers Everywhere, and multiple further permutations. The dreamer is the father of a family; with his wife, Anna Livia Plurabelle (ALP), a sometime personification of Dublin's River Liffey, he has three children, warring twin brothers Shem and Shaun, and a dangerously desirable daughter Issy. Other characters include two old servants, four wise old men, twelve pub customers and a tame hen called Biddy. The 'plot' of *Finnegans Wake* is always cast in shadows, but much of it circles around HCE's obscure, probably sexual crime, committed in the park with two girls and observed by a mysterious onlooker. Other mysteries adumbrate the text; a letter, perhaps written by Shem and entrusted to Shaun, and possibly containing a devastating family secret, has been lost in a middenheap – will it be discovered? What is the mysterious family secret – does it name HCE's incestuous desires for his daughter Issy? One of the central paradoxes of *Finnegans Wake* is how, while the text throws out references to the world's religions, histories, languages, cultures and philosophies, it also continually refers its readers back to that most familiar and intimate of locations, the family.

Finnegans Wake's compendious excess, its flouting of expectations about plot, language and even grammar, its punning layers of riddles, its vastness of allusions, its anarchic humour and its tremendous generosity together make a conventional reading experience impossible, which is perhaps one reason why the book responds so well to both audio recording and group readings. Faced with its notorious opening, 'riverrun, past Eve and Adam's, from swerve of shore to bend of bay, brings us by a commodius vicus of recirculation back to Howth Castle and Environs' (3: line 1–3), we are, in multiple senses, at sea. Yet *Finnegans Wake*, Joyce's final novel published barely two years before his death, is, in many senses, an entirely appropriate conclusion to Joyce's experiments with the novel form. In its persistent self-referentiality, in its encyclopeadic scope and in its style so emphasizing the increasing disassociation of author from text, *Finnegans Wake* elaborates and extends preoccupations already evident in his preceding fictions. With *A Portrait of the Artist as a Young Man*, *Ulysses* and *Finnegans Wake*, Joyce incrementally altered the landscape of the modernist, and, indeed, the modern novel. His impact and his influence is such that the term 'Joycean' has now become critical shorthand for the exciting, the experimental and the new.

Notes

1. Richard Ellmann, *James Joyce*, rev. edn (New York: Oxford University Press, 1982), p. 521.
2. See Ronald Bush, *The Genesis of Pound's Early Cantos* (Princeton: Princeton University Press, 1976), and Stanley Sulton, *Eliot, Joyce and Company* (New York: Oxford University Press, 1988).
3. James Joyce, *Ulysses*, ed. Hans Walter Gabler (London: The Bodley Head, 1986), chapter 1, lines 638, 643–4. Further references cited parenthetically by chapter and line number.
4. James Joyce, *Letters of James Joyce*, 3 vols., ed. Stuart Gilbert and Richard Ellmann (New York: Viking, 1957–66), vol. II p. 134, and James Joyce, *Dubliners*, ed. Terence Brown (London: Penguin, 1992), p. 35. Further references to *Dubliners* cited parenthetically.
5. James Joyce, *Letters*, vol. II, p. 134, and Joyce, *Letters*, vol. I, p. 63.
6. James Joyce, *A Portrait of the Artist as a Young Man* (London: Penguin, 1973), p. 175. Further references cited parenthetically.
7. Ellmann, *James Joyce*, p. 292.
8. Charles Dickens, *Great Expectations*, ed. Margaret Cardwell (Oxford: Oxford University Press, 1998), p. 1.
9. Hugh Kenner, *Joyce's Voices* (London: Faber and Faber, 1978), pp. 16–17.
10. Don Gifford, with Robert J. Seidman, *'Ulysses' Annotated: Notes for James Joyce's 'Ulysses'* (Berkeley: University of California Press, 1988).
11. See Austin Briggs, '"Roll Away the Reel World, the Reel World": "Circe" and Cinema', in Morris Beja and Shari Benstock (eds.), *Coping with Joyce: Essays from the Copenhagen Symposium* (Columbus: Ohio State University Press, 1989), pp. 149–56.
12. James Joyce, *Finnegans Wake* (London: Faber, 1939), p. 120, lines 9–14. Page and line numbers are the same in all editions and further references will be cited parenthetically in the text accordingly.
13. Joyce, *Letters*, vol. II, p. 146, and Colin MacCabe, 'An Introduction to *Finnegans Wake*', in John Harty (ed.), *A Finnegans Wake Casebook* (New York: Garland, 1991), p. 22.
14. Samuel Beckett, *Our Exagmination Round His Factification for Incamination of Work In Progress* (London: Faber and Faber, 1979), p. 14.
15. Margot Norris, '*Finnegans Wake*', in Derek Attridge (ed.), *The Cambridge Companion to James Joyce* (Cambridge: Cambridge University Press, 2004), p. 150.

7

MEG JENSEN

Tradition and revelation: moments of being in Virginia Woolf's major novels

Virginia Woolf (1882–1941) was determined to produce not only something beautiful in her art but also something all her own. She was, as her numerous diaries and essays demonstrate, intrigued by notions of time, space and consciousness. The impact of such influences upon the creation of identity is a central theme in her work and the representation of these complicated ideas in fiction was her greatest challenge. Woolf wrote in 1921, 'If a writer were a free man and not a slave, if he could write what he chose, not what he must ... there would be no plot, no comedy, no tragedy, no love interest.' The traditional plot-led structure of 'the novel' was a source of frustration for her as she believed that it did not reflect what it felt like to be alive. 'Life', she wrote, 'is not a series of gig lamps symmetrically arranged; life is a luminous halo.' Woolf's nine novels represent her negotiation of, and response to, that persistent frustration as she worked towards forging a new form of writing, one that would reflect the 'halo', the 'uncircumscribed spirit' of life.[1] Her resultant experiments with narrative structure enabled her to explore new ways of representing time, space and consciousness in her works.

In 'A Sketch of the Past' (1941), Woolf suggested that most people spend their lives wrapped in a kind of 'cotton wool' that limits their perceptions, protecting them from strong sensations. 'From this,' she states, 'I reach what I might call a philosophy; ... that behind the cotton wool is hidden a pattern.'[2] For Woolf, this 'pattern' is a paradigm of connection, of universal meaning and purpose normally unseen or unnoticed in everyday life. The images Woolf uses in her novels to represent this paradigm differ, and evoke both benign and malign forces within it. But whether illustrated as waves, flames, clocks ticking or feet stamping, the pattern is always repetitive, rhythmic and wordless. By contrast, the 'cotton wool' that obscures that pattern is composed of words that embody allusions to literature and voices of the past. Her works highlight the interplay between these differing discourses through what she termed 'moments of being', moments in which the 'cotton wool' is lifted, and repetitive, wordless rhythms are revealed. Some of

Woolf's characters find comfort in these moments, as voices from the past are silenced and in their place a wordless connection to the universe is glimpsed. Other characters, however, refuse to let go of the safety of words, and are frightened by and unable to interpret the rhythmic discourse beneath the 'cotton wool'. As Woolf's novels examine the relations between the past, the present and hidden patterns, they employ experimental narrative techniques and complex symbolism, and in doing so have changed readers' perceptions of the novel form for ever. Which is just as Woolf intended.

The Voyage Out

The variety of forms that Woolf's novels take is evidence of her fascination with the way the experience of life is represented in, or even revealed by fiction. Her first novel, *The Voyage Out* (1915), follows a young English woman, Rachel Vinrace, through her passage 'out' towards adulthood, as she crosses the ocean, leaves her father's care, falls in love and dies tragically of a fever. The novel begins with Rachel's aunt and uncle, Helen and Ridley Ambrose, travelling across London to join Rachel on her father's ship the *Euphrosyne*. Helen stops along the Embankment and cries: she has left her children behind. The narrator remarks that, when standing by 'the river near Waterloo bridge', '[i]t is always worthwhile to look down and see what is happening. But this lady looked neither up nor down.' Helen, it seems, can see only 'a great welling tear' before her when suddenly 'there struck upon her ears:

> *Lars Porsena of Clusium*
> *By the nine Gods he swore –*

And then more faintly . . .

> *That the Great House of Tarquin*
> *Should suffer wrong no more*[3]

In this opening Woolf hints that Helen's sorrow distances her from the external world – she literally cannot see beyond her own thoughts. But as Helen overhears these lines from Macaulay's Horatius (verses well-known to more than one generation of British schoolboys) the words interrupt her, reminding her of duty in the midst of her tears: 'Yes, she knew she must go back to all that, but at present, she must weep' (3).

The words that Helen overhears in this scene represent any number of concerns that may be considered 'Woolfian'. Macaulay's verses are a Victorian reimagining of a heroic imperial past, handed down to the privileged male heirs of Britain's own empire, through an education system unavailable to working-class men or to women of Woolf's time. As such, these verses and similar lines that appear in Woolf's novels from, among others, Shakespeare, Milton and Pope can be read as patriarchal, authoritarian and oppressive interruptions of characters' private thoughts – of their 'moments of being'. Such words from the past work like 'cotton wool' obscuring her characters' view, preventing the revelation of hidden truths and patterns. As Terence Hewitt suggests to Rachel later in the text, '[W]e want to know what's behind things don't we?' (266), and when the sound of Macaulay's 'stanza instantly stop[s]', Helen is able to do just that: 'this was the skeleton beneath', she thinks (3–4).

A similar reading of oppressive interruption may help to identify the origin of the fever that later kills Rachel. Her illness begins soon after her fiancé, Terence, 'was reading Milton aloud, because he said the words of Milton had substance and shape' (347), and Rachel's 'chief occupation' during the first day of her illness was 'to try to remember how the lines went' (350). As Jane Marcus has argued, Woolf saw the figure of Milton as a 'ferocious male patriarch'.[4] Indeed, in A Room of One's Own (1929) it is the narrator's attempt to seek out 'the manuscript of one of Milton's poems' that leads her to be barred from the 'Oxbridge' library.[5] If The Voyage Out is informed by this sense of Milton as destructive, then Rachel's death could be connected with her exposure to the contagion of Milton's poem, which itself inscribes patriarchal images: 'Sabrina' 'the virgin pure'; 'the daughter of Locrine' (347). Milton's words, passed on to Rachel through the lips of her fiancé, cause her collapse, drowning out the wordless rhythms of her piano and the 'steady beat of her own pulse … beating, struggling, fretting' (315). In The Voyage Out the words of the literary past are figured as dangerous external interruptions to the characters' internal 'moments of being', of seeing 'what's behind things'.

Jacob's Room

Jacob's Room (1922) is frequently referred to as Woolf's first experimental novel. This new work would be, in part, a response to the death of Woolf's brother Thoby Stephen in 1906, and as she began upon it Woolf outlined her new ideas: 'I figure that the approach will be entirely different this time; no scaffolding; scarcely a brick to be seen.'[6] As Hermoine Lee has noted, 'The form of Jacob's Room is the subject: an alternative to the false reality of the biography of fact … a biography of fragments', and this fragmented form mirrors the novel's attempt to draw together the pieces of a life unexpectedly torn apart.[7]

Jacob's Room begins, like *The Voyage Out*, with a mother, near the water, unable to see through her tears. While Helen Ambrose was portrayed as missing her children, in *Jacob's Room* Betty Flanders's tears articulate a different kind of loss. Sitting on a beach in Cornwall, half-ignoring her sons, Jacob and Archer, playing near by, the widow Betty weeps as she pens a letter. Betty's tears are, like Helen's, also interrupted, but rather than the words of Macaulay, Betty overhears Archer's cry: "'Ja-cob! Ja-cob!" ... The voice had an extraordinary sadness. Pure from all body, pure from all passion.'[8] Just as Helen's tears foretell Rachel's death, so, too, does this scene predict the text's conclusion: the novel will end as it begins, with an unanswered cry, with a vain search for Jacob.

If *The Voyage Out* suggested a divide between the oppressive external influence of the past and hidden rhythms, in *Jacob's Room* these opposing forces collide. While Betty's tears cause her view of the lighthouse and the bay to 'wobble', Archer's cry makes her newly aware of the external world. Here Betty's private grief is elided with and projected on to the larger canvas of world history; the 'extraordinary sadness' of Archer's cry laments not only the loss of Jacob in this moment on the beach, but the 'extraordinary' tragedy of all the young men who will, like Jacob, later come to rest in Flanders fields.

In *Jacob's Room* Woolf's 'moments of being' are more than private revelations of a hidden pattern: they function to imply and explore a universal link between internal and external, public and private experiences and identities. Later in the novel, Jacob, now a nineteen-year-old at Cambridge University, is standing looking out of his window when his thoughts are interrupted. At first, he can see little beyond the window, 'there was nothing at all, except the enclosing buildings', but then he discovers an altogether different view: 'the bared hills of Turkey – sharp lines, dry earth ... the women, standing naked-legged in the stream to beat linen on the stones' (43). Jacob's glimpse of this wordless pattern is, like that of Helen and Rachel before him, obscured:

> But none of that could show clearly through the swaddlings and blanketings of the Cambridge night ... The stroke of the clock even was muffled; ... as if generations of learned men ... issued it, already smooth and time-worn, with their blessing, for the use of the living. Was it to receive this gift from the past that the young man came to the window ... It was Jacob. (43)

Like Rachel, who memorizes Milton, Jacob will be made to pay for his acceptance of this gift from the past, for the 'Cambridge night' obscuring the view of the bared hills. And what of the women pictured in Jacob's reverie – what is it that they can see, 'standing naked-legged' and beating their 'linen on the stones'? If their presence in this scene seems a foreshadowing of Jacob's death, the end of the novel finds them prophetesses of horror on a much larger scale. There, Betty Flanders awakes, hearing a strange noise 'far away, she heard the dull sound, as if nocturnal women were beating great carpets ... Seabrook dead; her sons fighting for their country ... The nocturnal women were beating great carpets' (175). These women, repetitively beating, reflect not only the loss of Jacob, but also death itself, British military history and the passage of time – all without the use of words. By invoking Macaulay, Milton and Jacob's 'learned men', Woolf reminds us that certain words and voices are privileged and immortalized in her culture. But Woolf's texts also suggest that women may employ a different language to pass down knowledge: a wordless system of rhythm and repetition.

Mrs Dalloway

Woolf's fourth novel, *Mrs Dalloway* (1925), suggests that negotiating hidden patterns and the influences of the past is mostly a matter of interpretation, of reading. This novel also begins with a solitary woman's reverie – that of Clarissa Dalloway, the fifty-something wife of a Conservative MP, living in a fine house in Westminster. The tale unfolds over the course of one day in which Clarissa prepares for a party she will give in the evening. As she sets out in the morning, the sound of squeaking hinges sends her back to a summer long ago when she 'burst open the French windows and plunged at Bourton into the open air. How fresh, how calm ... and yet (for a girl of eighteen as she then was) solemn, feeling as she did, standing there at the open window, that something awful was about to happen.'[9] As Clarissa is thrown back in time, Woolf highlights the power that the past, in sounds and words, has over her central character, while Clarissa's sense of 'something awful' hints at the novel's tragic climax. That terrible ending will not in any simple sense be hers, however – Clarissa lives. Her 'solemn' feeling, then, seems to point instead to the tragedy of another character: the suicide of Septimus Smith.

Woolf used the term 'double' to describe the relation between the characters of Clarissa and Septimus[10] and noted that the novel would study 'the sane and insane side by side'.[11] As Harold Bloom has argued, this structure is the novel's 'peculiar virtue' in that Clarissa and Septimus 'share what might seem a single consciousness, intense and vulnerable, each fearing to be consumed by a fire perpetually about to break forth'.[12] Throughout the text both characters are haunted by a verse from Shakespeare's *Cymbeline*, 'Fear no more the heat o' the sun', and both see images of flames in moments of sudden revelation.[13] If Woolf's earlier novels implied that words from the past obscure hidden patterns, Woolf's doubling of Clarissa and Septimus suggests something very different: here, it is not the words, but the way those words are *read*, that matters.

Early on in the novel, a 'violent explosion' on Bond Street makes Clarissa jump – the sound of a motor car, carrying 'a face of the greatest importance', back-firing (16). Septimus also hears this explosion, and as he looks upon the car sees 'this gradual drawing together of everything to one centre ... as if some horror had come almost to the surface and was about to burst into flames' (18). As the car moves on, Clarissa imagines a calling card engraved with 'the name' of the important person, and wonders if this powerful name had 'by force of its own lustre, burnt its way through' the crowd. The image of the engraved card then reminds Clarissa that she, 'too, gave a party' (20).

In the next moment Clarissa's experience of the explosion connects her to a world in 'which, at this very moment ... strangers looked at each other and thought of the dead; of the flag; of Empire' (21). Septimus, however, finds no such comforting connection – for him, the 'gradual drawing together of everything' breeds 'horror' (18). Clarissa also sees flames, but to her they are purifying, burning their 'way through' (20). For Septimus, the flames reveal potential destruction, 'almost coming to the surface', 'about to burst into flames', and their different interpretations of this scene foretell their respective fates. Both characters are, as Bloom notes, 'intense and vulnerable', but while Septimus is horrified by the patterns revealed to him, Clarissa's ability to read in this moment evidence of her connections and her place in society ('the flag', the 'Empire', she, 'too, gave a party') ensures her safety and survival. While this scene draws a distinction between the two characters' readings of hidden patterns, elsewhere Woolf explores how each character interprets words from the literary past, in the guise of the verse from *Cymbeline*. As Clarissa sits sewing in the afternoon, she thinks: 'So on a summer's day waves collect, overbalance, and fall; collect and fall; ... until even the heart in the body ... says too, That is all. Fear no more, says the heart ... And the body alone listens ... the waves breaking; the dogs barking, far away barking and barking' (44–5). Here, we find not only the appearance of a system of sound and repetition, but also a subtle rewriting of the verse from *Cymbeline*. 'Fear no more the heat o' the sun' becomes 'Fear no more, says the heart.'

Later, Septimus's suicide elicits a further rewriting of the verse, as in the midst of his growing madness he thinks, 'Every power poured its treasures on his head ... while far away on the shore he heard dogs barking and barking far away. Fear no more, says the heart in the body; fear no more' (154). In these two passages both Clarissa and Septimus hear similar words, but read them differently. For Clarissa, the phrase 'Fear no more' offers comfort, a connection to the collective. Clarissa, moreover, appears to make a distinction between the heart, which offers its burdens to the sea, and the body, listening to the waves. In Septimus's hearing the heart and the body are not separated – for him, the heart is 'in the body', which is perhaps why he must throw them out of the window together. And while his vision offers him powers and treasures (like Jacob's 'gifts from the past') it does not allow him to unburden his fears to the collecting sea of sorrows, as Clarissa does.

The final appearance of this verse occurs in the midst of Clarissa's party, soon after she hears of Septimus's suicide. Before withdrawing from the room, Clarissa envisions a purifying fire: 'Always ... when she was told, first, suddenly, of an accident; her dress flamed, her body burnt'(202). Once alone, Clarissa 'pulled the blind ... The clock began striking ... and the words came to her Fear no more the heat of the sun. She must go back to them ... She felt glad he had done it; thrown it away. The clock was striking ... But she must go back. She must assemble' (204–5). Here, Clarissa confronts the two major landscapes of Woolf's novels in the lingering words and the relentless ticking of the clock. While in this passage Clarissa's 'gladness' at Septimus's suicide is troubling, it makes sense when seen as further evidence of her ability to read loss, death and flames as purification, and to hear in the words from *Cymbeline* a connection, a call to assembly, a duty to 'go back'.

Clarissa, that is, is able to convince herself that she is linked to the past even while her easy acceptance of Septimus's death paints her readings as suspect. This sense of connection ensures her survival, which can be seen in stark contrast not only to Septimus's fate, but also to the victims in the earlier novels. While Helen Ambrose withstands the interruption of Macaulay's verses and continues her weeping, Rachel memorizes the words of Milton and ends by being consumed by fever. Likewise, Jacob's acceptance of 'gifts from the past' ends with the 'fitful explosions' that kill him (*Jacob's Room*, 175). Thus in these early novels, the characters that survive are those who refuse to be overwhelmed by the power of the past or subsumed by hidden patterns.

To the Lighthouse

In each of Woolf's novels, structure and theme are closely linked. The relatively traditional form of *The Voyage Out*, for example, uses an omniscient third-person narrator to communicate the *Bildungsroman* of Rachel Vinrace's journey towards adulthood. Nevertheless, the oppressive role of the words of Macaulay and Milton in the novel, as they interrupt Helen's tears and invade Rachel's fevered dreams, complicates the relation between the novel's traditional narrative structure and the tale it tells. In Woolf's work references to traditional storytelling techniques or well-known literature are always a source of narrative tension. The fragmented form of *Jacob's Room*, part fictionalized biography, part elegy, similarly mimics the story it tells: through narrative gaps and leaps in time, the tale evokes both private loss and public mourning by conflating Jacob's death with the death of a generation, and Betty's tears with those of mothers throughout Europe. *Mrs Dalloway* takes place over the course of a single day, with flashbacks and visions expanding and/or contracting each character's sense of the speed with which that day passes. While the novel unfolds in finite time, in the present, 'life; London; this moment' (6), the form nevertheless hints that time itself is a matter of interpretation.

The structure of *To the Lighthouse* (1927), Woolf's fifth novel, is bound in an equally complex manner to her concerns and interests, and is composed of layer upon layer of narrative and linguistic 'scaffolding'. Arranged in three major sections, 'The Window', 'Time Passes' and 'The Lighthouse', the text is further subdivided into numbered passages of varying length, echoing perhaps the three-volume, chapter-driven novels so beloved of the Victorians. Nevertheless, the language of the text problematizes any attempt to read it in a traditional, linear manner. Through repetition of phrases and images (the words 'sudden' and 'interruption'; the figure of the lighthouse), Woolf demands that the reader look backwards as well as forwards when turning the pages of this work, her most personal story: a portrait of her family.[14]

To The Lighthouse, then, has two differing, even competing narrative strategies – a traditional framework of progression, demonstrated in the tight arrangement of sections and chapters, and an equally tight formulation of repetition, of return, that alludes to a desire to remained unfinished, unresolved. These two strategies are themselves linked through structure on the one hand, and image on the other, to the characters of Mr and Mrs Ramsay, respectively. If Woolf's earlier texts chronicle moments that reveal hidden patterns to her characters, the structure of *To the Lighthouse* makes such patterns explicit, and illustrates that there is more than one version of the past or one 'universal' pattern.

Mr Ramsay at first appears to embody a traditional narrative progression, through his constant physical movement and his shouting aloud verses from Tennyson's well-known poem 'The Charge of the Light Brigade'. As the novel continues, however, his attempts at moving forward are frustrated, and his link to the past is shown to be one of repetition rather than movement, as he returns to recite the same verses time and time again. Mr. Ramsay is 'for ever walking up and down, up and down', compelled to repeat even as he tries to progress, and his thoughts, too, adhere to this pattern. His 'splendid mind had no sort of difficulty in running over those letters, one by one ... until it had reached, say, the letter Q. He reached Q ... But after Q? What comes next?'[15] Later, in the moving passage that reveals the death of his wife, Mr Ramsay is again shown in aimless, frustrated, motion: '[Mr Ramsay, stumbling along a passage one dark morning, stretched his arms out, but Mrs Ramsay having died rather suddenly the night before, his arms, though stretched out, remained empty.]'[16] The final image of him in the novel confirms this association, as at long last he takes his children on the promised trip to the lighthouse. 'He rose and stood in the bow of the boat, very straight and tall ... as if he were leaping into space ... he sprang, lightly, like a young man' (318).

Similarly, Mrs Ramsay is at some points in the text aligned with repetition, with return, like the beam of the lighthouse at which she finds herself 'sitting and looking, sitting and looking with her work in her hands until she became the thing she looked at' (100–1). Earlier in the novel, though, she has sensed an interruption to that rhythm, as frustrating as the stasis that Mr Ramsay fights against. As she listens, 'the monotonous fall of waves on the beach which for the most part beat a measured and soothing tattoo to her thoughts ... seemed consolingly to repeat over and over "I am guarding you, I am your support" but at other times ... had no such kindly meaning, but like a ghostly roll of drums remorselessly beat the measure of life' (29–30).

Throughout the text Woolf both parallels and elides these two narrative designs and their respective versions of experience: Mrs Ramsay's rhythmic repetition, in which all is connected and therefore eternal, and Mr Ramsay's forward movement, which beats out the measure of finite time. The negotiation of this division is, more importantly, made manifest not only in the structure of Woolf's text, but also in the image of Lily Briscoe's painting – a portrait of Mrs Ramsay sitting in the window with James. It had been left behind incomplete in the years following the deaths of Mrs Ramsay, Prue and Andrew, but at the end of the novel, Lily returns to it. Looking at the window where Mrs Ramsay once posed, Lily is sure that she sees her once again – casting 'her shadow on the step. There she sat' (310). Lily then thinks of Mr Ramsay's journey to the lighthouse. 'He has landed', she said aloud. 'It is finished.' Then, turning to her canvas, and 'with a sudden intensity', Lily sees 'it all clear for a second'. And what does she see? The eventual success of Mr Ramsay's forward motion ('He has landed')? Or the ghostly but continued presence of the late Mrs Ramsay? Perhaps, in Lily's sudden moment of clarity, she has seen both, for taking up her brush, 'she drew a line there, in the centre. It was done; it was finished. Yes, she thought ... I have had my vision'(319). This 'line' in the centre of Lily's painting may thus imply the irreconcilable divide between two forms of experience, one progressive and one repetitive, or it could suggest something less divisive: here, Woolf's Lily has composed a single work of art, able to incorporate, to reveal, two parts of a single vision – one aligned with the mother, one with the father, and both entirely the artist's own.

The Waves

Like Archer's cry in *Jacob's Room*, the voices of the six characters of *The Waves* (1931), Susan, Jinny, Rhoda, Bernard, Neville and Louis, rise and fall in a manner seemingly detached from external reality. In this novel each of these characters offers a series of monologues that surface and ebb away over the course of their lives like the waves of the title. It is a complex structure, and one that leaves many readers baffled – so trained are we, like Mr Ramsay, to look for progression. But the vision of this text owes little to Mr Ramsay or the literature of the past.

Indeed, the patterns at work in *The Waves* are more convincingly aligned with the 'monotonous fall of waves' heard by Mrs Ramsay (*Lighthouse*, 29). Woolf considered the purpose of this strategy as she began the novel. 'I am not trying to tell a story,' she wrote. 'A mind thinking . . . life itself . . . I can tell stories. But that's not it. Also I shall do away with exact place and time.'[17] These reflections are themselves given voice in the novel, as the character of Bernard, a writer, proclaims, 'How tired I am of stories!'[18] Bernard is unsure of his own identity – he is, he thinks '[a] man without a self . . . a dead man' – and wonders 'how to describe the world seen without a self? There are no words' (314). A similar question is raised in the novel's prelude, which presents an image of the sun rising over the sea. It begins, 'The sun was indistinguishable from the sky except that the sea was slightly creased as if a cloth had wrinkles in it' (5). The voice of this passage, and the others that appear periodically as counterpoints to the characters' monologues, offer impersonal imagery – sun, sea, waves, the rhythms of nature over the course of a single day. But, troublingly, this voice articulates singular, subjective readings of those seemingly impersonal tropes: the sun 'was indistinguishable' but to whom? The sea here is 'creased as if a cloth', but in whose view? The agent of seeing, of poeticizing is never named. Who is it that sees a 'woollen sky'? This is a question that problematizes a novel given over to the revelation of identity through voice. For the unnamed 'self' that interprets this sunrise will continue, like the interruptions that startle Mrs Ramsay, to 'beat out the measure of time' in Woolf's text. In this opening Woolf presents a dilemma that her novel will debate if not resolve: if the passage of time and the need to connect to some universal pattern are the powers that shape identity, who is in charge of those powers? Who is it that speaks of the waves breaking on the shore?

The six named characters in the novel first appear as children, recounting sensory perceptions: "'I see a ring" said Bernard, "hanging above me. It quivers and hangs in a hoop of light." "I see a slab of pale yellow," said Susan, "spreading away until it meets a purple stripe" ... "I hear something stamping," said Louis. "A great beast's foot is chained. It stamps and stamps, and stamps"' (7). This last image is repeated in various ways throughout the text, and appears to function like the march of time – a beat that attempts to override the repetitive pattern of the characters' voices. As this stamping appears alongside the recurrence of the word 'now' – 'Now you trail away' (16); 'Now the wind lifts the blind' (17); 'Now the time has come' (31); 'Now to sum up' (260) – it seems to signal the irreconcilable desires of the text: to stay still and to progress, to tell a story without coming to an end. As Bernard claims at the end of the novel, '[H]ow tired I am of phrases that come down beautifully with all their feet on the ground ... I begin to long for ... broken words, inarticulate words like the shuffling of feet on the pavement' (261). Bernard's complaint makes explicit Woolf's own frustrations as a writer attempting to explore the tension between movement and stasis, unrealistic wholeness and fragmentary reality in her novels. For Bernard, like Woolf, factual storytelling is of little use in representing life – 'it is a mistake', he says, 'this extreme precision, this orderly and military progress; a convenience, a lie. There is always deep below it ... a rushing stream of ... street cries, half-finished sentences' (279).

If the interludes of sea, sun and waves that mark the passing of time in the text raise the question of identity – of the agent of seeing and interpretation – this dilemma is then spun out through the development, troubled though it is, of the separate identities of its six central characters. Louis's intelligence and conservatism, Rhoda's visions and anxieties, Susan's connection to the natural world, Jinny's sensuality and artifice, Neville's solipsism are all sketched through their monologues. The most fully realized of the characters, Bernard, searches for identity and meaning throughout, but is foiled in his attempt, ironically, through his reliance on storytelling. *The Waves* culminates in Bernard's retelling of the events of the novel. In his solitary voice, however, we hear the echoes of the other characters as he uses Neville's term 'globe' repeatedly to describe life (260, 274, 280), and invokes Rhoda's phrase 'my spine is like soft wax' (37) when he argues that '[t]he wax ... that coats the spine melted in different patches for each of us' (264). Although Bernard tells of the trauma of their individuation, 'We suffered terribly as we became separate bodies' (264), one wonders if this is an illusion, as he asks, 'Who am I? ... am I all of them? Am I one and distinct? I do not know' (316).

The notion of the world seen without a self, and the elucidation of what comprises identity are thus bound up in *The Waves* with the equally troublesome evocation of duelling patterns of power and influence. As Bernard charges to his death at the end of the text, confronting the inevitable conclusion of life told as a story, he is also aware of another kind of narrative calling to him: 'some sort of renewal ... another general awakening' (324). Hesitant in his language here, Bernard nevertheless recounts his glimpse of this perpetual, collective rhythm. But, being a writer, a storyteller, he interprets this rising of the waves, this 'incessant rise and fall and fall and rise again' as an enemy, pulling him back as he struggles to go forward, to complete his narrative. Unable to defy the drive towards resolution, Bernard 'flings' himself against this enemy and rides forward towards the end of the novel and his own death, as the unnamed speaker reminds us that the *'waves broke on the shore'* (325).

Between the Acts

If in *The Waves* Woolf explores the relations among hidden patterns, the influence of the past and the shaping of individual identity, her last novel engages with these concerns alongside the notion of collective identity. *Between the Acts* was written between 1938 and 1940, and published after Woolf's suicide in 1941. She conceived of the work as 'a centre: all literature discussed ... but "I" rejected: "We" substituted ... we all life, all art, all waifs and strays – a rambling capricious but somehow unified whole – the present state of my mind? And English country ... facts and notes.'[19]

In this 'centre' the figure of the English country house between the wars is placed. Pointz Hall belongs not to 'the old families' of the village but to relative newcomers the Olivers, and then for 'only something over a hundred and twenty years'.[20] And it is at this house over the course of the day that the novel unfolds, suggesting as it does so not only the long record of England's literary and military history, but also the manner in which such history is handed down to the 'present state of [...] mind'. This novel, like *The Waves*, is concerned with storytelling and it moves throughout among Isa's recitations of her poetry, the rhymes of the village idiot and the snippets of literature provided by the actors in Miss La Trobe's pageant.

The pageant itself offers 'Scenes from English History' (99) told with makeshift costumes, wobbling scenery, laughable props and a gramophone in poor repair. Miss La Trobe's production, it seems, echoes the feeble grip her audience has upon its own sense of history. Like the Olivers, who hang purchased portraits of unrelated grand ladies and gentleman in their hallways, the audience plays at a sense of connection to England's past. Thus the pageant allows Woolf not only to make use of her central tropes, but also to employ those tropes in the task of social critique. '*Dispersed we are*'

(115–16), repeats the broken gramophone, and the lacklustre rendition of 'God Save the King' at the end of the production cannot remedy the audience's sense of such dispersion. For in perhaps the most explicit moment of being and revelation, of the convergence of the past and hidden patterns portrayed in any of Woolf's novels, Miss La Trobe concludes her pageant with a singular stage-trick: '"Look! Out they come" cries the audience. "Holding what? Tin cans? Bedroom candlesticks? ... What's the notion? Anything that's bright enough to reflect, presumably, ourselves? Ourselves! Ourselves!"' (214). In order to suggest that the audience, too, is part of English social and literary history, Miss La Trobe has concluded her production by turning mirrors upon them. But the effect is not what she or the audience would wish: 'the audience saw themselves, not whole by any means, but at any rate sitting still' (216). At this point, rather than being able to see themselves as part of a continuum, whole and progressive, the fractured mirrors show the 'we' of the novel, the audience, in fragments, sitting still. The wartime England of which Woolf wrote was, in this critique, playing at its sense of history, unable or at least unwilling to confront itself: '"Ourselves?", they cry, "But that's too cruel!"' (214).

This, then, is Woolf's final figure in her project of reflecting 'life itself'. For all the power of the past and the pull of the beat of time, the irreconcilable desires for progress and for repetition, Woolf suggests, 'we all', artist and audience, find ourselves stuck in the present and 'sitting still'. In Woolf's novels literary tradition and the words of the past function as oppressive influences, limiting her characters' view of a hidden pattern of connection and belonging. What those texts obscure, however, Woolf, like Miss La Trobe, attempted to uncover: moments of being in which Woolf's words are themselves the mirror, the agents of revelation.

Notes

1. Virginia Woolf, 'Modern Fiction', in Woolf, *The Common Reader: First Series* (London: Hogarth Press, 1925), p. 189.
2. Virginia Woolf, 'A Sketch of the Past', in Woolf, *Moments of Being*, ed. Jeanne Schulkind, 2nd edn (London: Hogarth Press, 1985), p. 72.
3. Virginia Woolf, *The Voyage Out* (London: Hogarth Press, 1915), pp. 2–3. Further references cited parenthetically.
4. Jane Marcus, 'Niece of a Nun: Virginia Woolf, Caroline Stephen and the Cloistered Imagination', in Marcus (ed.), *Virginia Woolf and the Languages of Patriarchy* (Bloomington: Indiana University Press, 1987), p. 128.
5. Virginia Woolf, *A Room of One's Own* (London: Hogarth Press, 1928), p. 7.
6. Virginia Woolf, *The Diary of Virginia Woolf*, 5 vols., ed. Anne Olivier Bell (London: Hogarth Press, 1977–84), vol. II, p. 13.

7. Hermione Lee, *The Novels of Virginia Woolf* (London: Metheun, 1977), p. 72.
8. Virginia Woolf, *Jacob's Room* (London: Hogarth Press, 1925), pp. 8–9. Further references cited parenthetically.
9. Virginia Woolf, *Mrs Dalloway*, (London: Hogarth Press, 1925), p. 5. Further references cited parenthetically.
10. Virginia Woolf, 'Introduction', in Woolf, *Mrs Dalloway*, Modern Library Edition (New York: Random House, 1928), p. iv.
11. Woolf, *Diary*, vol. II, p. 207.
12. Harold Bloom, 'Introduction', in Bloom (ed.), *Modern Critical Interpretations: Virginia Woolf's 'Mrs Dalloway'* (New York: Chelsea House, 1988), p. 2.
13. For the trope of the flame as 'an agent of purification and refinement', see Perry Meisel, *The Absent Father: Virginia Woolf and Walter Pater* (New Haven: Yale University Press, 1980), pp. 56–7.
14. Woolf, *Diary*, vol. III, pp. 18–19.
15. Virginia Woolf, *To the Lighthouse* (London: Hogarth Press, 1927), pp. 17, 56–7. Further references cited parenthetically.
16. For clarity, I use here the version of the passage as corrected by Woolf for the first American edition of *To the Lighthouse* (New York: Harcourt Brace, 1927), p. 194.
17. Woolf, *Diary*, vol. III, p. 232.
18. Virginia Woolf, *The Waves* (London: Hogarth Press, 1931), p. 188. Further references cited parenthetically.
19. Woolf, *Diary*, vol. V, p. 135.
20. Virginia Woolf, *Between the Acts* (London: Hogarth Press, 1941), p. 11. Further references cited parenthetically.

8

REBECCA BEASLEY

Wyndham Lewis and modernist satire

Lewis's alternative modernism

The inclusion of Wyndham Lewis (1884–1957) in this *Companion* reflects a significant shift in our conception of the modernist novel over the past fifteen years. Although Lewis himself has frequently appeared as a major personality in narratives of modernism, his literary works have not had the wide readership of the novels of James Joyce, D. H. Lawrence or Virginia Woolf. Since the mid-1990s, however, Lewis's work has been cited in mainstream modernist studies with increasing regularity. This can be explained in part by the Black Sparrow Press's republication of Lewis's work, a large proportion of which had been out of print since its first publication. In addition, although many of Lewis's novels existed only on the margins of the modernist canon, they had over the intervening years accumulated a strong body of scholarly material generated by a small group of dedicated scholars, on which recent criticism has built. Finally, changes in modernist studies, and indeed in literary studies more generally, have created a congenial climate for Lewis's work.

Lewis's writing is no longer the aberration it evidently appeared to many in 1954, when Hugh Kenner defended Lewis's inclusion in Methuen's 'The Makers of Modern Literature' series as follows:

> No historian's model of the age of Joyce, Eliot, and Pound is intelligible without Lewis in it. More than any of these men, whose craft functioned with comparative freedom within the time, Lewis reveals the time's *nature*. He does this as much by disregarding nearly everything the artist is officially supposed to undertake, as by succeeding – so far as he has succeeded – in what he chose to do instead.[1]

Here, Kenner indicates the incompatibility between Lewis's view of what 'the artist is officially supposed to undertake' and the view that dominated literary studies in the mid-twentieth century. While the major Anglo-American critics of the period preferred to interpret fiction in terms of formal irony rather than social commentary, Lewis's novels foreground contemporary critique. As literary studies discarded the fantasy of autonomous literary works, and scholars of modernism sought to rebut the charge that modernist literature had 'altogether detached itself from the praxis of life', Lewis's novels were rediscovered as emphatically engaged works, which yet also displayed the commitment to formal experiment that is characteristic of modernist fiction.[2]

But Lewis's appropriation as a major modernist novelist is not without its difficulties. First, the progress of his career does not fit the accepted modernist chronology: his literary output was relatively slight during the main period of modernist production. Before the First World War, during the avant-garde stage of British modernism, Lewis's reputation was as a painter. He studied for two and a half years at the Slade, followed by seven years on the European continent, mainly in Paris, returning to London in 1908. In 1914 he launched Vorticism, the English response to Cubism and Futurism, and his most secure place in literary modernism has been as editor and main contributor to Vorticism's short-lived periodical, *Blast* (1914–15). However, the impact of Vorticism has tended to overshadow Lewis's literary work during the same period. Between 1909 and 1918 Lewis also published short fiction, a play and a poem in periodicals that were central to defining literary modernism: the *English Review*, the *Tramp*, the *New Age* and the *Little Review*, as well as *Blast*. In 1908–9 he wrote a 'potboiler' novel, *Mrs Dukes' Million*, published posthumously in 1977. Following the publication of his first novel, *Tarr*, in 1918, Lewis's reputation as a major experimental writer began to be established. But unlike Joyce, whose *A Portrait of the Artist as a Young Man* (1916) had preceded *Tarr*'s serialization in the *Egoist* during 1916–17, Lewis did not consolidate this success in the next few years with a second major novel. In 1916 he enlisted in the Royal Garrison Artillery, and in 1917–18 he worked as a war artist for the Canadian and British War Memorials Committees. While the other 'Men of 1914' were publishing the key works of canonical literary modernism in the early 1920s, Lewis's career stalled: he later remarked that the war 'caught me before I was quite through with my training. And although in the "post-war" I was not starting from nothing, I had to some extent to begin all over again.'[3] It was not until 1928 that Lewis's next novel, *The Childermass*, was published.

A further difficulty in understanding Lewis as a modernist novelist is suggested by his forceful repudiation of the work of most of his modernist contemporaries. In *Time and Western Man* (1927) and *Men Without Art* (1934) the literature of William Faulkner, Ernest Hemingway, Henry James, Joyce, Lawrence, Ezra Pound, Marcel Proust, Gertrude Stein and Woolf is criticized for its Romantic passivity, its failure to engage with present realities. In opposition to the 'internal method' of these writers, Lewis advocates the 'external method' of satire, thereby setting himself apart from the main line of Anglo-American modernist innovation and inviting comparison instead with the continental European, especially German, modernism of Expressionism.[4] In fact, it is probably true to say that Lewis has been represented most consistently as a major modernist figure in criticism that is explicitly antagonistic to modernism. A passage in *The Art of Being Ruled* (1926), and the notorious *Hitler* (1931), have made Lewis a favourite example for those who see modernism and fascism as part of the same trajectory. But, as the substantial scholarship on this topic attests, here, too, Lewis resists easy categorization.[5]

But it is precisely the difficulty of fitting Lewis into a modernist template that has aided his recuperation in recent years. As the category of modernism has expanded, Lewis's oeuvre has become more legible and his critique of the modernist project more pertinent. Indeed, for some scholars this critique not only adds interest to Lewis's work, it is suggestive of an alternative modernism. So for Tyrus Miller, for example, Lewis is the main protagonist of 'late modernism', an interwar modernism characterized by a 'growing scepticism about modernist sensibility and craft as means of managing the turbulent forces of the day', which 'reopens the modernist enclosure of form onto the work's social and political environs, facilitating its more direct, polemical engagement with topical and popular discourses'. As several critics, including Miller, have pointed out, Lewis's theorizing of art frequently bears a greater similarity to the modernism of mid-century Marxist critics, such as the Frankfurt School or the Situationists, than it does to that of his high modernist contemporaries.[6]

The inhuman artist

Lewis's oeuvre represents one of the most sustained and rigorous examinations of that favourite modernist concern: the role of the artist-intellectual in contemporary life. In the interwar period during which he produced his most important works, Lewis followed the French critic Julien Benda in arguing that the artist had a duty to take up a stance of intellectual opposition to the status quo. 'There is no real *criticism* of existing society,' he wrote. 'Politics and the highly organized, deeply entrenched, dominant mercantile society has it all its own way.' In his novels and in his voluminous critical writings, Lewis sought to stimulate intellectual exchange by adopting the antagonistic position of 'the Enemy', the name he also used as the title for his third periodical (1927–9). Yet at the same time, Lewis insisted on an essential division between art and politics, envisioning a future in which the artist would be viewed as an 'intellectual workman', left free to generate the intellectual source material needed to nourish civilization (*Art of Being Ruled* 360, 374).

Lewis's best-known and most studied novel, *Tarr*, was written before these arguments had taken on their specific interwar character, but it nevertheless introduces themes and techniques that Lewis would pursue in the later stages of his career. *Tarr* is traditionally regarded as the most straightforwardly modernist of Lewis's novels, a Dostoevskyan revision of the *Künstlerroman* that presents the competitive sexual exploits of two artists, the English Frederick Tarr and the German Otto Kreisler, against a background of bohemian life in prewar Paris. In the figure of Tarr himself we seem to encounter the artist-intellectual in his most familiarly modernist form, arguing for the primacy of art over life and mind over body, and enacting his argument by casting off his latent Romanticism, embodied by his fiancée Bertha Lunken and Kreisler. Yet this comfortable reading is troubled by two related factors: Kreisler's domination of the narrative, and Tarr's ultimate inability to perform the role of protagonist for the reader.

Lewis thwarts our identification with Tarr at precisely those points where his self-revelation as modernist appears imminent. Near the beginning of the novel, Tarr argues that humour is 'nothing but a first rate means of evading reality ... a system of *deadening feeling*', that, while it protects its wearer, also allows the underlying sensibility to soften. He resolves to 'swear off Humour for a year', to 'discard this husk and armour'. However, although discarding this armour to enable an engagement with reality might seem a typically modernist move, the nature of the reality revealed departs from modernist convention. Reality for Tarr (and for Lewis), is not located in a revelation of human consciousness, as it is in the works of Joyce, Lawrence or Woolf, for example. In *Tarr* reality is to be found in the inhuman: Tarr will 'gaze on Bertha inhumanly, and not humorously'. In the final section of the novel, Tarr expands this point into a theory of art:

> *Deadness* is the first condition of art ... The second is absence of *soul*, in the sentimental human sense. The lines and masses of the statue are its soul. No restless, quick flame-like ego is imagined for the *inside* of it. It has no inside. This is another condition of art; *to have no inside*, nothing you cannot *see*. Instead, then, of being something impelled like an independent machine by a little egoistic fire inside, it lives soullessly and deadly by its frontal lines and masses.[7]

In this speech, typically Lewisian in its emphatic tone, art-critical vocabulary, and philosophical ambition, Tarr makes explicit the novel's argument against the primacy of the self as the ground for art. It is an argument Lewis also explores through the bohemians' incessant role-playing, and the trope of the double, or split self, represented by Tarr's relationship with Kreisler, and also Kreisler's with Louis Soltyk. The vacuum that Tarr's inhumanity leaves in the novel is to a certain extent filled by the psychologically complex portrait of Kreisler, much admired by critics. Despite the novel's title, Lewis's letters indicate that when he began working on the novel in 1907 or 1908, he conceived it as a study of Kreisler; the story of Tarr and Bertha appears to have been introduced in 1911 and expanded in 1915.[8] But if Kreisler remained the emotional core of the novel, Lewis nevertheless invalidates him as the *Künstlerroman*'s hero: Kreisler's claustrophobic analyses of his obsessive relationships lack any self-knowledge, and the trajectory of his humiliation and eventual suicide is depicted as inevitable. Lewis presents the reader with two parallel plots, Tarr's in the tradition of the *Künstlerroman*, Kreisler's in that of the Romantic novel of disintegration, but both are undermined. Neither the philosophizing modernist nor the Romantic artist can provide an uncompromised model for the intellectual artist.[9]

Satire and the novel

In his 1937 autobiography, *Blasting and Bombardiering*, Lewis famously claimed that after the publication of *Tarr* in the last year of the war, he 'buried' himself, then 'disinterred' himself 'in 1926, the year of the General Strike – but as a philosopher and critic'. Although Lewis overstates the extent of his withdrawal – *The Caliph's Design* (1919), the two issues of his journal *The Tyro* (1921), and sections of his third novel, *The Apes of God*, were published during this period – the remarkable series of books that he published between 1926 and 1930 testifies to a sustained period of reflection on the postwar situation. The war had given him, he said, 'a *political* education', and the preservation of the artist-intellectual now became a political imperative (*Blasting* 5, 186).

During his 'burial', Lewis worked on a political and philosophical treatise entitled 'The Man of the World'. Although the project was abandoned, Lewis published parts of it as 'The Dithyrambic Spectator' (1925), 'Creatures of Habit and Creatures of Change' (1926), *The Art of Being Ruled*, *The Lion and the Fox* (1927) and *Time and Western Man*.[10] In 1928 he published his first novel since *Tarr*, the 'theological science fiction' of *The Childermass*, and in 1930 *The Apes of God*.[11] The continuities between the fiction and nonfiction are strong: *Time and Western Man*'s analysis of what Lewis called 'the time-cult' in contemporary literature and philosophy is explored in *The Childermass*; its related rebuttal of 'the child-cult' is revisited in *The Art of Being Ruled* and dramatized in the relationship between Pullman and Satterthwaite in *The Childermass*, and the Finnian Shaws in *The Apes of God*. Taken all together, these works provide a sustained critique of postwar Western society.

Lewis argued that Western civilization was disintegrating: symptoms of its decay included the popularity of Bergson's time philosophy (with its valuing of change over stability and intuition over intellect), a desire to retain the irresponsibility of childhood, and a general feminization of society (evidence of which Lewis located in the success of the suffrage movement, the 'fashion' of homosexuality and the break-up of the family). The emasculation of society led directly to a lowering of intellectual standards and 'a levelling, standardization, and pooling of the crowd-mind' (*Art of Being Ruled*, 166). The intellectual, whose role it was to maintain standards of value, was no longer engaged with life and had left a vacuum filled by second-rate thinkers.

It is these second-rate thinkers who are the protagonists of the novel that is arguably Lewis's masterpiece, *The Apes of God*. If the role-playing of the 'bourgeois bohemians' is deployed in *Tarr* primarily as an anti-Romantic trope, in *The Apes of God* it is made to carry the force of a more sustained argument. Lewis focuses on the '*societification*' of art, where 'the idlest of the rich', lacking both talent and taste, have taken up the practice of art, imitating (aping) genuinely talented artists. The chief target is the Bloomsbury group, broadly conceived, which Lewis held particularly responsible for the complacency and narrowness of literary culture, and that culture's resistance to his own writing. *Tarr* had contained a brief parody of Roger Fry in the character of the Cambridge-educated Alan Hobson, but in *The Apes of God* Lewis directs a much more wide-ranging attack on his contemporaries, including Lytton Strachey and Dora Carrington (satirized as Matthew Plunkett and Betty Bligh), Sidney and Violet Schiff (Lionel and Isabel Kein), Clive and Vanessa Bell (Jonathan and Mrs Bell), and – at greatest length – Edith, Osbert and Sacheverell Sitwell (the Finnian Shaws).[12]

The reader perceives these 'Apes' through the uncomprehending eyes of the Irish *naïf* Daniel Boleyn, under the tuition of Horace Zagreus with whom he is infatuated. In a key explanatory section, 'The Encyclical', Pierpoint, the novel's permanently absent genius and Lewis's mouthpiece, explains that the 'Apes' or 'New Bohemians' are responsible for the decline of art and intellectual activity, because they take up the amenities and the market needed by genuine artists, and, more importantly, because their self-representation as artists enables them to wield an unearned cultural authority. Their ill-educated opinions promote the second-rate art that they and their fellow Apes produce, and undermine the work of the genuine artists they imitate (120–5).

In his second autobiography, *Rude Assignment* (1950), Lewis remarked that *The Apes of God* was 'the only one of my books which can be described as pure Satire', but in fact Lewis's conception of satire is central to his entire oeuvre.[13] He distinguished his satirical works from Proust's, which he thought accurate but insufficient: Proust was too partisan, Lewis argued, 'he likes every odour that has ever reached him from the millionaire society he depicts' (*Art of Being Ruled*, 360). In *The Apes of God* Zagreus and Lionel and Isabel Klein discuss Proust at length: Zagreus argues that Proust's satire has no effect because his targets are always able to feel themselves exempt. In the transitional, interwar period, a far stronger satire is necessary to pierce 'the rhinoceros hides grown by a civilized man and a civilized woman' (*Apes* 255).

Lewis set out his definition of satire in *Satire and Fiction* (1930), a privately published pamphlet he brought out to publicize *The Apes of God*, and *Men Without Art*, into which much of the pamphlet was subsequently incorporated. Although he admits that 'to "Satire" I have given a meaning so wide as to confound it with "Art"', and indeed there is much in common here with the definitions of art in *Tarr*, Lewis's account is distinctive. A key point arises from his consideration of William Hazlitt's lecture on Shakespeare and Ben Jonson. Hazlitt criticizes Jonson's characters as 'machines, governed by mere routine, or by the convenience of the poet, whose property they are', and compares Jonson's plays unfavourably with Shakespeare's, in which 'we are let into the minds of his characters, we see the play of their thoughts ... His humour (so to speak) bubbles, sparkles, and finds its way in all directions, like a natural spring. In Ben Jonson it is, as it were, confined in a leaden cistern.' However, it is precisely the mechanical effect Hazlitt criticizes in Jonson that for Lewis is the mark of successful satirical characterization: 'is it not just because they are such *machines, governed by routine* ... that the satirist, in the first instance, has considered them suitable for satire? He who wants a jolly, carefree, bubbling, world chock-full of "charm," must not address himself to the satirist!' (*Men Without Art* 13, 91, 93).[14]

Lewis's explanation of his preference for the mechanical here is instructive: his point is that the satirist is most interested in those aspects of life where we are least conscious (and self-critical). In an earlier essay Lewis had reversed Bergson's influential theory of laughter to argue that the root of comedy was to be found in observing 'a thing behaving like a person', with the result that 'all men are necessarily comic: for they are all things, or physical bodies, behaving as persons'.[15] Indeed, the representation of bodies as ludicrously mechanical matter is a striking characteristic of Lewis's writing, both in his vivid close-ups of individuals, as when Anastasya laughs in *Tarr* ('this commotion was transmitted to her body as though sharp, sonorous blows had been struck on her mouth', 99), and in his analysis of group behaviour, as in the depiction of the 'peons' in *The Childermass*.[16] In *The Apes of God* we are invited to see every character as a mechanical doll ('clockwork answering clockwork', 8); so severe is the satire that the only place from which Lewis's artist-intellectual mouthpiece can speak is outside the action of the novel. Pierpoint is the only figure who is not compromised by his involvement in the Apes' society.

Lewis's machine aesthetic is the most striking effect of his '*external* approach' to fiction by which he aimed to combat the too-flattering '*internal* method of approach' of his contemporaries. While acknowledging that *Ulysses* (1922), for example, was a significant achievement, Lewis claimed that it demonstrated the limitations of the internal method, which robbed the novel of 'all linear properties', 'all contour and definition' (*Men Without Art* 103–4, 120). As these phrases suggest, the realization of the '*external* approach' owes much to Lewis's work as a painter. Indeed, writing on Joyce in *Time and Western Man*, he noted that 'it is a good deal as a pictorial and graphic artist that I approach these problems; and a method that does not secure that definition and logical integrity that, as a graphic artist, I require, I am, I admit, hostile to from the start' (*Time* 109).

The political spectacle

The significance of Lewis's machine aesthetic extends beyond issues of style and genre; by the time Lewis wrote *The Apes of God*, the metaphor had become literalized and Lewis perceived interwar Europe as separating into two groups, the individualized potential rulers and the mechanical mass of the ruled. He argued that liberal democracy had repressed natural competitive instincts and standardized human variety, leading the majority of people to seek a poor semblance of freedom by retreating from responsibility and embracing a childlike attitude of obedience to the state. This state in which the majority is subject to the will of the few would have been called slavery in earlier periods, Lewis remarks, but since it appears to have been freely chosen in a democratic society, rather than enforced in an authoritarian one, it is erroneously perceived as freedom. In reality, he argues, the masses are expertly manipulated by the ideological apparatus of the state (*Art of Being Ruled* 137, 131, 74).

However, according to Lewis this situation was not necessarily to be regretted by the intellectual. If the masses continued to be marshalled into their standardized 'system of clans, societies, clubs, syndics, and classes', the independent thinkers who could not be absorbed into these groups might form their own. This, Lewis comments, 'will be the moment of the renascence of our race, or will be the signal for a new biological transformation ... A natural separation will then occur, and everybody will get what he wants' (264). Although Lewis emphasizes that one group is not inferior to the other, this is clearly a deeply unsettling argument, and one that, in its biological turn, strangely undermines the sociological and political analyses that preceded it.[17] While Lewis's idiosyncratic account of the interwar social crisis was much more astute than is sometimes allowed, the same cannot be said of his political recommendations.

The most notorious of these is his assertion in 1926 that 'for anglo-saxon countries as they are constituted today some modified form of fascism would probably be best' (*Art of Being Ruled* 320–1), followed by the depiction, in 1931, of Hitler as a 'Man of Peace' whose policies could prevent a second world war.[18] The former statement was made briefly in the course of an argument against liberal-democratic hypocrisy, and Lewis publicly repudiated National Socialism in *The Hitler Cult* (1939): his support for National Socialism was temporary and, he admitted, misguided. Nevertheless, it must be faced that during the 1930s Lewis argued that Hitler's policies should be given a hearing in Britain, and that he believed a form of fascism could provide a version of the stable state conducive to intellectual production described in *The Art of Being Ruled*. Fredric Jameson's argument that 'the structural place of fascism' remains in Lewis's writings and 'is not altered by his later (and impeccable) anti-Nazi convictions' continues to be a major point of debate.[19]

It is on Lewis's most critically acclaimed work, *The Revenge for Love* (1937), that the discussion of Lewis's fascism has focused. Set in London and pre-Civil War Spain, the novel places Victor Stamp, an impoverished Australian artist, and his lover, Margot, among a fashionable clique of '*salon*-revolutionaries' epitomized by the artist Tristram Phipps and his wife Gillian.[20] As in *Tarr* and *The Apes of God*, Lewis depicts a world in which roles are taken for selves and self-promotion for truth, directing his sharpest criticism at Communist Party ideologues and capitalist war profiteers. Although the novel's 1934–5 date of composition precludes a specifically pro-Franco reading, it has been read as more broadly supportive of fascism. Critics have pointed variously to the identification of Victor with Germany in section six, 'The Fakers', the stereotypical presentation of Jewish characters in the novel, including that of Isaac Wohl in the same chapter, and the critique of ordinary politics.[21]

But in this novel there is no Pierpoint, nor even a Tarr, through which Lewis speaks. The novel's original title was 'False Bottoms', and Lewis systematically removes every stable ground on which a positive answer to the novel's critique might be based. If Margot is the closest to articulating

Lewis's revulsion towards the all-pervasive deceptions, the 'immense *false-bottom* underlying every seemingly solid surface, upon which it was her lot to tread' (155), she is by no means represented as an artist-intellectual. Her idealization of Woolf is for Lewis symptomatic of her sentimentality. In this sense *The Revenge for Love* reflects Lewis's increasing pessimism about the political situation and the potential for the intellectual to intervene.

Lewis's career did not recover from the publication of *Hitler* in 1931, though he continued to publish essays, short stories and novels (including one of his best, *Self Condemned*, 1954) until his death in 1957. When he reviewed his oeuvre in *Rude Assignment*, Lewis argued that his works were united by 'a pattern of thinking' that set out what he had earlier named 'a politics of the intellect'. His writing had engaged him, he wrote, in an 'analysis of what is obsessional in contemporary social life; in composing satiric verse; exposing abuses in art politics; celebrating in fiction picturesque parasites; in weighing, to the best of his ability, contemporary theories of the State' (153, 12). While elements of Lewis's views shifted more than he allowed in this retrospective glance, his fiction and nonfiction alike remained committed to the critique of ideology. Lewis's work requires us to ask uncomfortable questions of early twentieth-century history and of modernism's response to it, and his answers rarely make easy reading. For that reason they are fundamental to a nuanced understanding of modernism. Lewis was one of modernism's most innovative practitioners and simultaneously its most incisive critic.

Notes

1. Hugh Kenner, *Wyndham Lewis* (London: Methuen, 1954), p. xiv.
2. Peter Bürger, *Theory of the Avant-Garde*, trans. Michael Shaw (Minneapolis: University of Minnesota Press, 1984), p. 23.
3. Wyndham Lewis, *Blasting and Bombardiering* (London: Calder, 1982), pp. 292, 213. Further references cited parenthetically.
4. Wyndham Lewis, *Men Without Art*, ed. Seamus Cooney (Santa Rosa: Black Sparrow Press, 1987), pp. 98–9, and Peter Nicholls, *Modernisms: A Literary Guide* (London: Palgrave Macmillan, 1995), p. 273.
5. See Fredric Jameson, *Fables of Aggression: Wyndham Lewis, the Modernist as Fascist* (Berkeley: University of California Press, 1979); David Ayers, *Wyndham Lewis and Western Man* (London: Macmillan, 1992); Andrew Hewitt, *Fascist Modernism: Aesthetics, Politics, and the Avant-Garde* (Stanford: Stanford University Press, 1993), and, for a strong counterargument, Reed Way Dasenbrock, 'Wyndham Lewis's Fascist Imagination and the Fiction of Paranoia', in Richard J. Goslan (ed.), *Fascism, Aesthetics and Culture* (Hanover: University Press of New Hampshire, 1992), pp. 81–97.
6. Tyrus Miller, *Late Modernism: Politics, Fiction, and the Arts Between the World Wars* (Berkeley and Los Angeles: University of California Press, 1999), pp. 20, 44,

and Reed Way Dasenbrock, 'Afterword', in Wyndham Lewis, *The Art of Being Ruled*, ed. Dasenbrock (Santa Rosa: Black Sparrow Press, 1989), pp. 423–47 (p. 438). Further references cited parenthetically.

7. Wyndham Lewis, *Tarr: The 1918 Version*, ed. Paul O'Keeffe (Santa Rosa: Black Sparrow Press, 1990), pp. 42–3, 299–300.

8. Paul O'Keeffe, 'Afterword', in Lewis, *Tarr*, pp. 361–85 (pp. 380–2, 361–5).

9. Paul Peppis, 'Anti-Individualism and Fictions of National Character in Wyndham Lewis's *Tarr*', *Twentieth Century Literature* 40:2 (1994), pp. 226–55 (p. 239).

10. Paul Edwards, 'Afterword', in Wyndham Lewis, *Time and Western Man*, ed. Edwards (Santa Rosa: Black Sparrow Press, 1993), pp. 455–508 (pp. 481–98).

11. Jameson, *Fables of Aggression*, p. 6.

12. Paul Edwards, 'Afterword', in Wyndham Lewis, *The Apes of God*, ed. Edwards (Santa Barbara: Black Sparrow Press, 1981), pp. 629–39 (pp. 635–6). Further references cited parenthetically.

13. Wyndham Lewis, *Rude Assignment: An Intellectual Autobiography*, ed. Toby Foshay (Santa Barbara: Black Sparrow Press, 1984), p. 56. Further references cited parenthetically.

14. William Hazlitt, 'Lecture II: On Shakespeare and Ben Jonson,' in *The Selected Writings of William Hazlitt*, 9 vols., ed. Duncan Wu (London: Pickering and Chatto, 1998), vol. V, pp. 26–43 (p. 34).

15. Wyndham Lewis, 'The Meaning of the Wild Body,' in Lewis, *The Complete Wild Body*, ed. Bernard Lafourcade (Santa Barbara: Black Sparrow Press, 1982), pp. 155–60 (p. 158).

16. Wyndham Lewis, *The Childermass* (London: Calder, 2000), p. 26.

17. Andrzej Gasiorek, *Wyndham Lewis and Modernism* (Tavistock: Northcote House, 2004), pp. 80–1.

18. Wyndham Lewis, *Hitler* (London: Chatto and Windus, 1931), p. 32.

19. Jameson, *Fables of Aggression*, p. 183.

20. Wyndham Lewis, *The Revenge for Love*, ed. Reed Way Dasenbrock (Santa Rosa: Black Sparrow Press, 1991), p. 195. Further references cited parenthetically.

21. David Ayers makes the strongest charge of anti-Semitism against Lewis, in *Lewis and Western Man*, pp. 30–53. See also Dasenbrock, 'Wyndham Lewis's Fascist Imagination', p. 93.

9

HUGH STEVENS

D. H. Lawrence: organicism and the modernist novel

Can fiction be modernist when it aims to help us to recapture a premodern, or even 'primitive', relationship with nature and with our own bodies, and dissolve boundaries between the self and the world? This is the question we must answer in considering D. H. Lawrence's (1885–1930) conflictual relationship with literary modernism. In Lawrence's most challenging statements about the purpose of the novel, he emerges as something like an ecological antimodernist, continuing a tradition of Romantic organicism which modernism often appears to leave behind.

The novel, in Lawrence's view, goes astray when it affiliates itself with specific types of experimental modernism, because its real benefits derive from its potential to help us to resist the damaging effects of modernity. The novel's immediate task might be to offer us aesthetic representations of the world in all its complexity, but this task, for Lawrence, is part of a greater project of cultural regeneration. In a series of essays written in 1923 and 1925, including 'Art and Morality' and 'Why the Novel Matters', Lawrence shows an unrestrained contempt for the modernist novel, at least as it is practised by some of his celebrated contemporaries.[1] He argues that there are three categories of modern fiction: 'serious', 'popular' and 'valuable'. 'Serious' and 'popular' fiction represent fiction as it is being written in the 1920s, and both derive from and propagate the self-consciousness which Lawrence regards as the great problem of modern culture. Self-consciousness, and here Lawrence is influenced by his reading of Friedrich Nietzsche,[2] is an awareness of self as separated from the natural world, a mental condition arising from the influence of modern, rational, scientific thought, with its dualisms and harsh delineation of subject and object. In an early draft of an essay on John Galsworthy, Lawrence complains that the 'real individual' is destroyed by self-consciousness, which in turn is a product of what Lawrence calls 'the social consciousness'. Modern 'social individuals' are diminished creatures, 'always aware of the "you" set over against the "me," always conscious of the "it" which the "I" is up against . . . The social consciousness can only be analytical, critical, constructive but not creative, sensational but not passionate, emotional but without true feeling.' Lawrence complains that the modern novel contains no 'real individuals'. The modern novel is complicit in the process whereby 'the real individual lapses out, leaving only the social individual'.[3]

Lawrence's examples of 'serious' modern novelists include many of those we would now think of as defining 'modernism' – James Joyce, Marcel Proust, and Dorothy Richardson – and their fiction is described as 'dying in a very long-drawn-out fourteen-volume death agony, and absorbedly, childishly interested in the phenomenon', a 'dismal, long-drawn-out comedy' made up of 'self-consciousness picked into such fine bits that the bits are most of them invisible'. This modernist fiction is artificial, 'senile precocious', an unhealthy extension of adolescent absorbed self-consciousness into adulthood. On the other hand, popular novels (Lawrence's examples include Edith Maude Hull's *The Sheik* (1919) and Sinclair Lewis's *Babbitt* (1922) are spurious and conventional, 'just as self-conscious', only with 'more illusions about themselves'. Their heroines and heroes are 'lovelier, and more fascinating, and purer ... more heroic, braver, more chivalrous, more fetching' than those in the 'serious' novel, and present a series of hackneyed identities in which the 'mass of the populace "find themselves"'.[4]

Like Goldilocks, Lawrence finds his first two categories of 'serious' and 'popular' unhelpful precursors to the ideal third. The third category, of 'real valuable fiction', is what fiction should aspire to: this is a fiction which can reveal 'life'. This revelation requires first a move into somewhere secret, private and dark, whence we will emerge renewed, cleansed and freshened. In 'The Novel and the Feelings', Lawrence argues that 'unless we proceed to connect ourselves up with our own primeval sources, we shall degenerate', and the novel – or at least the *real* novel – can help us in this process: 'If we can't hear the cries far down in our own forests of dark veins, we can look in the real novels, and there listen-in. Not listen to the didactic statements of the author, but to the low, calling cries of the characters, as they wander in the dark woods of their destiny.'[5] In Lawrence's organicist metaphors self, nature and the novel are all harmoniously entwined: our veins are forests, fictional characters' destinies are dark woods. A historical and cultural dimension is present in these metaphors, as the forest and the woods stand for the natural world in English and German ecological thinking; in England the woods are nostalgically equated with an old England which has been lost; in German ecological thinking the forest is often figured as the soul of the German people.

There is a paradox at work here, as Lawrence's intentions for the novel are didactic, but he believes the novel's success depends on its being, in essence, a nondidactic form. The novel is the key artform which will help us to escape degeneration by reconnecting us with our primeval sources.[6] The reader plays an important role in this process, as the reader must differentiate between inauthentic authorial views and the authentic voices of characters. If we 'listen in' in the correct manner, we will shed the harmful self-consciousness that Lawrence associates with modernity. On the other hand, modernist fiction's efforts to trace the mental processes of sophisticated and self-conscious sensibilities destroy what Lawrence sees as the novel's main strength.

Another paradox is present in Lawrence's argument, because the novel – the literary form with which he is most identified – is itself a modern form, dependent on modern technology for its production and circulation, on modern education and a skilled workforce for its readership. In addition, the novel requires the felling of trees and the production of paper through modern industrial methods; put crudely, novels destroy the very trees they should be enabling us to discover. Lawrence's polemic on behalf of the novel works alongside his more general attack on technological and industrial modernity, so it is not surprising that the examples he gives of the 'real novel' are the Gospels of Matthew, Mark, Luke and John, Plato's *Dialogues* and Augustine's *Confessions*, all narratives from a time before the invention of printing or the development of the novel as a genre.[7] Lawrence's frequent polemical statements arguing for a preindustrial social organization, if taken seriously, would rob him of his own vocation as effectively as state censorship did during the First World War. The 'real valuable' novel will save humanity from modernity, but only this modernity enables the production of the novel. The novel finds readers because the population has become literate, but universal education is abhorred by Lawrence as an institution which stops the child from growing up with a creative and imaginative relationship to the natural world. Lawrence's views on education are implicit in several portrayals of teachers and unhappy school pupils (above all in *The Rainbow*, 1915), and are stated explicitly in 'Education of the People' and *Fantasia of the Unconscious*, a polemical essay of 1922.[8] Here universal education is identified as 'so uncouth, so psychologically barbaric, that it is the most terrible menace to the existence of our race'. Lawrence advocates that all schools should be closed for an indefinite period, 'elementary education should be stopped at once', and fathers should 'see that [their] boys are trained to be men', just as mothers should 'see that [their] daughters are trained to be women'.[9] The growth of and success of the novel, however, coincides with and depends on growth in rates of literacy brought about by modern education, and by the reduction in average working hours achieved by modern forms of labour and specialization.

Lawrence's defence of the novel requires that it should be associated with a 'natural' humanity which modernity threatens to destroy. Lawrence advances a vitalist and organicist aesthetic for the novel which conforms to criteria prominent in European aesthetics since their foundation as a discipline by Alexander Gottlieb Baumgarten in 1735.[10] Terry Eagleton notes how, for Baumgarten, 'aesthetics mediates between the generalities of reason and the particulars of sense ... [I]n their organic interpenetration, the elements of aesthetic representation resist that discrimination into discrete units which is characteristic of conceptual thought.'[11] Lawrence's defence of the novel endows it with qualities remarkably similar to those that Baumgarten attributes to 'aesthetic representation'; his aesthetic ideals for fiction have as much in common with Romantic organicism and Victorian realism – the 'complex web' of society as represented in George Eliot's fiction – as with modernist radicalism. The 'business of art', Lawrence claims, 'is to reveal the relation between man and his circumambient universe, at the living moment', and the novel is the best form to carry out this business, as the novel is the 'highest complex of subtle inter-relatedness that man has discovered'.[12] The novel captures the 'interrelatedness' of life, but 'inherently is and must be', Lawrence argues, '[i]nterrelated in all its parts, vitally, organically'.[13] The novel 'is a perfect medium for revealing to us the changing rainbow of our living relationships. The novel can help us to live, as nothing else can: no didactic Scripture, anyhow.'[14] Lawrence's views anticipate the central claims made for his fiction by the generation of admiring critics writing under the influence of F. R. Leavis: the novel is valuable because it can reveal 'life' to us. 'The novel is the one bright book of life.'[15]

Lawrence's plea that we should not listen to 'the didactic statements of the author' is an idea frequently found in his writing. Its most celebrated appearance is the aphoristic command, in *Studies in Classic American Literature* (1923): 'Never trust the artist. Trust the tale.'[16] One might follow W. B. Yeats, however, in asking, 'How can we know the dancer from the dance?'[17] What parts of a novel are 'tale', and what parts are 'artist'? Moreover, the advice to trust the 'tale' is problematic, as a 'tale' is not a person whom one can trust or be suspicious of. Does one trust the tale to tell the 'truth'? Does one trust the tale's presentation of events, or does one trust the view of human nature presented in the tale? Is 'trust' a mode of reading which does not require interpretation, and is miraculously free of the problems of interpretation? How do we trust a tale when it presents different and contradictory views of a character or a situation? And, as narrative theory has taught us that a tale is a particular 'narration' of a 'plot' – a series of events which can be thought of as different from the tale itself – if one trusts the 'tale', does one trust the 'narration' or the 'plot', the 'fabula' or the '*sjuzhet*'?[18] It is unsurprising that Lawrence is often condemned for failing to follow his own advice. A common critical judgement prefers his short stories and short novels (such as *The Ladybird* or *The Captain's Doll*, both 1923), which show off his narrative gifts at their best, to novels like *Lady Chatterley's Lover* (1928) or *The Plumed Serpent* (1926), in which the tale is supposedly smothered by the interfering voice of the artist.

Lawrence's critical reputation has been going down a long slide since Kate Millett's *Sexual Politics*, first published in 1970, toppled it off the lofty heights it reached under the influence of F. R. Leavis, for whom Lawrence was (in 1955) 'incomparably the greatest creative writer in English of our time', and 'one of the greatest English writers of any time'.[19] This fall might have been less severe if Lawrence had only done less, written less, and pruned his own 'didactic statements' from his prose. Even Lawrence's most admiring readers find it hard to make sense of the great heterogeneous clutter which is his oeuvre. The high praise accorded *Studies in Classic American Literature* is accompanied by disdain for his *Study of Thomas Hardy*. His travel writing is much admired; his letters have received few critical assessments. His novels are regarded as uneven: most critics regard his novels of the 1920s as disappointing in comparison with his three most highly regarded novels, *Sons and Lovers* (1913), *The Rainbow* (1915) and *Women in Love* (1921), all written in the previous decade (*Lady Chatterley's Lover* has received a great deal of critical attention, but much of this attention has been less than admiring). Critics have admired his poetry, but figures such as Ezra Pound, T. S. Eliot, Marianne Moore and William Carlos Williams are more highly esteemed as the most innovative poets of modernism. His philosophical essays, such as *The Crown* (1915), have few readers.

The enormous disparity in critical assessments of Lawrence's writing is worth noting, not only because it suggests that his writing might vary in quality, but also because it arises from conflicting impulses at work within it. Readers who respond negatively to Lawrence's interfering voice in his fiction echo views advanced, but not followed, by Lawrence himself. The novel's ability to reveal 'the trembling and oscillating of the balance' will be threatened, Lawrence writes, if 'the novelist puts his thumb in the pan, for love, tenderness, sweetness, peace'.[20] If the novelist wants the novel to express the value of a particular ideal, like 'peace', the resulting work might fail to represent human relationships in all their complexity. These views are expressed frequently and persuasively. But, if one reads a range of Lawrence's work, it is impossible not to view him as a writer who has not stopped with his thumbs, whose arms are plunged deep into the pan, up to the elbow, so palpable are his designs upon the reader. In 'The Future of the Novel' Lawrence claims that 'it was the greatest pity in the world, when philosophy and fiction got split'.[21] His claim here echoes the more famous claim made by T. S. Eliot in his 1921 essay 'The Metaphysical Poets' that '[i]n the seventeenth century a dissociation of sensibility set in, from which we have never recovered' – though his examples of novelistic philosophy, or philosophical fiction, are much older than the seventeenth century. Echoing Eliot's complaint that recent poets such as Alfred, Lord Tennyson and Robert Browning 'do not feel their thought as immediately as the odour of a rose',[22] Lawrence wants the philosophical and fictional aspects of the novel to be inseparable; this return to an older mode of writing before the mythical separation will enable a *new* mode of writing to emerge which can 'present us with new, really new feelings, a whole new line of emotion, which will get us out of the old emotional rut'.[23] Lawrence wants to return to what he sees as an older mode of writing in order to achieve something new.

Lawrence's formulation of a novelistic aesthetics based on notions of organic form is consistent with his advocacy of organic social organizations and ways of living which will enable us to reconnect with 'nature'. His organicism has a complex genealogy. Anne Fernihough has demonstrated its philosophical affiliations with late nineteenth-century and early twentieth-century German organicist and *völkisch* philosophies.[24] It also has a social and biographical provenance, as it is in part a response to Lawrence's experiences of the industrialism of English coalfield society, and the social divisions and tensions of the collier community in which he grew up. Indeed, before one attempts to locate Lawrence's modernism, one needs to acknowledge how Victorian he is. His fiction continues a project begun by George Eliot and Elizabeth Gaskell, and continued by Thomas Hardy: an analysis of the impact of modern technologies on provincial communities, in which the 'shock of the new' was caused by the industrial revolution rather than by aesthetic revolutions. Lawrence was born and grew up in Eastwood, a mining village on the Nottinghamshire-Derbyshire border. His childhood gave him an intimate acquaintance with the rural industrialism of coalfield society, and his fiction describes the environment of the Midlands as one in which the traditional components of English pastoralism – flowers, trees and forests, water and pasture, country houses, cottages and gardens – brush up against the waste products and frantic activity of mines, steelworks and factories. These stark contrasts are explored in most depth in three key novels, *The Rainbow*, *Women in Love* and *Lady Chatterley's Lover*, all of which examine the impact of what Lawrence calls the 'mechanical' on the landscape and on our way of living. In these novels the modern has a demonic and fascinating power, an awful destructiveness.

Lady Chatterley's Lover, Lawrence's last novel, offers his bleakest realization of the destructiveness of the industrial and the modern. The impact of modernity is shown through Lawrence's portrayal of human lives and his descriptions of a ravaged landscape. Modern industrialism and modern war are devastating in their impact on the Midlands coalmining community described in the novel. The First World War kills the elder of the two Chatterley brothers and cripples the younger, Clifford, who is shipped back from Flanders 'more or less in bits ... the lower half of his body, from the hips down, paralysed for ever'.[25] Clifford's father 'chop[s] down his trees and weed[s] men out of his colliery, to shove them into the war' (11); the trees are used for 'trench timber' (42). Thus Lawrence connects the injuries to the natural world with injuries to the body. There is an awful continuity between the trenches and the mines. Mrs Bolton, the working-class woman who nurses Clifford, was widowed when her husband, aged only twenty-eight, 'was killed in an explosion down pit' (80).

Clifford Chatterley's estate, Wragby, has a 'fine old park of oak trees' (13) and a wood with game and gamekeeper, but from the house 'one could see in the distance the chimney of Tevershall pit with its cloud of steam and smoke, and on the damp, hazy distance of the hill the raw straggle of Tevershall village ... rows of wretched, small begrimed brick houses with black slate roofs for lids, sharp angles and wilful blank dreariness' (13). (Here, the novel differs significantly from *Sons and Lovers*, since the coalminers' houses are seen only 'in the distance', rather than from within.) The burning pit-bank emits a 'stench', a 'sulphureous combustion of something under-earth: sulphur, coal, iron or acid', which fills the house; the air smells of 'sulphur, coal, iron, or acid' and 'even on the Christmas roses the smuts settled persistently' (13).

Just as T. S. Eliot realized the linguistic excitement and literary energies that can be generated from a sordid, squalid, urban environment, Lawrence, in *Lady Chatterley's Lover*, makes poetry out of the stuff of modern industry. The 'utter soulless ugliness of the coal-and-iron Midlands' yields, paradoxically, writing of great energy, stylistic toughness and novelty, which poetically captures the violent clashes of the industrial environment, its smells, its sounds, its textures, its awful visual splendours, – 'the rattle-rattle of the screens at the pit, the puff of the winding-engine, the clink-clank of shunting trucks', the 'red blotches' of the furnaces that 'burned and quavered' in the night (13). We are accustomed to descriptions of the bad air, the smogs, or fogs, of the city, whether the yellow fog which, in Eliot's 'The Love Song of J. Alfred Prufrock' (1915), 'rubs its back upon the window-panes', or, in Elizabeth Bowen's *The Death of the Heart* (1938), the 'fog' which invades the houses of London, so that, in daytime, indoors, her young heroine, Portia, 'could hardly see the rest of the room ... it was not like night but like air being ill'.[26] Lawrence's writing reminds us that this pollution also affects small towns and the rural landscape, where the mud is 'black with coal-dust', the miners' cottages are 'blackened', and the skies fill 'with a whole array of smoke plumes and steam'. The 'open, rolling country, where the castles and big houses still dominated, but like ghosts' gives way to a 'tangle of naked railway-lines, and foundries and other "works"' and the soundscape is violent, dominated by the 'huge reverberating clank' of iron, 'huge lorries' which 'shook the earth', and whistles which 'screamed' (155). 'Nature' is not an obvious retreat from modern industry, as modern industry has contaminated the entire ecosystem.

Lawrence believes his critique of industrial modernity puts him at odds with the literary and artistic movements of modernism, which he sees as having a symbiotic relation with new technologies and what he calls the 'mechanical'. Lawrence's fiction, despite its political waverings and plethora of contradictory political identifications, is fairly consistent in its diagnosis of the ills of modernity. In *The Rainbow* and *Lady Chatterley's Lover* we see the same historical 'grand narrative' being presented. The narrator of the latter novel tells us that England's stately homes are abandoned and 'are being pulled down', England's cottages are replaced by 'great plasterings of brick dwellings on the hopeless countryside'. These changes are not haphazard changes in a local environment but, the narrator suggests, representative of a change in epoch, a change in 'meaning' itself. One grand order – the 'organic' – is supplanted by another – the 'mechanical':

> This is history. One England blots out another. The mines had made the halls wealthy. Now they were blotting them out, as they had already blotted out the cottages. The industrial England blots out the agricultural England. One meaning blots out another. The new England blots out the old England. And the continuity is not organic, but mechanical. (156)

Here, Lawrence condenses history into a single opposition: between the agricultural and the industrial, the organic and the mechanical. The impulse is nostalgic and elegiac, but it is unclear whether the elegy is for mere 'nature', or for a preindustrial, hierarchic ordering of society dominated by grand estates. According to this narrative, Lawrence's fiction is 'modern' because it shows a consciousness of this process of change; it is written, as it were, after the old meanings have been blotted out. And its central couple, Connie and Mellors, can show us the way to a new organic continuity.

The relationship between Connie and Mellors is important for several reasons. It involves a reawakening of the body, of the most 'secret places' of life. It involves a rejection of the conventional ordering of industrial society (though their plans at the close of the novel, to run a small farm, are hardly revolutionary). But the relationship is in itself a rejection of social ordering, as it breaks down the boundaries of class. In the process, however, it pushes them away from society; they do not respond to the problems of modernity by bringing about social change, but by fleeing. (Ironically, this gesture of flight – as exemplified by Stephen Dedalus in James Joyce's 1916 *A Portrait of the Artist as a Young Man* – can be seen as a characteristically 'modernist' response.) Connie, wife of the industrialist and aristocrat Clifford Chatterley, forms a relationship with Mellors, a collier's son who has (like Lawrence himself) moved away from his working-class roots. As a boy he won a scholarship to 'Sheffield Grammar School, and learned French and things'; during his career in the army 'some Indian colonel took a fancy to him, and made him a lieutenant'. His reading certainly makes him familiar with the culture, science and politics of modernity: it includes 'books about bolshevist Russia, books of travel, a volume about the atom and the electron, another about the composition of the earth's core, and the causes of earthquakes: then a few novels: then three books on India' (212). Together Connie and Mellors embark on a discovery of nature and primitive sexuality which, despite Lawrence's own loathing of 'self-consciousness', has an intellectual and philosophical genealogy in highly conscious modes of modern thought. They are absolutely Lawrentian in their belief that an exploration of each other's 'secret places' can undo the contamination of the new mechanical and industrial England. Mellors tells Connie, 'An' if I only lived ten minutes, an' stroked thy arse an' got to know it, I should reckon I'd lived *one* life, sees ter! Industrial system or not!' (223).

When Connie dances naked in the rain 'with the eurythmic dance-movements she had learned so long ago in Dresden' (221), when Connie and Mellors make love outside in the rain, when the lovers thread flowers through each other's genitals, we can recognize various social influences in their actions, even as these actions are intended to help them to escape the social. Their actions are flamboyant realizations of the ecological antimodernism of late nineteenth-century English thinkers such as William Morris and John Ruskin, or of Edward Carpenter, who lived with his male lover George Merrill in the Derbyshire village of Broadway, writing books on sex and sexuality as well as poems influenced by Walt Whitman in a little hut by the brook at the end of his garden.[27]

Early in the novel we are casually given some information about events in Connie's youth which anticipate the central events of the novel. At the age of fifteen – in 1910, according to the novel's somewhat dodgy chronology[28] – Connie is 'sent to Dresden ... for music among other things', and there, with her sister Hilda, she lives freely with students, argues with men 'over philosophical and sociological and artistic matters', and tramps 'off to the forests with sturdy youths bearing guitars, twang-twang! – they sang the Wandervogel songs, and they were free' (6). This Dresden sojourn is significant for a number of reasons. Late nineteenth-century Germany witnessed the formation of the *Wandervögel* movement, in which bands of youths would go hiking and tramping. William H. Rollins writes that hundreds of thousands of Germans 'engaged in "life-reform" (*Lebensreform*) activities ... vegetarians, nudists, temperance advocates, clothing- and life-style-reformers'.[29] Various ecological movements began working with the concept of *Heimat*, or 'homeland', and in 1904, in Dresden, these movements were unified with the formation of the *Bund Heimatschutz* (League for Homeland Protection). This movement was an ecological response to the rapid industrialization of Germany in the late nineteenth century, and its intellectual and political ideas drew not only from German Romanticism but also from Morris and Ruskin. Its vision is remarkably similar to Lawrence's and that of his fictional gamekeeper intellectual, Mellors. These movements are difficult to characterize ideologically, as their responses to industrialism vary from a conservative nostalgia to anticapitalist radicalism. One commentator notes that youth movements like the *Wandervögel* responded to the rapid changes of German industrialism with a belief in an 'ideal image of pre-industrial peasant-dominated cultivated landscapes'.[30] A more radical tendency was evident at the 1912 'Second International Heimatschutz Congress' held in Stuttgart; in his opening address Carl Johannes Fuchs, a professor of national economy in Tübingen, claimed, 'The really central problem of the Heimatschutz is simply one and the same in all modern civilized states: it is the struggle against a capitalism that mercilessly destroys what has grown up over time along with its beauty.'[31]

This environmental activism was accompanied by other forms of activity which aimed at developing the individual's relation to nature, such as reforms within education. Connie will have learnt her eurythmic dance movements at the Jaques-Dalcroze Institute at Hellerau, near Dresden, founded by Emile Jaques-Dalcroze in 1910. At the institute, which was internationally renowned, Jaques-Dalcroze's various unconventional pedagogic methods were taught. His teaching used body improvisations and movements in order to learn rhythm and harmony. Different bodily movements correspond to various musical concepts; under the Jaques-Dalcroze method the body itself becomes a musical instrument. The teachings were important not only in education but also in expressionist dance: music, movement and therapy come together in the work of figures such as Rudolf von Laban and Mary Wigman.[32]

At the close of *Lady Chatterley's Lover*, Mellors outlines a programme for reform, many of the elements for which – such as clothing reform, nudism and the use of dance and music – could have come from early twentieth-century German ecological political and cultural movements. Men should wear 'scarlet trousers', 'dance and hop and skip, and sing and swagger and be handsome', and 'learn to be naked and handsome . . . and to sing in a mass and dance the old group dances, and carve the stools they sit on . . . Then they wouldn't need money. And that's the way to solve the industrial problem: train the people to be able to live and live in handsomeness, without needing to spend' (299–300).

Despite Mellors's utopian sentiments, Connie's and Mellors's discovery of nature differs from early twentieth-century environmental movements, in that they discover the wild as an isolated couple, rather than as part of any meaningful community. This movement from an emphasis on the community to an emphasis on the individual can be traced throughout Lawrence's fiction. Although *The White Peacock* (1911), *Sons and Lovers* and *The Rainbow* – his three Nottinghamshire novels written before *Women in Love* – show tensions between individual and community, these novels also give some grounds to hope that these tensions might be resolved. In these three works of fiction, rural life, nature and agriculture evoke what Lawrence calls the 'blood-intimacy' of an organic community.[33] The industrialism of coalmining threatens and works against this organic integrity, but the opposition between healthy rural communities and damaging industrialism leaves an ideal of organicism intact.

In *Women in Love* and in most of his subsequent fiction, however, Lawrence's metaphysic of blood-consciousness no longer attaches itself to or works within any particular community. If it survives at all, it survives only as an unrealized ideal awaiting the discovery of or creation of a place in which it might be lived out; or within an individualism which is suspicious of community; or within sexual relations outside the dominant ordering of marital domesticity and familial life.

In *Women in Love* and in *Lady Chatterley's Lover*, there is no continuity between the romantic couple and a broader canvas of social life, no symbolic linking of marital union with procreation and the institution of the family. In *Women in Love* Rupert Birkin asks Ursula Brangwen to 'wander about for a bit', to 'set off – just towards the distance'; he tells her: 'I should like to go with you – nowhere . . . That's the place to get to – nowhere. One wants to wander away from the world's somewhere, into our own nowheres.'[34] Connie and Mellors have plans that are equally vague. Mellors urges Connie, 'Bit by bit, let's drop the whole industrial life, an' go back' (219). The novel, however, gives no indication of how one might actually lead a preindustrial lifestyle, of *where* it is one should go back to.

It seems that Lawrence was much more skilled at expressing his angry disgust at modernity than he was at suggesting solutions to the problems he identified. In 'A Propos of "Lady Chatterley's Lover"', he talks of our need to 'get back into relation, vivid and nourishing relation to the cosmos and the universe', a process which will take place through 'the ritual of the seasons, with the Drama and the Passion of the soul embodied in procession and dance, this is for the community, an act of men and women, a whole community, in togetherness'.[35] But the individualism, isolation and alienation of his fictional lovers go against any formation of community. Their discovery of sensuality leads to some kind of renewal and regeneration, but this is a regeneration of individuals, not a regeneration of society. It takes a utopian leap of the imagination to see how these stories of lovers cavorting naked in the woods will bring about cultural regeneration, but Lawrence, in *Lady Chatterley's Lover*, is prepared to make that leap. A striking authorial digression in that novel tells us:

> It is the way our sympathy flows and recoils that really determines our lives. And here lies the vast importance of the novel, properly handled. It can inform and lead into new places the flow of our sympathetic consciousness, and it can lead our sympathy away in recoil from things gone dead. Therefore the novel, properly handled, can reveal the most secret places of life: for it is in the *passional* secret places of life, above all, that the tide of spiritual awareness needs to ebb and flow, cleansing and freshening. (101)

Lawrence seems to be saying that reading his own novels will lead our sympathy away from 'things gone dead' into 'new places', and reveal for us 'the most secret places', unleashing a cleansing, freshening, spiritual awareness. What are these secret places, however? When Connie and Mellors are together in the woods, Lawrence tells us that Mellors touches the 'two secret openings to her body', 'her secret places' (223); later, in the scene (notorious among critics and readers of the novel) when the lovers have anal sex, Mellors is described as '[b]urning out the shames, the deepest, oldest shames, in the most secret places' (247). Lawrence's politics here are radical, idiosyncratic and fanciful. One way of understanding them is as a precursor to thinkers such as Herbert Marcuse, whose blend of Marxism and Freudianism connected sexual repression with political and social repression. Marcuse's *Eros and Civilization* (1955) was enormously influential in the 1960s, the decade in which the ban on *Lady Chatterley's Lover* was lifted and the decade in which Lawrence was taken most seriously as a cultural critic. If we consider that it was not until the 1960s that ideas of sexual liberation came to be popularly connected with notions of personal liberation and social regeneration, then Lawrence's novel, for all that it is rooted in the England of the 1920s, is strikingly radical for its own time, even if its belief in the messianic possibilities of sexual liberation now seems touchingly naïve and its vision of sexuality remains seriously discredited by subsequent feminist criticism of Lawrence. If Millett's *Sexual Politics* was the key text which began the decline in his critical reputation, Lawrence nevertheless was himself advancing an early version of sexual politics. And, if he is a key figure in the history of antimodernism, his fictional portraits of alienated individuals trying to find some redemption in the realm of personal relationships and sexuality remain central to modernism, and the way in which modernism is associated with a reimagining of the sexual self.

Notes

1. These essays are all reprinted in D. H. Lawrence, *Study of Thomas Hardy and Other Essays*, ed. Bruce Steele (Cambridge: Cambridge University Press, 1985).
2. For the influence of Nietzsche on Lawrence, see Anne Fernihough, *D. H. Lawrence: Aesthetics and Ideology* (Oxford: Clarendon Press, 1993), and Colin Milton, *Lawrence and Nietzsche: A Study in Influence* (Aberdeen: Aberdeen University Press, 1997).
3. Lawrence, 'John Galsworthy', *Study of Thomas Hardy*, pp. 250–1.
4. Lawrence, 'The Future of the Novel', in *Study of Thomas Hardy*, pp. 151–3.
5. Lawrence, 'The Novel and the Feelings', in *Study of Thomas Hardy*, pp. 204–5.
6. See Daniel Pick, *Faces of Degeneration: A European Disorder, c. 1848–c. 1918* (Cambridge: Cambridge University Press, 1989), and William Greenslade, *Degeneration, Culture and the Novel, 1880–1940* (Cambridge: Cambridge University Press, 1994).
7. Lawrence, 'Future of the Novel', pp. 154–5.
8. D. H. Lawrence, 'Education of the People', in *Phoenix: The Posthumous Papers of D. H. Lawrence*, ed. Edward D. McDonald (London: Heinemann, 1936), pp. 587–665.
9. D. H. Lawrence, *Fantasia of the Unconscious and Psychoanalysis and the Unconscious* (London: Penguin, 1971), pp. 81–2.
10. See Fernihough, *D. H. Lawrence: Aesthetics and Ideology*, p. 1.
11. Terry Eagleton, *The Ideology of the Aesthetic* (Oxford: Blackwell, 1990), p. 15.
12. Lawrence, 'Morality and the Novel', in *Study of Thomas Hardy*, pp. 171, 172.
13. Lawrence, 'The Novel', in *Study of Thomas Hardy*, p. 186.
14. Lawrence, 'Morality and the Novel', p. 175.
15. Lawrence, 'Why the Novel Matters', in *Study of Thomas Hardy*, p. 195.
16. D. H. Lawrence, *Studies in Classic American Literature* (London: Penguin, 1971), p. 8.
17. William Butler Yeats, 'Among School Children', in Yeats, *The Collected Poems of W. B. Yeats* (London: Macmillan, 1982), p. 242.
18. See Peter Brooks, *Reading for the Plot: Intention and Design in Narrative* (Oxford: Clarendon Press, 1984) for an exposition of these concepts in narrative theory.
19. F. R. Leavis, *D. H. Lawrence: Novelist* (London: Chatto and Windus, 1955), p. 18, and Kate Millett, *Sexual Politics* (Garden City, NY: Doubleday, 1970).
20. Lawrence, 'Morality and the Novel', p. 173.
21. Lawrence, 'Future of the Novel', p. 154.
22. T. S. Eliot, 'The Metaphysical Poets', in Eliot, *Selected Essays* (London: Faber and Faber, 1951), pp. 287–8.

23. Lawrence, 'Future of the Novel', p. 155.
24. See Fernihough, *D. H. Lawrence: Aesthetics and Ideology*, pp. 20–33.
25. D. H. Lawrence, *Lady Chatterley's Lover*, ed. Michael Squires (London: Penguin, 1994), p. 5. Further references cited parenthetically.
26. Elizabeth Bowen, *The Death of the Heart* (London: Vintage, 1998), p. 114.
27. See Emile Delavenay, *D. H. Lawrence and Edward Carpenter: A Study in Edwardian Transition* (London: Heinemann, 1971).
28. Michael Squires notes that Connie is eighteen in 1913, twenty-three in 1918, but only twenty-seven in 1924 (explanatory notes to Penguin edition of *Lady Chatterley's Lover*, p. 349).
29. William H. Rollins, *A Greener Vision of Home: Cultural Politics and Environmental Reform in the German Heimatschutz Movement, 1904–1918* (Ann Arbor: University of Michigan Press, 1997), p. 73.
30. Cited in Rollins, *A Greener Vision of Home*, p. 166.
31. *Ibid.*, p. 97.
32. For more on Jaques-Dalcroze, see Irwin Spector, *Rhythm and Life: The Work of Emile Jaques-Dalcroze* (Stuyvesant, NY: Pendragon Press, 1990), and Marie-Laure Bachman, *Dalcroze Today: An Education Through and Into Music* (Oxford: Clarendon Press, 1991).
33. D. H. Lawrence, *The Rainbow*, ed. Mark Kinkead-Weekes (London: Penguin, 1995), p. 10.
34. D. H. Lawrence, *Women in Love*, ed. David Farmer, Lindeth Vasey and John Worthen (London: Penguin, 1995), p. 315.
35. Lawrence, 'A Propos of "Lady Chatterley's Lover"', *Lady Chatterley's Lover*, p. 329.

10

JEREMY HAWTHORN
Joseph Conrad's half-written fictions

On 31 May 1902, the 44-year-old Joseph Conrad (1857–1924) wrote to William Blackwood of Blackwood's publishing house. In a respectful but nonetheless assertive letter, Conrad accepts that he is 'long in [his] development' (his first novel was published in 1895), cites the precedents of William Makepeace Thackeray, Sir Walter Scott and George Eliot, and then distinguishes himself from these illustrious predecessors.

> But these are great names. I don't compare myself with them. I am *modern*, and I would rather recall Wagner the musician and Rodin the Sculptor who both had to starve a little in their day – and Whistler the painter who made Ruskin the critic foam at the mouth with scorn and indignation. They too have arrived. They had to suffer for being 'new'.[1]

'*Modern*'. 'New'. The immediate force of these key words in Conrad's letter is, to put it bluntly, to explain the relative unprofitability of his fiction: in the paragraph prior to the one from which his comments are taken, Conrad refers ironically to the present as 'a time when Sherlock Holmes looms so big'. He was clearly aware that there were different ways in which a writer could be modern or new. On the one hand is the newness associated with technical or formal innovation and originality, and on the other hand the newness established by the use of aspects of social or cultural modernity as fictional subject matter. Both Conrad's lifelong friend John Galsworthy, and H. G. Wells, with whom his friendship was much more up and down, were clearly modern in the second of these two senses, but less so if at all in the first. (Along with Arnold Bennett, they form the trio of 'Edwardians' criticized by Virginia Woolf in her essay 'Mr Bennett and Mrs Brown', 1924, and dubbed 'materialists' in her essay 'Modern Fiction', 1919.)[2]

When Conrad wrote this letter, he had behind him his first two 'Malayan' novels (*Almayer's Folly*, 1895, and *An Outcast of the Islands*, 1896) plus *The Nigger of the 'Narcissus'* (1897) and *Lord Jim* (1900). He had also written and published a number of shorter fictions including 'An Outpost of

Progress' (one of the five tales published in book form as *Tales of Unrest*, 1898), 'Typhoon' (1902), *Youth*, and *Heart of Darkness*. What exactly is Conrad likely to have had in mind when laying claim to modernity so far as these works are concerned?

In his letter Conrad comments specifically on *Youth* and *Heart of Darkness*, first published in *Blackwood's Magazine* in 1898 and 1899 respectively. Of *Heart of Darkness* he comments that 'the interview of the man and the girl' in the last pages of the work 'locks in – as it were – the whole 30000 words of narrative description into one suggestive view of a whole phase of life and makes of that story something quite on another plane than an anecdote of a man who went mad in the Centre of Africa'. Moving to *Youth*, the first of four works in which his narrator-character Charles Marlow appears, he asserts, 'Out of the material of a boys' story I've made *Youth* by the force of the idea expressed in accordance with a strict conception of my method' (417). From these brief comments we can extract some important claims about his significance as a literary artist. Conrad claims that his fiction:

1. presents us with a suggestive view of a whole phase of life rather than an anecdote about one man;
2. involves the requisitioning of popular modes and subject matter (boys' stories) for more serious purposes;
3. is characterized by an insistence on intellectual seriousness (the idea) and artistic technique (method).

In addition, Conrad's mention of 'the Centre of Africa' treats as a matter of course one of the most distinctive features of his fiction. The work of few writers includes a concern with such a range of people and places as does Conrad's. This is not just a matter of geography. Which other novelist provides so many or such detailed fictional accounts of collective physical labour as does Conrad?

The first of the claims listed above seems at first sight simple enough: *Heart of Darkness* is not just an 'anecdote' about 'a man', but a work possessing some sort of unity (of purpose and effect) that is concerned with 'a whole phase of life'. This claim mirrors that made in the earlier (1898) Author's Note to *The Nigger of the 'Narcissus'* in which Conrad writes, 'To snatch in a moment of courage, from the remorseless rush of time, a passing phase of life is only the beginning of the task. The task approached in tenderness and faith is to hold up unquestioningly, without choice and without fear, the rescued fragment before all eyes and in the light of a sincere mood.'[3] In both cases the claims seem to involve, or threaten, a paradox: on the one side the partial, the incomplete (anecdote, passing phase of life, fragment), on the other side unity or totality (whole phase of life). The paradox is arguably typical of literary modernism: on the one hand the fragment, the part, the item plucked from the stream of existence, and on the other a sense of (or yearning for) aesthetic completeness and all-embracingness. The 'fragments I have shored against my ruins' at the end of T.S. Eliot's *The Waste Land* (1922) are representative of a modernist attempt to hold back total chaos and retain some sort of order with the help of bits and pieces salvaged from an earlier, disintegrating totality. As we shall see, fragmentariness and incompleteness are central to the demands that Conrad's works place on the reader.

Popular forms

The letter to Blackwood associates modernity and a concern for artistic value with limited popular appeal. This said, the relationship between modernism and popular forms and genres is a complex and ambiguous one; many modernist artists were interested in popular art and culture, both in the sense of 'of the people' (folk culture) and 'for the people' (commercial or 'mass' culture). The letter mentions 'a boys' story', and from the start of his writing career Conrad makes controlled use of the genre of adventure stories best exemplified by the extremely successful novels of Sir Henry Rider Haggard. But this use is never uncritical, and typically the criticism is so fundamental that it amounts to active subversion. At the start of *Lord Jim*, for example, the narrative links Jim's moral flaws with, among other things, the 'course of light holiday literature' that prompts a vocation for the sea to declare itself to him. This course of reading forms the substance of Jim's early dreams.

> On the lower deck in the babel of two hundred voices he would forget himself, and beforehand live in his mind the sea-life of light literature. He saw himself saving people from sinking ships, cutting away masts in a hurricane, swimming through a surf with a line; or as a lonely castaway, barefooted and half naked, walking on uncovered reefs in search of shellfish to stave off starvation. He confronted savages on tropical shores, quelled mutinies on the high seas, and in a small boat upon the ocean kept up the hearts of despairing men – always an example of devotion to duty, and as unflinching as a hero in a book.[4]

So vivid are these dreams that they prevent Jim from acting: the quoted passage is followed by a scene in which Jim fails to help save some drowning sailors, a scene in which he is unable to admit to, and thus to confront, the fear that lies behind his paralysis. Jim's failure to recognize and master his fear prefigures and prepares the ground for his cowardly abandonment of the *Patna* and its passengers later on in the novel. As Robert Hampson has pointed out, 'in the first part of the novel, [Conrad] produces a _nter-version of the sea-life of romance; in the second part of the novel, in Patusan, he recreates the colonial world of adventure romance'.[5]

If we understand the phrase metaphorically, there are many 'lonely castaways' in Conrad's fiction: Almayer, Willems (*Outcast*), Kurtz, Jim, Carlier and Kayerts ('Outpost'), the literal castaway Decoud (*Nostromo*, 1904), Razumov (*Under Western Eyes*, 1911) and Heyst (*Victory*, 1915). But none of these 'castaways' behaves like the hero of a boy's adventure story. In 'The Secret Sharer' (1910) the outcast Leggatt is a murderer not a hero, and when he asks the narrator-captain to maroon him, the captain protests, 'Maroon you! We are not living in a boys' adventure tale.'[6] In *Heart of Darkness* the progression from Kurtz's noble intentions as summarized in his Report for the International Society for the Suppression of Savage Customs to his scrawled afterword 'Exterminate all of the brutes!' is the progress from the world as seen in a boys' adventure tale to the world Conrad had witnessed at first hand in the Belgian Congo in 1890.

From omniscience to suggestion

Conrad's first two novels from 1895 and 1896 are told by narrators with seemingly unrestricted access to the minds of characters. Their plots unfold in more or less chronological fashion, though both readers and characters are often kept ignorant of important events. With *The Nigger of the 'Narcissus'* we see a move to far greater narrative complexity or even confusion, as the narrating voice is at one time that of a crew member and at another time that of a narrator with access to the unexpressed thoughts and experiences of his characters. Michael Levenson uses Conrad's novella to illustrate some key oppositions in modernism – between, for example, the values of consciousness exemplified by the narrator, and the values of unconsciousness as exemplified by the character Singleton, who is described, paradoxically, as 'meditative and unthinking'.[7]

Following *The Nigger of the 'Narcissus'*, Conrad displays a consistent willingness to vary and to complicate his narrative technique in the interests of his artistic aims. He does not abandon what in traditional terminology was known as an omniscient narrator – both *Nostromo* and *The Secret Agent* (1907) are narrated from a nonpersonified and extradiegetic (that is, 'outside of the world of the story') perspective that allows the reader to be taken into the minds of various characters. In both novels, however, the reader can construct a chronology of events only once most of the novel has been read, and even then the task is not straightforward. Moreover, if these two novels are the technical heirs of the early novels and the omniscient voice of *The Nigger of the 'Narcissus'*, other fictional works can be related to the 'I'/crew member voice of the same novella.

Youth and *Heart of Darkness* are, respectively, the first and second of the four works in which Conrad makes use of his personified narrator Charles Marlow. In both these works the framing of Marlow's narrative by the comments of an also personified but unnamed narrator gives us that distinctively Conradian sense that we are not perceiving the world and its people in unmediated form, but indirectly, either through one reporting consciousness, or through a chain of linked consciousnesses. And this leads us to Conrad's impressionism.

In the works in which use is made of a personified narrator, starting rather hesitantly with *The Nigger of the 'Narcissus'*, Conrad produces the fiction that is best known for its impressionist techniques and effects – though John Peters has argued that all of Conrad's fiction is essentially impressionist in nature.[8] In the Marlow narratives, and in *Under Western Eyes*, which is narrated by the anonymous but personified and intradiegetic ('inside the world of the story') 'Teacher of Languages', the reader is not presented with the world 'as it is', but with the world as it appears to a perceiving and involved consciousness or a chain of several such consciousnesses. Moreover, if such reporting consciousnesses are central to Conrad's impressionism, the effect of their narratives on both their listeners and on us, Conrad's readers, is inseparable from Conrad's use of suggestion.

The frame narrator of *Heart of Darkness* issues an early warning to the reader of the novella:

> The yarns of seamen have a direct simplicity, the whole meaning of which lies within the shell of a cracked nut. But Marlow was not typical (if his propensity to spin yarns be excepted), and to him the meaning of an episode was not inside like a kernel but outside, enveloping the tale which brought it out only as a glow brings out a haze, in the likeness of one of these misty halos that sometimes are made visible by the spectral illumination of moonshine.[9]

At first glance this might suggest a distinctly *un*modernist characteristic – a concern with outer context rather than with that inner, psychological complexity that is often associated with the modernist revolution. But Conrad's and Marlow's 'outside' is not the 'outside' of writers such as Bennett, Galsworthy and Wells. It consists not of solid, concrete objects (not that these are lacking in Conrad's fiction) but of a 'meaning' that is brought out by the tale in the way that moonshine makes a halo of mist visible. Like many key modernist declarations, the passage announces its profundity while tantalizing with its elusiveness. But it does seem to imply that meaning is not self-evident, to be read off from clear contextual information as in the novels of Woolf's 'Edwardians'. It is, rather, to be won through an act of interpretation that is specific to the time, place and perspective of the interpreter: both the frame narrator's remark and Conrad's own comment about his novella make use of visual-optical metaphors: 'suggestive *view*'[10], 'spectral *illumination*'. Conrad's liking for such metaphors is intimately related to his impressionism; a much-quoted claim in Conrad's Note to *The Nigger of the 'Narcissus'* is, 'My task which I am trying to achieve is, by the power of the written word, to make you hear, to make you feel – it is, before all, to make you *see!*' (130).

Ian Watt has coined the phrase 'delayed decoding' to describe one particular favoured impressionistic technique of Conrad's. Watt's example of this technique is the scene in *Heart of Darkness* in which Marlow, travelling upriver in charge of his steamer, believes that '[s]ticks, little sticks, were flying about' – until it dawns on him (and the reader) that the sticks are actually '[a]rrows, by Jove! We were being shot at!'.[11]

In many ways, however, Conrad's use of suggestion is more interesting than his use of impressionist techniques such as delayed decoding. In the 'sticks' passage the reader and Marlow do eventually share a knowledge of 'what really happened'. But where suggestion is used, the reader is left without any final confirmation of his or her responses. Throughout Conrad's letters and essays, we find a succession of comments stressing the fundamental importance of literary suggestion. In a letter to Hugh Clifford written on 9 October 1899, for example, Conrad makes the following pronouncement on a piece of Clifford's prose:

> The word *frightened* is fatal. It seems as if it had been written withought [*sic*] any thought at all. It takes away all sense of reality – for if you read the sentence *in its place on the page* You will see that the word *frightened* (or indeed any word of the sort) is inadequate to express the true state of that man's mind. No word is adequate. The imagination of the reader should be left free to arouse his feeling. (*Letters* II 201)

Almost exactly eleven years later, in October 1910, Conrad writes to Helen Sanderson: 'In letters suggestiveness itself – a great quality – must be obtained by precise expression . . . To awaken a responsive feeling something exact must be said.'[12] If we take a classic textual crux from *Heart of Darkness* – Kurtz's dying ejaculation, 'The horror! The horror!' – we may have to accept that attempts to fix exactly what the words mean are doomed to failure. The misty meaning must be made visible by the spectral illumination of our varied readings.

The creative reader

For Conrad, the suggestiveness of his fiction is premised upon readers who are prepared to exercise their creativity. In a letter written to R. B. Cunninghame Graham at the very start of his writing career, on 5 August

1897, he declares, 'To know that *You* could read me is good news indeed – for one writes only half the book; the other half is with the reader.'[13] The sentiment is by no means original: the opening paragraph of the eleventh chapter of the second volume of Laurence Sterne's *The Life and Opinions of Tristram Shandy, Gentleman* (1759–67) advances the claim that 'the truest respect which you can pay to the reader's understanding, is to halve this matter amicably, and leave him something to imagine'.[14] Although Conrad had certainly read some eighteenth-century British novels (by Tobias Smollett, for example), there is no evidence that he had read *Tristram Shandy*. Nevertheless, Sterne's proto-modernist commitment to a creative reader clearly chimes well with the spirit of early modernism; it is echoed not just by Conrad, but by his friend Henry James who, in his Preface to the 1908 New York edition of *The Turn of the Screw* explains, 'Make him [the reader] *think* the evil, make him think it for himself, and you are released from weak specifications.'[15] There is a striking moment towards the end of Conrad's early tale 'Karain' (1897) when the narrator is describing his parting from the title-character: 'He [Karain] stood up in the boat, lifted up both his arms, then pointed to the infallible charm. We cheered again; and the Malays in the boats stared – very much puzzled and impressed. I wonder what they thought; what he thought … what the reader thinks?'[16] The ellipsis is Conrad's, and it is followed by the surprising and direct appeal to the reader. Conrad has a great liking for ellipses, and they typically require the reader to provide a missing element. But here the ellipsis indicates not just missing information but also a violent shift of perspective. In spite of the use of the past tense, the narrator could not have wondered what the reader thought when saying goodbye to Karain: this is what he thinks in the 'now' of the narrative.

If the novelist has to write half-books, he or she must practise the virtue that Marlow has to exercise in the heart of Africa: restraint. A letter of Conrad's to the *New York Times* 'Saturday Review', published on 25 August 1901, includes the revealing claim, 'Fiction, at the point of development at which it has arrived, demands from the writer a spirit of scrupulous abnegation' (*Letters* II 348). Five years later, James Joyce was famously to claim of the as-yet unpublished *Dubliners* (minus 'The Dead'), 'I have written it for the most part in a style of scrupulous meanness.'[17] Scrupulous abnegation, scrupulous meanness: early literary modernism involves self-denial and restraint from the novelist; it indeed requires that he or she hold back from the provision of comprehensive information in order to force the reader to complement the labour of the author.

The gaps left to be filled in rarely involve simple facts. The nearest that Conrad comes to this is perhaps in a tale that he himself described in a letter as a 'trick' – 'Il Conde' (1908) (*Letters* IV 104). It was a trick that took in readers for more than sixty years, as it was only in the 1970s that critics pointed out that the Count of the title was not a saintly old man who suffered the horrible indignity of being robbed at knifepoint, but an old roué cruising for sex who is robbed by a young man he attempts to pick up.[18] In the Author's Note written for the volume in which 'Il Conde' was collected, Conrad writes, 'All I can say is that the personality of the narrator [i.e. the Count, not the narrator of the tale] was extremely suggestive quite apart from the story he was telling me.'[19] Conrad seems clearly to be playing with the reader here, encouraging him or her to look for meanings that may not be immediately apparent (the *OED* gives 'apparently to suggest something indecent' as one euphemistic meaning of 'suggestive').

His young friend and protégé Richard Curle infuriated the novelist when, using his knowledge of Conrad's personal history, he specified the location of the port to which the shipwrecked sailors in *Youth* sail. In a letter dated 24 April 1922, Conrad exploded, 'Didn't it ever occur to you, my dear Curle, that I knew what I was doing in leaving the facts of my life and even my tales in the background? Explicitness, my dear fellow, is fatal to the glamour of all artistic work, robbing it of all suggestiveness, destroying all illusion.' He later elaborates, 'The paragraph you quote of the East meeting the narrator is all right in itself; whereas directly it's connected with Mintok it becomes nothing at all. Mintok is a damned hole without any beach and without any glamour.'[20] The protest raises troubling questions for students and teachers using editions of *Heart of Darkness* which dutifully map out the history of the Belgian Congo. We must at least weigh the possibility that some aspects of what we know as scholarly research are in tension with the artistic aims of a writer such as Conrad.

From method to idea

In Conrad's major fiction a technique predicated on omission and incompleteness produces responses in the reader that mirror a more general human response to what he seems to have perceived as the existential condition of humankind. In another much-quoted comment, in the 'Familiar Preface' to *A Personal Record* (1908–9), Conrad notes, 'Those who read me know my conviction that the world, the temporal world, rests on a few very simple ideas; so simple that they must be as old as the hills. It rests notably, among others, on the idea of Fidelity.'[21] But strictly speaking, fidelity, with or without a capital letter, is not so much an idea as a virtue or a standard of conduct. And it is a standard of conduct that guides those who cannot plan their actions on the basis of total knowledge. It is not hard to see here a parallel between the always-ignorant human being, covering the gaps in his or her knowledge with the guide to correct conduct provided by a capitalized Fidelity, and the struggling reader who has to respond to hints and suggestions without receiving any final confirmation that his or her response is correct.

In Conrad's 'A Smile of Fortune' (1911), for example, the captain-narrator meets the impenetrable ship-chandler Alfred Jacobus who offers to provide the captain with the sacks that he desperately needs for his cargo, persuades him to buy a consignment of potatoes, and introduces him to his daughter Alice. The captain never discovers whether Jacobus is using the promise of the sacks in an attempt to marry him off to his daughter, or is using the lure of his daughter to ensnare the captain into buying the overpriced potatoes. The reader, too, is never able finally to confirm which of these alternatives (or both, or neither) is the case.

More profoundly, in *Lord Jim* Conrad's narrator Marlow draws pointed attention to the fact that he can never see Jim clearly – he is always in a mist or under a cloud. To a certain extent the title-character of Conrad's novel is like the title-character of Virginia Woolf's later novel *Jacob's Room* (1922): a partly empty space around whom more well-defined characters move, and in relation to whom they are defined. Jim and Jacob exemplify that central modernist belief in – or fear of – the 'unknowableness' of other people, but they may have more in common than this. Their blankness may also result in part from the impossibility of stating openly that they are the object of homoerotic desire, and a number of recent critics of Conrad have paid close attention to the interrogation – and subsequent blurring – of fixed gender characteristics in what had previously been considered archetypically masculine fictions. Geoffrey Galt Harpham claims that in the Marlow of *Heart of Darkness* and *Lord Jim*, 'Conrad had inaugurated British literary modernism in part by exploring a masculine way of being that "included" the feminine'.[22]

Harpham also suggests that the novelist blurs other distinctions and oppositions, arguing that after Conrad 'Western literature begins to think of itself as deracinated, as properly belonging not to a national tradition but to a more comprehensively conceived community that can best be represented by the exile or émigré' (184). Cultural exile is certainly no bad training for those concerned to explore and depict existential exile. Writing to his friend Cunninghame Graham on 20 December 1897, Conrad takes issue with Graham's optimistic social vision in another much-quoted conceit.

There is a – let us say – a machine. It evolved itself (I am severely scientific) out of a chaos of scraps of iron and behold! – it knits. I am horrified at the horrible work and stand appalled. I feel it ought to embroider – but it goes on knitting. You come and say: 'this is all right; it's only a question of the right kind of oil.

Let us use this – for instance – celestial oil and the machine shall embroider a most beautiful design in purple and gold.' Will it? Alas no. You cannot by any special lubrication make embroidery with a knitting machine. (*Letters* I 425)

Conrad concludes, 'It knits us in and it knits us out.' The vision is not so very far removed from Franz Kafka's penal colony in 'In the Penal Colony' (1919), with its scriptive torture-machine, and in spite of their many and major differences these two great modernists share a tragic sense of the need to affirm a belief in moral conduct while possessing no confidence in its efficacy. We find another parallel in the work of a third great modernist novelist. Woolf's *The Waves* (1931) ends with Bernard's defiant, 'Against you I will fling myself, unvanquished and unyielding, O Death!', followed by the final line of the novel: '*The waves broke on the shore.*' Conrad the seaman knew that the waves – literal or metaphorical – were stronger than any human being. But he shared Woolf's heroic commitment to a human effort that, like her, he believed incapable of altering the tragic lot of humankind.

Global systems, individual solitude

By the time of the publication of *Nostromo* in 1904, the settings of Conrad's fictional works had included the different cultures of the Malay Archipelago, London, Brittany, Africa and South America, along with life on ships sailing between Bombay and London and in the China seas. He was to go on to set stories in Russia and Geneva, and (without naming them) in Australia and Mauritius. But what distinguishes Conrad's fiction from that of his predecessors (and of many of his contemporaries and successors) is not the range of different geographical settings so much as his understanding of that process to which we now give the comfortably neutral name of globalization – that binding together of different lands and peoples by global economic and political systems more accurately, if less comfortably, termed imperialism.

Already in Conrad's first published novel *Almayer's Folly*, we find the following wistfully ironic comment: 'The deliberations conducted in London have a far reaching importance; and so, the decision issued from the fog-veiled offices of the Borneo Co. darkened for Almayer the brilliant sunshine of the Tropics and added another drop of bitterness to the cup of his disenchantments.'[23] From the very beginning of his writing career, Conrad saw the world in a process of transformation from a number of independent and autonomous economic units to a network of different cultural groups increasingly in the power of global economic and political systems controlled from Europe and North America. The almost Kafkaesque alienation of many Conradian heroes is directly related to this perception of the world as governed by political and economic units and forces that are impersonal and morally neutral – and thus *inhuman*. Towards the end of *Nostromo*, the desperate Mrs Gould asks Dr Monygham if there is to be no peace – presumably for Costaguana and its people. His answer shows how Conrad could adapt his vision of the heartless knitting machine to the political and economic working of imperialism. "'No!' interrupted the doctor. "There is no peace and no rest in the development of material interests. They have their law, and their justice. But it is founded on expediency, and is inhuman; it is without rectitude, without the continuity and the force that can be found only in a moral principle."'[24] Conrad's great political novels from *Heart of Darkness* through *Nostromo* and *The Secret Agent* to *Under Western Eyes* depict a world increasingly dominated by processes that have a logic that in the most profound of senses is neither human nor moral.

It is in *Nostromo* that Conrad will subject the growth of imperialism to the most sustained analytical scrutiny, but his fiction is consistently concerned to draw the reader's attention to the global reach of European and North American economic and political power. One of the reasons why 'Lord' Jim cannot escape to a place where no one knows of his disgrace is that there are no longer any places in which to hide. When at the end of Part First of *Under Western Eyes* Razumov tells his inquisitor Mikulin that he intends to 'retire', Mikulin's soft answer is chilling in its unanswerability: 'Where to?'[25] Mikulin knows, and Razumov knows – just as Conrad and his readers know – that there is nowhere truly to retire to in the modern world. When in *Victory* Axel Heyst withdraws to his abandoned island with the rescued Lena, they are not alone for long. Accompanied by his two disreputable partners, 'Mr Jones' bursts in on their seclusion, telling Heyst, 'I am the world itself, come to pay you a visit.'[26]

It may seem odd that the vision that terrifies Conrad's heroes beyond any other – the prospect of a total separation from other people – should be one that his fiction constantly suggests is impossible to achieve because sooner or later the world will always pay a visit. But the solitude and loneliness that terrify both Conrad and his characters are not of a sort that can be prevented by the company of other human beings. Two of Conrad's most lonely characters – Verloc in *The Secret Agent* and Razumov in *Under Western Eyes* – are secret agents in a literal sense, and the secret agent is always alone, even when surrounded by others. A crucial aspect of Conrad's modernity is his recognition that the modern world puts pressure on us all to be secret agents. Conrad's *personal* loneliness and fear of solitude are certainly linked to the fact of his exile: the son of a Polish nationalist, writing in English and living far from a Polish nation that did not even enjoy statehood. In a literal sense, being an alien, Conrad experienced alienation. But the alienation of so very many of his characters is one that is linked to the alienating forces of modernity that engage those who never leave the country of their birth. 'Karain' ends with a depiction of the Englishman Jackson's profound sense of unreality in the midst of other people. He experiences this sense of non-belonging, however, not in the Malay Archipelago, where the story opens, but in his native England, in the Strand in the heart of London:

> The whole length of the street, deep as a well and narrow like a corridor, was full of a sombre and ceaseless stir ... Innumerable eyes stared straight in front, feet moved hurriedly, blank faces flowed, arms swung. Over all, a narrow ragged strip of smoky sky wound about between the high roofs, extended and motionless, like a soiled streamer flying above the rout of a mob.[27]

From the early, 'exotic' part of the story and its romantic, nineteenth-century, boy's-story milieu, suddenly we are transported not merely to the heart of London but to the heart of the modernist vision and perhaps, too, to the heart of darkness. The lost, blank faces of a painting by Edvard Munch, Eliot's crowd flowing over London bridge – here is the modernist nightmare of mechanized, alienated, lost souls in its most chilling form. And it is chilling because it forces us to recognize the uncanny, the alien, the *unheimlich* (literally 'unhomely') not in a foreign setting, but in the very place where we should feel least alone and most at home.

If one of the classic moments in the modernist novel occurs at the start of Kafka's *The Trial* (1925) when the knock at the door announces that K's home and life are about to be invaded by the representatives of a system he cannot understand, in Conrad's *Under Western Eyes* the student Razumov does not even have the benefit of a knock at the door. Returning home to his student room, he finds it already occupied by a political assassin who will place Razumov at the mercy of opposed subversive and repressive movements for which he has no personal sympathy. This mixture of global control and local blindness and disempowerment is fundamental to Conrad's modernist vision: the world will, sooner or later, come to visit, but before it does so the individual is blithely ignorant of what to expect. If Conrad's reader often feels confused and abandoned, the feeling models a more general alienation engendered in the hearts and lives of its subjects by a modern world controlled by increasingly impersonal forces. If Conrad's fictions are difficult, this may remind us – may be meant to remind us – that so, too, is modern life.

Notes

1. Joseph Conrad, *The Collected Letters of Joseph Conrad*, 8 vols., *Volume II: 1898–1902*, ed. Frederick R. Karl and Laurence Davies (Cambridge: Cambridge University Press, 1986), p. 418. Further references cited parenthetically.

2. Virginia Woolf, 'Mr Bennett and Mrs Brown', in Peter Faulkner (ed.), *A Modernist Reader: Modernism in England 1910–1930* (London: Batsford, 1986), and 'Modern Fiction', in Woolf, *The Common Reader: First Series*, ed. Andrew McNeillie (London: Hogarth Press, 1984), pp. 147–8.

3. Joseph Conrad, *The Nigger of the 'Narcissus'*, ed. Allan Simmons (London: J. M. Dent, 1997), p. 130. Further references cited parenthetically.

4. Joseph Conrad, *Lord Jim: A Tale*, ed. Jacques Berthoud (Oxford: Oxford University Press, 2002), p. 5.

5. Robert Hampson, *Cross-Cultural Encounters in Joseph Conrad's Malay Fiction* (Basingstoke: Palgrave Macmillan, 2000), p. 129.

6. Joseph Conrad, *'Twixt Land and Sea: Three Tales* (London: J. M. Dent, 1947), p. 131.

7. Michael H. Levenson, *A Genealogy of Modernism: A Study of English Literary Doctrine 1908–1922* (Cambridge: Cambridge University Press, 1984), pp. 32–3.

8. John G. Peters, *Conrad and Impressionism* (Cambridge: Cambridge University Press, 2001), pp. 32–3.

9. Joseph Conrad, *Heart of Darkness and Other Tales*, ed. Cedric Watts (Oxford: Oxford University Press, 2002), p. 105.

10. Conrad, *Collected Letters, Volume III: 1903–1908*, ed. Karl and Davies, (1983), p. 417.

11. Ian Watt, *Conrad in the Nineteenth Century* (London: Chatto and Windus, 1980), pp. 175–8.

12. Conrad, *Collected Letters, Volume IV: 1908–1911*, ed. Karl and Davies (1983), p. 376.

13. Conrad, *Collected Letters, Volume I: 1861–1897*, ed. Karl and Davies (1983), p. 370.

14. Laurence Sterne, *The Life and Opinions of Tristram Shandy, Gentleman*, ed. Melvyn New and Joan New (London: Penguin 1997), p. 88.

15. The Preface is reprinted in part in Henry James, *The Turn of the Screw*, eds. Deborah Esch and Jonathan Warren, 2nd edn (New York: Norton, 1999), pp. 123–9 (p. 128).

16. Joseph Conrad, 'Karain', in Conrad, *Heart of Darkness and Other Tales*, ed. Watts, pp. 64–5.

17. James Joyce to Grant Richards, 5 May 1906, in Joyce, *Letters of James Joyce*, 3 vols., ed. Stuart Gilbert and Richard Ellmann (New York: Viking, 1957–66), vol. II, p. 132.

18. See, for example, Douglas A. Hughes, 'Conrad's "Il Conde": "A Deucedly Queer Story"', *Conradiana* 7 (1975), pp. 17–25.

19. Joseph Conrad, *A Set of Six* (London: J. M. Dent, 1954), p. v.

20. Joseph Conrad, *Collected Letters Volume VII: 1920–1922*, ed. Davies and J. H. Stape (2005), p. 457.

21. Joseph Conrad, *A Personal Record: Some Reminiscences* (London: J. M. Dent, 1946), p. xix.

22. Geoffrey Galt Harpham, *One of Us: The Mastery of Joseph Conrad* (Chicago: University of Chicago Press, 1996), p. 131. Further references cited parenthetically.

23. Joseph Conrad, *Almayer's Folly: A Story of an Eastern River*, ed. Floyd Eugene Eddleman and David Leon Higdon (Cambridge: Cambridge University Press, 1994), p. 28.

24. Joseph Conrad, *Nostromo: A Tale of the Seaboard*, ed. Keith Carabine (Oxford: Oxford University Press, 1984), p. 511.

25. Joseph Conrad, *Under Western Eyes*, ed. Jeremy Hawthorn (Oxford: Oxford University Press, 2003), p. 74.

26. Joseph Conrad, *Victory: An Island Tale*, ed. Mara Kalnins (Oxford: Oxford University Press, 2004), p. 285.

27. Conrad, 'Karain', in *Heart of Darkness*, p. 66.

I I

DEBORAH PARSONS

Djuna Barnes: melancholic modernism

'I believe this may be our last chance to do something remarkable in the way of imaginative literature,' T. S. Eliot declared, when recommending Djuna Barnes's (1892–1982) *Nightwood* (1936) for publication with Faber and Faber in 1935.[1] Initial readers, while acknowledging the virtuosity of the novel's style, were yet largely bemused by the obscurity of its 'plot' and discomforted by a pervasive overtone of the profane and the sacrilegious. In his introductory Preface for the American edition the following year, Eliot set about elucidating the structure and method of the novel, downplaying its more controversial subject matter and forestalling charges of unreadability. *Nightwood*, he explained, 'demands something of the reader that the ordinary novel-reader is not prepared to give', because 'it is so good a novel that only sensibilities trained on poetry can wholly appreciate it'.[2] To understand the novel as a masterpiece of modern art, in other words, the reader should be prepared to suspend any expectation of conventional linear narrative and recognize that it is constructed according to the formalist principles of modern poetry. *Nightwood* having been claimed by Eliot as the final expression of high modernism, American reviewers followed his lead with palpable relief, the *Brooklyn Eagle* going so far as to recommend it as 'an excellent companion piece for "The Waste Land"'.[3]

A majority of readers since then, however, have struggled to reconcile the canonizing implications of Eliot's Preface with aspects of the text itself that strain against such easy assimilation. Barnes's arcane and figural language; her flamboyantly ornamental use of metaphorical and allegorical techniques; her eccentric characters, caught in attitudes of restless, ponderous despair; and her evocation of the melancholia of love and loss and the desperate confession of sin and shame, seem far removed from Ezra Pound's advocacy of 'straight talk' or Eliot's own argument for the disciplinary logic of the modern novel. Yet in describing *Nightwood* as the 'great achievement of a style', and drawing attention to 'the beauty of [its] phrasing, the brilliance of wit and characterization, and a quality of horror and doom very nearly related to that of Elizabethan tragedy', Eliot himself acknowledges an at once technically mannered and emotionally excessive quality to Barnes's writing in which its very exaggeration of modernist form and themes fore-shadows their end ('Preface' xiv). Through the overstatement of its own artistry, this singularly stylish text exposes the myth of modernism's claim to aesthetic mastery over the chaos of history.

Djuna Barnes was born in 1892 in Cornwall-on-Hudson, New York State. Her upbringing (in a household that consisted of her grandmother Zadel, her dilettante father Wald, his wife Elizabeth *and* his mistress and their numer-ous offspring) was unorthodox, and she would always remember her child-hood with pain, revisiting the trauma of her father's philosophy of polygamy in both her first novel *Ryder* (1928) and her late dramatic work *The Antiphon* (1958). In 1912 a need for family economies resulted in the enforced removal of Elizabeth and her children to New York, where Barnes studied briefly at the revolutionary liberal arts college the Pratt Institute and then the Art Students League before embarking on a career as a journalist and illustrator. Regular posts at the *Brooklyn Daily Eagle* and *New York Press* proved her to be an original and sardonic commentator on New York life, and she was soon a sought-after and well-paid freelancer, contributing feature articles and interviews to all the city's leading news-papers and glossies. At the same time, however, she was establishing herself as a prominent figure within the Greenwich Village bohemia of the day, furnishing its avant-garde literary journals and magazines with poetry, prose, drawings and all but unperformable drama that mimicked the Decadent style and themes of the 1890s. In 1921 she was offered a lucrative position as a correspondent for the prestigious *McCall's* magazine in Paris. This was the city that she would make home, literally for the next decade and spiritually for the rest of her life, and it was here that she would meet two of the biggest influences on her art: Thelma Wood, with whom she embarked on a passionate yet stormy love affair, and James Joyce, whom she inter-viewed for *Vanity Fair* a month after the publication of *Ulysses* in 1922 and who would become a long-term friend and drinking partner. 'I hope you will suffer prettily in Paris,' a young girl tells Barnes in an account of her first impressions of the French capital. She would, but she would also mature as a writer.[4]

Barnes was already lauded for her witty parodies of aestheticist ennui when she joined the Parisian expatriate community in the early 1920s – 'a legendary personality that has dominated the intellectual night-life of Europe for a century is in town' Ernest Hemingway commented sarcastically in an editorial for the *transatlantic review* – but she had little substantial work to her name other than a pamphlet of illustrated poems, *A Book of Repulsive*

Women (1915), and a collection of her short stories, *A Book* (1923). When she read *Ulysses* (1922), the novel about which the literary world was currently agog, she announced, 'I shall never write another line. Who has the nerve to after this?'[5] Yet her long and extraordinary talks with Joyce – 'of rivers and of religion ... of women ... of Ibsen, of Strindberg, Shakespeare ... of death, of rats, of horses, the sea; languages, climates and offerings. Of artists and of Ireland', as she recalls in her *Vanity Fair* interview – would seem to have proved the artistic stimulus that she needed.[6] The result was *Ryder* (1928), an autobiographical family saga written not from her familiar pose of decadent ennui but instead in the robust tones of Geoffrey Chaucer, Laurence Sterne, Henry Fielding and the King James Bible. Unconventional even by contemporary standards, Barnes described it as a 'female *Tom Jones*', her own attempt at a comic-epic novel that significantly exchanges Joyce's use of the classical Homeric genre for its parody in the writing of the English Restoration.[7] Boni & Liveright, the American publisher from which Barnes had already secured an agreement on the novel when it published *A Book*, was wary but finally honoured publication. With the dubious benefit of intervention by the New York Post Office, which demanded the expurgation of words, passages and illustrations referring most explicitly to bodily fluids and religious blasphemy, *Ryder* in fact briefly became a bestseller and Barnes's writing was lauded as comparable in its virtuosity and wit with that of Joyce.

After the success of the 1920s, for Barnes the 1930s were marked by cumulative trauma: separation from Thelma Wood, an affair with the young writer Charles Henri Ford, severe appendicitis, an abortion, and the physical toll of increasingly heavy drinking, which would eventually result in breakdown and an enforced return to New York in 1940. It was within this context that *Nightwood* was conceived, much of the first draft being written at Hayford Hall, the English mansion in Dartmoor rented by American art patron Peggy Guggenheim in the summers of 1932 and 1933. 'I wrote it you must remember', she recalled in a letter to fellow guest Emily Coleman, 'when I did not know whether Thelma would come back to me or not ... whether I could live with her again or not; in that turmoil of Charles and Morocco, sickness, Hayford Hall – everything, then the end here in New York ... when I realised that being here was death (and is) for me.'[8] The company at Hayford Hall, which also included the writer Antonia White, whose first novel *Frost in May* appeared in 1933, and the critics John Holms and Edwin Muir, made for an environment of supportive aesthetic intensity and astute if often brutal commentary on both the high points and the faults of Barnes's manuscript. Holms, the charismatic centre of the group, compared it to Robert Burton's *Anatomy of Melancholy* (1621), the extraordinary compendium, at once treatise and confessional narrative, of the symptoms and treatment of depression caused by love, jealousy and religious guilt that was undergoing something of a renaissance amid a generation fluent in the more popularized concepts of psychoanalysis.[9] Indeed, Floyd Dell, one of Barnes's associates from her years in Greenwich Village, described Burton in his New York translation of the *Anatomy* in 1927 as a precursor of Sigmund Freud, his interests 'identical with that of our great modern analyst of the psyche'.[10]

Burton's account, told through the narrative persona of Democritus Jr, begins with the Fall of Man, and his condemnation by God's wrath to misery, fear and death. The harsh irony of life is that it ends only in death, in punishment of the original sin for which man must submit to God's mercy. While Freud's definition in his essay 'Mourning and Melancholia' (1917), translated into English in 1925, is both secular and more clinical, the traits of self-revulsion and self-negation that he identifies with the melancholic disposition reiterate those outlined by Burton in 1621. Freud conceptualizes melancholia as a pathological reaction to loss, distinguished from mourning in that it is focused not on the actual object of that loss but in on the self. The melancholic, Freud argues, suffers 'an impoverishment of his ego on a grand scale', marked by an insistent self-exposure and self-criticism of everything in himself that he deems morally reprehensible. Thus he

> represents his ego to us as worthless, incapable of any achievement and morally despicable; he reproaches himself, vilifies himself and expects to be cast out and punished. He abases himself before everyone and commiserates with his own relatives for being connected with anyone so unworthy. He is not of the opinion that a change has taken place in him, but extends his self-criticism back over the past; he declares that he was never any better.[11]

Barnes, who always claimed that the *Anatomy* was her favourite book, was a self-professed melancholic. 'Having life is the greatest horror,' she wrote to her mother, 'I cannot think of it as a "merry, gay & joyous thing, just to be alive" – it seems to me monstrous, obscene & still with the most obscene trick at the end.'[12] Melancholia, for both Burton and Freud, is symptomatic of a deviation from the norm of reason, and both thus make rational explanation and understanding the basis of its cure. Barnes was highly ambivalent towards the explanatory narratives of psychoanalysis, however, seemingly agreeing with Joyce's comment to her that it was 'neither more nor less than blackmail' ('James Joyce' 65). The extravagant multiplicity of fragmentary references, quotations and plagiarisms with which Burton piles up his study, by contrast, serve to overwhelm explanation, and while ostensibly advocating reason, restraint and conformity to God's word as the ideal means for avoiding melancholy, Democritus Jr's ultimately more sanguine strategy, as befitting the namesake of the 'laughing philosopher', is to look upon the state of man with ridicule, and to counter melancholy with humour. In *Ryder* Barnes had similarly met the bleakness of human existence with resilient, earthy frivolity. The theme, form and writing of *Nightwood*, however, would be increasingly dominated by the melancholic muse. 'Melancholia, melancholia, it rides me like a bucking mare,' Barnes would write to Coleman.[13] There is certainly no suggestion of an aloof and objective paring of modernist fingernails (see page xxx) in her accounts of her authorship. 'It lies here on the floor, and I circle around it like the murderess about the body,' she said of her attempts to revise the manuscript in 1935. 'I seem to have no will power, only an awful despair.'[14]

Dedicated to Guggenheim and Holms, *Nightwood* was the fruit of this far from impersonal aesthetic; a metaphysical exploration of man's condemnation to knowledge of sin, shame and death since the Fall, and of his desperate search for spiritual salvation amid the dark terror that thus constitutes postlapsarian existence, mapped on to the increasingly exclusionary politics of contemporary history and the personal story of melancholic loss with which Barnes perceived her relationship with Wood. What there is of conventional 'plot' in the novel begins in 1880, with the death of an Austrian baroness shortly after giving birth to her Jewish son. Reintroduced in his thirties, Felix Volkbein hides the shame of his heritage beneath a fake coat of arms, making obeisance to the Austria of the Habsburg dynasty. As if unable to erase an instinctive racial memory, however, he drifts around urban Europe in the company of a motley collection of actors and circus performers, for whom 'the immense disqualification of the public' (11) is similarly a way of life. Attending a bedside with cross-dressing, quack gynaecologist Dr Matthew-Mighty-grain-of-salt-Dante-O'Connor, he meets and marries the beautiful and enigmatic Robin Vote, with the intention that through her young American blood 'she might bear sons who would recognize and honour the past' (40) and in so doing consolidate his counterfeit lineage. Robin is soon driven to restless wandering around the ancient capitals of Europe, seeking escape from some weight of which she is only half-consciously aware. She finally gives birth to a weak and mentally backward child and disappears, turning up some time later in Paris in the company of Nora Flood, an American heiress. While dependent on the security of Nora's love, Robin is yet driven from its consuming intensity into drunken dissipation and promiscuity. When she finally leaves for another woman, Jenny Petheridge, Nora appeals despairingly to O'Connor for an explanation of her loss, and his long part-comic/part-melancholic monologues on the literal and metaphorical 'night-world' that Robin inhabits constitute most of the second half of the book. Narrative action is resumed only in the notorious final chapter, in which Nora, who has returned to the USA, is drawn by the barking of her dog to a chapel on her New England estate, where she finds Robin sinking on all fours before the cowering animal in front of the altar.

'I have a narrative but you will be put to it to find it' (87), the loquacious O'Connor tells Nora, a statement that might serve as a self-reflexive comment on *Nightwood* itself. '[T]hey all say that it is not a novel,' Barnes wrote in exasperation to Coleman as the manuscript was rejected by one literary editor after another, 'that there is no continuity of life in it, only high spots and poetry – that I do not give anyone an idea what the persons wore, ate or how they opened and closed doors, how they earned a living or how they took off their shoes and put on their hats. God knows I don't.'[15] Even T. R. Smith at Boni & Liveright, the far from conservative publisher which had brought out *Ryder*, was unconvinced. The manuscript contained 'much brilliant writing', Smith acknowledged, but he continued with regret that after the opening pages he thought it collapsed into 'a rambling, obscure, complicated account of what the average reader will consider "God only knows"'.[16] It was Muir who finally suggested offering it to Eliot. Of anyone, Coleman wrote to Barnes optimistically, 'Eliot is the man who <u>might</u> risk it.'[17] After a selection of passages failed to draw much response, Coleman sent him a copy of the full manuscript, even marking passages that she thought he would particularly like, accompanied by a carefully crafted letter in which she strategically outlined its formal weaknesses at the same time as highlighting its metaphysical questioning. 'Perhaps you will conclude that the book is worthless – as a novel, or whatever it was intended to be,' she finished, '[b]ut I think you will agree with me that it contains as extraordinary writing as has been done in our time: that the human truths revealed in it (the light it sheds on the relations of good and evil, in this life) make it a document which absolutely must be published.'[18] Reading the novel as a whole, Eliot did agree, with the proviso that Barnes submit to the omission or toning down of some of its more profane allusions and language, which he expected would incite censorship.

Although Barnes's refusal of any obligation to provide details of character, time or place seems to echo the self-definition of the modern novel in the 1920s, her interest is in the soul and the passions rather than the consciousness, and her manner of characterization is allegorical rather than mimetic. There is no privileged insight into the individual mind in *Nightwood*, none of the focus on the 'stream of consciousness', for example, that characterized the narrative method of Virginia Woolf, Dorothy Richardson or the early Joyce. For Barnes's concern is not with the capturing of life as it is directly experienced by the mind, an essentially realist principle, and she refuses even her chief protagonists the memory of and reflection upon the kind of tangible personal past that so constitutes selfhood for Woolf and Richardson. Her method is figural rather than impressionistic, and her narrative style obsessively confessional rather than structured according to the objective principle of Jamesian 'point of view'. Felix, Nora and Jenny, for example, are depicted through patterns of associated imagery that serve to emphasize the role of each as representative of universal states of melancholy: shame, loss and jealousy. The introduction of Robin, moreover, one of the ornamental setpieces of the novel, entirely refuses literal interpretation in its abundance of extravagant metaphor:

> The perfume that her body exhaled was of the quality of that earth-flesh, fungi, which smells of captured dampness and yet is so dry, overcast with the odor of oil of amber, which is an inner malady of the sea, making her seem as if she had invaded a sleep cautious and entire. Her flesh was the texture of plant life, and beneath it one sensed a frame, broad, porous, and sleep-worn, as if sleep were a decay fishing her beneath the visible surface. About her head there was an effulgence of phosphorous glowing about the circumference of a body of water – as if her life lay through her in ungainly luminous deterioration – the troubling structure of the born somnambule, who lives in two worlds – meet of child and desperado. (31)

Nothing in this passage provides any meaningful referent for situating Robin as a character in either a conventionally or psychologically realist sense. Caught in the unconsciousness of heavy sleep, 'her unknown life more nearly tuned to its origin' (52), she is instead made the allegorical embodiment of man's dormant primeval memory, suppressed and disavowed by rational consciousness and the social, religious and historical narratives that serve it. 'With the correct artist we contemplate life, with the poetic artist we make a new one,' Barnes stated in 1939, contrasting the mimetic principle of realist art with the archetypal image patterns that structure and convey meaning (in Eliot's terms the poetic 'mythic method') in an alternative tradition of symbolic art: 'Realistic values sit before one, to interpret or not, as the eye is good or off focus; with the spiritual life the critic (or novelist) has to more than record, he has to understand with a sixth sense that is almost a kind of collusion, not an appraisal, the one is safe, the other danger.'[19] Realist and poetic fiction are here defined as undertaking separate endeavours, the former observing and re-presenting the surface of life from a detached and empirical perspective, however experimental, while the latter acts as a means of figurative expression for the mute, nonrepresentational quality of the human soul or (in its post-Freudian incarnation) primordial unconscious, dependent on the visionary eye of the melancholic artist.

For much of the novel Robin remains 'La somnambule', her actions instinctive rather than intentional, propelled like those of a sleepwalker by some unfathomable inner compulsion, 'in her speech and her gestures ... a desperate anonymity' (151). Her lack of ego is what contributes to her seeming only half human, but it is also fundamental to her complete lack of awareness of moral responsibility, an amorality implicitly likened to man's state of innocence prior to the self-consciousness with which he is endowed by the Fall, by history and by socialization. To articulate and guide the reader through this syncretic 'narrative' of the human condition Barnes turns to O'Connor, and the extended metaphor of the 'night' through which he tells the story of man's self-awareness and self-hatred after the loss of his original innocence. The paradox of man's condition, O'Connor and Barnes imply, is that he is condemned to come to self-knowledge only through sin and shame. Shame, Eve Kosofsky Sedgwick argues, at once defines the self and is defined by a desire for the effacement of that self. 'Shame is a bad feeling attaching to what one is,' she explains, 'one therefore *is something*, in experiencing shame ... the structure "identity," marked by shame's threshold between sociability and introversion, may be established and naturalized in the first instance *through shame*.'[20] As the doctor observes of Robin, '[t]o be utterly innocent, would be to be utterly unknown, particularly to oneself' (125). Because Robin has no comprehension of sin, she also lacks the sense of shame that in Sedgwick's terms becomes the standard for socialized identity, in direct contrast to Felix's and his father's embarrassed refusal of their Jewishness and careful construction of a counterfeit yet socially acceptable 'identity'. Indeed, far from being abnormal freaks, the quacks, circus performers and other dissemblers that populate *Nightwood*'s shady night-world embody to a grotesque degree the condition of *all* mankind, parodying its shameful performance of social identity in 'splendid and reeking falsification' (10).

'Doctor, I have come to ask you to tell me everything you know about the night,' Nora asks, arriving at his room at three in the morning and remarkably unsurprised to find him rouged and bewigged, and wearing a woman's nightgown (71). While put out at having been thus interrupted, the doctor is quick to elaborate on his favourite topic. 'Well, I, doctor Matthew-Mighty-grain-of-salt-Dante-O'Connor, will tell you how the day and the night are related by their division,' he replies. 'The very constitution of twilight is a fabulous reconstruction of fear, fear bottom-out and wrong side up' (72). The reasoned, civilized world of the day literally brings itself into being by separating off from the primal, instinctive origins that it finds shameful and thus wilfully 'forgets', but that remain indestructible if dormant within the 'night' of the unconscious soul. Sensing that something has been lost from within himself, man is condemned to inescapable melancholia, though occasionally there are those who are more aware of this loss than others, and like

Robin instinctively resist it. French nights are so fascinating for the world over, O'Connor suggests, exactly because in them man catches a glimpse of that lost self, his 'sediment, vegetable and animal' (76). The French alone do not deny the content of the night for the values of the day, and indeed 'leave testimony of the two in the dawn' (74), able to do so, according to Barnes's religious philosophy, because of the ritual of confession at the heart of the Catholic faith that promises absolution as reward for the acknowledgement of sin. The puritan American by contrast 'separates the two for fear of indignities', disavowing rather than expressing his sin, and as a result 'will find no comfort until the night melts away' (76). Thus Nora, 'without the joy and safety of the Catholic faith' (54), suffers the agony of having internalized the day's 'thought upon and calculated' (72) negation of her night self. '[W]hat of our own sleep?' the doctor challenges her. 'We go to it no better – and betray her with the virtue of our days' (78). For it is indeed with just such virtue that Nora betrays Robin, finally forcing her to see herself through the shamed eyes of society. As she recounts in horror to the doctor, in a parodic blend of Catholic confession and psychoanalytic talking cure, '[s]he was asleep and I struck her awake. I saw her come awake and turn befouled before me, she who had managed in that sleep to keep whole ... No rot had touched her until then, and there before my eyes I saw her corrupt all at once and withering, because I had struck her sleep away' (131). Nora's desire for Robin is in part a desire for reconciliation with the primal innocence of the night, her loss described as 'an amputation that [she] could not renounce' (53). Yet she is also the cause of the corruption of that innocence. 'You were a "good woman",' the doctor declares, 'and so a bitch on a high plane' (131).

In appearance, attitude and language, O'Connor was closely modelled on the figure of Dan Mahoney, who was, according to expatriate legend, 'the most-quoted homosexual in Paris, a man who combined the professions of pathic, abortionist, professional boxer and quasi-confessor to literary women', and whose talk consisted of 'an extraordinary harangue revolving around unmentionable subjects and indescribable practices'.[21] Mahoney's combination of melancholy and garrulous wit recalled for Barnes that of the laughing Democritus Jr of the *Anatomy*, who declares that without 'mirth, which is the life and quintessence of Physick', any treatment of melancholy is 'dull, dead, and of no force ... It begins with sorrow ... it must be expelled with hilarity' (*Anatomy* 485). 'I hope that you are not too somber,' Barnes wrote to Mahoney shortly before his death in 1959, 'that you have some of your former hilarious sorrow.'[22] The doctor's spiritually, psychologically, historically and politically embedded explanation of 'the night', however, bears the influence of another Irishman obsessively engaged in giving expression to man's collective dream-memory of his primal origins: Joyce. *Finnegans Wake*

(1939), Joyce declared, was his 'night-book', as *Ulysses*, in its focus on the stream of the conscious mind, had been his 'day-book'. Barnes would have known of his use of the metaphor of the night from the instalments of *Work in Progress*, and her own construction of the night as the repository of all that man finds shameful is, in focus and argument if not in stylistic expression, markedly similar. 'We believe that it is in the abnormal that we approach closer to reality,' Joyce reportedly observed:

> When we are living a normal life we are living a conventional one, following a pattern which has been laid out by other people in another generation, an objective pattern imposed upon us by the church and state. But a writer must maintain a continual struggle against the objective: that is his function. The eternal qualities are the imagination and the sexual instinct, and the formal life tries to suppress both.[23]

Barnes's association of an instinctive life, forgotten yet eternal, with the night, and of conscious, modern civilization with the day, coheres strikingly with Joyce's reference here to the exclusionary accounts of existence offered by religion and history.

'All great talkers', Joyce told Barnes in 1922, 'have spoken in the language of Sterne, Swift or the Restoration'. Joyce himself she thought of as just such a voice, noting however that 'because no voice can hold out over the brutalities of life without breaking' he had turned to writing, 'for so he could arrange, in the necessary silence, the abundant inadequacies of life' ('James Joyce' 65). Eliot's critical account of *Ulysses* the following year credited him with exactly the same such saving arrangement, a function he also claimed for his own Tiresias in *The Waste Land* and subsequently O'Connor, whom he suggested drew together Barnes's 'deeper design, that of the human misery and bondage which is universal' ('Preface' vii–viii). By the writing of *Nightwood*, however, for Barnes the 'mythic method' seemed as futile as psychoanalysis and the religious confessional for giving meaning to and absolution from the 'immense panorama of futility and anarchy' that was human history, as Eliot described it.[24] 'Destiny and history are untidy', O'Connor notes, 'we fear memory of that disorder' (106). O'Connor in *Nightwood*, like Joyce's Shem the Penman in *Finnegans Wake*, gives ludic voice to the chaos of primal memory and disavowed history regarded as taboo by the world of the 'day' and repressed by the formal narratives of man's civilization.

Eliot's critical endorsement of course resulted in *Nightwood* being appropriated early to the formalist canon of literary modernism, notably by Joseph Frank in his 1945 essay 'Spatial Form in Modern Literature'. For Frank, the novel was the apotheosis of the classical Imagist aesthetics that he identified developing from the early modernism of Pound and T. E. Hulme, through Eliot, Proust and Joyce, and culminating in the mid-1930s. Whereas in the novels of Proust or the early Joyce, Frank argues, there remained a persistent concern with the 'naturalistic' principle, through which formal experimentation was put to the service of the faithful portrayal of modern life, in *Nightwood* the fine balance of form and verisimilitude gives way to a preponderance of symbolic significance, in which the reader is 'asked only to accept the work of art as an autonomous structure giving us an individual vision of reality; and the question of the relation of this vision to an extra-artistic "objective" world has ceased to have any fundamental importance'.[25] F. R. Leavis, writing with far less enthusiasm for modernist stylism than Frank, noted a similarly baroque exhaustion of high modernist principle in *Nightwood*, citing Barnes alongside Henry Miller and Lawrence Durrell as writers influenced by what he regarded as a disintegration of the organic principle in art in the work of Joyce and a 'regrettable (if minor) strain' of world-weary decadence in that of Eliot.[26]

Thanks to Leavis's decisive influence, *Nightwood* fell into cult obscurity for several decades, until the rise of feminist literary criticism reappropriated it as a lesbian classic and Barnes herself as one of the figureheads of the project to establish an alternative canon of female modernism. Among contemporary critics keen to embrace both the aesthetically and the socially subversive potential of the marginal and the performative, Barnes's thematic depiction of a prelapsarian/pre-Oedipal sexuality, presented as 'innocent' yet also grotesque and shameful, has been celebrated for its social and political dissidence and inversion of the normalized oppositions of a dualistic social order; day and night, human and beast, male and female, the sacred and the profane. As *Nightwood* proves increasingly 'Joycean' in its refusal of critics' attempts to appropriate it straightforwardly for the canon of either a formalist or a gendered modernism, however, contemporary modernist studies have begun to emphasize its significance in relation to modernist narrative and received conceptions of what makes a 'modernist novel'. For Peter Nicholls, it is a text that stands outside literary criticism's dominant formal, transatlantic *and* gendered definitions of modernism, an example of what he sees as an alternative figural trend in modernism that 'seems always to mutate into its opposite, to yield something which the structure cannot contain or speak'.[27] Tyrus Miller, meanwhile, notes that it also transgresses the *historical* parameters by which the modernist 'moment' has been conveniently yet arbitrarily defined, extending a self-consciously formally experimental trend in fiction well into the more broadly antimodernist literary temper of the 1930s. Late modernism, Miller suggests, presents 'disfigured likenesses of modernist masterpieces: the unlovely allegories of a world's end'.[28] In *Nightwood* pattern indeed remains at best fragile, and O'Connor's very exaggeration of his 'Tiresian' role always threatens to reveal itself as an empty mockery. 'I am my own charlatan' (86) the doctor admits, even his rollicking monologues eventually overwhelmed by the painful enormity of the human condition, and the authority of his diagnosis of the 'night' upon which the reader comes to depend undercut. Charles Baxter recognizes that in the doctor's drunken breakdown at the end of the novel Barnes articulates her lack of faith in the redemptive power of the modernist writer, 'the defrocked priest (or priestess) of words, whose formulas once seemed to recreate, to turn words into flesh, and now simply turn upon their speaker'.[29] His ever more maniacal diatribes expose what in the contemporary history of the 1930s was becoming increasingly apparent beneath modernism's formal scaffolding: '*nothing, but wrath and weeping!*' (149).

'I writ of melancholy, by being busy to avoid melancholy,' Burton declares at the beginning of *Anatomy of Melancholy* (16). As implicit in O'Connor's final collapse, however, for Barnes words ultimately failed to shore up the ruins of existence, which remained both 'the greatest horror' and the source of her art. 'You make horror beautiful – it is your greatest gift,' Coleman wrote to her after reading the manuscript of *Nightwood* in 1935.[30] Yet shortly before its publication, she recorded in her diary that Eliot had said to her that he did not think Barnes would ever write again; 'he felt the pressure so great in this; as though she had writen [sic] herself out'.[31] His words were prophetic; it would be another two decades before she completed *The Antiphon*, after which she lived in almost total seclusion. 'How do writers keep on writing?,' she asked in 1963. 'I don't see how my kind can – the "passion spent," and even the fury – the passion made into *Nightwood*, the fury (nearly) exhausted in *The Antiphon* . . . what is left? "The horror," as Conrad put it.'[32]

Notes

1. T. S. Eliot, Letter to Geoffrey Faber, quoted in Phillip Herring, *Djuna: The Life and Works of Djuna Barnes* (New York: Viking, 1995), p. 231.
2. T. S. Eliot, 'Preface' to Djuna Barnes, *Nightwood* (London: Faber and Faber, 1996), p. x. Further references cited parenthetically.
3. C. L. Watson, 'Mr Eliot Presents Miss Barnes', *Brooklyn Eagle*, 7 March 1937, Papers of Djuna Barnes [PDB], Special Collections, University of Maryland Libraries: Series II.
4. Djuna Barnes, 'Vagaries Malicieux', *The Double-Dealer*, May 1922, p. 256.
5. Quoted in Louis F. Kannenstine, *The Art of Djuna Barnes: Duality and Damnation* (New York: New York University Press, 1977), p. 48.
6. Djuna Barnes, 'James Joyce', *Vanity Fair*, April 1922, p. 65. Further references cited parenthetically.

7. Quoted in Andrew Field, *Djuna: The Life and Times of Djuna Barnes* (New York: Putnam's, 1983), p. 127.

8. Djuna Barnes to Emily Coleman, 20 September 1935, The Emily Holmes Coleman Papers [ECP], Special Collections, University of Delaware: Series I.2, Box 2, Folder 11.

9. There are two copies of the *Anatomy* in the personal library bequeathed by Barnes to the University of Maryland.

10. Robert Burton, *The Anatomy of Melancholy*, ed. Floyd Dell and Paul Jordan-Smith (New York: Tudor, 1927), p. xiii.

11. Sigmund Freud, 'Mourning and Melancholia', in *Penguin Freud Library, Volume 11: On Metapsychology* (London: Penguin, 1991), p. 254.

12. Djuna Barnes to Elizabeth Chappell Barnes, 19 February 1923, PDB: Series I, Box 5, Folder 2.

13. Djuna Barnes to Emily Coleman, 21 May 1938, PDB: Series II, Box 3, Folder 12.

14. Djuna Barnes to Emily Coleman, 17 May 1935, PDB: Series II, Box 3, Folder 7.

15. Djuna Barnes to Emily Coleman, 20 April 1934, ECP: Series I.2, Box 2, Folder 9.

16. T. R. Smith to Djuna Barnes, 29 August 1934, PDB: Series II, Box 3, Folder 10.

17. Emily Coleman to Djuna Barnes, 5 November 1935, PDB: Series II, Box 3, Folder 8.

18. Emily Coleman to T. S. Eliot, 25 October 1935, ECP: Series I.2, Box 2, Folder 13.

19. Djuna Barnes to Emily Coleman, 5 January 1939, PDB: Series II, Box 3, Folder 14.

20. Eve Kosofsky Sedgwick, 'Queer Performativity: Henry James's *The Art of the Novel*', *GLQ: Journal of Lesbian and Gay Studies* 1 (1993), p. 12.

21. John Glassco, *Memoirs of Montparnasse* (Oxford: Oxford University Press, 1995), p. 20.

22. Djuna Barnes to Daniel Mahoney, 14 November 1958, PDB: Series II, Box 11, Folder 31.

23. Arthur Power, *Conversations with James Joyce* (Dublin: Lilliput Press, 1999), p. 86.

24. T. S. Eliot, 'Ulysses, Order and Myth' (1923), in Peter Faulkner (ed), *A Modernist Reader: Modernism in England 1910–1930* (London: Batsford, 1986), p. 103.

25. Joseph Frank, 'Spatial Form in Modern Literature', in Frank, *The Widening Gyre: Crisis and Mastery in Modern Literature* (Bloomington: Indiana University Press, 1963), p. 28.

26. F. R. Leavis, *The Great Tradition* (London: Penguin, 1962), p. 36.

27. Peter Nicholls, *Modernisms: A Literary Guide* (London: Palgrave Macmillan, 1995), p. 12.

28. Tyrus Miller, *Late Modernism: Politics, Fiction, and the Arts Between the World Wars* (Los Angeles: University of California Press, 1999), p. 15.

29. Charles Baxter, 'A Self-Consuming Light: *Nightwood* and the Crisis of Modernism', *Journal of Modern Literature* 3 (1974), p. 1176.

30. Emily Coleman to Djuna Barnes, 27 August 1935, PDB: Series II, Box 3, Folder 7.

31. ECP: Series II, Box 79, Folder 644.

32. Djuna Barnes to Peter Hoare, 18 July 1963, PDB: Series II, Box 9, Folder 33.

CATHERINE GUNTHER KODAT

William Faulkner: an impossibly comprehensive expressivity

> I went to the dresser and took up the watch, with the face still down. I tapped
> the crystal on the corner of the dresser and caught the fragments of glass in
> my hand and put them into the ashtray and twisted the hands off and put
> them in the tray. The watch ticked on ... Father brought back a watch-charm
> from the Saint Louis Fair to Jason: a tiny opera glass into which you
> squinted with one eye and saw a skyscraper, a ferris wheel all spidery,
> Niagara Falls on a pinhead.
> William Faulkner, *The Sound and the Fury* (1929)[1]

> As regards any specific book, I'm trying primarily to tell a story, in the most
> effective way I can think of, the most moving, the most exhaustive. But I
> think even that is incidental to what I am trying to do, taking my output
> (the course of it) as a whole. I am telling the same story over and over, which
> is myself and the world ... This I think accounts for what people call the
> obscurity, the involved formless 'style', endless sentences. I'm trying to say
> it all in one sentence, between one Cap and one period. I'm still trying to
> put it all, if possible, on one pinhead.
> William Faulkner, Letter to Malcolm Cowley[2]

By 1944 the literary critic Malcolm Cowley had been reading the novels of
William Faulkner (1897–1962) for some time, and 'gradually and with
errors of judgment' he had begun to 'perceive a pattern' in the novels that
had largely escaped him on first reading (6). Among the first to describe the
emergence of literary modernism in America, Cowley was struck by the
inverse relationship between his own growing certainty of the importance
of Faulkner's fiction and what he termed the author's 'quoted value on the
literary stock exchange' (as he noted, by 'the later years of World War II ...
[Faulkner's] seventeen books were effectively out of print'), and he decided
'to write a long essay on Faulkner ... to see whether it mightn't redress the
balance between his worth and his reputation' (5–6). To that end, he wrote
to the author asking for an interview; three months later Faulkner replied,
indicating his willingness to assist Cowley as he could. A kind of collaboration between author and critic ensued, and the result was something of
much greater substance than an essay: *The Portable Faulkner* (1946), an

anthology comprised of short stories and excerpts from the major novels, all chosen by Cowley and framed by his exegesis of the creation and meaning of Faulkner's 'mythical' Yoknapatawpha county. The rest is literary history.

The revaluation of Faulkner's work set in motion by Cowley can, in retrospect, be viewed as only one instance of a critical constant, for Faulkner's reputation has been subject to frequent and radical revaluation. Largely dismissed (even reviled) during the 1930s as a purveyor of macabre tales of 'rape, mutilation, castration, incest, patricide, lynching, and necrophilia', author of 'a series of horror stories that are essentially false ... diffused through the brilliant technique that promises us everything and gives us nothing',[3] Faulkner saw his reputation undergo a complete volte-face in the years after the Second World War, thanks largely to Cowley, whose work on *The Portable Faulkner* did indeed realize his dream of discovering a neglected artist such 'that other voices will be added to the critic's voice, in a swelling chorus' of praise (*Portable Faulkner* 3). In 1950, on the occasion of receiving the Nobel Prize, Faulkner delivered a brief address that called for a literature based on 'the old universal truths lacking which any story is ephemeral and doomed – love and honour and pity and pride and compassion and sacrifice',[4] and in doing so he appeared to ratify the claims of those critics who followed Cowley in arguing that, far from being 'a combination of Thomas Nelson Page, a fascist, and a psychopath gnawing his nails', Faulkner was a model of liberal humanism, an affirmative author whose novels were best read not as peculiarly regional effusions of the gothic but rather as universalist articulations 'of issues which are common to our modern world'.[5]

A generation later, Faulkner's reputation again underwent serious revision, as literary scholars who came of age during the civil rights and feminist movements turned a critical eye on those American cultural figures whose work seemed suspiciously consonant with a political and economic establishment that demanded rigorous interrogation. Faulkner's novels certainly address the race and gender ideologies of the USA, but they can hardly be said to deliver morals quick to hand, and attempts to clarify matters by examining his extraliterary engagements with civil rights through the 1950s muddy the waters even more. For example: 1956 was an especially busy year in Faulkner's civil rights work, and was spent mostly in efforts to control the fall-out from a late February interview with the London *Sunday Times* correspondent Russell Warren Howe, in which, addled with drink and anxiety over Autherine Lucy's efforts to become the first black student enrolled at the University of Alabama, Faulkner asserted, '[I]f it came to fighting I'd fight for Mississippi against the United States even if it meant going out into the street and shooting Negroes.'[6] In an essay published some months later in *Ebony*, a rather penitent Faulkner characterized his comment as 'a statement which no sober man would make nor any sane man believe'; yet his plea, one paragraph later, for black civil rights leaders to 'go slow now'[7] drew widespread criticism (including Nina Simone's scornful 1963 ballad 'Mississippi Goddam'). To this day, listserve anecdotes about Faulkner's supposed eagerness to 'pick up a shotgun, go into the streets, and kill a few Negroes if he had to' are not difficult to find.[8]

As the civil rights movement spurred an increasingly critical examination of Faulkner on issues of race, so, too, the rise of feminism prompted heightened attention to his representations of women: was the theme of *Sanctuary* (1931) truly that women have, as a character claims in another Faulkner novel, 'an affinity for evil' (*Sound and the Fury* 59)? Thus by the middle of the 1980s a new critical consensus on Faulkner began to take shape: far from being an author articulating universal truths, he was a deeply flawed product of an equally flawed time, a problem in need of explanation.[9] In this re-revaluation, the rise of Faulkner's reputation after the Second World War was seen as symptomatic of the blindness, the willed 'innocence', at the heart of the USA's Cold War imperial project. Lawrence H. Schwartz's 1988 study *Creating Faulkner's Reputation* offers the strongest version of this claim: 'Faulkner's work was championed and canonized because his often supremely individualistic themes and technically difficult prose served an ideological cause,' he writes. 'Unintentionally, he produced a commodity of enormous value as a cultural weapon in the early years of the Cold War' (210).

It is probably too soon to predict the shape it will take, or the critical judgements it will produce, but all the signs indicate that today, yet again, Faulkner's work – and so, his reputation – is undergoing reexamination. The selection of three Faulkner novels –*The Sound and the Fury* (1929), *As I Lay Dying* (1930), and *Light and August* (1932) – as the summer 2005 reading selections for Oprah Winfrey's book club is probably the strongest (if not also the strangest) indicator that something is afoot. Advertised as 'A Summer of Faulkner', Oprah's promotion of the novels included a special packaged edition of the texts, a linked series of websites filled with historical information about Faulkner and the South, and the services of three distinguished American scholars (Thadious Davis, Robert W. Hamblin and Arnold Weinstein), who provided brief online interpretative essays and answered email questions from readers. This is a cultural development that few would have predicted, given Oprah's status as an African-American television celebrity and sometime actress whose best-known involvement in the world of literature is her faithful devotion to the work of Toni Morrison, and it perhaps indicates that one strand of what could be called the 'identity critique' of Faulkner has run its course. At the very least, it raises the possibility that the past half-century's worth of stark rises and precipitous falls in Faulkner's 'literary stock' finally tells us little about the merits of the work itself. Rather, it illustrates an ongoing critical habit wherein particular aspects of that stock are picked out for over- or undervaluation by particular readers making judgements at particular historical moments.

For Faulkner's work brings complex expectations into play, expectations driven equally by the novels' formal properties – clearly connected to modernist literary techniques developed in Europe – and by their content: which is, speaking generally, the disjunction between the vaulted promises of American democracy and equality and the lived realities of American injustice, a disjunction demonstrated perhaps most profoundly in the country's ongoing racial struggle in its peculiarly virulent Southern strain. Thus what is important about Faulkner's fiction – and what is alarming about it also – is its uncanny ability to highlight the relationship between form and content such that each not only animates the other (in traditionally good, modernist formalist fashion) but each also reveals the inadequacies of a reading strategy that would value one aspect of the text more than the other. This is to say, in other words, that in Faulkner's novels history and literature emerge as projects simultaneously opposed and conjoined, sometimes violently, terrifyingly so. If this is to emphasize that Faulkner is crucial to contemporary critical efforts to rethink literary modernism's relationship to history, it is also to demonstrate the importance of Faulkner's engagement with literary modernism to his effort to 'tell about the South'.[10]

In what follows, I read Faulkner's major work (from *The Sound and the Fury* to *Absalom, Absalom!* (1936)) so as to emphasize not only what this work accomplishes in its own engagements with modernist literary technique and Southern American history but also what it has made possible in the work of others. Thus I have divided the remainder of this chapter into two sections, one focusing on the life and the work, the other on the legacy.

But first, a word about the two quotations standing at the start of the chapter. The first, drawn from the Quentin Compson section of *The Sound and the Fury* ('June 2, 1910'), describes Quentin's effort to destroy his grandfather's watch, a family heirloom passed down to him by his father and described as 'the mausoleum of all hope and desire', the 'reducto absurdum [*sic*] of all human experience' (47). The second comes from a letter Faulkner sent to Cowley in November 1944, at the very beginning of the process that would result in *The Portable Faulkner*. There is much to say about both these passages, but what interests me here is the unusual and startling figure they share: the image of a pinhead supporting an impossibly comprehensive expressivity.

In *The Sound and the Fury*, Quentin's recollection of his brother Jason's watch-charm emerges in almost classically modernist fashion out of the flow of associations catalysed by his attempt to destroy his own paternal souvenir. The absurdity of an effort to measure (and so contain) time conjures up the absurdity of an effort to contain (and so measure) space; the ludicrous impossibility of 'Niagara Falls on a pinhead' suggests the ludicrous impossibility of Quentin's 'time' (in 1910) resembling in any way that of father and grandfather. Still, the fact that these impossibilities exist (and, in the case of the grandfather's watch, seem oddly resistant to destruction) signals, in *The Sound and the Fury*, the larger impossibility that the novel nevertheless takes as its central artistic challenge, which is, briefly put, to represent memory loosed from its moorings in time, space or even flesh.

In the second passage the effort to capture 'Niagara Falls on a pinhead' – an effort impossible in every dimension, involving the arrest of flow as well as the compression of space – becomes 'the attempt to say it all in one sentence', and so the figure for Faulkner's understanding of his own writing. Yet if the image of the pinhead in *The Sound and the Fury* connects Faulkner's work to a modernism influenced by Bergsonian notions of time, matter and memory, the second connects it to a near-reportorial realism and fanatical excess of detail grounded in Honoré de Balzac. The connections between Faulkner's fiction and the novels of Balzac are well known and do not need to be rehearsed here; my point is simply to note that Faulkner expresses his ambition in terms that are historical as well as aesthetic.[11] In sum, the image of the overloaded pinhead stands, as a kind of metonymy, for a literary practice concerned to puncture the membrane separating the historical and the literary, event and representation, fact and fiction, and it invites recognition of how Faulkner's prose works as a kind of verbal suture, a prosthetic aesthetic that draws attention to the gaps it ostensibly works to close. For the South is what Faulkner knows and so what he has to tell, and I use *has* here to mean both possession and compulsion: the South is what is given to him to tell and what he *must* tell. The challenge of reading Faulkner lies in grasping how his fiction refuses to reduce a bloody, criminal history to the status of a bourgeois fairy story (to paraphrase the critique of modernism articulated by Georg Lukács), even as it rejects the notion that history can be properly understood only in a single, 'realistic' way. Faulkner's best novels, produced in an almost white-hot frenzy out of the depths of the Depression, virtually vibrate in the intensity of this dialectical tension. Perhaps it is, finally, this grim, determined refusal, this neither/nor, that accounts for the lability of Faulkner's reputation, as readers continue to struggle with the challenge of squaring a horrific, historically insistent content with prose at once beautiful and obscure.

Faulkner's life and work

The oldest of four boys, Faulkner was born in 1897 in Mississippi, and except for a few sojourns of varying lengths (notably in New Orleans, Hollywood and Charlottesville, Virginia), he lived all of his life there, spending most of his adult years in a large antebellum house in the university town of Oxford that he bought in 1930 and christened Rowan Oak. The fictional Yoknapatawpha county has recognizable antecedents in the actual Lafayette county; the fictional county seat of Jefferson likewise bears a more than passing resemblance to Oxford, capital of Lafayette county. Like the Dublin of James Joyce's *Ulysses* (1922), then, Faulkner's Jefferson has strong roots in the actual; but, as with Joyce, Faulkner's literary concerns could not be said to begin, or end (or even to linger at some middle point) in verisimilitude.

Still, abetting these links between fictional and actual biographies and geographies are the strong connections that can be drawn between Faulkner's family history and the lives of some of his characters. Attributes of the Sartoris family as reported in *Flags in the Dust* (first published in 1929 as *Sartoris*) and *The Unvanquished* (1938), and of Rev. Gail Hightower's grandfather in *Light in August* (1932), resemble in many particulars the more storied aspects of the lives of Faulkner's paternal great-grandfather, William Clark Falkner (a lawyer, politician, railroad entrepreneur and sometime author known as the 'old colonel' for his services to the Confederacy during the Civil War) and grandfather, John Wesley Thompson Falkner (the militarily innocent 'young colonel', also a lawyer and politician, and founder of the First National Bank of Oxford). (Faulkner added the 'u' to his own name.) For years shaped largely by the assumption that Faulkner's fictional engagements with his family history derived from the way his ancestors embodied the genteel 'cavalier' of Southern antebellum myth, critical attention to this history took a remarkable turn in 1993 with the publication of Joel Williamson's *William Faulkner and Southern History*, a study pointing out that the 'old colonel' was in truth more Snopes than Sartoris (a shrewd businessman, he owned slaves but never operated a plantation), and raising the possibility that the miscegenation and incest plot central to the narrative of *Go Down, Moses* (1942) is no pure fiction, but may rather represent Faulkner's meditation on the rumoured practices of that same forebear.[12]

Thus the usual caveats regarding the use of biography in the study of literature, confronted with the case of Faulkner, manage to seem simultaneously both excessively restraining and insufficiently cautious. In terms of the novels themselves, the difficulty is compounded by the persistence with which particular details of Faulkner's own life and family narrative are refigured both as intensely personal expressions of a scandalous and violent public history (involving slavery, white supremacy, vote rigging, environmental exploitation and patriarchal abuse) and as excruciatingly public manifestations of personal depravity (think, for instance, of the ravings of Doc Hines in *Light in August* or of Jason Compson in *The Sound and the Fury*). Cowley's reach for 'mythical' allegory is completely understandable in such a literary landscape; but allegory cannot, finally, account for all that is afoot in the fiction.

As literary apprenticeships go, Faulkner's was a rather prolonged one: *The Sound and the Fury*, universally regarded as his first great achievement, was his fourth novel and his fifth published work (his first publication, in 1924, was a collection of verse in a Symbolist vein, *The Marble Faun*). In a preface to the novel written several years after its first appearance and published only after his death, Faulkner tellingly likens the experience of writing *The Sound and the Fury* to the shutting of a door 'between me and all publishers' addresses and booklists and I said to myself, Now I can write. Now I can just write.'[13] Whatever its relation to the actual creation of *The Sound and the Fury* – and the novel's obvious differences from the work that preceded it would indicate that something transformative did indeed occur – this image of the scene of *writing* as a kind of ecstatic immuring in the world of Art, a world conceived as a region apart from all mundane economic concerns (those 'publishers' addresses and booklists'), does capture one aspect of the experience of *reading* it, as we move from the hermetic recesses of Benjy's conciousness through the gradually expanding spaces of Quentin's and Jason's narratives to the seeming amplitude of the third-person vista and its overview of the collapse of the house of Compson. This is a collapse punctuated, with no small irony, by the restoration of a traditional reading practice of a traditionally ordered text: 'and his eyes were empty and blue and serene again as cornice and façade flowed smoothly once more from left to right, post and tree, window and doorway and signboard each in its ordered place' (*Sound and the Fury*, 191). The novel seems, in this way, entirely a meditation on memory conducted outside of history, with the imposition of direct (i.e. linear) causality appearing as a kind of numbing betrayal of some higher 'truth'. Certainly, Jean-Paul Sartre's famous reading of the novel as an 'absurdity which is so un-novelistic and so untrue', a vision of 'suffocation and a world dying of old age' that flows from a faulty metaphysics, responds to this aspect of the work.[14] And Eric J. Sundquist's view that *The Sound and the Fury* is important 'only ... in the larger context of novels to which it gives rise'[15] – that is, those novels like *Light in August* and *Absalom, Absalom!* that more clearly address the Southern racial theme – echoes this sense that the central flaw of the work is its failure to confront history.

What Sartre's critique misses, however, and what more recent approaches to the novel work to capture, is the persistent sense in *The Sound and the Fury* that there is more at stake in the narrative than an expansion into prose of the possibilities of poetic dramatic monologue. In noting that novels like *Light in August, Absalom, Absalom!* and *Go Down, Moses,* all more directly engaged in issues of Southern history and American racial injustice, do indeed arise from the thematic concerns and literary techniques first deployed in *The Sound and the Fury,* Sundquist points the way towards a view of the novel that would track its swervings and silences precisely as indicators of something outside consciousness that the novel is 'trying to say', and that would attempt, however obscured that something may be in a psychological twilight, to acknowledge its presence and take some measure of its contours.

Recent work by John T. Matthews and Richard L. Godden has gone far towards making that presence more palpable. As Matthews notes, the very first sentence of *The Sound and the Fury* 'prefigures the whole novel's close concentration on the inner workings of the single mind',[16] but the Compson grounds are surrounded by a fence – not a wall – 'through' which Benjy can glimpse a world beyond that which encloses him. For Matthews, the fact that Benjy, Quentin and Jason attend to what lies beyond their yard only with reluctance and at considerable risk (Benjy is castrated as a consequence of his attempt to step outside the family gate) points precisely to the fetishization of the loss of their sister Caddy as a means of refusing to acknowledge other, larger, political, economic and social losses: '*The Sound and the Fury* appears to offer a case study of the breakup of the Southern rural aristocracy, a late but accurate example of the replacement of the agrarian economy by mercantile capitalism,' Matthews notes. And in its obsession with time past, the novel 'reflects the way in which the emergence of the New South created a nostalgically fictional version of the Old South that could thus be both honored and replaced' (*Lost Cause* 97).

That Faulkner returns to the character of Quentin Compson in his masterpiece *Absalom, Absalom!* – a sustained critical examination of Southern ideology whose remorseless demands on the reader are unprecedented in American fiction – is, perhaps, one clear indication that readings of *The Sound and the Fury* casting it as a modernist evasion of history are fundamentally flawed. As Godden has brilliantly demonstrated in three interrelated essays on the novel, the highly experimental technical methods of *Absalom, Absalom!* are intimately related to its historical project. It is a commonplace in readings of the novel to note the parallel between fiction-making and history (as efforts to tell the story of Thomas Sutpen pass from Mr Compson to Rosa Coldfield to Quentin and his Harvard roommate Shreve McCannon), but it is wrong to assume that, in doing so, Faulkner's novel means to question the knowability of history. As Godden notes:

> It would be a mistake to read the novel's difficulty as raising primarily episte-mological questions; while readers must ask, 'Who knows what, when, and how?' this should not – critics to the contrary – induce a crisis of knowledge culminating in some form of the unanswerable question 'How can they (or we) know at all?' In *Absalom, Absalom!*, a novel designed to explore a repressive class 'design', difficulty begs the altogether more answerable question 'How can those who know so much, repress so much of what they know?'[17]

The textual difficulty of *Absalom, Absalom!*, in other words, enacts not the difficulty of knowing as such but rather the difficulty of *remembering* when everything in one's social, political and economic surroundings demands a strategic and deliberate *forgetting*. Godden illustrates this point in his read-ing of the novel's postulate that Sutpen earned his fortune by working as an overseer on a sugar plantation in Haiti in the first third of the nineteenth century – a clear historical impossibility, given the Haitian revolution of 1791. In tracing the tale of Sutpen's Haitian adventures to its narrative source – a campfire conversation between Sutpen and Quentin's grandfather, like Sutpen a planter, slave owner and Confederate army officer – Godden demonstrates how the novel simultaneously elaborates and interrogates a deathly desire to forget black revolution in order to remember white supremacy.

I have lingered over *The Sound and the Fury* and *Absalom, Absalom!* because, taken together, the novels give us not only some of Faulkner's finest writing but also his most sustained engagement with the full range of tech-niques of literary modernism; they also bookend the years commonly regarded as Faulkner's most fruitful. Other important novels from this period can usefully be seen as local investigations into particular aspects of the relationship between literature and history. *As I Lay Dying*, which Faulkner himself termed a 'deliberate ... tour-de-force',[18] pushes to the limit the investigation of individual consciousness begun in *The Sound and the Fury*. In its exploration of communal voice and the logics of conformity, *Light in August* presses off on quite a different tack; the daring aspects of this novel lie less in its technical properties than in its direct treatment (Faulkner's first) of Southern racism – an issue almost literally embodied in the character of Joe Christmas, whose doom arises from his status as a racially indeterminate subject caught in a world that demands racial certainty. Between *As I Lay Dying* and *Light in August* came *Sanctuary*, a *succès de scandale* whose spectacular tale of a young woman raped with a corncob brought Faulkner to the attention of Hollywood (where he worked as a scriptwriter, off and on, from 1932 well into the 1940s). Although Faulkner himself called the book 'a cheap idea ... deliberately conceived to make money',[19] the novel remains startling in its diagnosis of the parallels between the *noir* sensibilities of the pulp bestsellers of the day and the ostensible rectitude of the Southern patriarchial order.

Between *Absalom, Absalom!* and the appearance of Cowley's *Portable*, Faulkner produced three more novels of significance – *The Wild Palms* (1939; republished in 1990 under its original title, *If I Forget Thee, Jerusalem*), *The Hamlet* (1940), and *Go Down, Moses*. They can be viewed as discrete chapters of a continuing exploration of the dialectic between form and content in its engagement with the relationship between fiction and history, with each novel addressing a different social front: *The Wild Palms* develops technical modes and thematic territory first explored in *Light in August* (the double plot) and *Sanctuary* (the commercialization of sexuality in popular culture); *The Hamlet* revisits issues of class, gender and rhetoric first touched on in *As I Lay Dying*; and *Go Down, Moses* (like *Absalom, Absalom!* structured around a racial secret) narrates Southern racial and environmental exploitation as related aspects of a single crime. Although Faulkner produced a considerable body of work in the years following the appearance of the *Portable* and the receipt of the Nobel Prize, critical opinion on the quality of these novels remains unsettled.

Faulkner's legacy

Rather than trying to adjudicate this question of the value of Faulkner's late work in any sort of direct fashion, I would like to approach the issue obliquely through a different consideration of what might be meant by successful 'late' modernist work in a Faulknerian vein, and in doing so to conclude with a gesture back toward the observations with which I began this chapter on the lability of Faulkner's reputation. For even as contemporary literary *scholars* work to establish some method for judging the worth of Faulkner's challenging oeuvre, *writers* read Faulkner, and use him, in ways that complicate efforts to ground his work in a singularly (or single) American frame of reference.

Schwartz's assessment of the ideological valences of the Cold War renovation of Faulkner's reputation does not attend in any systematic fashion to the shape of that reputation outside the USA. But as Sartre's review of *The Sound and the Fury* indicates, Faulkner's work was read with interest in France well before the onset of the Cold War; and as Pascale Casanova's recent study makes clear, the rise of 'global Faulkner' can be viewed as a prewar French phenomenon as much as a Cold War American one. Maurice Coindreau's *Nouvelle revue française* essay, which marked the beginning of serious critical attention to Faulkner in France, came out in June 1931, shortly before the appearance of his translation of *As I Lay Dying*, the first of Faulkner's novels to be published in French. It was the French translations of Faulkner published through the 1930s and 1940s that impressed authors as various as Juan Benet, Gabriel García Márquez, Carlos Fuentes, Ricardo Piglia, Juan Carlos Onetti, Juan José Saer, Jorge Luis Borges, Rachid Boudjedra and Kateb Yacine. According to Casanova, these authors found in Faulkner's formally daring approach to intransigent historical problems literary 'tools of liberation':

> Faulkner's work ... reconciles properties that normally are thought to be incompatible. As a citizen of the most powerful nation in the world, and as a writer consecrated by Paris, Faulkner nonetheless evoked in all his books ... characters, landscapes, ways of thinking and stories that exactly coincided with the reality of all those countries said to lie in the 'South' – a rural and archaic world prey to magical styles of thought and trapped in the closed life of families and villages. ...
>
> Faulkner thus helped a primitive and rural world that until then had seemed to demand a codified and descriptive realism to achieve novelistic modernity.[20]

However, and to return to the American frame, it is African-American authors who provide the most complicated and interesting testimony regarding Faulkner's legacy. In his famous essay 'The World and the Jug', published a little over a year after Faulkner's death in 1962, Ralph Ellison sought to distinguish between those authors he considered 'relatives' and those he considered 'ancestors': 'while one can do nothing about choosing one's relatives, one can, as artist, choose one's "ancestors". [Richard] Wright was, in this sense, a "relative"; Hemingway an "ancestor". Langston Hughes ... was a "relative"; Eliot ... and Malraux and Dostoievsky and Faulkner were "ancestors" – if you please or don't please!'[21] A little more than twenty years after Ellison claimed Faulkner as a literary ancestor, Toni Morrison, who has taken considerable pains to make clear that she does not regard herself as an author 'influenced' by Faulkner, reported that his work had 'an enormous effect' on her.[22] She continued:

> there was in Faulkner this power and courage – the courage of a writer, a special kind of courage. My reasons, I think, for being interested in and deeply moved by all his subjects had something to do with my desire to find out something about this country and that artistic articulation of its past that was not available in history .... And there was something else about Faulkner which

I can only call 'gaze.' He had a gaze that was different. It appeared, at that time, to be similar to a look, even a sort of staring, a refusal-to-look-away approach in his writing that I found admirable. (296–7)

In other words, the importance Faulkner has for Morrison lies not in his public prescriptions for social change – and how could it, given the tortured nature of those prescriptions, delivered late in the life of a man who, however aghast and ashamed, accepted a certain definition of what it meant to be a white man in Mississippi? Rather, the importance lies in Faulkner's willingness to attempt a particular kind of 'artistic articulation' of American history – an articulation grounded in the understanding that if one may not awaken from history's nightmare, the least one can do is acknowledge it as one's own.

Notes

1. William Faulkner, *The Sound and the Fury*, ed. David Minter (New York: W. W. Norton, 1987), p. 49. Further references cited parenthetically.
2. Malcolm Cowley, *The Faulkner-Cowley File: Letters and Memories 1944–1962* (Harmondsworth: Penguin, 1978), p. 14. Further references cited parenthetically.
3. Lawrence H. Schwartz, *Creating Faulkner's Reputation: The Politics of Modern Literary Criticism* (Knoxville: University of Tennessee Press, 1988), p. 13. Schwartz quotes Bernard De Voto's 'Witchcraft in Mississippi' from the *Saturday Review of Literature*, 31 October 1936. Further references cited parenthetically.
4. William Faulkner, 'Address Upon Receiving the Nobel Prize for Literature', in Faulkner, *Essays, Speeches, and Public Letters*, ed. James B. Meriwether (London: Chatto and Windus, 1967), p. 120.
5. Robert Penn Warren's *New Republic* review of *The Portable Faulkner*, cited in Cowley, *The Faulkner-Cowley File*, pp. 94, 93. Thomas Nelson Page's turn-of-the-century 'Marse Chan' stories were sentimental apologias for slavery.
6. Joseph Blotner, *Faulkner: A Biography* (New York: Random House, 1974), p. 1591.
7. William Faulkner, 'A Letter to the Leaders in the Negro Race', in *Essays, Speeches and Letters*, p. 107.
8. See, for example, the Saturday 30 June 2001 postings on H-AMSTDY, the American Studies listserve maintained at the University of Michigan H-NET website, http://www.h-net.org/.
9. See, for example, John Carlos Rowe, 'The African-American Voice in Faulkner's *Go Down, Moses*', in Gerald Kennedy (ed.), *Modern American Short Story Sequences: Composite Fictions and Fictive Communities* (Cambridge: Cambridge University Press, 1995), pp. 76–97.
10. William Faulkner, *Absalom, Absalom!: The Corrected Text*, ed. Noel Polk (New York: Vintage International, 1990), p. 142.

11. For a discussion of the connections between Faulkner and Balzac, see Merrill Horton, 'Faulkner, Balzac and the Word', *The Faulkner Journal* 19:2 (2004), pp. 91–106.

12. Joel Williamson, *William Faulkner and Southern History* (New York: Oxford University Press, 1993).

13. William Faulkner, 'An Introduction to *The Sound and the Fury*', *Mississippi Quarterly* 26 (1973), reprinted in Faulkner, *The Sound and the Fury*, p. 222.

14. Jean-Paul Sartre, 'On *The Sound and the Fury*: Time in the Work of Faulkner', in Faulkner, *The Sound and the Fury*, p. 259.

15. Eric J. Sundquist, *Faulkner: The House Divided* (Baltimore: Johns Hopkins University Press, 1983), p. 9.

16. John T. Matthews, *'The Sound and the Fury': Faulkner and the Lost Cause* (Boston: Twayne, 1991), p. 90. Further references cited parenthetically.

17. Richard L. Godden, *Fictions of Labour: William Faulkner and the South's Long Revolution* (Cambridge: Cambridge University Press, 1997), p. 78.

18. Faulkner, 'An Introduction to *The Sound and the Fury*', p. 219.

19. William Faulkner, *Sanctuary: The Corrected Text*, ed. Noel Polk (New York: Vintage International, 1993), pp. 321–2.

20. Pascale Casanova, *The World Republic of Letters*, trans. M. B. DeBevoise (Cambridge, MA: Harvard University Press, 2004), pp. 336–7.

21. Ralph Ellison, *Shadow and Act* (New York: Vintage Books, 1972), p. 140.

22. Toni Morrison, 'Faulkner and Women', in Doreen Fowler and Ann J. Abadie (eds.), *Faulkner and Women: Faulkner and Yoknapatawpha 1985* (Jackson: University Press of Mississippi, 1986), p. 296.

13

HOWARD FINN

Writing lives: Dorothy Richardson, May Sinclair, Gertrude Stein

The early modernist novel, with its variations on the 'stream-of-consciousness' method, attempted to capture the inner life with an immediacy and authenticity that preceding realisms had lacked. This emphasis on documenting the subjectivity of the individual was also, however, potentially problematic. The modernist novel increasingly had to perform the difficult trick of rendering subjectivity while at the same time distancing and universalizing it. This 'objectifying' was for some novelists to be achieved through the power of aesthetic form, a would-be classicism in which the artwork becomes autonomous from the subjective vagaries of its creator, an aesthetic of 'impersonality', to use T. S. Eliot's term.[1] For this 'late' version of modernism, the autobiographical becomes almost an anathema, because the value of the work of art now lies precisely in its transcendence of the personal. And this view, continued in the traditions of New Criticism and poststructuralism, has remained powerful until quite recently. If reading a novel in relation to the biographical is to be guilty of being reductive, then writing a novel as autobiographical expression is tantamount to original sin.

The relationship between the autobiographical impulse – the desire to write one's life – and modernist conceptions of objectifying form was particularly vexed for women writers. It is striking that at the precise moment when they tried to give voice to the self at its most personal, women modernists also invariably embraced an extreme formalism. In part, this formalism was an attempt to raise the private to the public register of a literary discourse. In the work of Dorothy Richardson (1873–1957), May Sinclair (1862–1946) and Gertrude Stein (1874–1946), we will see both the importance of the autobiographical dimension in their writing and also the ways in which modernist formalist strategies are bound up in their novels with the attempt to both articulate and disavow traumatic material being 'worked through' in the act of writing a life. But looking at the example of Richardson, Sinclair and Stein, it is also as if in giving voice to the self they simultaneously gave voice to doubts about the self. Avowing one's life became inextricably bound up with the disavowing of unacceptable aspects of that life, and writing one's life became a kind of cathartic writing-cure analogous to the early Freudian talking-cure. As their common investment in redemptive epiphanic 'moments of being' (to use a term associated with Richardson and Virginia Woolf) might suggest, modernist women writers seem haunted by the possibility that in representing one's life in all its 'authentic' detail it may turn out that the life had little value or meaning; that it was an unlived life. Looked at from this point of view, the formalist excess and obscurantism of the modernist novel resembles a strategy for working through these contradictions, a strategy through which the auto-biographical impulse is both avowed and disavowed.

Dorothy Richardson: overwriting lives

The narrative of Dorothy Richardson's multivolume *Pilgrimage* (1915–67) charts Miriam Henderson's life from adolescence to her thirties, covering a period from the mid-1890s to 1912. This is a journey through family crisis, social decline, the institutions/ideologies of school and church, and anxieties over nation, race and gender, love, sex and guilt. Miriam encounters Jewish intellectuals, Russian revolutionaries, Fabian socialists, suffragettes and lit-erati. She has relationships with at least six men and three women. She faces major traumas, including her father's bankruptcy, her mother's suicide and her own nervous breakdowns. But the narrative focus is not directly on these key events but overwhelmingly on the everyday and the mundane: washing at a basin, drinking a cup of tea, eating a sandwich in an ABC café, opening a window, walking down a street. Or simply sitting in a chair and thinking – the everyday rhythms of the mind. This is, in part, an emphasis concerning gender: assigning value to the domestic and the everyday because this is what patriarchy dismisses as a feminized realm and trivial. Richardson was also influenced by her time with the Quakers and takes as one of her models for *Pilgrimage* the tradition of Puritan spiritual autobiography, in which every-day actions, such as walking up a flight of stairs, can be a site of struggle for the soul. Miriam's struggle is a quest for the existential self, a quest marked by epiphanic moments in which a heightened awareness of existence or being is evoked. This series of 'moments of being' in response to events both extraordinary and utterly ordinary constitute a continuity in (self)conscious-ness. It is these subjective responses to events that are 'objectified' by the narrative, not the events themselves, and it is perhaps because of this need to focus so rigorously on responses evoked that Richardson more often than not does not actually give us the event. The reader has to experience Miriam's reaction first and then on the basis of that experience reconstruct the events that provoked it – hence the difficulty many readers initially have with *Pilgrimage*.

At the end of *Honeycomb* (Book III, 1917), Miriam attends the double wedding of her sisters and then accompanies her ailing mother, who is suffering from depression, to Brighton. When they are walking home one evening to their guesthouse, '"It is too late," said Mrs Henderson with clear quiet bitterness, "God has deserted me." They walked on, tiny figures in a world of huge grey-stone. "He will not let me sleep . . . He does not care."'² In the next paragraph Miriam grapples with the implications of her mother's words and their plight. She is too young to understand and can only respond to her mother's torment with her own feelings of acute physical discomfort. Nothing more can be articulated; they are walking 'in a world full of perfect unanswering silence'. There is then a gap on the page, a missing paragraph, a silence. The text then resumes: 'The bony old woman held Miriam clasped closely in her arms. "You must never, as long as you live, blame yourself, my gurl." She went away' (489). As readers we are not sure of who the old woman is or why she is holding Miriam in her arms and telling her not to feel guilt for the rest of her life. We do not know what event has happened, only that an overwhelmed Miriam is lost in a dreamlike state: 'Perhaps she dreamed that the old woman had come in and said that. Everything was a dream; the world. I shall not have any life. I can never have any life; all my days. There were cold tears running in her mouth' (489). This passage moves from third person to free indirect, to first person and then back to third person. The shifts mark not only shifts of narrative perspective, but shifts in registers of subjectivity, the first person 'I shall not have any life' being the most intensified, a kind of direct address. And with this paragraph *Honeycomb* ends.

It was May Sinclair, writing about the end of *Honeycomb* in her 1918 *Egoist* article 'The Novels of Dorothy Richardson', who applied the phrase 'stream of consciousness' to a work of literature for the first time. Sinclair commends Richardson's decision to 'plunge in' to the reality of the mind, arguing that the aim is not only to capture the inner life 'first hand' as it happens, but to reproduce or simulate these effects of subjectivity in the act of reading.³ But many readers, after experiencing 'first hand' Miriam's trauma at the end of *Honeycomb*, will want to know and understand what it was that traumatized Miriam, and why. Subsequent *Pilgrimage* books will provide some of the necessary information as well as a retracing of the preceding narrative. A process of reconstructing the event can begin. After walking home in the 'unanswerable silence' to the guesthouse, Miriam fell asleep. In the gap on the page, the missing paragraph, Mrs Henderson died. Miriam awoke in the arms of the old woman, the landlady. Miriam is there and not there: in a dream state. The event, the mother's death, is repressed but is present in the mark of its repression: the blank paragraph. The symptoms of this repression will return in a network of displaced references to the moment of trauma – it could even be argued that the whole of *Pilgrimage* is generated by this proliferation of displacements.[4]

Richardson was trying to capture the 'inner life' of a particular individual by presenting an experience of consciousness 'as it happens', but much more than this she was, like her main influence Henry James, trying to capture the experience of subjectivity as being constituted by layers of disavowal and displacement. If *Pilgrimage* often resembles an act of writing as interminable analysis, a 'working through', then reading *Pilgrimage* tends to put the reader in the position of analyst, determined to reconstruct the text in such a way that its displacements are interpreted and its underlying meanings understood. In *Honeycomb* Miriam is 'absent', lost in sleep, fatigue and delirium at the exact moment when Mrs Henderson dies, while in the actual events of 1895 Dorothy had literally been absent – had gone out for a walk – when Mrs Richardson committed suicide by cutting her throat with a kitchen knife in the lodgings where they were staying.[5] In the novel the death is acknowledged in the act of the old woman telling Miriam not to feel guilty for the rest of her life, implying, as Miriam says, that she *will* feel guilty for 'all my days'. Dorothy had been entirely absent from the scene, but in the novel Miriam is brought into the scene and her absence is staged in terms of her innermost subjective responses: as disavowal and guilt.

Although *Pilgrimage* is comprehensible as a self-contained work of art, the autobiographical dimension, far from reducing the text, enables us to see what is at stake in transforming autobiographical reality into a modernist fictional narrative, how this transformation or 'working through' might be carried out, and why. The complexity of this play between the autobiographical and its literary expression is particularly evident in *Clear Horizon* (Book XI, 1935, set in 1907) since it deals with a highly charged set of personal relationships in which the autobiographical is impossible to separate from the literary or intertextual. Richardson had a long personal and political relationship with H. G. Wells, who is represented in *Pilgrimage* by the character Hypo Wilson. In 1906 Richardson met Veronica-Leslie Jones (a character called Amabel in the novel), a young militant suffragette. Hypo tells Miriam and Amabel of his curiosity about the independent lives they lead and seems fascinated, if perplexed, by Amabel's suffragette activism – hence his enthusiastic suggestion, often taken as a statement of intent for *Pilgrimage*, that Miriam 'document' in a novel her life amid these changing times for women.[6]

In 1909, however, Wells wrote his own document of the new era for women, the novel *Ann Veronica*.[7] Wells's heroine was scandalously based on the young Fabian Amber Reeves, but readers of Richardson cannot help but notice that entire episodes from *Ann Veronica* crop up in the Hypo-Miriam-Amabel sections of *Pilgrimage*, albeit from a radically different perspective.[8] For example, the Amabel-in-prison chapter from Richardson's *Clear Horizon* is clearly a rewriting of the Ann Veronica-in-prison chapter in Wells's novel. But the intertextual relations are also biographical in complicated ways. Readers familiar with Richardson's biography may notice that many details of the character Ann Veronica seem to correspond to Richardson and Jones rather than Amber Reeves (even the names suggest some conflation: Amber becomes Veronica in Wells, Veronica becomes Amabel in Richardson). Wells thought his somewhat unflattering portrait in *Pilgrimage* was accurate and well achieved. Not all the interested parties were so sanguine. When Richardson died in 1957, Veronica (now Grad) contacted Richardson's relative, Rose Odle, to demand the wedding ring from Richardson's finger (Richardson having eventually married). A correspondence ensued in which Veronica recounts her closeness to Richardson and mentions a crucial night they spent together, the morning after which Richardson set in motion a plan for Veronica to marry a man, Benjamin Grad, whom Richardson had refused to marry and wished to pass on to Veronica. This tangled web is treated at length in *Pilgrimage*. In 1957 Veronica Grad told Odle that she felt the arranged marriage (arranged by Richardson that is) had ruined her life: 'Maybe it was all worth it as a sacrifice to her "Art". I can't judge of that . . . I am even able to believe she thought she loved me – but first everyone was "copy" material not only for books but for stimulation for Dorothy.'[9]

In their letters Veronica and Odle constantly allude to the fact that at the heart of these old events is a lesbian affair between Richardson and Veronica, only to then deny this fact as unseemly and better hidden from the prying eyes of biographers and posterity – indeed, to deny this fact to themselves. The love affair between Miriam and Amabel is presented obliquely in *Clear Horizon*, as is the current of lesbian desire throughout *Pilgrimage*. As Joanne Winning has shown in her recent discussion of this issue, in the transition from draft versions into final text the lesbian narrative of the later *Pilgrimage* books is 'overwritten' by erasures and ellipses, transformed into a subtext.[10] It is not the case that in reality Richardson and her friends lived an openly lesbian life, which had to be toned down for publication in novel form. Neither is it true that Richardson and her friends lived a repressed life, which was then played out as suggestive fantasy in fiction. Rather, a complex set of avowals and disavowals located in the social codes and mores of the time (and quite probably internalized in the attitudes and consciousness of the participants) are developed and worked through in the fiction. The novel provides a space for fantasy, like trauma, to be played out but not resolved; fiction reproduces, albeit in an imaginatively modified form, the equivocal logic of disavowal that marks 'real life' itself.

May Sinclair: the way of sublimation

May Sinclair achieved popular and critical acclaim at the turn of the twentieth century with a series of novels dealing with the breakdown of Victorian social and moral certainties – reflected in issues such as the New Woman, religious doubt and family tensions. Her involvement in the suffragette campaign provided material for a more radical kind of novel, *The Tree of Heaven* (1917), dealing with the same suffragette demonstrations, imprisonments and ideological issues as Richardson's *Clear Horizon* and Wells's *Ann Veronica*. This led to her association with the emerging modernist grouping around the journal the *Egoist*. As an established writer of an older generation, her promotion of Richardson and advocacy of Imagism, T. S. Eliot, Ezra Pound and H. D. (Hilda Doolittle), was valuable at a time when early modernism was under attack. Her writing became strongly influenced by these younger writers and it is her later modernist novels, *Mary Olivier: A Life* (1919) and *The Life and Death of Harriett Frean* (1922), for which she is remembered today rather than the earlier bestsellers.

Sinclair's outlook was informed by German idealist philosophy and by psychology – initially the ideas of William James, then Sigmund Freud and Carl Jung. She combined these interests in a philosophical approach that she termed New Idealism and which countered the loss of belief in religious and social absolutes with a privileging of the self and (self)consciousness: reality is meaningful only in as far as it is manifested in the unfolding of self-realization. *Mary Olivier* traces its heroine's life from infancy to middle age. After a happy childhood, the family home disintegrates as Mary's brothers depart one by one and the father declines into alcoholism. Mary educates herself in languages and philosophy, the book documenting the progress in her reading, from Plato to Spinoza, Kant and Hegel. As her appalled mother predicts, such 'unwomanly' intellectual interests discourage a series of potential suitors. As the men of the family meet premature deaths, Mary gives up the possibility of marriage to Richard Nicholson, the love of her life, to care for her ailing mother. When her mother dies, Mary is left alone. Events are described from Mary's point of view in an attempt to capture her interiority both as a response to particular experiences and as a developing sense of selfhood – and as Sinclair told her French translator, 'all this description of the *inner life* is autobiographically as accurate as I can make it' (italics in original).[11] To achieve this Sinclair follows Richardson's method: events both extraordinary and mundane are selected as being illustrative of the heroine's unfolding consciousness and rendered as short imagistic episodes without narrative transitions, mixing free indirect narration with first-person stream-of-consciousness passages. Sinclair uses pronoun shifts in a more systematic way than Richardson, often employing the second person, a 'you' to suggest a retrospective objectification of the 'I', as in the opening of the novel where Mary is a baby in her cot being held by her father and then breastfed by her mother: 'Mamma's breast: a smooth, cool, round thing that hung to your hands and slipped from them when they tried to hold it. You could feel the little ridges of the stiff nipple as your finger pushed it back into the breast.'[12]

For the reader, the overall effect of these constant pronoun shifts is to make Mary appear to be a divided self or a multiplicity of selves, something she recognizes in adolescence when she has 'queer glimpses of the persons that were called Mary Olivier' – she is dutiful daughter to Mrs Olivier, a girl on the verge of womanhood to her watchful aunts, a tomboy playmate to her brother Mark – but 'her secret happiness had nothing to do with any of these Mary Oliviers' (110), her true self is independent of these public selves. Self-realization therefore becomes synonymous with a move towards separation and independence from the family and assigned social roles. And, most of all, this necessitates a struggle to free herself from the need to love and be loved by her mother.

Arguably it is this tortuous relationship of mother and daughter that is the trauma at the heart of the novel rather than the terrible deaths of father and brothers or the disappointed romantic affairs. Initially Mary believes that although, externally, she 'claws on to' her mother and other relatives, her inner life is free (290). But the Olivier family history is marked by fatal medical conditions, madness, depression and alcoholism and, later, after her father and brothers have died and her Aunt Charlotte has gone mad, Mary realizes that she may never be free. The 'I' is predetermined by factors located in Mary's family, in her childhood, in the past; factors that lie beyond her own agency in the present. She had thought of herself as an 'independent and separate entity, a sacred, inviolable self' (333), but now realizes that this was an illusion – she is doomed to act out what the family history has determined: 'You were part of it; you were nothing that they had not been before you. It was no good struggling. You were caught in the net; you couldn't get out' (333). Mary realizes with horror that the lives of her mother and father were probably determined by the lives of her grandparents and beyond that by generations unknown. However, this leads her to a sense of compassionate resignation. It is wrong to judge, nobody is to blame, everyone is 'caught in the net': 'Mamma, Papa and Aunt Charlotte, Dan and

Roddy, they were caught in the net. They couldn't get out' (333). And this resignation prefigures the peculiar kind of self-realization or transcendence which Mary achieves at the end of the novel. She sacrifices her life and chance of love in order to look after a mother whose broken mind has disappeared into 'a black hole' and will now never acknowledge her dutiful daughter (426). Mary achieves happiness precisely through an act of renunciation: by 'letting go' she gains her 'real self' (436).

For Sinclair, the key concept in psychoanalysis was sublimation. If life is inherently traumatic, the answer is to transcend psychological disturbance by sublimating it into a project of self-realization. To the celibate Sinclair, following Freud, the obvious example is of unsatisfied libido or sexual energy being transferred via sublimation into intellectual or artistic endeavour. But, as Suzanne Raitt argues in her recent biography of Sinclair, by proposing that in a more general sense sublimation can channel a whole life into a higher consciousness Sinclair explicitly aligns herself with Jung rather than Freud.[13] So where does 'positive' sublimation end and 'negative' repression begin? For Mary on the final page of the novel, as with Miriam in *Pilgrimage*, the realization of the self takes the form of an epiphany, a transcendent moment of being. And, as in *Pilgrimage*, this existential epiphany is a 'letting go' of worldly happiness that can be read as a displaced form of letting go of worldly trauma, one denial substituting itself for another, and a stoical resignation is played out as the precarious ecstasy of self-realization: 'I tried to doubt away this ultimate passion, and it turned my doubt into its own exquisite sting, the very thrill of the adventure. Supposing there's nothing in it, nothing at all? That's the risk you take' (437). Is this really what Sinclair praised as 'the way of sublimation'? Here, the ultimate passion is renunciation and doubt becomes a masochistic pleasure. And if this is the self-realization, was it worth the struggle? The thrill seems less convincing than the doubt since transcendence – or sublimation – might be merely an illusion, with 'nothing in it, nothing at all'.

Sinclair's doubts get the upper hand in *The Life and Death of Harriett Frean*, where she presents the opposite scenario in which a life of sublimation turns out to have been a life of repression based on illusion, creating only paralysis and stagnation. Although less directly autobiographical, *Harriett Frean* abstracts the main lessons of *Mary Olivier* and simplifies them into Freudian archetypes. With its simple, repetitive narrative voice the novel resembles Stein's *Three Lives* (1909) rather than *Pilgrimage* and the overall effect is that of a decidedly disturbing fairy tale. As a child Harriett lives to be good in the eyes of her mother and father. She can continue to bask in this triad only by renouncing anything external to it. As a young woman she rejects the advances of Robin Lethbridge, the fiancé of her best friend

Priscilla Heaven. The ostensible moral justification is clear, but Harriett's motivation is actually to enjoy the pleasure of renunciation in the eyes of her parents and to sustain her ecstatic dependence on them. For Robin and Priscilla, the outcome is disastrous. Their unhappy marriage becomes a relationship of sordid dependence. Priscilla's denial takes the form of falling into hysteria and paralysis, while Robin's takes that of becoming her resentful carer. When Priscilla dies, Robin, in turn, forces his second wife to become *his* tormented servant. Harriett's moral act of renunciation thus initiates a chain of repression and unhappiness. Harriett's life is also doomed. After her father's death, she is left as carer to her mother, this relationship of life-denying subservience leading to a gradual withdrawal from the world. When her mother dies, a weakened Harriett becomes utterly dependent on a housekeeper and companion, Maggie, who effectively has to renounce *her* life to look after Harriett.

Towards the end of the novel, Harriett is forced to confront the possibility that her whole life has been determined by an idealized image of her mother and father – and their love – that turned out to be illusory, but such an idea is always couched in denial: 'She clung to the image of her mother; and always beside it, shadowy and pathetic, she discerned the image of her lost self.'[14] Whereas Mary Olivier believed that she had found her life and her real self through the act of 'letting go' as an act of sublimation, Harriet Frean finds out that letting go was an act of repression through which she lost for ever her real self and any chance of a life – and destroyed several other lives into the bargain. Ironically for a writer dedicated to representing her life as a quest for self-realization, what links *Mary Olivier* and *Harriet Frean* is the sense that, for Sinclair, agency is located in the unconscious, in factors of childhood and preceding generations, and that the choice between sublimation and repression has already been determined by factors of which the individual is not aware until it is too late. *Harriett Frean* draws on Sinclair's own past, the all-consuming relationship with her mother, but it is also uncannily autobiographical in terms of Sinclair's future. A few years later, she would begin to suffer the debilitating effects of Parkinson's disease and withdraw into seclusion and silence, spending the long twilight years until her death in 1946 in absolute dependence on her housekeeper and companion Florence Bartrop.

Gertrude Stein: everybody's autobiography

Like Richardson and Sinclair, Gertrude Stein acknowledged the crucial influence of Henry James and William James, studying psychology under the latter at Harvard, conducting laboratory experiments on automatic writing, and deriving from them the idea of the stream of consciousness as well as a mechanistic psychological typology. These ideas produced an ambivalence characteristic of literary modernism. On the one hand, the privileging of consciousness led Stein to see her writing as an attempt to capture the inner life in all its depth and individuality, its *presence*. On the other hand, her psychological typology led her to see her writing as an attempt to capture the behavioural surface; 'character' for Stein consists less in introspective contemplation than in habitual behaviour – how people perform everyday tasks and, most of all, how people talk. Many of the usual attributes of the novel, including plot and, especially, symbolism of any kind, are stripped away to leave only what is essential: the vernacular small talk of the characters. Stein retains the narrator, usually a laconic version of the author's voice, fulfilling a role which resembles that of a storyteller in an archaic oral tradition. In Stein's oeuvre this voice soon came to mediate or incorporate the voices of characters and so her narrative becomes either a kind of 'objective' monologue reporting in quasi-scientific fashion its findings about 'character', or a deliriously self-reflexive – and implicitly autobiographical – description of the act of writing and the subjectivity of the narrator.

Stein surmised that everyday small talk is for most of us basically an endless monologue consisting of slight permutations of repetitive phrases concerning a tiny set of habitual topics. Such speech patterns form the basis of Stein's 'continuous present' writing style, but she takes that repetitive style to such an extreme that naturalism disappears, engulfed by a syntax ever more detached from its ostensible referents. In this way the style quickly becomes another version of modernist formalism.[15] Although Stein's elimination of romantic symbolism in favour of simplified vernacular had an influence on the American novel via Ernest Hemingway, it is the supposed liberation of language from overdetermined referents, especially psychological or social meaning, that made Stein such an abiding influence on the American avant-garde across the arts. It has generally been those critics dismissive of Stein who have argued that her formalist strategies were a 'trick' concealing a 'secret' – the trick being automatic writing and the secret being lesbianism. More recently, however, the idea that Stein's writing encodes lesbian desire has brought her work back into critical connection with other modernist women writers and the contemporary concerns of gay and lesbian studies. To privilege the autonomy of form over the autobiographical dimension here is to miss a very real content or meaning to the work and to be complicit in repression at an ideological level.

Stein's first novel, *Q.E.D.* (1903), based on an affair from Stein's college days and drawing on material derived from her diaries and love letters, is a conventionally written *roman à clef* outlining, unconventionally, an

unhappy lesbian love triangle. Adele (Stein) is forced to confront the realization that her condemnation of her lover's decadence is simply a projection of
guilt over her own desire. Worse still, the lover, Helen, knows this and
accuses Adele of being repressed and living an unlived life.[16] Adele finally
confesses to Helen that 'I want nothing of you except what you give me of
your need' (128) – but will Helen, as the desired one, ever have such a need?
The affair and the novel end in 'deadlock' (133). *Q.E.D.* sets up Stein's
favoured psychological archetypes: aggression/passivity, independence/
dependence, domination/submission – positions adopted in relation to the
circulation of need. Such behavioural polarities can coexist within an individual or become inverted – as in, for example, what today would be termed
a 'passive aggressive' position. The original affair led to a breakdown and
depression for Stein. Her troubled adolescence had been marked not only by
the intensity of unrequited taboo desire, but also by the early deaths of her
parents. She left this past behind when she left the USA with her brother Leo
to embark on what would eventually become the legend of her Parisian life as
writer and art collector. In Paris she began to write the critically acclaimed
Three Lives (1909) and the critically vilified *The Making of Americans*
(1925), one of the most extreme and excessive novels ever written in terms
of its style and length.

Three Lives, which could justifiably be called the first truly modernist
novel, is actually three novellas, each given over to the writing of a single life
from birth to death. Two were based on sometime servants in the Stein
households: 'The Good Ana' and 'The Gentle Lena'. They tell of women of
recent immigrant stock trying to make a life in the German community of
Bridgepoint (Baltimore). A third story, 'Melanctha', tells the tale of a love
affair in a black community and was, Stein claimed, based on her observation
of life in such a neighbourhood when she was a medical student at Johns
Hopkins Medical School (she left after two years in 1901, without qualify-
ing).[17] The reader might initially assume that these are social realist render-
ings of women's lives as objects of social oppression. But if so, it is a very odd
kind of social realism. The narrator makes no moral judgement and the
narratives actually focus on Stein's behavioural archetypes; writing a life
means showing how personality traits determine that life. Servant Ana is
constantly engaged in struggles of dominance and submission with a succession of masters and mistresses, acting in ways that Stein translates as dependent, independent, passive, aggressive, etc., but finally her defining
characteristic is indeed 'goodness' – she spends her life giving to others and
in the end her 'strained worn-out body' dies, like Sinclair's Harriett Frean, on
the operating table having given her life to others.[18] Lena's defining characteristic is 'gentleness', which means an absolute passivity. Having been sent

from Germany to the USA, she is then married off in sordid circumstances, has three children and dies giving birth to a fourth. She is exploited by everyone. Her being or inner life is not acknowledged by anyone. The story ends with the widower content with his three surviving children without the distraction of a superfluous wife. 'Melanctha' was hailed by many, including Richard Wright, as the first serious literary representation of African-American culture.[19] This reading has understandably fallen out of favour and the story is now regarded as notable for marking the appearance of Stein's formalism (the serial variation of repetitive sentences in unorthodox syntax). It is also notable in being the most autobiographical of the three lives – it is a transposition of the love triangle documented in *Q.E.D.* and several key episodes from the earlier novel are revisited, including the pivotal scene where power shifts after spontaneous, impulsive Melanctha accuses the intellectual Jeff Campbell of living only superficially, of not understanding real depths of feeling. Accepting this revelation, Campbell begs Melanctha to be his teacher, as Adele had begged Helen in *Q.E.D.*[20] The story allows Stein to play out her idea of behavioural polarities at length, showing how lack of compatibility between character types can lead only to an emotional and erotic impasse. As with Richardson and Sinclair, it is telling that Stein's attempt to grapple with these still traumatic autobiographically based issues should have given rise to a modernist and formalist style. In Stein's case, the style represented, in what she termed its 'insistence', a kind of incantatory reverie in which language becomes an erotic fetishizing of the object of desire, but also an act of obscuring or distancing the true object or traumatic kernel of the discourse.

Equipped with a set of psychological archetypes and a radical new literary formalism, Stein turned to *The Making of Americans*. This book begins with an amended version of an early 1903 manuscript introducing two families: the Dehnings and the Herslands, both based on the Stein clan. The reader assumes that these families are the 'particular' that will represent the 'universal' of how America came to be 'made'. But the story of migration and the successive generations soon gives way to lengthy descriptions of each character making a passing appearance in the narrative (including neighbours, servants, dressmakers) and each character is described almost exclusively in terms of archetypal personality traits ('bottom natures') that belong to them: one has 'dependence', another 'attacking' or 'resisting', one has a 'hole in their being', another is 'whole in their living' and so on. Everyone lives in a mode of 'repeating'. The psycho-biographical aspect periodically gives way, in turn, to exercises in Stein's 'insistent' style, where syntactical permutations centring on selected words such as dependent, attacking, living, loving, being, etc. can go on for several pages – a formalist investigation of language superseding character analysis as the object of the exercise. Characters become nameless, reduced to 'this one' or 'that one', as if identifiable selves have become unmentionable. The narrator frequently interrupts to comment on how happy or miserable she is at how the book is shaping up.

Stein toyed with titles such as 'The Making of a Book' or 'The Making of an Author', which suggests that the book might be read as a record of its own writing.[21] For example, a 1904 manuscript, 'Fernhurst' (concerning another scandalous love triangle from Stein's college days), is pasted into the middle of *The Making of Americans* but followed by an editorial comment declaring that this narrative and its words are empty and no longer have meaning.[22] There then follows a rewriting of the episode using Stein's current 'insistent' style. But even this is interrupted by one of the narrator's admissions of 'despair' at the impossibility of 'realising the being in anyone' (458). The fact that Stein was acutely depressed during much of the period spent writing the novel (1903–11) indicates that it could also be approached as the document of a writer trying to write her way out of a personal crisis. This would explain why much of the narrative seems to be an attempt to 'work through' Stein's feelings towards her mother, father and brothers. According to *Everybody's Autobiography* (1937), the death of the parents meant little to the Stein children: 'Then one morning we could not wake up our father. Leo climbed in by the window and called out to us that he was dead in his bed and he was ... Then our life without a father began a very pleasant one.'[23] The earlier death of the mother had meant even less; she had long been sick, 'so when she died we had all already had the habit of doing without her' (142). But the casually repressed returns with a vengeance in the excess of *The Making of Americans*, where Mrs Hersland is the focus of a lengthy and tortuous attempt to come to terms with the idea of a sweet but weak and passive mother who has little 'being' or 'living' in her and Mr Hersland is one of a long line of Stein's representations of the father as a weak but authoritarian, even brutal figure. Although the characters in the novel are shifting composites, it is evident that the Hersland daughter, Martha, is, in part, another of Stein's self-portraits, while the penultimate chapter dedicated to the 'death' of David, the Hersland son, appears to contain a portrait of Leo Stein.[24] Stein was Leo's disciple until their breach over purchasing Cubist paintings, but it was Leo's violent criticism of Stein's writing rather than his criticism of Picasso that made any reconciliation impossible. The David Hersland chapter is a long set of permutations on what it means to have become 'a dead one' in the 'middle of one's living' and seems to mark the break with Leo, who, having failed to find his artistic vocation – or any vocation – has betrayed the potential of his youth and is doomed to fall into the ineffectual neurosis of an unlived life. The implication being that Stein herself is no longer 'a dead one' (a fear expressed earlier in the novel); through the cathartic writing-cure that is *The Making of Americans* she has found her vocation and herself.

Self-belief was assured when Leo and his doubts were replaced by the enthusiastic support of Stein's new partner Alice B. Toklas. The next phase of Stein's output, including *Tender Buttons* (1914), *Bee Time Vine* (1913–27) and pieces such as 'Lifting Belly' (1917) have often been interpreted as operating via lover's code words shared by Stein and Toklas concerning their sexual relationship. This is autobiographical writing at its most private. Autobiographical writing at its most public came with the publication of *The Autobiography of Alice B. Toklas* (1933) in which Toklas appears to recount a collection of anecdotes about Stein's Parisian life and friendships with Picasso et al. The twist revealed on the final page is that Toklas was too busy to write her autobiography, so Stein wrote it for her. Thus Stein got to play Boswell to herself as Johnson. *The Autobiography of Alice B. Toklas* constructs Stein's life in terms of anecdote, celebrity, digression and gossip – to masculinist modernism sure signs of an abjectly feminized realm – and Stein later followed up with *Everybody's Autobiography*, a book that constructs Stein more in terms of responses to the mundane and everyday, as well as musing on the success of the previous autobiography and the superficiality of its genre. It is striking that both autobiographies often refer to *The Making of Americans* as their authoritative reference on Stein's life.

Writing and living

The act of writing a life is to turn private experience into public expression. For modernist women writers, the aim was to *retain* the essential individuality and subjectivity of the private experience rather than losing it in the transition to public 'literary' discourse. But despite the writers' emphasis on the specificity of interiority and selfhood, it is evident that these representations of the self are haunted by trauma and the behavioural archetypes of the immediate family and of generations lost to all but the unconscious. The act of writing about a life happening in the 'present continuous' of the everyday becomes a retrospective act of salvaging the self from a haunted afterlife. Miriam Henderson declares, 'I can never have any life', and the whole of *Pilgrimage* is finely balanced on whether this turns out to be true or not. Mary Olivier salvages her life through the very act of renouncing it, a position reversed by Harriett Frean, whose renunciation is a form of death, the unlived life to which Stein's 'dead ones' also succumb. While eschewing the overtly romantic existential epiphanies of Richardson and Sinclair, in Stein's repetitions of insistence it is still a heightened being or presence in the here and now that divides the living from the living dead. For Richardson, Sinclair and Stein, 'writing a life' is an attempt to map out this dividing line between the lived and unlived life.

Notes

1. T. S. Eliot, 'Tradition and the Individual Talent', in Eliot, *Selected Prose of T. S. Eliot*, ed. Frank Kermode (London: Faber and Faber, 1975), pp. 42–3.
2. Dorothy Richardson, *Pilgrimage*, 4 vols. (London: Virago, 1977), vol. I, p. 489.
3. May Sinclair, 'The Novels of Dorothy Richardson', in Bonnie Kime Scott (ed.), *The Gender of Modernism: A Critical Anthology* (Bloomington: Indiana University Press, 1990), p. 444.
4. See, for example, Richardson, *Pilgrimage*, vol. IV, p. 155.
5. Gloria G. Fromm, *Dorothy Richardson: A Biography* (Urbana: Illinois University Press, 1977), p. 22.
6. Richardson, *Pilgimage*, vol. IV, p. 397.
7. H. G. Wells, *Ann Veronica* (London: Dent/Everyman, 1966).
8. Stephen Heath, 'Writing for Silence: Dorothy Richardson and the Novel', in Susanne Kappeler and Norman Bryson (eds.), *Teaching the Text* (London: Routledge, 1983), pp. 126–47.
9. Gillian Hanscombe, *The Art of Life: Dorothy Richardson and the Development of Feminist Consciousness* (London: Peter Owen, 1982), Appendix, Letter 9, p. 179.
10. Joanne Winning, *The Pilgrimage of Dorothy Richardson* (Madison: University of Wisconsin Press, 2000).
11. Cited in Suzanne Raitt, *May Sinclair: A Modern Victorian* (Oxford: Oxford University Press, 2000), p. 216.
12. May Sinclair, *Mary Olivier: A Life* (New York: Review Books, 2002), p. 6. Further references cited parenthetically.
13. Raitt, *May Sinclair*, pp. 230–3.
14. May Sinclair, *The Life and Death of Harriett Frean* (London: Virago, 1993), p. 110. See also pp. 152–6.
15. Marianne DeKoven, *A Different Language: Gertrude Stein's Experimental Writing* (Madison: University of Wisconsin Press, 1983).
16. Gertrude Stein, *Fernhurst, Q.E.D., and Other Early Writings* (London: Peter Owen, 1972), p. 60. Further references cited parenthetically.
17. Gertrude Stein, *The Autobiography of Alice B. Toklas* (London: Grey Arrow, 1960), p. 86.
18. Gertrude Stein, *Three Lives* (New York: Dover, 1994), p. 46.
19. Alice B. Toklas, *What Is Remembered* (1963) (London: Cardinal, 1989), p. 183.
20. Stein, *Three Lives*, pp. 70–2; *Q.E.D.*, p. 60. See Richard Bridgman, *Gertrude Stein in Pieces* (New York: Oxford University Press, 1970), chapter 3.
21. Steven Mayer, 'Introduction' in Gertrude Stein, *The Making of Americans* (Illinois: Dalkey Archive, 1995), p. xxvi.
22. Stein, *Making of Americans*, p. 441.
23. Gertrude Stein, *Everybody's Autobiography* (Cambridge: Exact Change, 1993), p. 146. Further references cited parenthetically.
24. Bridgman, *Stein in Pieces*, chapter 4.

14

ANNA SNAITH

C. L. R. James, Claude McKay, Nella Larsen, Jean Toomer: the 'black Atlantic' and the modernist novel

> The posing went along famously. Soon the students began making
> polite conversation with me. They were all fierce moderns. Some of them
> asked if I had seen the African Negro sculptures ... They seemed interested in
> what I had to say and talked a lot about primitive simplicity and color and
> 'significant form' from Cezanne to Picasso. Their naked savage was
> quickly getting on to civilized things.
>
> Claude McKay, *Banjo* (1929)[1]

Modernism is often discussed in terms of movement: the increased speed brought about by new technologies and new modes of transport; the endlessly circulating networks of international capitalism; the global migrations of peoples. Anglo-American literary modernism, in particular, can be understood through transatlantic journeys, and the expatriate artistic communities created by these voyages. Yet despite this, modernist studies has continued to employ a nationally bounded methodology.[2] This chapter's focus on the 'black Atlantic' – African-American and Afro-Caribbean modernist writers and their literal and metaphorical transatlantic journeys – necessarily complicates the relationship between discrete nations and cultural production. In the epigraph to this chapter, taken from Jamaican Claude McKay's *Banjo* (1929), West Indian Ray is working as a nude model in Paris. While the student artists signal their modernity through their knowledge of primitivism, their construction and objectification of the nonmodern, black body here does not allow for Ray's entry into 'civilized' discourse. Similarly, modernist studies has not yet adequately accounted for the symbolism of Ray's presence in Paris: the contact between black and white writers, or modernity and racial difference.

Attention to such contact puts pressure on many other frameworks within which modernism has been defined and debated: the city, the relationship between politics and aesthetics and between high and low culture. The migrations of intellectuals such as Trinidadian C. L. R. James or African-American Nella Larsen across the Atlantic in the 1930s were about creative opportunities just as they were for T. S. Eliot or H. D. (Hilda Doolittle), but they were also predicated upon, and resonant with, the racial terror of slavery which brought about the transportation of millions of Africans to the 'New World'. The modernism of black Atlantic writers speaks of a particular relationship to Western modernity, not only because of the centrality of slavery to capitalist modernity, but also because of differently inflected motives for cultural regeneration and artistic revolution. Not only Atlantic crossings are at issue here, but also the crossing of the national and racial boundaries that have tried to contain modernist studies. Alternative modernisms, and the alternative geographies which inform them, force a reevaluation of the relationships between canonical and noncanonical writers.

Questions of race and aesthetics have been slow to impact on modernist studies. Work on the specific interrelationships of modernism and empire has only recently emerged in the field, which is surprising given the ruptures in imperial relationships that occurred in the late nineteenth and early twentieth centuries.[3] Initially, critical emphasis was placed on the depiction of racial difference in the work of white metropolitan writers, such as Eliot's use of Hinduism in *The Waste Land* (1922), E. M. Forster's Indian connections in *A Passage to India* (1924) or African sculpture in D. H. Lawrence's *Women in Love* (1921). Such evocations of the 'primitive' other in British metropolitan modernism invariably signify cultural subversion, but are often also predicated on homogenization, romanticization or eroticism.

British modernism's fascination with 'primitivism', seen for example in Roger Fry's attendance, with Virginia Woolf, at an exhibition of 'Negro' art at the Chelsea Book Club in 1920, and his essay on the subject in *Vision and Design* that year, has been mirrored in modernist studies through a focus on the appearance of 'primitive' cultural artefacts and artistic representations in the metropolis rather than the appearance of human beings.[4] Racial difference appears in modernist London via French art, rather than through Claude McKay's appearance at the 1917 Club. Tracing the journeys and networks of communication of black and Asian writers in Britain is, however, necessary for a reconsideration of the modernist period. As W. E. B. DuBois wrote in *Crisis* magazine: 'This Empire is a coloured Empire ... and more and more the streets of London are showing this fact.'[5]

Attention to work by black writers in the period has largely been confined to the Harlem, or 'New Negro', Renaissance. A variety of socioeconomic factors in the USA post-Reconstruction, including the expansion of corporate capitalism, led to the 'Great Migration' of African-Americans from the rural South to northern industrial centres. The search for greater economic opportunities also saw the migration of thousands of people from the Caribbean to American cities during the same period. By the 1920s Harlem had become the 'black metropolis' and by the end of the decade 164,000 black people lived in the area of north Manhattan.[6] The 'rent parties', jazz venues like the Cotton Club and speakeasies on 133rd St's Jungle Alley were the sites where black was in vogue and where African-American art and politics flourished. Langston Hughes, Zora Neale Hurston, Claude McKay and Countee Cullen, writers associated with the Renaissance – the 'Niggerati', as Hurston called them – generated an explosion of black writing including anthologies such as *The New Negro* (1925) and *The Book of American Negro Poetry* (1922), novels, collections of poetry and periodicals such as DuBois's *Crisis*, or Charles Johnson's *Opportunity*.

The relatively short-lived and geographically focused nature of the Harlem Renaissance has meant that work on black modernist writing has been segregated within modernist studies and has not been fully alive to the international networks which fuelled writing by people of African descent in this period. The Harlem Renaissance was as much about transnational links, particularly to Africa and to a wider European black diaspora, as it was about American identity and the place of the black population in a changing USA. This chapter will explore the work of four writers who contributed significantly to the internationalism of black writing in this period: two Afro-Caribbean writers, C. L. R. James and Claude McKay, and two African-American writers, Nella Larsen and Jean Toomer. All four deal with the articulation of racial difference in the context of growing modernization and increased contact between the 'New World' and Europe.

The chapter takes its title and conceptual framework from Paul Gilroy's influential *The Black Atlantic* (1993), which reconsiders the relationship between black intellectuals and Western modernity. Gilroy argues for a transnational and intercultural perspective. Taking the Atlantic as 'one single, complex unit of analysis' moves discussion beyond the ethnic absolutisms which, he argues, have governed cultural studies. Black Atlantic writing deals in 'cultural mutation and (dis)continuity': the transformation of cultural forms during the passage from Africa or Europe to the Americas, or vice versa.[7] Gilroy complicates a simple binary between African-American/Afro-Caribbean and European American cultural production, positing the interdependency of black and white writers, rather than a situation of mimicry or the simple adoption of Western literary conventions.

The issue of interracialism is a key topic in accounts of the Harlem Renaissance. The success or failure of this movement is often linked to the motives behind relations between black and white intellectuals. For George Hutchinson, the 'response to the exclusion of African American writers from modernism, for example, has been to polemically position African American modernism as the subversive "other" to a white modernism conceived along very traditional lines'.[8] A more nuanced account of the relationships and collaborations between black and white writers, patrons and editors does not necessarily idealize the cultural terrain, but allows for the positioning of black writers within various cultural institutions. The writers considered here, as well as other novelists who might have been (Jessie Fauset, Langston Hughes) were not coming to Europe to experience modernity but were a constituent part of it. The links between colonization and modernity in a Caribbean context in particular lead to a modernism, predicated on creolization, which both engages with and resists the forms of British modernism.[9]

A writer such as C. L. R. James, given his 'British' education in Trinidad, works within as well as against European literary traditions. James's position in London reminds us that 'some of the most potent conceptions of Englishness have been constructed by alien outsiders' (*Black Atlantic* 11). By and in response to. It was during the modernist period that London, heart of empire, became the crucible for some of the most effective and radical articulations of anticolonial and pan-African thought.[10] The concept of the 'black European', to use James's term, requires 'some specific forms of double consciousness' (1). What was a contradiction to Woolf, as seen in her depiction of a distinctly un-English 'negress' in London in *A Room of One's Own* (1929), was not so for James.[11] Indeed, his oeuvre can be seen as contributing to a 'counterculture of modernity': alternative social models that reject racial violence but also assert their entitlement to a Western intellectual heritage (*Black Atlantic* 36).

Modernism is an urban phenomenon. Cities provided the sites for artistic collaboration (the cafés, the galleries, the bookshops) that generated the manifestos and periodicals that characterize modernism. But the urban environment was also crucial for the black rights organizations and the Pan-African conferences that provided the political underpinnings to black modernist writing, for example DuBois's Pan-African conference in London in 1900, James's International Friends of Abyssinia (formed in London), or the League of Coloured Peoples, led by the black doctor Harold Moody. Events such as the race riots of 1919 in London and Cardiff or the invasion of Abyssinia by Italy in 1935 served to crystallize radical anti-imperialism in the metropolis. Traditions of free speech and a free press brought political activists to London, and African-American and Afro-Caribbean writers met African intellectuals and students as well as Irish and Indian nationalists. As the Caribbean Ras Makonnen put it, 'What was it like to be a Black man in the Britain of 1930s? . . . Imagine what it meant for us to go to Hyde Park to speak to a race of people who were considered our masters, and tell them right out what we felt about their empire and about them . . . all this when you knew very well that back in the colonies even to say "God is love" might get the authorities after you!'[12] Such contexts produce alternative narratives of the familiar sites of modernist London, as well as refocusing the map, so that the East End, home of the *Workers' Dreadnought*, for which Claude McKay worked as a field reporter, becomes a pivotal site, as do Amy Ashwood Garvey's Florence Mills café on Oxford Street[13] and the Erskine Club on Whitfield Street[14], examples of the places where black people gathered in the metropolis.

The critical approach to black modernism as the 'other' of Anglo-American modernism has been precipitated by a focus on content with the former and form with the latter.[15] Such categories rapidly break down, however, in the face of the fluidity that characterizes black modernism. Toomer's *Cane* (1923), for example, sits among the most formally experimental novels of the period, yet its avant-garde form is intimately linked to its celebration of black folk culture. Whereas James's *Minty Alley* (1936) and McKay's three novels (*Home to Harlem*, 1928, *Banjo*, 1929, and *Banana Bottom*, 1933), all of which depict black working-class cultures, might be considered as social realism, James's use of narrative voice and McKay's incorporation of music and folk tale challenge the novel form itself. The combination of a modernist concern with newness and a desire to represent cultural traditions thus creates a fusion of realism and experimental form.

C. L. R. James

In 1932 the Trinidadian Marxist, social theorist, dramatist, novelist, biographer, sports commentator and political activist Cyril Lionel Robert James (1901–89) arrived in London. James's transatlantic voyage is central to the history of anticolonial thought; the moment in which the black colonial intellectual engages first hand with metropolitan modernism and British politics. During the 1930s James, through interaction with the cricketer Learie Constantine, fellow West Indian revolutionary George Padmore, and the International Labour Party, developed his Trotskyism and his anticolonialism. He published *The Black Jacobins* (1938), about the 1791 Haitian revolution, and his play *Toussaint L'Ouverture*, about the leader of that revolution, was performed on the West End stage starring Paul Robeson in 1936.

James was a polymath, moving with similar intensity from writings on world revolution to cricket commentary, but it is as a novelist that we need to

consider him here. When he arrived in London he was carrying the manuscript of a novel, *Minty Alley*, which was to be published by Secker and
Warburg in 1936. Writing later in his autobiography, *Beyond a Boundary*
(1963), James described his first transatlantic voyage: 'In March 1932
I boarded the boat for Plymouth. I was about to enter the arena where I
was to play the role for which I had prepared myself. The British intellectual
was going to Britain. About Britain I was a strange compound of knowledge
and ignorance.'[16] His colonial education had trained him, and his West
Indian identity entitled him, to contribute to the modernity of the metropolis.

During his first weeks in London, living in Bloomsbury, James wrote a
series of articles for the *Port of Spain Gazette* (collected as *Letters from
London* in 2003) documenting his reactions to the city and Bloomsbury in
particular. These articles are full of markers of cultural capital and his
fervour for intellectual debate seems unbounded. In 'The Bloomsbury
Atmosphere' he recounts attending a lecture by Edith Sitwell, at which he
is quick to demonstrate his knowledge by filling the gaps in her lecture with
the names of contemporary writers and composers.[17] While James does not
mention his racial difference in this account, his urgency to prove himself in
Bloomsbury implicitly suggests his fear that his black West Indian identity
might be seen to preclude him from such debate.

Some accounts of James's arrival in London have stressed his initial awe at
and acceptance of the high culture of Bloomsbury, feelings which eroded
with his political radicalization. But in fact, his early enthusiasm for
Bloomsbury is tempered by his attacks on the empty experimentation of
literary modernism (*Letters* 27–8) and his description of Bloomsbury living
as 'highly artificial' (52). He continued to have faith in the association of
Britishness with equality, justice and a revolutionary tradition, but his early
experiences confirmed that those values were not to be found in official or
mainstream culture (deadened by the effects of capitalist modernity) but in
the northern working-class communities he encountered, as well as in the
colonies (124).

While James was writing for a Trinidadian audience about London's
literary intelligentsia, he was writing for a London audience about working-class life in the West Indies, emblematic of his position as a black
European. In 1932 a small northern press published James's *The Life of
Captain Cipriani*, about the Trinidadian Labour leader, which was then
picked up by Leonard and Virginia Woolf, who published it as a pamphlet
entitled *The Case for West Indian Self Government* in the Hogarth Press's
Day to Day series in 1933. This document of colonial nationalism and the
ignorance about the West Indies which *The Case* rightly assumes of its
metropolitan readers tempers the celebration of 'intellectual ferment' in

Letters from London. Minty Alley sits alongside *The Case* in reminding us of James's commitment to working-class West Indians, but also of his disloca-tion: 'a British intellectual long before I was ten, already an alien in my own environment among my own people' (*Beyond* 18).

Minty Alley depicts the black middle-class bookseller Haynes's move to No. 2 Minty Alley, a house in the slum area, or 'barrack-yards' of Port of Spain, after the death of his mother, who had hoped to send her son to England to become a doctor. Cut off from his middle-class environment, Haynes becomes a detached observer of the economic and sexual tribulations of the inhabitants of the house. In particular, he observes a destructive and violent love triangle between the landlady, Mrs Rouse, her boyfriend Benoît and a nurse. He is gradually drawn into the drama by his love for Maisie, Mrs Rouse's niece, who eventually leaves for the USA.

The house is a microcosm of Trinidadian society, complete with racial tensions between Asians and Afro-Caribbeans, and suggestive of James's argument that the small scale of the islands contributed to their modernity by allowing for a more entire, and therefore developed, social vision.[18] The novel documents the economic hardship of Trinidadian life, as well as mourning its eclipse by a rising black middle class. As he wrote in his short story 'Triumph' (1929): 'No longer do the barrack-yarders live the pictur-esque life of twenty-five years ago ... The policeman is to the stick-fighter and "pierrot" as the sanitary inspector to mosquito larvae ... Barrack-yard life has lost its savour.'[19] At the end of the novel, Haynes, nostalgic for 'old times', returns to look through the windows of the house now represented by a new demographic: 'husband and wife and three children lived there and one of the children was sitting at the piano playing a familiar tune'.[20] James represented an urban black working class, but insisted on their modernity and internationalism rather than a nostalgic primitivism.[21]

Minty Alley is a realist novel, but its narrative perspective is limited to that of its protagonist, thereby eschewing the narratorial direction common to much social realism. The novel consists primarily of dialogue, as James gives voice to a community and takes it with him to Britain. Furthermore, as C. L. Innes argues, Haynes 'fails to take upon himself the authority his education and status give him; he desires to remain an onlooker' (*Black and Asian* 205). Haynes's alienation is similar to James's own. He embodies the pitfalls and benefits of the West Indian intellectual: 'Their attachment to the lower classes could be greater than that almost anywhere else, due to the intimacy of the surroundings. But it inevitably had a vicarious quality. That was their achievement and their limitation.'[22] James's position as a black Marxist anti-imperialist intellectual in London in the 1930s, alienated from a culture in whose model he had been educated, creates his countercultural position. As he put it, '[W]e are members of this civilization and take part in it, but we come from outside ... And it is when you are outside, but can take part as a member, that you see differently from the ways they see, and you are able to write independently.'[23]

Claude McKay

Like James, the Jamaican Claude McKay (1889–1948) in his politics and writing was dedicated to socialism and the representation of a global black working-class culture. Unlike James, he came to Britain via Harlem where he had published poetry, including his incendiary 'If We Must Die' (1919), in periodicals such as the *Masses* and the *Liberator*. He was to become a leading figure of the Harlem Renaissance, particularly with the publication of his collection of poetry *Harlem Shadows* in 1922, but between 1919 and 1921 he lived in London. McKay was outspoken about his hatred of England and the severe racism he encountered there, but, as he put it, 'if there was no romance for me in London, there was plenty of radical knowledge'.[24] At the International Socialist Club in Shoreditch he met Sylvia Pankhurst and became involved in the Workers' Socialist Federation, publishing poems and articles in its periodical, the *Workers' Dreadnought*. In his capacity as a reporter, McKay spent time at the London Docks interviewing African sailors. McKay was at the heart of British Communism, and mixed with anarchists, Sinn Féin supporters and anti-imperialists. It was in London that he developed his interest in Africa and his knowledge of Marxism, which led to his travels in the Soviet Union in 1922. He frequented the Drury Lane Club, established for nonwhite colonials and African-American soldiers, and the 1917 Club, a haunt of Fabians and Bloomsbury intellectuals. Despite the radicalism of his surroundings, as a gay black man he was certainly unusual, and socialism did not preclude racism. McKay was outspoken about the racism he encountered in the left-wing *Daily Herald*, for instance. One finds none of the celebration of London expressed by James; the severe racism he experienced caused him to feel embattled. McKay left London to travel through Europe, Africa and the Soviet Union, living in Morocco for several years before returning to the USA.

McKay's three novels, *Home to Harlem*, *Banjo: a Story Without a Plot* and *Banana Bottom*, all deal with black working-class culture and contact with Europe. The place of the black man in the modern world, the alienation of the black intellectual and the identification of a redemptive folk culture are all subjects addressed in his fiction. The links between form and politics are complex here, in that McKay was initially encouraged to write dialect poetry by Walter Jekyll, a white Jamaican (who appears as Squire Gensir in *Banana*

Bottom). In his introduction to McKay's 1920 collection of poetry, *Spring in New Hampshire*, I. A. Richards called him a 'pure-blooded Negro', representing the 'authentic' voice of the Jamaican peasant.[25] His use of the sonnet form, however, raises questions about the possibility of reclaiming conventional forms (as with the Jamaican poet Una Marson), as opposed to performing a primitivism created by a white intelligentsia. Behind McKay's representation of modern art and race in *Banjo* is his denunciation of modern primitivism: 'The slogan of the aesthetic art world is "Return to the Primitive." The Futurists and Impressionists are agreed in turning everything upside down in an attempt to achieve the wisdom of the primitive Negro ... Homage is rendered to dead Negro artists, while the living must struggle for recognition.'[26]

McKay's first two novels caused controversy among a black middle class who felt that he was simply reinforcing the demeaning stereotypes they were fighting to undo. DuBois wrote that '*Home to Harlem* ... for the most part nauseates me, and after the dirtier parts of its filth I feel distinctly like taking a bath ... McKay has set out to cater to that prurient demand on the part of white folk for a portrayal in Negroes of that utter licentiousness which conventional civilisation holds white folk back from enjoying.'[27] But McKay's novels engage in debates about class and racial identity that undermine the very dichotomies that DuBois's comments reinforce.

Banjo, set in the Ditch area of Marseilles in 1926, depicts the diversity and vibrancy of a diasporic black culture: 'in no other port had he ever seen congregated such a picturesque variety of Negroes. Negroes speaking the civilized tongues, Negroes speaking all the African dialects, black Negroes, brown Negroes, yellow Negroes' (56). The relationship between the eponymous protagonist, an African-American seaman, and Ray, a Haitian intellectual (who also appears in *Home to Harlem*) allows for the depiction of debates around class, race and social change. Ray politicizes Banjo (teaches him about the Haitian revolution and Abyssinia, and rids him of stereotypes about Africa), but is also drawn to the immediacy and determination of Banjo's existence. Like Haynes, Ray is the alienated black intellectual. He relies on writing about Banjo as the answer to racial awareness: 'if this renaissance we're talking about is going to be more than a sporadic and scabby thing, we'll have to get down to our racial roots to create it' (172). Modern civilization, for Ray, dehumanizes the black man by degrading him and cutting him off from his culture. Through Banjo, Ray can reconnect if not with his past then with the immediacy associated with that past.

But as with James, McKay's representations of black working-class communities are not idealized. His Harlem embodies dynamism: 'The sugared laughter. The honey-talk on its streets. And all night long, ragtime and "blues" playing somewhere, singing somewhere, dancing somewhere. Oh, the contagious fever of Harlem.'[28] But his characters' struggle in the face of pervasive racism is ever present. His novels, like James's *Minty Alley*, deal with cultural change, in particular the conflict between modernity and folk culture. For McKay, folk culture enables his characters to deal with the dehumanizing elements of modern life.

McKay's double consciousness can be seen in the fluctuation between high and popular culture in his novels. In *Home to Harlem* Jake identifies with the linguistic refashioning of James Joyce or D. H. Lawrence: he 'dreams of making something with words' (158). In wordcraft is the beginning of social revolution. But his novels are also collages of folk tales, songs and fables. The subtitle of *Banjo*, 'A Story without a Plot', indicates the impossibility of harmonious resolution or linear narrative.

In his third novel, *Banana Bottom*, Bita Plant returns to her native Jamaica after being educated in England. Resisting the attempts by her adoptive white missionary parents to arrange a suitable marriage for their protégée, Bita releases herself from constraints imposed on her and reconnects with the island and its folk traditions. The novel traces the conflict between European belief systems and Jamaican folk culture and religion. Critics have seen this novel as a resolution of the problems presented in the preceding two: Bita marries Jubban, who works on the land, but maintains 'the intellectual side of her life'.[29] The black intellectual is no longer a misfit. At the close of the novel, Bita is reading Pascal: her 'European' education has relevance for her rural Jamaican existence because she has learnt to separate its intellectual content from the value systems that contain it. With belief and confidence in her background, she can reread and reassess European thought.

Nella Larsen

Some obscurity surrounds the details of Nella Larsen's (1891–1964) mixed-race parentage, but her Danish West Indian origins led to movement between diverse ethnic communities. She grew up in a Scandinavian community in Chicago, but her blackness became an issue after her mother's second marriage, to a white man. After Larsen's estrangement from her family, she moved to New York where she became a key figure of the Harlem Renaissance and published two novels, *Quicksand* (1928) and *Passing* (1929). She was always keen to stress her European *and* West Indian ancestry, and her novels can be characterized by cross-cultural movement, depicting an international black identity. Harlem appears in both novels, but it is portrayed in the context of a global black diaspora. Between 1930 and 1932 Larsen travelled around Europe on a Guggenheim Fellowship, working on a novel called 'Mirage', which was never published.

Larsen's mixed-race background is crucial for her novels, which need to be placed in the context of 'passing' literature. Larsen rejects the figure of the 'tragic mulatto' caught between races, supposedly evidence of the disastrous effects of miscegenation. Instead, her aesthetic vision centres on the fluctuation and instability of racial categories and their particular effects on women. Like Jean Rhys, her attention to the restrictions placed on women because of both race and gender, and to the psychological consequences of these, make her novels unusual for the period.

Quicksand follows its protagonist, mixed-race Helga Crane, on a journey from the American South, to Chicago, to Harlem, to Copenhagen and back to the South. Helga, like Larsen, has a black father who has abandoned her but whose racial identity she fully accepts. In the novel Helga's mother, again like Larsen's, has married a white man and subsequently disengaged from her black child. Each of the geographical sites in the novel represents not only a stage in Helga's development, but also a range of attitudes towards racial identity. Helga resigns from Naxos College, modelled in part on the Tuskegee Institute where Larsen worked briefly. She cannot accept its philosophy of racial uplift, based on Booker T. Washington's policies of accommodation, cleanliness, good manners and labour as the key to the social progress of African-Americans.

The novel then moves to Harlem, via Chicago, where Helga is excited by the 'gorgeous panorama' but haunted by an inability to find a place which offers her a fulfilling life as a black woman: 'somewhere, within her, in a deep recess, crouched discontent'.[30] She works as a speechwriter for Mrs Hayes-Rore, who is involved in black women's political organizations. Helga confronts the hypocrisy of those who are driven by the 'race problem' and by a burning hatred of whites, yet mimic their bourgeois lifestyle and reject 'the songs, the dances, and the softly blurred speech of the race' (51). From Harlem, Helga goes to Copenhagen, where she is displayed as an exotic object by her aunt and uncle. She becomes a sign of their modernity: 'a decoration. A curio ... her dark, alien appearance was to most people an astonishment' (75). This connects her to the only other black people she sees in Copenhagen: at the circus she is filled with 'a fierce hatred for the cavorting Negroes on the stage' (85). From the opening passage of the novel, in which Helga is framed by patterns of light and shade, the text slips between her own aesthetic appreciation of beauty, and her exhibition by others. 'The blue Chinese carpet ... the bright covers of the books ... the oriental silk which covered the stool at her slim feet'; these are the markers of her modernity, her cosmopolitanism, her middle-class status (5). But in Copenhagen those silks turn her into an exotic commodity: 'she was dressed in the shining black taffeta with its bizarre trimmings of purple and cerise' (71).

The novel traces the black Atlantic. The journeys that Helga makes suggest both the opportunities open to working women and the restrictions imposed on her by her race. Larsen portrays the commodification and exhibition of women, and the difficulties for women who attempt to reject marriage and motherhood. As a black woman Helga occupies an overdetermined position in terms of illicit, uncontained or pathological sexuality.[31] Her one disastrous attempt to express her sexuality results in a retreat into submissive motherhood. The novel ends with her pregnant with her fifth child, married to a preacher in rural Alabama.

Larsen's second novel, *Passing*, subtly explores the psychology of the denial of racial identity. It foregrounds the economic and class contexts for 'passing', as well as its particular significance for women, including the fear of childbirth as a moment of exposure: 'nobody wants a dark child'.[32] Two childhood friends reconnect in Harlem's Sugar Hill district in 1927. Irene Redfield lives a comfortable, black middle-class existence with her physician husband and two sons. Clare Kendry, to escape from her black working-class origins, has married wealthy white John Bellew, who is unaware of her African-American identity. Their reencounter makes each woman aware of her dissatisfaction with her life: Clare desires the company of black women, and enters Irene's world of parties and charity events, thereby threatening her 'white' existence, and Irene is attracted to Clare's risk-taking in contrast to her own conventional lifestyle. Clare represents a threat not only to Irene's marriage, but also to her identity. In the final scene, just as Clare's husband has realized that she is black, Irene pushes Clare, who falls from a window and dies.

The anonymity of the city facilitates racial performance. In a chance encounter between the two women, which takes place on the roof terrace of a whites-only hotel in Chicago, both women are passing for white. Irene, despite her charity work for the racial uplift organization the Negro Welfare League (based on the National Urban League), denies her racial background for reasons of social convenience. Even when not literally 'passing', Irene's social aspirations become a kind of denial, or mimicking, of white bourgeois codes. The novel, and this scene in particular, hovers over the fear of exposure. Clare's willingness to flirt with this fear, by rekindling her friendship with Irene, threatens the codes of propriety that govern Irene's existence. Irene cannot have Clare free, as she puts it.

The modernity of Larsen's novels revolves around her depiction of the constructedness of racial boundaries and categories, and the performance of racial identity. On the advice of Carl Van Vechten, Larsen sent an advance copy of *Quicksand* to Gertrude Stein, expressing admiration for her 'performance' of blackness in 'Melanctha' (1909).[33] Larsen explores the silences and distortions occasioned by racial oppression, particularly in the context of female friendship and desire. The economics of skin colour that runs through her work has particular implications for women in terms of marriage and social mobility. Clare passes for white to gain the privileges of her black middle-class friends, denied her by her black working-class background. However, Clare crosses not only a racial divide, but also the codes of female behaviour. For this reason Clare instigates both attraction and repulsion in Irene; Irene both wants to be her, and to extinguish the threat she represents to her existence. She desires Clare – 'the soft white face, the disturbing scarlet mouth, the dreaming eyes, the caressing smile, the whole torturing loveliness that had been Clare Kendry' (111) – and her bravery: 'she wanted, suddenly, to shock people, to hurt them, to make them notice her, to be aware of her suffering' (92).

Jean Toomer

Jean Toomer (1894–1967) occupies a complex position in the history of African-American writing. He has been seen as emblematic of the Harlem Renaissance, and his 1923 novel *Cane* feted as its pinnacle. However, his complicated racial ancestry and rejection of the label 'black' has led to doubts as to whether this is the most appropriate context for his work. Although both Toomer's parents had African-American (and Indian) blood, they were light skinned and could therefore pass for white. Toomer's childhood reinforced this racial ambiguity when, after his parents' divorce, his mother's remarriage and later death, he moved from middle-class white neighbourhoods to less affluent black ones. Toomer's life can be characterized by movement between communities and systems of belief. As he himself put it, 'I am locomotive, nomadic.'[34]

Critics have seized on Toomer's statement to Nancy Cunard, 'I am not a Negro', as a denial of his race rather than a renunciation of what he saw as the restrictions of racial categorizing.[35] He was reluctant to be part of her *Negro* anthology (1934), preferring to think of himself as American: 'There is a new race in America. I am a member of this new race. It is neither white nor black nor in-between. It is the American race' (*Reader* 105). Toomer's life and writings, as well as his transatlantic voyages, were motivated by a search for spiritual fulfilment, which led him to the Russian mystic Georgi Ivanovich Gurdjieff and his philosophical system based on the attainment of higher levels of consciousness through rigorous mental and physical exercises.[36] He became a disciple of Gurdjieff and led workshops on his teachings in New York (attended at one point by Larsen) and in 1924 he made his first trip to the Gurdjieff Institute for Harmonious Development of Man in Fontainebleau, France, where Katherine Mansfield had died from tuberculosis the year before. Toomer was to attend the Institute again in 1926 and 1927.

Toomer's devotion to religious and spiritual thought dominated and directed his writings (essays, pamphlets and poems) after the publication of his only novel and by far his most famous publication. *Cane* was inspired by Toomer's work at an agricultural college in Sparta, Georgia, and his exposure to black folk culture. Just as problems of classification have preoccupied discussions of Toomer's racial identity, critics have puzzled over the generic definition of this text. The work is a collage of short stories, sketches, poems and drama and is usually classified as a novel (though Toomer never described it in this way), as it is here, but has alternatively been called a 'novel-poem', a 'mosaic of poems, short stories, and intense sketches' and a 'collage of fiction, songs and poetry'.[37] Many of the pieces in *Cane* were published separately in periodicals such as *Crisis*, *The Liberator* and *Broom* before Waldo Frank persuaded Toomer to approach Boni & Liveright about publication. *Cane* made debates about Toomer's racial identity public, debates that were to plague him throughout his life, particularly after his marriages to white women.

While Toomer resented Frank's emphasis on the author's racial identity in his introduction to *Cane*, the impetus for the novel came from his belief that the folk culture of the African-American South represented what was authentic and meaningful in the face of modernization and mechanization. The poetic sections of the text, often ignored in favour of the prose, are nostalgic and elegiac in tone: 'O land and soil, red soil and sweet-gum tree, / So scant of grass, so profligate of pines, / Now just before an epoch's sun declines / Thy son, in time, I have returned to thee.'[38] However, while *Cane* celebrates aspects of Southern black culture, it certainly does not wholly romanticize it. The text is full of racial violence, from lynchings to other murderous effects of racial segregation. Furthermore, Toomer recognized that his ideas about a new American race lay not in a retreat from modernity: 'If anything comes up now, pure Negro, it will be a swan song. Dont [*sic*] let us fool ourselves, brother: the Negro of the folk-song has all but passed away' (*Reader* 24).

Cane is divided into three sections, the first and third set in rural Georgia and the second section, written after the other two, in the urban North (Washington, DC and Chicago). Section one includes sketches about a number of rural women, who embody the vanishing beauty of the folk-spirit and proximity to the land but are also victimized and made outcasts by the racial tensions and sexual codes which pervade their communities. The first sketch, 'Karintha', depicts a woman whose extraordinary beauty and vitality is coopted by the desire of men to 'bring her money'. In another sketch Becky, a white woman with two black sons, is socially ostracized and eventually killed when the cabin she has been forced to live in collapses. Toomer's characters are invariably mixed-race or caught between communities or ways of life. *Cane* depicts the movement beyond racial boundaries, but also the destruction that can result from such movement in a culture riven by the distinction between black and white. 'Fern', with a Jewish father and black mother, is the embodiment of sorrow, and 'Esther', whose father is the richest coloured man in town, is caught between communities: a black bourgeoisie predicated on white values and black folk culture represented by the preacher Barlo. The section ends with the lynching and mutilation of Tom Burwell, violent racism brought about by the violent reaction to inter-racial sexual rivalry.

In section two the reader makes the migration north and the pace of the text changes. Here, Toomer introduces jazz and dramatic forms, to parallel the changed forms of black cultural expression in the context of urbanization. His sketches focus on relationships which cross racial or class divides as they are played out in various urban sites, such as 'Seventh Street' in Washington, DC or the Howard Theatre where Toomer was briefly manager. The third section consists of one story, 'Kabnis', originally written as a play, in which Ralph Kabnis, a mixed-race Northerner, returns South to reconnect with his roots, but instead finds a community disfigured by racial violence and terrorized by the fear of lynchings. Kabnis fails to see strength in the black community, and the story ends in self-hatred and despair at the situation in the South.

Cane is a text that fuses hope and despair. It celebrates the strength and vitality of African-American culture at the same time as it acknowledges the destructive forces of both racial violence and modernity. Its form, too, mirrors this fusion, in its interplay between fragmentation and wholeness, the formal experimentation associated with high modernism and folk culture. As the text weaves together various dichotomies – North/South, male/female, rural/urban, black/white – their rigidity is called into question. *Cane* has troubled critics, who have had problems finding a vocabulary to encompass its multigeneric form, or have found it hard to square its role as inaugurator of the Harlem Renaissance with Toomer's own description of his racial identity.

Cane is an apt place to leave our discussion, as it signals the impossibility of any neat categorization of 'black Atlantic' modernism. As evoked in the epigraph to this chapter, Ray's 'pose' comes to life. He breaks the containment of his objectification as black male and speaks, as a metropolitan subject and participant in the city's intellectual and cultural debates. The diverse reasons for the transatlantic crossings made by these four writers echo the diversity of their engagement with racial difference as it impacts on questions of class, sexuality, literary form, urbanization and national identity. In a recent anthology of modernist writing, Lawrence Rainey makes an editorial decision to exclude black writers on the grounds that 'any attempt to include them [Langston Hughes, Zora Neale Hurston] in an anthology containing Joyce, Eliot, Woolf, and Stein would inevitably smack of tokenism'.[39] The implication of unity behind Rainey's 'them' does more damage than would the inclusion of Larsen or McKay in his anthology. Furthermore, to refuse to provoke consideration of the transnational *and* transracial contact points of modernist writing obscures key aspects not only of the work by the four novelists considered in this chapter, but also work by the four canonical modernists cited by Rainey. For James, McKay, Larsen and Toomer, those moments of contact, literal or metaphorical, are moments of double consciousness, of conflict and collaboration, but they speak nevertheless to the impossibility of talking about Western modernity or Anglo-American modernism as discrete from the history of black writing.

Notes

1. Claude McKay, *Banjo* (London: The X Press, 2000), p. 112. Further references cited parenthetically.
2. See Andreas Huyssen, 'Geographies of Modernism in a Globalizing World', in Peter Brooker and Andrew Thacker (eds.), *Geographies of Modernism: Literatures, Cultures, Spaces* (London: Routledge, 2005), p. 9.
3. See Howard Booth and Nigel Rigby (eds.), *Modernism and Empire* (Manchester: Manchester University Press, 2000).
4. Jane Marcus, *Hearts of Darkness: White Women Write Race* (New Brunswick: Rutgers University Press, 2004), p. 50.
5. C. L. Innes, *A History of Black and Asian Writing in Britain* (Cambridge: Cambridge University Press, 2002), p. 167.
6. Cary D. Wintz, *Black Culture and the Harlem Renaissance* (Houston: Rice University Press, 1988), pp. 14, 20.
7. Paul Gilroy, *The Black Atlantic: Modernity and Double Consciousness* (London: Verso, 1993), pp. 15, 2. Further references cited parenthetically.
8. George Hutchinson, *The Harlem Renaissance in Black and White* (Cambridge, MA: Harvard University Press, 1995), p. 14. For an alternative view, see Houston A. Baker, *Modernism and the Harlem Renaissance* (Chicago: University of Chicago Press, 1987).
9. See Simon Gikandi, *Writing in Limbo: Modernism and Caribbean Literature* (Ithaca: Cornell University Press, 1992).
10. See Anuradha Dingwaney Needham, 'Inhabiting the Metropole: C. L. R. James and the Postcolonial Intellectual of the African Diaspora', *Diaspora* 2:3 (1993), pp. 281–303.

11. Virginia Woolf, *A Room of One's Own and Three Guineas*, ed. Morag Shiach (Oxford: Oxford University Press, 1992), p. 65.

12. Ras Makonnen, quoted in Cedric Robinson, *Black Marxism* (London: Zed, 1983), pp. 372–3.

13. Alison Donnell, 'Una Marson: feminism, anti-colonialism and a forgotten fight for freedom', in Bill Schwarz (ed.), *West Indian Intellectuals in Britain* (Manchester: Manchester University Press, 2003), p. 116.

14. Sukhdev Sandhu, *London Calling: How Black and Asian Writers Imagined a City* (London: HarperCollins, 2003), p. 120.

15. See Michael North, *The Dialect of Modernism: Race, Language and Twentieth-Century Literature* (Oxford: Oxford University Press, 1994), p. 101.

16. C. L. R. James, *Beyond a Boundary* (London: Serpent's Tail, 1994), p. 111. Further references cited parenthetically.

17. C. L. R. James, *Letters from London* (Oxford: Signal Books, 2003), p. 25. Further references cited parenthetically.

18. Stephen Howe, 'C. L. R. James: Visions of History, Visions of Britain', in Schwartz (ed.), *West Indian Intellectuals*, p. 157.

19. *The C. L. R. James Reader*, ed. Anna Grimshaw (Oxford: Blackwell, 1992), pp. 29–30.

20. C. L. R. James, *Minty Alley* (London: New Beacon Books, 1994), p. 244.

21. See 'A National Purpose for Caribbean Peoples', *At the Rendezvous of Victory: Selected Writings* (London: Allison and Busby, 1984), pp. 143–58.

22. Paul Buhle, *C. L. R. James: The Artist as Revolutionary* (London: Verso, 1988), p. 33.

23. C. L. R. James, 'Discovering Literature in Trinidad: the 1930s', in *Spheres of Existence: Selected Writings* (London: Allison and Busby, 1980), pp. 237–44.

24. Claude McKay, *A Long Way From Home* (London: Pluto Press, 1985), p. 69.

25. I. A. Richards, 'Preface', in Claude McKay, *Spring in New Hampshire* (London: Grant Richards, 1920), p. 5.

26. Claude McKay, *The Negroes in America*, ed. Alan L. McLeod, trans. Robert J. Winter (Port Washington, NY: Kennikat Press, 1979), pp. 63–4.

27. W. E. B. DuBois, 'Two Novels', *Crisis* 35:6 (1928), p. 202.

28. Claude McKay, *Home to Harlem* (London: The X Press, 2000), p. 10. Further references cited parenthetically.

29. Claude McKay, *Banana Bottom* (London: Pluto Press, 1986), p. 313.

30. Nella Larsen, *Quicksand* (Harmondsworth: Penguin, 2002), p. 50. Further references cited parenthetically.

31. See Amelia DeFalco, 'Jungle Creatures and Dancing Apes: Modern Primitivism and Nella Larsen's *Quicksand*', *Mosaic* 38:2 (2005), pp. 19–36.

32. Nella Larsen, *Passing* (Harmondsworth: Penguin, 2003), p. 36. Further references cited parenthetically.

33. Jessica G. Rabin, *Surviving the Crossing: (Im)migration, Ethnicity and Gender in Willa Cather, Gertrude Stein and Nella Larsen* (New York: Routledge, 2004), pp. 136–7.

34. Jean Toomer, *A Jean Toomer Reader*, ed. Frederik L. Rusch (New York: Oxford University Press, 1993), p. 3. Further references cited parenthetically.

35. Toomer, quoted in North, *Dialect*, p. 150.

36. Charles R. Larson, *Invisible Darkness: Jean Toomer and Nella Larsen* (Iowa City: University of Iowa Press, 1993), p. 37.
37. Brian Joseph Benson and Mabel Mayle Dillard, *Jean Toomer* (Boston: Twayne, 1980), p. 50.
38. Jean Toomer, *Cane* (New York: Liveright, 1975), p. 12.
39. Lawrence Rainey, *Modernism: An Anthology* (Oxford: Blackwell, 2005), p. xxxi.

15

LOIS OPPENHEIM

Situating Samuel Beckett

However astute Friedrich Nietzsche's observation that 'the big problems [are] like cold baths; you have to get out as fast as you [get] in', one would be ill advised to withdraw too rapidly from the 'big problem' of modernism.[1] There is much to be gained, as we have seen in the preceding chapters, by framing the fiction of a given author in accordance with the historical, stylistic and thematic parameters of the modernist aesthetic. Yet just where a writer as slippery as Samuel Beckett (1906–1989) lies on the spectrum that extends from early to late, from low to high and then post, has prompted considerable debate in recent years.[2] It will not be the purpose of this chapter to enter that debate, but rather to suggest a means of access into Beckett's novels that will reveal the essence of their link to modernism, regardless of the prefix one assigns to the term.

We might begin by noting that Beckett's fiction clearly exhibits the oppositional spirit fundamental to the modernist enterprise. In fact, his experimentation with novelistic form reveals an opposition to the conventional rules of narration so extraordinary that when he began writing novels it provoked a veritable crisis of genre. That is to say, the congruence of form and content – such as is found in the dissolution, at once, of any coherent storytelling and of any real character identity – threw into question the very nature of the novel itself. Already in his 1931 essay *Proust*, which appeared in print several years before his first novel, one perceived the preoccupation with the recovering of lost selves in which the primary tension of his own novelistic concerns would originate. If reality in Proust's masterwork depended upon the projection of an individual's subjective awareness and, at the same time, every individual was revealed to be a succession of individuals, reality maintained nonetheless a veneer of constancy. This discovery of conflict between reality and our perception of it made an extraordinary appearance in Proust's novel that Beckett described, with his characteristically intelligent wit, thus: 'The mortal microcosm cannot forgive the relative immortality of the macrocosm. The whisky bears a grudge against the decanter.'[3] And it was precisely this opposition that would impel Beckett's own novelistic vision.

Residing from the late 1930s in France, Beckett was not alone in upending that country's tradition of the well-made novel so eloquently served by Honoré de Balzac, Stendhal and Emile Zola in the preceding century. Among the earliest practitioners of what would become known in the 1950s as the *nouveau roman* (or 'new novel'), he shared with Alain Robbe-Grillet and others the will to free the novel from its subservience to a reality all too familiar to author, character and reader alike. But Beckett's oppositional penchant was unique in not being restricted to a rupture with that novelistic tradition. For what is deeply embedded in all his fiction is a resistance to his own writing, and to the opacity of language more generally, and it is in this self-resistance that the source of the modernist/postmodernist debate with regard to his work lies.

The psychoanalyst Bennett Simon has called ours 'the age of the schizoid' and situated the characteristic features of Beckett's writing – depersonalization, ego fragmentation, blocked affect and communicative dysfunction – well within it.[4] The novelist's earliest critics, though, sought to situate his writings within the tradition of twentieth-century continental philosophy. It made good sense in 1961 for the critic Martin Esslin to write apropos of Beckett's play *Waiting for Godot* (1956), 'There is here a truly astonishing parallel between the Existentialist philosophy of Jean-Paul Sartre and the creative intuition of Beckett.'[5] It also made good sense in 1963 for Robbe-Grillet to relate that intuition to philosopher Martin Heidegger's notion of being-in-the-world, or *Dasein*. If Georg Hegel had conceived of a pure being and a pure nonbeing, two opposing abstractions whose unification was the basis of reality, Sartre dismissed any presupposition of the simultaneity of these abstractions. Heidegger, however, went even further in establishing the existence of nothingness in anxiety, the affective manifestation of its apprehension by the self. And when Beckett's novels were read as allegorical equivalents of such philosophic theses, as parables of the (post?) modernist (or at least post-Cartesian) philosophic tradition very much in the air at the time, it seemed undeniable that sense could be made of a literary oeuvre seemingly devoted to its own denial. What better critical handle for reading Beckett than the increasingly refined proof of the reality of absence? After all, beginning with *Murphy* (1938) and continuing into the 1950s with the trilogy *Molloy* (1951), *Malone Dies* (1951), and *The Unnamable* (1953), almost nothing was left of the dialogue, character and action that had previously constituted the genre. Whether contextualized psychosocially or philosophically, then, it was Beckett's fictive *un*writing of narrative,[6] and his depiction of the negative impulse itself, that his mid-century readers were seeking to frame.

In the decades following, Jean-François Lyotard, Jürgen Habermas and Gianni Vattimo debated the 'end of modernity' and Beckett's critics were quick to fall in step. Was Beckett a modernist? Was he rather neo- or postmodernist? As the twentieth century neared its close, a kind of desperate attempt to locate his work on a spectrum ill-defined from the start was felt. Porter Abbott, one of the smartest writers on Beckett around, gave us 'Late Modernism: Samuel Beckett and the Art of the Oeuvre'. Breon Mitchell offered 'Samuel Beckett and the Postmodern Controversy'. Nicholas Zurbrugg jumped in with the judicious 'Seven Types of Postmodernity: Several Types of Samuel Beckett'. And books by Steven Connor, Leslie Hill, Thomas Trezise, and Richard Begam all tackled the question of Beckett's subversive projecting of nothing in one form or another.[7] The circumscription of Beckett's perpetually slippery writing – by which I mean his resistance to his own previously written word, which took the form both of a perpetual undoing of text within a given work and a rewriting of one text within the next – had found a new critical forum.

Concomitantly, though, the philosopher Richard Rorty was calling for an end to the postmodern, the author Umberto Eco was claiming that the confusion surrounding the terms 'modern' and 'postmodern' was post-modern in and of itself, and the sociologist Bruno Latour went so far as to argue that 'No-one has ever been modern', that 'Modernity has never begun.'[8] Perhaps they had good cause to reduce the dichotomy. Perhaps not. But in the interest of establishing the extent to which Beckett's novels reveal not only the modernist preoccupation with the plasticity of narrative structure, but also the modernist fascination with the expressivity of language itself, one might rethink his fiction in terms of what follows here.

Insofar as Beckett was explicit in defining art, whether verbal or visual, not as object or thing, but as *agent* of both the artist and the reader/spectator's perception, art was not to be construed as inherently representational. It was not, in other words, to be conceived as successfully re-presenting the world as an objectively knowable phenomenon; viewed thus, it was doomed to failure from the start. Artistic legitimacy, rather, could reside for Beckett only in the depiction of the absence of such representation; in short, in the depiction of nothingness – which necessarily produces a profoundly uncanny effect. In his writings on literature and painting, and in a now celebrated letter to an acquaintance, Axel Kaun, Beckett set forth this thinking and in his novels he put it to the test. Indeed, it is precisely his persistent effort to achieve in his fiction the representation of nothingness, to attain his ideal of 'a literature of the unword', that challenges the critic in any attempt to qualify Beckett's modernism as early, high, late, or post.[9] For Beckett's novels reveal no more or less than the very uncanniness of his creative purpose. Of what, though, does the uncanny effect in Beckett's work consist?

Beckett's uncanny

In *Being and Time* Heidegger locates the uncanny within *Dasein*'s encounter with the 'nothing' of the world. '[A]nxiety', he writes, 'brings [*Dasein*] back from its absorption in the "world"' and, as '[e]veryday familiarity collapses' and *Dasein* is individualized, it enters 'the existential "mode" of the "*not-at-home*"'.[10] Similarly, in his 1919 paper on the subject, Sigmund Freud focuses on the horrifying quality of that which is unhomelike or unhomely (on the 'un' of the *unheimlich* that serves not to oppose it to the *heimlich*, but to reveal its origin within it): 'the "uncanny" is that class of the terrifying which leads back to something long known to us, once very familiar'.[11] In a word, then, the uncanny originates in a reemergence of the negated or repressed.

Freud describes a number of circumstances in which the familiar becomes frightening and uncanny. These include confusion between inanimate and animate objects; the doubling that arises, for example, from critical self-observation; involuntary or random repetition (as in the recurrence of the same number in several events of close succession); the projection of envy on to others that is betrayed in the fear of the evil eye; and the overestimation of the power of one's thinking or the belief in the omnipotence of one's mental processes. What is remarkable is the consistency with which these circumstances are traceable in Beckett's fiction and the regularity of their uncanny effect.

While what Freud had in mind with regard to confusion between living and lifeless objects was more on the order of a child's treatment of a doll as a person, Beckett's characters (to the extent they can be termed that) relate to inanimate objects as though they were extensions of themselves. Crutches and bicycles, bowler hats and tattered garments: all are quite inseparable from their owner in Beckett's fiction and they muddle the animate/inanimate boundary to elicit a similarly uncanny result. Consider the relation of the principal character to his rocking chair in Beckett's first published novel: not only is Murphy bound to the chair by seven scarves that restrict his movements to 'only the most local', but insofar as it is 'his own', the chair 'never [leaves] him'. In fact, it is the attachment of the chair to his thereby 'appeased' body that frees him to 'come alive in his mind'.[12] Likewise, the narrator of *How It Is* (1964) holds steadfastly to his sack as he makes his way, belly down, in the mud because it is equated with his life. More extreme is Molloy who, in the novel of the same name, conceives of himself only in relation to the infinite parameters of the universe with which he is fused. The uncanny in Beckett's fiction derives, then, from instances where psychic and physical demarcation, like those of ego and world or self and other, is blurred.

Doubling is so frequently employed by Beckett as to have become a platitude in critical analyses of his work. Self-awareness, splitting and twinning lend a palpable fragility to the Beckettian speaking subject. Indeed, it is the precariousness of the ego and the need for self-preservation that provoke the defence: like the setting of voices on tape in certain of Beckett's plays (most notably *Krapp's Last Tape* and *Rockaby*, published in 1959 and 1981 respectively), the flow of identities from one self to another in his novels, particularly in the trilogy, harbours a terror of extinction. The title alone of the third of those novels gives an ironic name to the dreaded annihilation of self whence the doubling evolves. Beckett's penultimate work, *Stirrings Still* (1988) – where the lone image is of one who sees himself seeing his previous comings and goings – is also a case in point. In focusing the character's (mental) eyes on himself and, specifically, on a self whose only real activity is (mentally) visual, the narrative makes doubling a means of triumphing over ego dissolution or death: 'One night as he sat at his table head on hands he saw himself rise and go. One night or day. For when his own light went out he was not left in the dark.'[13]

Doubling takes still other forms in Beckett's fiction. There is, for example, the 'ghosting' (Ruby Cohn's term) – in other words, the ghostly presences, ghostly decors and ghostly language – that runs throughout the texts.[14] I will return shortly to the negation of such uncanny elements, for therein resides the key to Beckett's undoing of narrative structure and the unwriting that he so strategically shapes. My point here is simply that doubling, a rich motif in Beckett's novels, extends from ego-splitting to revenants and beyond, and that it not only serves a self-preservational purpose but can become, as Freud notes in his essay, 'the ghastly harbinger of death' (141).

It goes without saying that repetition is an important aesthetic strategy in Beckett that is neither involuntary nor random. His play on the (ad nauseam) repetition of night and day, for example, continually unveils the passage of time (the *sine qua non* of his texts) as something familiar yet new or foreign, eerie even, to lend an uncanny effect. So, too, the 'repetition by distortion' or 'misremembering' (as Abbott calls it) that is Beckett's means of creating – or, more accurately, decreating, insofar as it is a dismantling of previously used material – is deliberate. Beyond tropic variations and readaptations of narrative themes, though, less determined philosophic and artistic leitmotifs also unleash the uncanny effect: the manias for measuring and symmetry – as seen in *Watt* (1953) and *The Lost Ones* (1970) for instance – may be noted in this regard.[15] And Molloy's obsessive repositioning in his pockets of his sixteen sucking stones is another obvious example. In their subtle reminiscence of the compulsive nature of human instincts and of certain pathologies as well, these repetitions are perceived as uncanny to the extent that they bring to the brink of consciousness wishes formerly deeply repressed in the unconscious mind.

One has only to consider the short prose text that dates to 1956, 'From an Abandoned Work', to know just how nefarious the dreaded gaze or evil eye can be. Oedipal thoughts of uniting with the mother are impeded in the short story by a paternalized roadman who sends the narrator a petrifying 'look'. Having gone 'in terror of him as a child', the narrator exclaims, 'Now he is dead and I resemble him.'[16] As Michel Bernard has noted, 'The son has interiorized the threat, and what the narrator now fears is punishment by his superego as a by-product of castration.'[17] Even more explicit is the disturbing quality of Beckett's aptly titled *Film* (1967) where the uncanny stems from the indulgence of O (object) in the agony of being visually perceived and from the extreme measures taken by him to avoid the scrutiny of E (eye). Again, the connection to the threat of castration is evident; so, too, is the link to the last instance of the uncanny that Freud describes – the narcissistic overestimation of the power of subjective thought and the concomitant risk posed by one's mental potency with respect to the external world. For such fearful intensity can stem only from a belief in the synonymy of intention and act, a belief in the magical powers of self and others comparable to the animistic notion of the world that the maturing mind, with its increasing faculty of judgement, comes to reject.

It almost goes without saying that belief in the omnipotence of mentation is the compelling force in Beckett's novels. The predominance of mind in this fiction ensues from an overwhelming awareness of (and defensive manoeuvring against) what victimizes the human being and defines, in fact, the human condition: time. As Beckett explained in *Proust*, 'the world [is] a projection of the individual's consciousness' and is thus created and recreated continually by way of those laws of memory and habit that, 'never integrally and at once' but bit by bit, allow for its possession (12, 17–18). With the body in various states of disintegration as it voyages through time towards its demise, the mind of the Beckett character flows through the formlessness of thought to triumph over the decomposing physical reality. So fluid is the mind, in fact, so synonymous is it with existence, that the Beckettian character is poignantly and forever in search of the self, of the 'I' that it inhabits. As the Unnamable puts it, '[W]e must have walls, I need walls, good and thick, I need a prison, I was right, for me alone, I'll go there now, I'll put me in it, I'm there already, I'll start looking for me now, I'm there somewhere, it won't be I, no matter, I'll say it's I, perhaps it will be I ...'[18] However transient and ephemeral the identity of self, though, however many Murphys, Molloys, Malones, Mahoods, and, ultimately, Unnamables the Beckettian 'I' assumes, there is always recognition of a core self, a return to the fold. To put it somewhat differently, it is the uncanny familiarity of the psychic self that has been or will be other that impels continuance, that allows one to 'go on'.

Space prevents a closer examination of these manifestations of the uncanny in Beckett's fictive work. My purpose thus far has been simply to establish ground for the observation that the uncanny may be said to account for the frequently cited primary conundrum associated with this author – namely, how it is that his novels result from a continual *un*writing of narrative. For the confusion between inanimate and animate, the doubling, repetition, fear of the look, and omnipotent thinking characteristic of his work all display an eerie familiarity within the strange *nonassumption of identity* and *nonoccurrence of event* that constitute the Beckett text.[19] Having referred, however, to a higher order of the oppositional impulse that aims precisely at undoing the uncanny element – or, more precisely, at revealing the creative process as a (however paradoxical) representation of the failure of representation – I turn now to this dimension of Beckett's modernist enterprise and to the function it may be said to serve.

Undoing the uncanny

Beckett's primary narrative purpose – to create 'a literature of the unword' – may be understood in terms of a three-step process. The first is the representation of absence that I have qualified in terms of the uncanny effect. I have said that the uncanny is linked to anxiety as the source of repression and to a reemergence of the repressed in familiar guise. The representation of this anxiety-laden repression, the imaging of absence in an uncanny form, is what Sidney Feshbach has called the 'projection in a visual image such that the image seems to take on a life of its own'.[20] And, indeed, Beckett's aesthetic figuration of the body's uncanny extension through objects outside it, of the eerie gaze of the evil eye, and of the many uncanny doublings and ghosts are indelibly marked on the mind of the reader.

We have only to consider Beckett's persistent play in his narratives with the generic mother to appreciate how powerful his images of repression or absence may be. Despite her missing persona, the unspecified mother in his work continually poses a formidable threat of engulfment. In *Film*, where objects project the undepicted mother in all her phantom glory, this is put in high relief on the screen. But it is just as vividly imaged on the written page. Take, for example, the postwar short story *First Love* (1946) whose Oedipal title is by no means gratuitous. It is precisely the inconspicuous presence of the mother and her wifely reincarnation (as ghost of an already ghosted mother) that render the narrator-son's response (or lack thereof) to her abandonment of him profound. The son's affective unresponsiveness (which he humorously refers to as 'anxiety constipation') is a protective mechanism and the ghosting of the maternal imago is undertaken in self-defence. The birth of the child that ultimately sends the narrator fleeing at the close of the story repeats the process insofar as the protagonist-son ignores the ghosted maternal figure – now his wife, the mother of his infant – erasing her in much the same way as he had erased his own mother. This brings us to the second of the three steps involved in Beckett's narrative process: the negation of the representation of absence.

It is interesting to note how consistently strong is the need in Beckett's fiction to erase what is not visibly present. A constancy of memory erasure runs as a leitmotif throughout all Beckett's novels and plays.[21] The following passage, from *Murphy*, is characteristic in this regard:

> When he was naked he lay down in a tuft of soaking tuffets and tried to get a picture of Celia. In vain. Of his mother. In vain. Of his father (for he was not illegitimate). In vain ... He tried again with his father, his mother, Celia, Wylie, Neary, Cooper, Miss Dew, Miss Carridge, Nelly, the sheep, the chandlers, even Bom and Co., even Bim, even Ticklepenny and Miss Counihan, even Mr. Quigley. He tried with the men, women, children and animals that belong to even worse stories than this. In vain in all cases. (251)

Beckett's impersonal characterizations (however oxymoronic the concept) reveal struggles for identity embedded in obliteration: if affect is flat and numbness prevails as a primary feature of Beckett's narratives, it is not that structures of familial conflict are denied, but rather that a kind of massive decathexis, what the psychoanalyst André Green has described as 'a striving towards the zero state', is revealed as a powerful affective defence against them.[22] Indeed, the notion of negative hallucination – which Green defines not as the absence of representation, such as a nonreflected mirror image, but as the representation of the absence of representation[23] – is precisely what Beckett's dissociative and decathected writing continually projects.

Abbott's notion of 'narratricide', the 'disassembling [of] narrative', describes well the author's means of unwriting phantom or uncanny effects (43). For characteristic of Beckett is not only the aborted happening or nonevent, but a discourse that self-reflectively focuses on its own undoing of narrative, its *un*writing of writing – in writing. Beckett's creative process is said to have been 'decreative' in the sense that it was motivated by the need to rewrite and continually finetune previous texts in new ones. (So it was that Beckett's American director Alan Schneider could rightly observe, 'Every line of Beckett contains the whole of Beckett.')[24] But it is also 'decreative' in the sense that negation is what the author aims to depict. Consider the late prose texts where, for example, the white on white of *Ping* (1967); the blueless sea and sky, greenless grass, and colourless flowers that lie 'beyond the unknown' in *Ill Seen Ill Said* (1981); and the immeasurable dark of certainty of *Fizzles* (1976) and *Company* (1980) visually work against a narrative mode already doomed to fail because of its inherent incapacity to represent. The imagining of the unimaginable that this colourlessness evokes is evidence that the process of negating the original evolves into a process of representing the act of negating itself.

The third and final stage in Beckett's depiction of his idealized notion of creative capacity is what transpires in the actual writing of the process of unwriting, the narrative structuring of the 'narratricide' that both the uncanny object and its erasure represent. The ultimate triumph of creativity, in other words, consists of the representation of the denial of representation, the revelation of the aesthetic process itself.

In 'Negation', a short paper of 1925, Freud refers to the 'lifting' of repression that occurs when a repressed image or idea, a representation or ideation of something absent or lost, is negated. Although not an acceptance of the content that the conscious mind has repudiated, the negation serves as 'a way of taking cognizance of what is repressed'.[25] Already in 'Beyond the Pleasure Principle' (1920), the process was illustrated in Freud's recounting of the famous 'fort-da' game played by his eighteen-month-old grandson. With the child's exclamations of *fort* and *da* ('gone' and 'there') as he made a wooden reel disappear and return, he mastered absence, which is to say he mastered the anxiety produced by the prospect of his mother's departure. More important for our present purposes, however, is that with the disappearance and reappearance that the play with the toy afforded, the repression which the anxiety over the potential loss of mother had given rise was itself removed. In being elevated to the higher level of the game, in other words, subliminal awareness of the repressed content (separation from mother) was achieved.

As Paul Ricoeur noted, 'The work of art is also a *fort-da*, a disappearing of the archaic object as fantasy and its reappearing as a cultural object.'[26] And it is in this aesthetic *Aufhebung*, the term used by both Freud and Hegel, that what Beckett himself referred to in *Proust* as 'the core of the onion' – and the key to his own modernist enterprise (whether high, neo or post!) – is to be found. Beckett's so-called second trilogy – the late short novels *Company, Ill Seen Ill Said* and *Worstward Ho* (1983) – perhaps most clearly illustrates the interplay of negation and reconstitution that is his creative process. *Company* plays on (imaginary) visions perceptible only in the dark; only with closed eyes, in 'his little void', does the narrator see and hear, for the company of *Company* is a fable, 'the fable of one fabling of one with you in the dark'.[27] Similarly, *Ill Seen Ill Said* plays on the unwording and wording of the inexpressible void: 'Suddenly the look . . . Look? Too weak a word. Too wrong. Its absence? No better. Unspeakable globe. Unbearable.'[28] With *Worstward Ho* we are even closer to the 'literature of the unword' necessitated by the impediment of words to seeing. These textual 'assault[s] against words' of which Beckett wrote in 1937 to Kaun is the culmination of the following reflection: 'more and more my own language appears to me like a veil that must be torn apart in order to get at the things (or the Nothingness) behind it'.[29] The paradox, of course, is that the potential for such destruction lies solely within the province of articulation, a reality responsible for Beckett's often cited, often misunderstood notion of the failure of art. What Ricoeur has called the 'denying-overcoming of esthetic creation', comparable to the 'disappearing-reappearing' of the *fort-da* game (316), then, is precisely the negation, but also the simultaneous retaining and surpassing, of a given reality. Thus, as Freud theorized, is the uncanny, in the return of something repressed, produced; thus, as Beckett demonstrated, is the uncanny, in the triumph over the repression, itself erased and the aesthetic process revealed.

The representation of absence

I have aimed to establish a connection between Beckett's novel writing and Freud's notion of the uncanny because it offers a means of access into the writer's narrative process. Such a connection is unrelated to the pathography practised by psychoanalytically oriented critics seeking understanding of literary content through the psyche of the author. Rather, it is a point of convergence not at all surprising when traced historically to its source: both men were profoundly interested in philosophy. The impression made on Beckett by René Descartes, Arnold Geulincx, Immanuel Kant, Jean-Paul Sartre and Arthur Schopenhauer is well-documented. And phenomenology was very much in the air when Beckett was in his most productive period in Paris after the Second World War, the German influence of Hegel, Edmund Husserl, and Heidegger having been brought there (directly) by Sartre and (indirectly) by Maurice Merleau-Ponty. So, too, the impact of phenomenology on Freud was significant. Like Husserl, Freud was a student in Vienna of Franz Brentano, the philosopher/psychologist for whose 'fruitful influence', as Freud himself referred to it, the analyst was exceedingly grateful. (A 'remarkable man', a 'damned clever fellow', a 'genius in fact', 'in many respects, an ideal human being' is how Freud described Brentano to a friend.)[30] Recounting a visit to his professor, Freud wrote of Brentano's application of the scientific method to philosophy and psychology and of his merciless taking to task of those who 'had picked up the wrong end of

Descartes's philosophy, his complete separation of body and soul'.[31] The importance of the correlation of mind and body for Freud's development of psychoanalysis hardly needs mentioning. But the influence of Brentano on the evolution of Freud's thought should not be overlooked. And the impact of phenomenology on the origin of Beckett's preoccupation with subject and object in his novels, its bearing on his simultaneous insistence upon and resistance to the dualistic thinking of Descartes, is strikingly similar.

My point is that both Beckett and Freud struggled with radical dualities: those of the primary/secondary psychic processes and the pleasure/reality principles most important to Freud; those of subject/object and mind/body of greatest consequence to Beckett. Each found in negation the means to overcome the impasse which the Cartesian legacy had bestowed upon modern thought. As Harold Bloom has observed, 'Few insights, even in Freud, are so profound as this vision of negation, for no other theoretical statement at once succeeds as well in tracing the epistemological faculty convincingly to so primitive an origin.'[32] The same could be said of Beckett's creative praxis wherein negation unveils the epistemological core of the relation of reality to art.

The question remains as to what Beckett's depiction of this epistemological core – the creative energy or force – consists of. What do we have when the negation that is the representation of absence (the uncanny as resurfaced repression) has itself been negated? In a word, we have a 'prosereality' (the narrative counterpart to Ruby Cohn's famous neologism, 'theatereality') that reflects an utterly nonconceptual and primarily visual thinking. In 'The "Uncanny"' Freud claimed that the uncanny effect is 'often and easily produced by effacing the distinction between imagination and reality' (152). The congruence of narrative and real imagery in Beckett's early and late fiction (like the congruence of dramatic and real time in *Godot* and other Beckett plays) is proof. In fact, Beckett's privileging of sight alone – the unifying force of all his work – is given to uncanniness from the start: no other sense removes as definitively the imagination/reality distinction as that which serves as the quintessential ontological metaphor and the paradigm of aesthetic creation as well.

Indeed, this is why Freud's metapsychology aimed, first topologically and then structurally, to figure the mind. Even the more recent theorists of psychoanalytic theory, those of the object relations school, were compelled to construct a model – intersubjectivity being no less apprehensible by the mind's eye – for the figurative handle is a necessary point of departure. I need not review here the many instances of Beckett's own figurations of the psyche to be found in his novels, and in *Murphy* and *Watt* (1953) most notably. But I do want to emphasize that Beckett goes beyond symbolic representation

(*Watt*'s final line, 'no symbols where none intended', is a caveat not to be ignored)[33] to delineate the empirical, imaging not only the mind but its energy, too. This, then, is precisely where Beckett's double negation leaves us – before the dynamic discharge of psychic activity that is the creative act.

From *Murphy* to the late prose works, the feasibility of representing an objectively known world in language is Beckett's primary concern. The only certainty to which the early protagonist subscribes is the 'partial congruence of the world of his mind with the world of his body', a subjective consonance that sets the stage for all the works to come (*Murphy* 109). In the short narratives of the mid- to late 1960s – specifically, *Imagination Dead Imagine, Enough, Ping, Lessness*, and *The Lost Ones* – the flow of creative energy from soma to psyche is distilled through a cosmic negation of earthly existence. In *Ill Seen Ill Said* Beckett renders the 'silence at the eye of the scream' (73) at least as successfully as Edvard Munch does. Projecting the bodily source of psychic function, the late works further depict the constellation wherein ideation is negated and fantasy is the concrete manifestation of somatically rooted drive. Therein lies Beckett's essentially modernist enterprise, be it early, high or post.

In summary, a double negation occurs in Beckett resulting in a three-stage process depicting psychic energy or creative force. The unwriting that we associate with the nonassumption of identity and the nonoccurrence of event in his texts, a narrative deconstruction seen by some as characteristic of what Simon refers to as the schizoid age, is describable in terms of the interplay between the representation of absence and of the reemergence of what has been negated or repressed. The consequence of this uncanniness and its undoing is a focus on psychic function, a visualization projecting at once fantasy and actuality, both the concrete expression of drive and the reflection of its own epistemological core. It is this that promotes the perception of Beckett's novels as exceedingly complex and yet simple – beyond words.

Notes

1. Cited by Bruno Latour in *We Have Never Been Modern*, trans. Catherine Porter (Cambridge, MA: Harvard University Press, 1993), p. 12.
2. See Lois Oppenheim, *The Painted Word: Samuel Beckett's Dialogue With Art* (Ann Arbor: University of Michigan Press, 2000), pp. 13–27.
3. Samuel Beckett, *Proust* (London: Calder and Boyars, 1970), pp. 21–2. Further references cited parenthetically.
4. Bennett Simon, *Tragic Drama and the Family: From Aeschylus to Beckett* (New Haven: Yale University Press, 1988), pp. 235–47.
5. Martin Esslin, *The Theatre of the Absurd* (New York: Doubleday, 1961), p. 26.
6. See H. Porter Abbott in 'Narratricide: Samuel Beckett as Autographer', *Romance Studies* 11 (1987), pp. 35–46, and the first chapter of Abbott, *Beckett Writing*

Beckett (Ithaca: Cornell University Press, 1996). Further references to 'Narratriude' cited parenthetically.

7. Porter Abbott, 'Late Modernism: Samuel Beckett and the Art of the Oeuvre', in Enoch Brater and Ruby Cohn (eds.), *Around the Absurd* (Ann Arbor: University of Michigan Press, 1990), pp. 73–96; Breon Mitchell, 'Samuel Beckett and the Postmodern Controversy', in Matei Calinescu and Douwe Fokkeme (eds.), *Exploring Postmodernism* (Amsterdam: John Benjamins, 1990), pp. 109–22; Nicholas Zurbrugg, 'Seven Types of Postmodernity: Several Types of Samuel Beckett', in Joseph H. Smith (ed.), *The World of Samuel Beckett* (Baltimore: Johns Hopkins University Press, 1991), pp. 30–52; Steven Connor, *Samuel Beckett: Repetition, Theory and Text* (Oxford: Blackwell, 1988); Leslie Hill, *Beckett's Fiction: In Different Words* (Cambridge: Cambridge University Press, 1990); Thomas Trezise, *Into the Breach: Samuel Beckett and the Ends of Literature* (Princeton: Princeton University Press, 1990); and Richard Begam, *Samuel Beckett and the End of Modernity* (Stanford: Stanford University Press, 1996).

8. Richard Rorty, *New York Times*, 1 November 1997, p. B13; Umberto Eco cited in Mitchell, 'Postmodern Controversy', p. 109; and Latour, *We Have Never Been Modern*, p. 47.

9. Beckett, 'Letter to Axel Kaun', in Beckett, *Disjecta*, ed. Ruby Cohn (New York: Grove Press, 1984), p. 173.

10. Martin Heidegger, *Being and Time*, trans. John Macquarrie and Edward Robinson (New York: Harper and Row, 1962), pp. 321, 233.

11. Sigmund Freud, 'The "Uncanny"', in Freud, *On Creativity and the Unconscious: Papers on the Psychology of Art, Literature, Love, Religion* (New York: Harper and Row, 1958), pp. 123–4. Further references cited parenthetically.

12. Samuel Beckett, *Murphy* (New York: Grove Weidenfeld, 1957), pp. 1–2. Further references cited parenthetically.

13. Samuel Beckett, *Stirrings Still* (New York: Blue Moon Books, 1989), p. 1.

14. See Ruby Cohn, 'Ghosting Through Beckett', in Marius Buning and Lois Oppenheim (eds.), *Beckett in the 1990s* (Amsterdam: Rodopi, 1993), pp. 1–11.

15. See William Thomas McBride, 'This Mania for Symmetry: Beckett's Homo Mensura', *Romance Studies* 11 (1987), pp. 77–85.

16. Samuel Beckett, 'From an Abandoned Work', in S. E. Gontarski (ed.), *Samuel Beckett: The Complete Short Prose 1929–1989* (New York: Grove Press, 1995), p. 163.

17. Michel Bernard, 'The Hysterico-Obsessional Structure of "From an Abandoned Work"', *Journal of Beckett Studies* 4 (1994), p. 95.

18. Beckett, *The Unnamable* (New York: Grove Press, 1958) p. 173.

19. Abbott refers to the 'not-taking-on of an identity' and the 'not-taking-place' or 'textual non-event' in 'Narratricide', pp. 41–3.

20. In an email communication to Lois Oppenheim, 2 June 2000.

21. See Lois Oppenheim, 'A Preoccupation with Object-Representation: The Beckett-Bion Case Revisited', *The International Journal of Psychoanalysis* 82 (2001), pp. 767–84.

22. André Green, *On Private Madness* (Madison, CT: International Universities Press, 1986), p. 59.

23. André Green, *Le Travail du negative* (Paris: Editions de Minuit, 1993), p. 376.

24. Cited by Enoch Brater, *Beyond Minimalism: Beckett's Late Style in the Theatre* (Oxford: Oxford University Press, 1987), p. 176.
25. Freud, 'Negation', in *The Freud Reader*, ed. Peter Gay (New York: Norton, 1989), p. 667.
26. Paul Ricoeur, *Freud and Philosophy: An Essay on Interpretation*, trans. Denis Savage (New Haven: Yale University Press, 1970), p. 314. Further references cited parenthetically.
27. Samuel Beckett, *Company*, in Beckett, *Nohow On* (London: Calder Publications, 1992), pp. 51–2.
28. Samuel Beckett, *Ill Seen Ill Said*, in *Nohow On*, pp. 51–52, 95. Further references cited parenthetically.
29. Samuel Beckett, 'Letter to Axel Kaun', in Cohn (ed.), *Disjecta*, pp. 173, 171.
30. Sigmund Freud, *The Letters of Sigmund Freud to Eduard Silberstein 1871–1881*, ed. Walter Boehlich, trans. Arnold J. Pomerans (Cambridge, MA: Harvard University Press, 1990), p. 95.
31. *Ibid.*, pp. 102–3.
32. Harold Bloom (ed.), *Sigmund Freud* (New York: Chelsea House, 1985), p. 160.
33. Samuel Beckett, *Watt* (London: John Calder, 1976), p. 255.

General

Armstrong, Tim. *Modernism: A Cultural History*. Cambridge: Polity Press, 2005.

Ayers, David. *Modernism: A Short Introduction*. Oxford: Blackwell, 2004.

Berman, Jessica. *Modernist Fiction, Cosmopolitanism and the Politics of Community*. Cambridge: Cambridge University Press, 2001.

Brooker, Peter and Andrew Thacker (eds.). *Geographies of Modernism: Literatures, Cultures, Spaces*. London: Routledge, 2005.

Brooks, Peter. *Reading for the Plot: Intention and Design in Narrative*. Oxford: Clarendon Press, 1984.

Goldman, Jane. *Modernism, 1910–1945: Image to Apocalypse*. London: Palgrave Macmillan, 2004.

Greenslade, William. *Degeneration, Culture and the Novel, 1880–1940*. Cambridge: Cambridge University Press, 1994.

Hale, Dorothy J. *The Novel: An Anthology of Criticism and Theory*. Oxford: Blackwell, 2005.

Keating, Peter. *The Haunted Study. A Social History of the English Novel 1875–1914*. London: Secker and Warburg, 1989.

Latham, Sean. *'Am I a Snob?': Modernism and the Novel*. Ithaca: Cornell University Press, 2003.

Levenson, Michael (ed.). *The Cambridge Companion to Modernism*. Cambridge: Cambridge University Press, 1999.

Levenson, Michael H. *A Genealogy of Modernism. A Study of English Literary Doctrine, 1908–1922*. Cambridge: Cambridge University Press, 1984.

Matz, Jesse. *Literary Impressionism and Modernist Aesthetics*. Cambridge: Cambridge University Press, 2001.

Miller, Jane Eldridge. *Rebel Women: Feminism, Modernism and the Edwardian Novel*. London: Virago, 1994.

Nicholls, Peter. *Modernisms: A Literary Guide*. London: Palgrave Macmillan, 1995.

Pykett, Lyn. *Engendering Fictions: The English Novel in the Early Twentieth Century*. London: Arnold, 1994.

Rainey, Lawrence (ed.). *Modernism: An Anthology*. Oxford: Blackwell, 2005.

Scott, Bonnie Kime (ed.). *The Gender of Modernism: A Critical Anthology*. Bloomington: Indiana University Press, 1990.

Stevenson, Randall. *Modernist Fiction: An Introduction*. Hemel Hempstead: Harvester Wheatsheaf, 1992.

Sumner, Rosemary. *A Route to Modernism: Hardy, Lawrence, Woolf*. Basingstoke: Macmillan, 2000.

Tratner, Michael, *Modernism and Mass Politics: Joyce, Woolf, Eliot, Yeats*. Stanford: Stanford University Press, 1995.

Trotter, David. *The English Novel in History 1895–1920*. London: Routledge, 1993.

White, Allon. *The Uses of Obscurity. The Fiction of Early Modernism*. London: Routledge, 1981.

Williams, Raymond. *The Politics of Modernism: Against the New Conformists*, ed. Tony Pinkney. London: Verso, 1989.

James Joyce

Attridge, Derek. *Joyce Effects*. Cambridge: Cambridge University Press, 2000.

Blamires, Harry. *The New Bloomsday Book: A Guide Through Ulysses*, 3rd edn. London: Routledge, 1996.

Ellmann, Richard. *James Joyce*, rev. edn. Oxford: Oxford University Press, 1982.

Gibson, Andrew. *Joyce's Revenge: History, Politics and Aesthetics in 'Ulysses'*. Oxford: Oxford University Press, 2002.

Mahaffey, Vicky. *Reauthorising Joyce*. Cambridge: Cambridge University Press, 1988.

Nolan, Emer. *James Joyce and Nationalism*. London: Routledge, 1995.

Norris, Margot. *Joyce's Web: The Social Unravelling of Modernism*. Austin: University of Texas Press, 1992.

Virginia Woolf

Bowlby, Rachel. *Virginia Woolf: Feminist Destinations and Further Essays on Virginia Woolf*. Edinburgh: Edinburgh University Press, 1997.

Hanson, Clare. *Virginia Woolf*. Houndmills: Macmillan, 1994.

Lee, Hermoine. *The Novels of Virginia Woolf*. London: Methuen, 1977.

Marcus, Laura. *Virginia Woolf*. Plymouth: Northcote House, 1997.

Marcus, Jane (ed.). *Virginia Woolf and the Languages of Patriarchy*. Bloomington: Indiana University Press, 1987.

Zwerdling, Alex. *Virginia Woolf and the Real World*. Berkley: University of California Press, 1986.

Wyndham Lewis

Ayers, David. *Wyndham Lewis and Western Man*. London: Macmillan, 1992.

Corbett, David Peters (ed.). *Wyndham Lewis and the Art of Modern War*. Cambridge: Cambridge University Press, 1998.

Edwards, Paul. *Wyndham Lewis: Painter and Writer*. New Haven: Yale University Press, 2000.

Foshay, Toby. *Wyndham Lewis and the Avant-Garde: The Politics of the Intellect.* Montreal: McGill-Queen's University Press, 1992.

Gasiorek, Andrzej. *Wyndham Lewis and Modernism.* Tavistock: Northcote House, 2004.

Jameson, Fredric. *Fables of Aggression: Wyndham Lewis, the Modernist as Fascist.* Berkeley and Los Angeles: University of California Press, 1979.

Meyers, Jeffrey (ed.). *Wyndham Lewis: A Revaluation.* London: Athlone Press, 1980.

Miller, Tyrus. *Late Modernism: Politics, Fiction and the Arts Between the World Wars.* Berkeley and Los Angeles, CA: University of California Press, 1999.

D. H. Lawrence

Chaudhuri, Amit. *D. H. Lawrence and 'Difference': Postcoloniality and the Poetry of the Present.* Oxford: Oxford University Press, 2003.

Fernihough, Anne. *D. H. Lawrence: Aesthetics and Ideology.* Oxford: Clarendon Press, 1993.

Kinkead-Weekes, Mark. *D. H. Lawrence: Triumph to Exile 1912–1922.* Cambridge: Cambridge University Press, 1996.

Milton, Colin. *Lawrence and Nietzsche: A Study in Influence.* Aberdeen: Aberdeen University Press, 1997.

Sheehan, Paul. *Modernism, Narrative and Humanism.* Cambridge: Cambridge University Press, 2002.

Shiach, Morag. *Modernism, Labour and Selfhood in British Literature and Culture, 1890–1930.* Cambridge: Cambridge University Press, 2003.

Worthen, John. *D. H. Lawrence: The Life of an Outsider.* London: Allen Lane, 2005.

Joseph Conrad

Dryden, Linda. *Joseph Conrad and the Imperial Romance.* Basingstoke: Palgrave Macmillan, 2000.

Erdinast-Vulcan, Daphna. *Joseph Conrad and the Modern Temper.* Oxford: Clarendon Press, 1991.

Lothe, Jakob. *Conrad's Narrative Method.* Oxford: Clarendon Press, 1989.

Peters, John G. *Conrad and Impressionism.* Cambridge: Cambridge University Press, 2001.

Roberts, Andrew Michael (ed.). *Joseph Conrad.* London: Addison Wesley Longman, 1998.

Schneider, Lissa. *Conrad's Narratives of Difference: Not Exactly Tales for Boys.* New York and London: Routledge, 2003.

Djuna Barnes

Broe, Mary Lyn (ed.). *Silence and Power: A Revaluation of Djuna Barnes.* Carbondale: Southern Illinois University Press, 1991.

Chait, Sandra M. and Elizabeth M. Podnieks (eds.). *Hayford Hall: Hangovers, Erotics, and Modernist Aesthetics.* Carbondale: Southern Illinois University Press, 1995.

Kaivola, Karen. *All Contraries Confounded: The Lyrical Fiction of Virginia Woolf, Djuna Barnes, and Marguerite Duras.* Iowa City: University of Iowa Press, 1991.

Kaup, Monika, 'The Neobaroque in Djuna Barnes'. *Modernism/Modernity* 12:1 (2005), pp. 85–110.

Parsons, Deborah L. *Djuna Barnes.* Plymouth: Northcote House Press, 2003.

Plumb, Cheryl J. (ed.). *Nightwood: The Original Version and Related Drafts* Normal, IL: Dalkey Archive Press, 1995.

Scott, Bonnie Kime. *Refiguring Modernism I: The Women of 1928.* Bloomington: Indiana University Press, 1995.

William Faulkner

Duvall, John N. *Faulkner's Marginal Couple: Invisible, Outlaw, and Unspeakable Communities.* Austin: University of Texas Press, 1990.

Glissant, Edouard. *Faulkner, Mississippi*, trans. Barbara Lewis and Thomas C. Spear. Chicago: University of Chicago Press, 1996.

Kolmerten, Carol A., Stephen M. Ross and Judith Bryant Wittenberg (eds.). *Unflinching Gaze: Morrison and Faulkner Re-envisioned.* Jackson: University Press of Mississippi, 1997.

Matthews, John T. *The Play of Faulkner's Language.* Ithaca: Cornell University Press, 1982.

Moreland, Richard C. *Faulkner and Modernism: Rereading and Rewriting.* Madison: University of Wisconsin Press, 1990.

Spillers, Hortense J. 'Faulkner Adds Up: *Absalom, Absalom!* and *The Sound and the Fury'*, in Spillers, *Black, White, and in Color: Essays on American Literature and Culture.* Chicago: University of Chicago Press, 2003.

Wagner-Martin, Linda (ed.). *New Essays on 'Go Down, Moses'.* Cambridge: Cambridge University Press, 1996.

Dorothy Richardson, May Sinclair and Gertrude Stein

Bridgman, Richard. *Gertrude Stein in Pieces.* New York: Oxford University Press, 1970.

DeKoven, Marianne. *A Different Language: Gertrude Stein's Experimental Writing.* Madison: University of Wisconsin Press, 1983.

Fullbrook, Kate. *Free Women: Ethics and Aesthetics in Twentieth-Century Women's Fiction.* London: Harvester, 1990.

Hanscombe, Gillian. *The Art of Life: Dorothy Richardson and the Development of Feminist Consciousness.* London: Peter Owen, 1982.

Radford, Jean. *Dorothy Richardson.* Hemel Hempstead: Harvester Wheatsheaf, 1991.

Raitt, Suzanne. *May Sinclair: A Modern Victorian.* Oxford: Oxford University Press, 2000.

Watts, Carol. *Dorothy Richardson.* Plymouth: Northcote House, 1995.

Winning, Joanne. *The Pilgrimage of Dorothy Richardson.* Madison: University of Wisconsin Press, 2000.

C. L. R. James, Claude McKay, Nella Larsen and Jean Toomer

Baker, Houston A. *Modernism and the Harlem Renaissance*. Chicago: University of Chicago Press, 1987.

Booth, Howard and Nigel Rigby (eds.). *Modernism and Empire*. Manchester: Manchester University Press, 2000.

Buhle, Paul. *C. L. R. James: The Artist as Revolutionary*. London: Verso, 1988.

Doyle, Laura and Laura Winkiel (eds.). *Geomodernisms: Race, Modernism, Modernity*. Bloomington: Indiana University Press, 2005.

Gikandi, Simon. *Writing in Limbo: Modernism and Caribbean Literature*. Ithaca: Cornell University Press, 1992.

Gilroy, Paul. *The Black Atlantic: Modernity and Double Consciousness*. London: Verso, 1993.

Larson, Charles R. *Invisible Darkness: Jean Toomer and Nella Larsen*. Iowa City: University of Iowa Press, 1993.

North, Michael. *The Dialect of Modernism: Race, Language and Twentieth-Century Literature*. Oxford: Oxford University Press, 1994.

Schwarz, Bill (ed.). *West Indian Intellectuals in Britain*. Manchester: Manchester University Press, 2003.

Samuel Beckett

Begam, Richard. *Samuel Beckett and the End of Modernity*. Stanford: Stanford University Press, 1996.

Connor, Steven. *Samuel Beckett: Repetition, Theory and Text*. Oxford: Basil Blackwell, 1988.

Hill, Leslie. *Beckett's Fiction: In Different Words*. Cambridge: Cambridge University Press, 1990.

Oppenheim, Lois. *The Painted Word: Samuel Beckett's Dialogue With Art*. Ann Arbor: University of Michigan Press, 2000.

Smith, Joseph H (ed.). *The World of Samuel Beckett*. Baltimore: Johns Hopkins University Press, 1991.

Trezise, Thomas. *Into the Breach: Samuel Beckett and the Ends of Literature*. Princeton: Princeton University Press, 1990.

INDEX

Cambridge Companions to...

AUTHORS